Everyday Law for
Gays and Lesbians

The Everyday Law Series
Edited by Richard Delgado and Jean Stefancic
University of Pittsburgh Law School

Everyday Law for Individuals with Disabilities
Ruth Colker and Adam Milani (2005)

Everyday Law for Children
David Herring (2006)

Everyday Law for Consumers
Michael L. Rustad (2007)

Everyday Law for Gays and Lesbians
Anthony C. Infanti (2007)

Forthcoming
Everyday Law for the Elderly
Lawrence Frolik

Everyday Law for Latino/as
Steve Bender, Joaquin Avila, and Raquel Aldana-Pindell

Everyday Law for African Americans
Harold McDougall III

Everyday Law for
Gays and Lesbians
and Those Who
Care About Them

Anthony C. Infanti

Paradigm Publishers
Boulder • London

Copyright © 2007 Paradigm Publishers

Published in the United States by Paradigm Publishers, 3360 Mitchell Lane Suite E, Boulder, CO 80301 USA.

Paradigm Publishers is the trade name of Birkenkamp & Company, LLC, Dean Birkenkamp, President and Publisher.

Library of Congress Cataloging-in-Publication Data
Infanti, Anthony C., 1968–
Everyday law for gays and lesbians (and those who care about them) /
Anthony C. Infanti.
    p.   cm.—(Everyday law series)
  Includes bibliographical references and index.
  ISBN 978-1-59451-436-4 (hardcover : alk. paper)
    1. Homosexuality—Law and legislation—United States.   2. Gay rights—United
States.   3. Gays—Legal status, laws, etc.—United States.   I. Title.

KF4754.5.I54 2007
342.7308'7—dc22
2007016918

Printed and bound in the United States of America on acid-free paper that meets the standards of the American National Standard for Permanence of Paper for Printed Library Materials.

Designed and Typeset by Mulberry Tree Enterprises.

11   10   09   08   07   1   2   3   4   5

Contents

Preface and Acknowledgments

When my colleagues Richard Delgado and Jean Stefancic first approached me about writing this book, I was intrigued by the project because of a keen personal interest in the law as it applies to lesbians and gay men. At the same time, however, I was daunted by the idea of researching and writing a book that covers so many, and such disparate, areas of the law. I also wished to do more than simply write a summary of the law; I wished to take the genre a step further by empowering and encouraging lesbians and gay men (and those who care about them) to embrace the struggle for change in their daily lives. After much thought, I ultimately decided to undertake the project, and I'm glad I did because it has proved to be quite a rewarding experience. Now that the book is complete, I can only hope that you find it to be a worthwhile and helpful read.

Before we begin in earnest, a few words are in order with regard to the scope of the book. As the title indicates, this book focuses on the legal concerns of lesbians and gay men. With the exception of passing references, I do not consider the peculiar legal concerns of either bisexual or transgendered persons, despite their inclusion within the broader lesbian, gay, bisexual, and transgendered (LGBT) community. This is the result of a deliberate choice. Being neither bisexual nor transgendered, I simply do not feel that I can adequately address the ways in which the law impacts the lives of bisexual and transgendered persons; I leave that task to those who are in a better position to do so.

Even with respect to lesbians and gay men, I have chosen to focus the substantive legal discussion in this book on the interaction between their sexual orientation and the law, and I have purposefully ignored the potentially complex interactions between and among the law and other characteristics that might form part of their identities (e.g., race, ethnicity, class, and gender). I have limited the scope of the book in this way for the sake of producing a manuscript of manageable length and depth. Continuing in this vein, please bear in mind as you read the book that none of the chapters provides an exhaustive treatment of how the law applies to lesbians and gay men. Moreover, the book is not meant to provide legal advice because, to be meaningful, such advice must be tailored to your specific circumstances. This book is best taken as a starting point for further thought, research, or informed discussion with others—whether family, friends, coworkers, or your attorney. To this end, I have included in the appendix to this book a list of resources that you might find useful in gathering further information or in seeking help to resolve specific problems. This list includes the many organizations mentioned throughout the course of the book—along with a few others—and provides a description of each organization as well as its contact information.

Before closing this preface, I would like to thank some of the many people who have made this book possible. I would like to thank Richard Delgado and Jean Stefancic for offering me the opportunity to write this book. I would like to thank my partner, Hien, for encouraging me to undertake this project and for providing me with his love and support while I was working on it. I would like to thank my sister, Elyse, and her partner, Cindy, as well as my former student and able research assistant Lacy Wilbur for contributing to the narratives that begin each chapter of the book. I would also like to thank Elyse and Cindy for being so kind as to provide the photograph of their family that appears on the cover of this book. I would like to thank Jennifer White, Deanne Yocum, and Bryan Oklin for their assistance in researching various chapters of the book. I would like to thank Susan Broms and her staff of student research fellows at the University of Pittsburgh School of Law's Barco Law Library for providing additional research support. I would like to thank Michele Kristakis of the Barco Law Library for making sure that I never missed new contributions to the legal academic literature in the areas covered by this book. I would like to thank all who have provided comments on drafts of chapters for the book, including Debbie Brake, Ben Bratman, Dan Friedson, Darryll Jones, Margaret Mahoney, Martha Mannix, Stella Smetanka, and Lu-in Wang. Finally, I would like to thank the University of Pittsburgh School of Law for providing me with financial and academic support that facilitated the writing of this book, and I would like to thank the University of California at Santa Barbara's Center for the Study of Sexual Minorities in the Military (now the Michael D. Palm Center) for awarding me a grant to support the research for Chapter 4.

Parts of this book are adapted from my previous work. The narratives that open Chapters 3 and 5 are adapted from Anthony C. Infanti, "The Internal Revenue Code as Sodomy Statute," 44 *Santa Clara L. Rev.* 763 (2004), where they first appeared. Parts of Chapters 6 and 7 are also adapted from that article as well as from Anthony C. Infanti, "Tax Protest, 'A Homosexual,' and Frivolity: A Deconstructionist Meditation," 24 *St. Louis U. Pub. L. Rev.* 21 (2005), which is reprinted with the permission of the *St. Louis University Pub-*

lic Law Review; Anthony C. Infanti, "A Tax Crit Identity Crisis? Or Tax Expenditure Analysis, Deconstruction, and the Rethinking of a Collective Identity," 26 *Whittier L. Rev.* 707 (2005), which is reprinted with the permission of the *Whittier Law Review;* Anthony C. Infanti, "*Baehr v. Lewin:* A Step in the Right Direction for Gay Rights?" 4 *Tul. J.L. & Sexuality* 1 (1994), which is reprinted with the permission of the *Tulane Journal of Law and Sexuality,* which holds the copyright; and Anthony C. Infanti, "Marriage or Bust," which was published on *Jurist* (http://jurist.law.pitt.edu) on March 23, 2004.

1
Introduction

It is easy to concede the inevitability of social injustice and find the serenity to accept it. The far harder task is to feel its intolerability and seek the strength to change it.

—Judge David Bazelon

My mother passed away when I was thirty years old. She was the kind of woman who could embarrass you and make you laugh all at once—even after she had passed away. At my mother's funeral, a middle school teacher told me stories from the time when my mother had worked in her special education class. The teacher chuckled as she confessed her amazement at the things my mother would say to the students—things she herself would never dare to say. My mother would suggest to the students that it might be time to take a bath or buy some deodorant and once even asked a particularly troublesome student if he ever got sick, clearly implying that his absence from class would be a welcome occurrence.

A few years before her death, while she was still working at the school, my mother returned home from work one day visibly upset. When my father asked what was wrong, she recounted a tirade that she had heard in the teachers' room. One of the teachers had been loudly disparaging lesbians and gay men. This upset my mother because, by that time, I had been out of the closet for a number of years, and my partner and I had been visiting my parents most weekends. My parents liked having us around and always tried to cajole us into staying the entire weekend. So my mother knew that this teacher's acerbic remarks were not meant only for the disembodied "homosexuals" that she kept assailing but applied equally to me and my partner.

Even though my mother took these remarks personally, she did not speak up or counter them in any way—she just sat there suffering in silence.

1

My father, who had initially had a very difficult time accepting my homosexuality, was rather surprised at my mother's reaction (or, more precisely, lack thereof). For a few moments, he sat shaking his head in a mixture of disappointment and disbelief. When he finally looked up at the outspoken woman whom he had been married to for more than thirty years, he asked her how she could have remained silent. Why hadn't she defended me? Why had she chosen to hold her tongue this one time when she had never before hesitated to speak her mind—whether for good or for ill?

I share this story with you because it fills me simultaneously with sadness and hope. For me, it both exemplifies the current predicament of the American lesbian and gay movement and demonstrates the potential for positive change in straight attitudes toward lesbians and gay men. To explore these themes more fully, in the first part of this chapter I survey the social and legal landscape that surrounds us, explain why I view our current situation as a predicament, and consider the source of that predicament. In the second part of the chapter, I set the stage—and the tone—for the remainder of the book by suggesting that our individual lesbian and gay narratives can be a radical and powerful tool for promoting positive change in how society and the law view and treat lesbians and gay men. The ultimate goal of this book is to empower and inspire each of us to deploy these narratives in the most effective way possible.

The Predicament

The *Oxford English Dictionary* defines a "predicament" as a "state of being; condition, situation, position; esp. an unpleasant, trying, or dangerous situation." When I examine the social and legal terrain that surrounds us, I find us situated somewhere far short of the unqualified acceptance that we seek and a mere stone's throw from the unadulterated hostility that defines our past. This proves to be an unpleasant, trying, and dangerous situation indeed.

Measuring Our Progress: How Far We Have Come
To some, this assessment may sound bleak.[1] After all, you might counter, the lesbian and gay movement in the United States did not coalesce until the late 1960s and early 1970s.[2] In the short span of the past several decades, the movement has made remarkable strides in normalizing homosexuality. Straight society has gone from treating homosexuality as the taboo "love that dare not speak its name" to routinely talking about the increasing "acceptance" of lesbians and gay men into the "mainstream." Once reviled, the lesbian and gay community is now considered a "niche" advertising market.[3] There appears to be no shortage of lesbian and gay characters in film and on television, and there was recently a race to create the first lesbian and gay cable television channel. In addition, an ever growing number of

employers are offering domestic partner benefits to their employees; many have also added sexual orientation to their nondiscrimination policies.

With high-profile successes in the courts, the legal tide likewise appears to be turning in favor of the lesbian and gay movement. In a stunning reversal of its decision in *Bowers v. Hardwick*,[4] the U.S. Supreme Court in *Lawrence v. Texas*[5] struck down the remaining state sodomy laws. Not even a year later, in *Goodridge v. Department of Public Health*,[6] the Massachusetts Supreme Judicial Court extended the right to marry to same-sex couples in Massachusetts. A number of other jurisdictions—including California, Connecticut, the District of Columbia, Hawaii, Maine, New Hampshire, New Jersey, Oregon, Washington, and Vermont—have enacted domestic partnership or civil union regimes that provide legal recognition to same-sex couples.

And, comparatively speaking, one would expect the United States to be more advanced than many other countries in its treatment of lesbians and gay men. Why else would lesbians and gay men who are persecuted in their native countries seek—and, in a number of cases, be granted—refuge here?[7] Moreover, many people in non-Western countries perceive gay identity and gay pride to be a threatening Western, and particularly American, export.[8]

Measuring Our Progress: How Far We Have to Go

Further embracing the geographic sense of "situation," we could easily imagine ourselves to be on a journey away from a dark, suffocatingly oppressive place that gives shape to the unadulterated hostility of our past and to be traveling down a road (with all of its twists, turns, detours, and dead ends) toward the bright hope of a future unqualified acceptance of lesbians and gay men. But as soon as we see ourselves as traveling down a road, it becomes clear that the upbeat assessment of our situation privileges a backward-looking measure of progress; in other words, by this measure, whether we have made progress (and how much) is determined by looking back to see how far we have come.

Progress can also be measured from a forward-looking perspective; in other words, whether we have made progress (and how much) can as easily be determined by looking toward our destination to see how far we still have to go. Yet this slight shift in perspective casts an entirely different light on our progress. In this new light, the advances made by the lesbian and gay movement over the past several decades no longer seem remarkable but instead appear fitful and slight. A great deal of hostility continues to be directed toward lesbians and gay men, and homosexuality continues to evoke feelings of shame and discomfort in both straights *and* gays. As the following discussion illustrates, this shame, discomfort, and hostility manifest themselves in a myriad of ways.

The Closet. Far too many lesbians and gay men still feel the need to live in the closet because they fear the repercussions of admitting their homosexuality.

James McGreevey, the former governor of New Jersey, is just one recent notable example. McGreevey resigned his office in 2004 after announcing both his homosexuality and an extramarital affair with another man.

The Media. Notwithstanding the increased frequency with which lesbians and gay men are portrayed on television and in film, the lesbian and gay characters that we do see too often replicate and reinforce stereotypes. The characters also fail to reflect the diversity of the lesbian and gay community and the real lives of lesbians and gay men. Societal discomfort with homosexuality is further evidenced by the comparative rarity of on-screen physical intimacy between members of the same sex.

Employment. Only twenty states and the District of Columbia have enacted laws that prohibit discrimination on the basis of sexual orientation in both public and private employment. Although it has been asserted that relatively few employment discrimination claims have actually been made under these laws, a recent empirical study maintains that when the raw number of complaints is adjusted to take into account the estimated number of lesbians and gay men in the workforce, "gay rights laws are used with greater frequency than the raw numbers imply."[9] In reality, claims of sexual orientation–based employment discrimination were made at about the same rate as claims of gender-based employment discrimination.

Furthermore, contrary to the stereotype of lesbians and gay men as economically privileged, studies have found that gay and bisexual men actually earn lower wages than other men and significantly lower wages than married men.[10] These and other studies have found, however, that lesbians and bisexual women earn higher wages than other women, married or unmarried, even though one would expect lesbians to do worse than heterosexual women in the labor market because of the additional disadvantage of their sexual orientation. It may be that any negative effects on wages caused by lesbians' and bisexual women's gender and sexual orientation are more than counterbalanced by positive effects due to their (actual or imagined) departure from stereotypical gender roles—particularly with regard to marriage and child-rearing, which are often perceived to reduce a woman's commitment to market labor.[11] In other words, several negatives (i.e., gender and sexual orientation discrimination plus what appears to be a bonus but is in essence more gender discrimination) may come together to produce a positive (i.e., higher wages). Thus, this anomalous result—which has been termed a "wage premium" for lesbians and bisexual women—should not necessarily be taken as a sign that they suffer less employment discrimination than heterosexual women.

Even those who remain in the closet in an attempt to pass as straight and avoid the adverse impact of sexual orientation–based employment discrimination might find themselves suffering the effects of indirect discrimination. It has been pointed out [that] passing [as straight] may require a conscious effort to avoid potentially awkward social interactions that contribute to job satisfaction or advancement for other workers. The isolation involved in many passing strategies could lead to higher absenteeism and job turnover, and the energy devoted to passing might reduce productivity. In this case, the behavior is not an intrinsic characteristic of the worker but an effect of indirect discrimination within a workplace perceived as threatening. Two individuals with equal productive abilities would have differential productivity and, therefore, differential wages because of the work environment's effect on the gay individual's productivity.[12]

Bias Crimes. Antigay violence persists at high levels. When the number of reports is adjusted for population size, lesbians and gay men report higher rates of bias crimes than do African Americans or Jewish people, and they report significantly more crimes against the person than either of those groups.[13] Consider, by way of example, the years 2003 and 2004: In the geographic area covered by the National Coalition of Anti-Violence Programs (which includes less than 30 percent of the national population), the number of incidents of violence against gay men, lesbians, bisexuals, and transgender individuals increased 8 percent from 2002 to 2003 and increased by another 4 percent from 2003 to 2004.[14] Although there was a 4 percent decrease in the number of victims suffering injuries in 2003, the number of victims suffering serious injuries rose 3 percent, and the number of murder victims rose 80 percent (from 10 in 2002 to 18 in 2003). Again in 2004, despite a 2 percent decrease in the number of victims suffering injuries, the number of victims suffering serious injuries rose an astounding 20 percent, and the number of murder victims rose 11 percent (to 20 in 2004). Disturbingly, it appears that antigay violence spikes whenever the lesbian and gay community finds itself in the spotlight. For instance, there was a noticeable spike in antigay violence in the latter half of 2003—when the *Lawrence* and *Goodridge* decisions were issued—and this increase continued into the first half of 2004.

The ability to physically menace and even kill lesbians and gay men with impunity stems from the fact that these crimes often go unreported because of the victim's fear of being outed or harassed by the police. Even when these crimes are reported, advocacy groups find it necessary to press for the investigation of complaints. According to the National Coalition of Anti-Violence Programs, in 2004, there was an 82 percent increase in the number of bias-crime complaints that police refused to take, and 66 percent of the bias-crime complaints that were taken resulted in no arrest. It should come as little surprise then to hear reports of reactionaries calling for an "open season" on lesbians and gay men.[15]

Legal Troubles. The lesbian and gay movement's high-profile legal successes have been matched by equally high-profile failures. To take a recent example, the same-sex marriage movement was dealt a significant series of blows in July 2006. Over the span of just a few short weeks, the New York Court of Appeals, which has a reputation for being progressive, held that New York law effectively bans same-sex marriage and upheld that ban against constitutional attack; the Washington Supreme Court upheld its same-sex marriage ban against constitutional attack; the Georgia Supreme Court upheld its state constitutional ban on same-sex marriage against a procedural attack that had been successful in a lower court; the Massachusetts Supreme Judicial Court ruled that, should it pass all of the necessary steps for approval, a voter-initiated amendment to the state constitution could prospectively ban same-sex marriage; and the U.S. Court of Appeals for the Eighth Circuit found that Nebraska's state constitutional ban on recognizing same-sex marriages, civil unions, domestic partnerships, or any other legal relationship between same-sex partners did not violate the federal constitution.[16]

An International Perspective. When our legal progress is viewed from a wider, international perspective, it becomes clear that the United States is far from being a leader (and, in fact, is only slowly becoming a follower) in recognizing and remedying lesbian and gay rights issues. In 1996, South Africa became the first country to include an explicit ban on sexual orientation discrimination in its constitution, providing a stark contrast to recent attempts in the United States to enshrine discrimination against same-sex couples in the federal constitution. Although Americans are generally hostile to the idea of same-sex marriage, the Netherlands, Belgium, Canada, South Africa, and Spain have all extended the right to marry to same-sex couples. A number of other countries (including Denmark, Norway, Sweden, Iceland, Finland, France, Germany, and Great Britain) have put in place quasi-marriage regimes, which afford almost all of the rights and obligations of marriage, or semimarriage regimes, which afford a limited selection of the rights and obligations of marriage.

More than twenty years before the U.S. Supreme Court's decision in *Lawrence v. Texas,* the European Court of Human Rights (ECHR) began the "development of international human rights law in the area of gay and lesbian sexuality"[17] by holding that Northern Ireland's sodomy law violated the European Convention for the Protection of Human Rights and Fundamental Freedoms.[18] In the late 1980s and early 1990s, the ECHR reaffirmed its interpretation of the European Convention when it found that the sodomy laws of Ireland and Cyprus also violated the convention.[19]

Over the past quarter century, the ECHR's decisions concerning sexual orientation have not been uniformly positive; however, commentators have noted that the ECHR has become "increasingly receptive to human rights claims brought by lesbian and gay applicants" since the late 1990s.[20] For example, the ECHR has held the following to constitute violations of the European Convention: (1) employing different ages of consent for heterosexual and homosexual relations, (2) the United Kingdom's ban on lesbians and gay men serving in the military, (3) a Portuguese appellate court's overturning of a lower court ruling that awarded custody of a young girl to her gay father, (4) the United Kingdom's criminalization of homosexual relations between more than two men in private, and (5) denying the surviving member of a same-sex couple the benefit of an Austrian rent law that permitted surviving life companions to succeed to decedent companions' tenancies.[21]

The United Nations Human Rights Committee has on several occasions considered the application of the International Covenant on Civil and Political Rights (ICCPR) to sexual orientation discrimination.[22] In 1994, nearly a decade before the decision in *Lawrence v. Texas,* the committee found that Tasmania's sodomy law violated the ICCPR.[23] In that decision, the committee also noted that the references to "sex" in the provisions of the ICCPR that guarantee equal protection of the law without regard to status also cover sexual orientation. The committee later reaffirmed this interpretation of the ICCPR in another case brought against Australia.[24] In that case, the committee held that Australia's denial of pension benefits to the surviving same-sex partner of a veteran violated the ICCPR because those same benefits would have been provided to the surviving opposite-sex partner of a veteran, whether or not the two had been married.

In a case brought against New Zealand, the committee held that the ICCPR does not obligate states that have ratified the treaty to extend the right to marry to same-sex couples.[25] This interpretation was based on language in the ICCPR that guarantees "the right of men and women of marriageable age to marry."[26] The committee noted that, in contrast to the other provisions of the ICCPR, this "is the only substantive provision in the [ICCPR] which defines a right by using the term 'men and women', rather than 'every human being', 'everyone' and 'all persons.'"[27] Two members of the committee wrote an opinion concurring in this interpretation but at the same time issued a warning that the opinion "should not be read as a general statement that differential treatment between married couples and same-sex couples not allowed under the law to marry would never amount to a violation of [the ICCPR]."[28] They explained that, where same-sex couples are not offered the choice to marry, "a denial of certain rights or benefits to same-sex couples that are available to married couples may amount to discrimination prohibited under [the ICCPR], unless otherwise justified on reasonable and objective criteria."[29]

Seeing the Predicament in Our Progress
But privileging this forward-looking measure of progress is equally misleading. The true measure of our progress cannot be found at either extreme; rather, it lies somewhere in between, in a blending of these opposing perspectives. Likewise, the true picture of our predicament emerges from that same hodgepodge of hostility, shame, discomfort, and normalization.

You may recall that "predicament" especially connotes "an unpleasant, trying, or dangerous situation." That our current situation is unpleasant and dangerous should be self-evident: Two of the ingredients in our hodgepodge are hostility and shame, and I have already amply illustrated their effects (e.g., the antigay tirade that my mother silently endured that day at school, the continuing need for many of us to remain in the closet, and the ever-present threat of financial or physical harm due to employment discrimination or antigay violence). To understand why these times are so trying—the last in the trio of adjectives and the one most in need of elaboration—we can draw on the discomfort and normalization that complete our hodgepodge to explain the enervating uncertainty that is a natural concomitant of society's grudging toleration of homosexuality.

In American society, there are people, like my mother, who sympathize with the lesbian and gay movement in its battle to inch toward unqualified acceptance. Shortly after I graduated from law school, my mother asked me whether I was gay. I answered her truthfully, and in spite of appearing initially troubled by my answer, she ultimately took the news well. My sexual orientation—though obviously not what she preferred it to be—was not going to change how much she loved me. People like my mother sympathize with lesbians and gay men because they see us as human beings and not as some disembodied and dehumanized "other" that can be vilified and scapegoated for society's problems. They are deeply troubled by antigay violence and other extreme manifestations of sexual prejudice (more commonly called "homophobia").[30] That's why coming out has proved to be such a powerful process for lesbians and gay men—studies have found a correlation between contact with lesbians and gay men, particularly close and frequent contact, and positive general attitudes toward lesbians and gay men.[31]

Yet there are limits to every straight person's sympathy for lesbians and gay men; the boundaries for each may be different, but they are boundaries nonetheless.[32] Notably, a study of the trends in public opinion concerning lesbians and gay men found that "over the past thirty years, American public opinion regarding gay people, gay rights and homosexual sex has moved unambiguously toward acceptance and tolerance. However, Americans remain deeply uncomfortable with gays as compared to other demographic groups, and their support for gay rights does not extend as strongly to the domains of sexuality and relationships."[33] At some point, even straight people who think of themselves as tolerant cannot help but fall prey to—or just cynically exploit—the shame that our society ingrains in each of us concerning the subject of homosexuality.

Consider, for example, former President Bill Clinton and Democratic presidential candidate John Kerry. In 1996, Clinton, who is generally considered to be a friend of the lesbian and gay community, signed the Defense of Marriage Act into law to prevent the Republicans from using the issue against him in his reelection campaign. Compounding the damage, Clinton then used his support for this law, which his own spokesman had earlier labeled "gay baiting," in an advertisement that was designed to garner votes from religious conservatives. As for John Kerry, in his campaign for the presidency, he likewise rejected the idea of same-sex marriage; however, Kerry would not go so far as to support a constitutional ban on same-sex marriage, even after Clinton advised him that announcing support for the measure would be politically expedient.

As these two examples illustrate, the contours of straight limited sympathy for lesbians and gay men vary from individual to individual. The boundary of my mother's limited sympathy was clear. She was bothered by what she heard that day at school but was clearly ashamed to speak up. She did not want to challenge the teacher's caustic remarks because doing so might entail an implicit or explicit public acknowledgment that she had a gay son. Despite being troubled by my mother's hesitancy to respond to an open attack on lesbians and gay men, I didn't blame her for remaining silent. How could I when I had lived in the closet for years because of the same shame? But although I could understand the existence of this boundary and could forgive my mother for crossing it, I have not found it quite so easy to forget the disappointment I felt when she told me this story.

Unfortunately, such disappointment is an unpleasant, though unavoidable, by-product of society's grudging toleration of lesbians and gay men. Because the limits of straight sympathy for lesbians and gay men vary from individual to individual, it is exceedingly difficult to tell who the enemy is — or, worse, when someone who appears to be an ally will reach her limit and suddenly transform into the enemy (or into an acquiescing accomplice, which is really no better). This difficulty is exacerbated by the nature of sexual orientation as a generally nonobvious characteristic, or "concealable stigma."[34] In our heterosexist society, people are assumed to be straight absent some clear evidence or indication to the contrary. This unspoken presumption effectively renders the coming-out process never ending; it requires us to reinvent our identities each time we come into contact with someone, whether that person is a new acquaintance or an old friend and, because of internalized antigay hostility and oppression, whether that person is straight or gay. I long ago stopped counting the number of times that I felt put upon when I had to answer what many straight people would consider to be the most banal of questions: Are you married? Do you have children? What did you do last weekend?

Whenever a response may reveal your sexual orientation or require you (directly or indirectly) to talk about your already revealed sexual orientation in more detail, you must decide how candid you can safely be when answering. How can you know whether a full and honest answer will be met with shock, disgust, or some level of sympathy? It is this constant nagging uncertainty that makes these times so trying for lesbians and gay men.

The Roots of the Predicament

According to the *Online Etymology Dictionary*,[35] the first recorded instance of "predicament" taking on the meaning of an "unpleasant situation" did not occur until 1586. Interestingly, although this modern negative connotation of the word is redolent of the current state of the lesbian and gay movement, it is the word's Latin roots that suggest why we find ourselves in a most unpleasant, trying, and dangerous situation. The word "predicament" has its roots in the Latin verb *prædicare*, which means to "assert, proclaim, [or] declare publicly." That verb, in turn, is derived from a combination of the Latin *præ-* ("forth, before") and *dicare* ("to proclaim"). As this etymology denotes, the current predicament of the lesbian and gay movement is firmly rooted in what has been proclaimed before—that is, in Western society's long-standing tradition of sexual prejudice.

Professor Byrne Fone documents the history of Western sexual prejudice in his book *Homophobia: A History*.[36] Fone traces the roots of sexual prejudice back to ancient Greece. In retrospect, Greece is often viewed "as a utopia in which homosexual love flourished without blame or censure";[37] however, Fone notes that the only homosexual activity accepted in ancient Greek society was that which conformed to, and reinforced, the primacy of the adult male citizen. Accordingly, "the adult male had the unquestioned right to penetrate and dominate his presumably weaker, usually younger, and socially inferior partner,"[38] who might be a younger man but not an underage boy. In contrast, it was not socially acceptable for an adult male to be effeminate, to accept the passive role in homosexual sex, or to engage exclusively in homosexual sex. Similar conventions prevailed in Roman society.

Nearer the end of Antiquity, even this limited acceptance of homosexual activity began to erode as attitudes toward homosexuality changed with the rise of antisexual asceticism. This erosion "culminate[d] in the legal prohibition of homosexual acts in an edict of 390 C.E. and the subsequent declaration by the Church that such acts were sinful because they were unnatural."[39] Referring to the biblical punishment of Sodom and Gomorrah, the edict directed that the offender was to "'expiate his crime in the avenging flames.'"[40] In 533 C.E., as part of his codification and revision of Roman law, the emperor Justinian formally applied the death penalty to homosexual acts. In the ensuing five hundred years, civil and ecclesiastical attempts to control homosexual activity expanded significantly, and homosexual acts generally came to be viewed as "heinous and occasionally [were] described as the worst of all sins."[41]

By the late Middle Ages, sodomy was no longer a sin that could be repented; it had become a sin without forgiveness. In the early thirteenth century, the Catholic Church called for civil (as well as ecclesiastical) punishment of sodomy. Civil punishments were enacted in Italy, France, Spain, and England during the thirteenth century. The extent to which homosexual activity was persecuted during that period remains unknown, which may be due in part to the fact that sodomy was considered such a horrible crime that the records of sodomy trials "were sometimes burned with the guilty sodomite."[42] Nonetheless, records of executions do go back as far as 1292, when a man was burned alive for committing sodomy.

Notwithstanding a "rediscovery of classical writings [that] prompted a cautious reexamination of male eros,"[43] the Renaissance saw the criminalization of sodomy throughout Europe and the enactment of truly horrific punishments for homosexual acts—ranging from castration to death by decapitation, hanging, or burning. During this period, "nearly sixteen thousand people were tried for sodomy . . . [and] about four hundred men and women are known to have been executed" in Spain, Portugal, France, Italy, and Geneva alone.[44] During the colonial period in New England, sodomy was punishable by death. There are records of men being executed as well as records of men being severely whipped, burned with a hot iron, and then made permanent outcasts for engaging in homosexual activity.

By the late eighteenth and early nineteenth centuries, many Western European nations had decriminalized sodomy; however, this decriminalization "did not mean that intolerance of sodomites also disappeared."[45] In any event, England bucked the trend toward decriminalization, retaining the death penalty for sodomy until 1861 and criminal sanctions for homosexual activity into the twentieth century. The United States likewise ignored the trend toward decriminalization, with many states abolishing the death penalty for homosexual activity but retaining criminal prohibitions of sodomy—in some cases into the twenty-first century.

In a series of articles, law professor William Eskridge has documented the history of the legal treatment of homosexuality in the United States from the late nineteenth century through the early 1980s.[46] In late-nineteenth- and early-twentieth-century America, arrests and convictions for "crimes against nature" rose, as did the use of other laws (e.g., those relating to disorderly conduct, vagrancy, loitering, indecent exposure, and solicitation) to regulate same-sex "degeneracy." Eskridge describes the chilling practical effects of this regulation of homosexual activity:

> More important, the consequences of arrest and more certain conviction of crimes associated with homosexuality often had tragic collateral consequences: jail time (several years if convicted of sodomy), incarceration and physical torture in a mental institution under a sexual psychopath law, loss of one's job and even livelihood if the arrest were publicized, court-martial or (more typically) administrative separation from the armed forces, deportation if one were a noncitizen, and continued surveillance and harassment by police officers and detectives. The homosexual was not only a sexual outlaw, but one who by World War II had clearly caught the eye of the government.[47]

Tracking the medical discourse of the period, American social understanding of homosexual activity shifted from "the *sinful sodomite* to the *degenerate invert* . . . [and then] from the degenerate invert to the *psychopathic homo-*

sexual."[48] Although the invert was considered a threat for challenging traditional gender roles (an invert might today be called a "gender bender"), the psychopathic homosexual was considered even more of a threat because he "was sexually out of control and even predatory."[49] In view of the threat to society posed by homosexuality, the government sought to "expunge homosexuality from the nation's public culture . . . [through] censorship of homophile publications, theatrical productions, and movies that depicted 'sex perversion'; disruption of homosexual socialization by state raids on homosexual haunts and by regulation of liquor sales; and finally direct interrogation, treatment, and exclusion during World War II."[50]

In the postwar years, homosexuals were the object of witch hunts at the federal and state levels. As antihomosexual panics swept cities from Boise, Idaho, to Miami, Florida, vice squads vigorously pursued homosexuals through spying, decoys, and raids. In addition, an increasing number of states enacted sexual psychopath laws that permitted indefinite detention and psychiatric treatment of homosexuals—treatment that included lobotomies, electric shock aversion therapy, pharmacological shock (induced vomiting when homoerotic images were shown), and the injection of hormones. At the same time, the federal government attempted to eliminate homosexuals from civil service employment and military service, and it further attempted to exclude alien homosexuals from entering the United States. These federal witch hunts had a broader impact because the government shared information with private employers, who often blacklisted individuals discharged for being homosexual. Whether on their own or cued by the federal government, the states also began witch hunts for homosexuals.

In the 1940s and 1950s, the federal government surveilled and harassed both individual homosexuals and homosexual organizations, and state and local governments attempted to suppress homosexual socialization by raiding gay bars and revoking their liquor licenses. During this period, the federal and state governments censored homosexual publications. Films were subjected to several layers of censorship: The federal government impounded foreign films dealing with homosexuality, the motion-picture industry adopted a voluntary censorship code that prohibited reference to homosexuality in films distributed domestically, and state and local licensing laws prohibited films dealing with homosexuality.

This barrage of police persecution, government employment discrimination, exclusion of homosexual aliens, suppression of homosexual socialization, and censorship of homosexual materials did not abate until the 1960s and 1970s.

Extricating Ourselves from the Current Predicament

Finding Reason to Hope

With literally thousands of years of fear, prejudice, and persecution behind us, there is little wonder that shame, discomfort, and hostility toward homosexuality seem to be encoded in our cultural DNA.[51] But the fact that these attitudes are deeply entrenched cannot mean that they are wholly unchangeable. There must be hope that societal attitudes can change and that human progress is possible. For one, I see that hope in the vignette that opened this chapter. Through the veil of disappointment at my mother's failure to stand up for all lesbians and gay men (and, vicariously, for me), I witnessed a sign of an amazing transformation that had occurred in my father, an opening wide of the boundaries of his sympathy for lesbians and gay men.

My father was a first-generation American whose parents had immigrated to the United States from Italy a few years before he was born. He was brought up in a highly traditional, patriarchal home where the husband and father ruled. Our home was run exactly the same way. My father's word was law: He would not tolerate our doing something without his permission or contrary to his views. After he found out about my sexual orientation, my father excoriated me for "doing this" to my family, as if I were intentionally trying to hurt or defy him. After I refused to speak to him for several months and failed to return home for the holidays, my father realized that I was not going to change or go back into the closet to make him happy. My father, a man who did not care to read much more than the morning paper, began to take trips to the library to do research on homosexuality and to learn more about a part of who I am. Eventually he called to apologize for the way he had treated me, and we reconciled.

For someone who had found it so difficult at first to accept a gay son, my father quickly became one of my strongest supporters. That day when my mother came home from school upset, I realized just how much he had changed. He did not worry about people finding out about my sexual orientation; what was important to him was protecting his son from a vituperative attack. Instead of directing his disappointment and displeasure at my being gay, he was now directing it at my mother for not speaking up in my defense. If someone so headstrong and set in his ways as my father could change his attitude toward lesbians and gay men, it gives me hope that broader change in societal attitudes is possible.

Reconsidering How We Go About Realizing This Hope

Thus far, the lesbian and gay movement has largely focused its efforts to realize this potential for change on advancing the legal rights of lesbians and gay men. The attraction of this approach is quite natural:

> For many of us who have suffered oppression or discrimination in any form it is easy to understand the attraction of rights-based approaches. Civil rights initiatives have an immediate, concrete appeal. They promise to secure the basic constitutional rights that lesbians and gay men have previously lived without: freedom from discrimination in areas such as housing, employment, child custody, military service, legal marriage, and spousal benefits. For individuals

who live in a country that ostensibly provides these protections to all of its citizens, yet in practice denies them to particular groups, the simple granting of
such rights often seems like the ultimate luxury: all we can hope for and, at the
same time, too much to hope for.[52]

Despite the attractiveness of this approach, we must recognize that the
ability to effect positive change through the legal system is (and always has
been) limited. The ability to effect social change through legislation or court
decisions has been the subject of intense academic debate.[53] Even setting
aside debates over cause and effect, the courts, to which we turn most often
for vindication of our rights, are an inherently limited tool for effecting
change. A recent empirical study of appellate court decisions confirmed
anecdotal evidence[54] that state courts are far more receptive than federal
courts to the claims of lesbian and gay litigants.[55] Indeed, a commentator has
characterized this study as indicating that "federal courts not only were less
receptive than state courts to gay rights claims, but that they were *systemati-
cally* hostile" to such claims.[56] As a practical matter, this hostility significantly limits the places where civil rights claims may be brought with some
chance of success, and it simultaneously increases the costs of litigation by
necessitating, in many cases, fifty separate state battles in lieu of a single federal battle. The chances of success are further limited by the possibility,
which exists in every case, that sexual prejudice will influence a judge's or a
jury's decision in a case brought by a lesbian or gay man.[57]

Even more discouraging, however, is the need for lesbians and gay men
to conform to the expectations of the legal system. To obtain a certain result,
lesbian and gay litigants may feel constrained to make arguments that will
help them win in the short term but that may do long-term harm. Moreover,
rather than telling their own stories in their own words, lesbian and gay litigants may be forced to tell a partial, stylized version of their stories that fits
what the legal system wants to hear. As my colleagues Richard Delgado and
Jean Stefancic have remarked, "the story you end up telling is not your own,
not the one you would recount if you were telling it to a friend. You do not
feel that comfortable with it; it is not you, in a way."[58] And this censorship
does not come from the legal system alone; lesbian and gay rights organizations are complicit in this silencing whenever they discourage individuals
from pursuing their legal rights for fear of suffering a loss in court or choose
a plaintiff for a test case in the belief that he embodies characteristics that
will make him sympathetic to a court.[59]

Changing Everyday Law Through Our Radical Everyday Lives
Given these questions and limitations, it seems unwise to place so much of
our focus on rights-based strategies—that is, on lobbying for (or against)
legislation when we think we can win an incremental victory (or stave off
defeat) and on seeking to bring that "right" case before the "right" court at

the "right" time in the hope of establishing favorable legal precedent. We would be better served by shedding our tendency to view legal change as an end in itself in favor of recognizing that legal change is no more than a single means of working toward our ends. For, in reality, the relationship between law and society is not unidirectional; rather, the relationship is more complex because the legal and social realms influence—and are influenced by—each other. Thus, legal decisions can create opportunities for social change, just as social change can alter how legal decisions are made.[60]

In place of our current, largely rights-based approach, we need to strike a more appropriate balance between pursuing legal and nonlegal avenues for change. In part, this will require us to shift the locus of action away from centralized efforts, which rely on the national civil rights organizations (e.g., the Human Rights Campaign, the National Gay and Lesbian Task Force, and Lambda Legal) for direction and guidance, toward a broader effort that enlists each of us to do all we can to effect change in our daily lives. Indeed, I will close this introductory chapter and open the remainder of the book by suggesting that our individual lesbian and gay narratives—the stories of our everyday lives—are a radical and powerful tool for enhancing our ability to effect favorable legal *and* social change.

A quick story will serve as an apt prelude to this discussion. During the early 1990s, I lived in San Diego, California, for a year while clerking for a federal judge after graduating from law school. Early that year, I purchased a T-shirt from the AIDS Coalition to Unleash Power (ACT UP) booth at a local event.[61] The T-shirt was emblazoned with the words "SILENCE = DEATH." On the back of the T-shirt, these words were translated into a number of different languages, behind which was an image of the globe. I felt strongly about HIV prevention and the message on the T-shirt because I had spent my last year of law school working at an AIDS law clinic to help people with HIV (almost all of whom were gay men and many of whom had already advanced to full-blown AIDS) to obtain Social Security disability benefits and to prepare wills, living wills, and powers of attorney for them.

Later in the year, I was at the grocery store standing in the checkout line when an attractive, impeccably dressed elderly woman tapped me on the shoulder. She had noticed my T-shirt and was wondering what the message meant. I explained to her that, for me, the message meant that failing to talk about HIV/AIDS would only lead to more deaths from the disease—progress in fighting the disease could come only from speaking out, talking about the disease, raising awareness, and demanding a cure. I am not sure that this elderly woman quite knew how to respond, but after she reflected for a moment, she acknowledged that the message was valuable.

The message on that T-shirt is not only applicable to HIV/AIDS; it applies equally to the larger lesbian and gay movement. Each time we choose to pass as straight or to cover our sexual orientation because we believe it will make someone else (e.g., a judge, an employer, a parent, or a friend) feel

more comfortable, we contribute to our own death—that slow and painful
death of our individual and collective identity that my mother had a taste of
in the teachers' room that day at school. Similarly juxtaposed with the adverse effects on us of silence are the benefits of speaking out: Recall that
studies have demonstrated a correlation between contact with lesbians and
gay men, particularly close and frequent contact, and positive general attitudes toward lesbians and gay men. Our experience with HIV/AIDS should
counsel us to take every opportunity, in court and out of court, to speak
out—to tell our stories and to make sure that those stories are told in our
own powerful and empowering words:[62]

> At stake here is not only the self-identity of lesbians and gay men as such but
> also the ability to tell our stories and share our lives. The ability to speak of
> oneself in one's own terms, to tell the story of one's life, marks the difference
> between existence and nonexistence, community and isolation, pride and
> shame. Both our self-images and the images others have of us depend on our
> freedom to share our stories. The importance of stories in changing others' at-
> titudes cannot be overestimated, for "our stories hold the power of persua-
> sion. We must counter disinformation with the truth of our lives."[63]

The more lesbians and gay men tell their individual stories—stories of discrimination and subordination; of love lost and found; of the banalities of
daily life with partners, parents, children, and friends—the harder it will be
for members of the heterosexual majority to view us as an undifferentiated
"other" that can be marginalized, demonized, stigmatized, or just forgotten.
They will begin to see us as both the same and different in a myriad of ways.
Our stories—*all* of our stories—are a woefully underutilized tool for eliminating the boundaries of straight sympathy for lesbians and gay men. Our
stories hold the promise of moving straight people beyond sympathy and toward empathy; in other words, our stories may convert what is really no more
than a form of pity into an understanding of what it is really like to be a lesbian or gay man living as an outsider in a generally hostile society. This understanding may shake straight people out of the complacency that their heterosexual privilege affords them and may help to extricate us from our current
predicament and move us closer to the unqualified acceptance that we seek.
    There is an additional advantage to telling our own stories in our own
words. The cramped, two-dimensional stories that have been told in the legal realm have too often privileged the experience of those who most closely
mirror the members of the majority who will be passing judgment on us. It
would be to our advantage to enrich the overall lesbian and gay narrative
with the many individual stories that compose the diverse rainbow that we
have adopted as the symbol of our movement. In this way, we can help others to see us not as "homosexuals" or "gays" (terms that tend to bring to
mind gay men and to obscure lesbians) but as multidimensional people. By

telling a multiplicity of stories, we can be seen not just through the single lens of our sexual orientation but as a complex amalgam of the characteristics and experiences that contribute to who we are as individual human beings, including those relating to our race, class, gender, religion, ethnicity, and physical ability (to name a few).[64] Through these stories, we can work to break down stereotypes, those "logjam[s] of overgeneralization inherent in arguments based on assumptions about a group identity."[65]

Naturally, this strategy involves risks and costs. It will require a conscious effort on all of our parts not just to "come out" but to "be out." As mentioned earlier, the coming-out process is ongoing and never ending. In our everyday encounters, we will have to strive not to take the easy road and to allow the prevailing presumption of heterosexuality to mask or cover who we are. Talking about what you did over the weekend with your partner, your vacation together, or the everyday obstacles that you encounter as a lesbian or gay man might not seem as important as protesting a bias crime, an instance of employment discrimination, or the inability to marry—*but it is.*

Over the long history recounted earlier, antigay fear, prejudice, and persecution have become entrenched in our society—to the point that heterosexuality is tacitly privileged in nearly every area of our lives. Because this privileging is an unspoken assumption upon which our society is built, the only way to combat its effects is to draw attention to the privileging and challenge it wherever and whenever we meet it. We cannot limit ourselves to speaking out only in "important" situations, when redress is required for some wrong that has been done, because these wrongs are not the problem—they are no more than symptoms of the problem. To effect lasting, positive change, we must attack the problem itself—the heterosexual hegemony that makes it so difficult for straight people to embrace and understand our point of view—by engaging in an active overturning and destabilizing of the privileging of heterosexuality that undergirds so much of our social structure.

Opportunities to overturn and destabilize this privileging abound. We encounter them each time we feel (internal or external) pressure to keep silent—to pass as straight or to cover our sexual orientation. We can choose to give in to that pressure and suffer the reaffirmation of the privileging as it is painfully reinscribed over our identity. Alternatively, we can choose to tell our stories in our own words, to call attention to the privileging of heterosexuality, and to challenge and subvert it. This latter alternative will require a very trying effort. We will not always be met with sympathy or understanding; indeed, each time that we speak out, we risk being met with unabashed verbal (or even physical) hostility. Although it would be truly unwise to speak out when we are certain that our physical safety would be jeopardized, we should recognize that the difficult situations will often be the ones in which our stories have the potential to move someone to recognize and question (and maybe someday reject or abandon) a privileging that she had never noticed before.

For example, simply talking about our lives in the same matter-of-fact tone and way that straight people speak about their own lives is often viewed as a threatening, radical act. Undoubtedly, when we do so, we may be accused of "flaunting" the "private" matter of our (homo)sexual orientation. Such a reaction should not be viewed as a mark of benign ignorance—it should be viewed as a mark of our oppression by straight society and the clearest evidence of every straight person's (witting or unwitting) sanctioning of it and participation in it. Instead of being cowed by this reaction, we should take it as an opportunity to point out the many ways in which the presumption and privileging of heterosexuality permeate our society and suffuse the words of straight people with (not-so-hidden) meaning. Their ability to speak freely about matters that implicate their (hetero)sexual orientation—whether it be about parents, grandparents, and grandchildren; dating, relationships, marriage, and divorce; or trying to get pregnant, the birth of children, and the ups and downs of raising children—stems from, and simultaneously reinforces, the presumption and privileging of heterosexuality. Furthermore, the flaunting of heterosexuality comes not only through speech; we also see it in symbols: the wedding rings that are visible on so many hands, the pictures of family on desks at work, the station wagon or minivan in the driveway, and the political metonym of the soccer (now security) "mom" and the NASCAR "dad." Unless and until the straight majority hears our perspective, we cannot expect them to question their own unspoken, unconscious privileging of heterosexuality in all that they say and do.

And, in keeping with a multidimensional view of the lesbian and gay community, we must recognize that different members of our community experience coming out and being out differently. Because of the intersection of sexual orientation with other characteristics (e.g., ethnicity, race, gender, or class), some members of our community may pay a higher price than others for pursuing a strategy of destabilizing outness.[66] As a result, we must also take the next step of engaging in a dialogue to see how the costs and burdens of coming out and being out can be lessened for them, and to see how we can work together to combat the other privilegings in our society that affect members of the lesbian and gay community.[67] One way in which the inherent risks and costs of this strategy can be mitigated is if we are not the only ones undertaking the task. If it is done carefully and with sensitivity, those who care about us—our straight family, friends, and colleagues—can themselves begin to identify and challenge the privileging of heterosexuality in our society as well.[68]

In the following pages, my goal is to highlight some of the many areas in which the privileging of heterosexuality manifests itself and to empower and inspire each of us to identify and challenge that privileging—to tell our own stories, in our own words, and in the most effective way possible. Thus, the title of this book notwithstanding, the remaining chapters will not focus narrowly on legal strategies or legal solutions to problems. Knowing our legal rights is important, but it is equally important to know when and how most effectively to press those rights and to know when and what nonlegal avenues of relief might be more appropriate alternatives. With these tools, we must engage in a constant overturning from within, a subversion through narrative of the privileging of heterosexuality in our society. Of course we should expect to meet with both success and failure along the way, and progress will often be incremental at best. Nonetheless, to paraphrase the epigraph with which this chapter began, we can neither accept our current predicament nor rely on others to extricate us from it—we must undertake the far harder task that is "to feel its intolerability and seek the strength to change it."

Notes

1. See, for example, Susan J. Becker, "Many Are Chilled, but Few Are Frozen: How Transformative Learning in Popular Culture, Christianity, and Science Will Lead to the Eventual Demise of Legally Sanctioned Discrimination Against Sexual Minorities in the United States," *Am. U. J. Gender Soc. Pol'y and L.* 14 (2006): 177.

2. Elizabeth Armstrong has provocatively challenged the conventional wisdom that the 1969 Stonewall uprising was the catalyst for gay liberation. Elizabeth A. Armstrong, *Forging Gay Identities: Organizing Sexuality in San Francisco, 1950–1994* (Chicago: University of Chicago Press, 2002), 56–80.

3. M. V. Lee Badgett, *Money, Myths, and Change: The Economic Lives of Lesbians and Gay Men* (Chicago: University of Chicago Press, 2001), 101–132; David M. Skover and Kellye Y. Testy, "LesBiGay Identity as Commodity," *Cal. L. Rev.* 90 (2002): 223.

4. *Bowers v. Hardwick*, 478 U.S. 186 (1986).

5. *Lawrence v. Texas*, 539 U.S. 558 (2003).

6. *Goodridge v. Dep't of Pub. Health*, 798 N.E.2d 941 (Mass. 2003); see also *Opinions of the Justices to the Senate*, 802 N.E.2d 565 (Mass. 2004).

7. For example, *Karouni v. Gonzales*, 399 F.3d 1163 (9th Cir. 2005); *Hernandez-Montiel v. Immigration and Naturalization Serv.*, 225 F.3d 1084 (9th Cir. 2000); *Pitcherskaia v. Immigration and Naturalization Serv.*, 118 F.3d 641 (9th Cir. 1997). But see Amnesty International, *Crimes of Hate, Conspiracy of Silence: Torture and Ill Treatment Based on Sexual Identity* (London: Amnesty International Publications, 2001) (including a number of occurrences in the United States among examples of torture and ill treatment of individuals based on their sexual orientation).

8. Sonia Katyal, "Exporting Identity," *Yale J.L. and Feminism* 14 (2002): 97, 98–102.

9. William B. Rubenstein, "Do Gay Rights Laws Matter? An Empirical Assessment," *S. Cal. L. Rev.* 75 (2001): 65, 68.

10. Sylvia A. Allegretto and Michelle M. Arthur, "An Empirical Analysis of Homosexual/Heterosexual Male Earnings Differentials: Unmarried and Equal?" *Indus. and Lab. Rel. Rev.* 54 (2001): 631, 644; Nathan Berg and Donald Lien, "Measuring the Effect of Sexual Orientation on Income: Evidence of Discrimination?" *Contemp.*

Econ. Pol'y 20 (2002): 394, 411; Dan A. Black, Hoda R. Makar, Seth G. Sanders, and Lowell J. Taylor, "The Earnings Effects of Sexual Orientation," *Indus. and Lab. Rel. Rev.* 56 (2003): 449, 463; John M. Blandford, "The Nexus of Sexual Orientation and Gender in the Determination of Earnings," *Indus. and Lab. Rel. Rev.* 56 (2003): 622, 628; Christopher S. Carpenter, "Revisiting the Income Penalty for Behaviorally Gay Men: Evidence from NHANES III," *Lab. Econ.* 14 (2007): 25, 29–32.

11. See Black et al., "The Earnings Effects of Sexual Orientation," 466–469; Blandford, "The Nexus of Sexual Orientation and Gender," 630, 639–640; and Letitia Anne Peplau and Adam Fingerhut, "The Paradox of the Lesbian Worker," *J. Soc. Issues* 60 (2004): 719, 721–727.

12. M. V. Lee Badgett, "The Wage Effects of Sexual Orientation Discrimination," *Indus. and Lab. Rel. Rev.* 48 (1995): 726, 728.

13. William B. Rubenstein, "The Real Story of U.S. Hate Crimes Statistics: An Empirical Analysis," *Tul. L. Rev.* 78 (2004): 1213. It is worth noting that Rubenstein's analysis uses the bias-crime statistics compiled by the Federal Bureau of Investigation (FBI). See note 14 for a discussion of the limitations of these statistics.

14. National Coalition of Anti-Violence Programs (NCAVP), *Anti-Lesbian, Gay, Bisexual, and Transgender Violence in 2004* (New York: NCAVP, 2005); NCAVP, *Anti-Lesbian, Gay, Bisexual, and Transgender Violence in 2003* (New York: NCAVP, 2004). The FBI also reports bias-crime statistics, including those motivated by sexual orientation bias; however, these reports significantly underreport the level of antigay violence in the United States. The FBI report for 2003, which covers a geographic area including nearly 83 percent of the national population, reported only 1,239 incidents of violence motivated by sexual orientation bias, which is far below the number reported by NCAVP with respect to a much smaller portion of the national population. U.S. Department of Justice, *FBI Hate Crime Statistics: 2003* (Washington, DC: FBI, 2004): 1, 9. The FBI's underreporting of sexual orientation–motivated bias crimes has been attributed to a number of factors, including the victim's desire not to be outed and lesbian women's and gay men's general distrust of the police due to a history of harassment at their hands. Donald Altschiller, *Hate Crimes: A Reference Handbook*, 2d ed. (Santa Barbara, CA: ABC-CLIO, 2005): 27–28.

15. Bob Hague, "Voicemail Message Suggests 'Open Season' on Gays," Wisconsin Radio Network, December 6, 2005, available at www.wrn.com/gestalt/go.cfm?objectid=E78DA9DB-FA31-41FE-835BAA01D956B977&dbtranslator=local.cfm; see also *Boyd County High School Gay-Straight Alliance v. Bd. of Educ.*, 258 F. Supp. 2d 667, 670 n.1 (E.D. Ky. 2003) ("One example of the harassment includes students in . . . English class stating that they needed to take all the fucking faggots out in the back woods and kill them"); American Civil Liberties Union, "2006 Workplan" (2006), 6 (indicating that the same "school's Model United Nations once adopted a resolution declaring an 'open hunting season' on gay students").

16. *Citizens for Equal Prot., Inc. v. Bruning*, 455 F.3d 859 (8th Cir. 2006); *Perdue v. O'Kelley*, 632 S.E.2d 110 (Ga. 2006); *Schulman v. Att'y Gen.*, 850 N.E.2d 505 (Mass. 2006); *Hernandez v. Robles*, 855 N.E.2d 1 (N.Y. 2006); *Andersen v. King County*, 138 P.3d 963 (Wash. 2006).

17. Kristen L. Walker, "Evolving Human Rights Norms Around Sexuality," *ILSA J. Int'l and Comp. L.* 6 (2000): 343, 344.

18. *Dudgeon v. United Kingdom*, app. 7525/76, 4 Eur. H.R. Rep. 149, 167–168 (1981).

19. *Modinos v. Cyprus,* app. 15070/89, 16 Eur. H.R. Rep. 485, 492 (1993); *Norris v. Ireland,* app. 10581/83, 13 Eur. H.R. Rep. 186, 201 (1988).

20. Laurence R. Helfer, "International Decision: *Salgueiro da Silva Mouta v. Portugal; A.D.T. v. United Kingdom,*" *Am. J. Int'l L.* 95 (2001): 422; see also Kristen Walker, "Sexuality and Human Rights in Europe: An Update," *N.Y.U. Rev. L. and Soc. Change* 26 (2000): 169, 185.

21. *B.B. v. United Kingdom,* app. 53760/00, 39 Eur. H.R. Rep. 635 (2004); *Karner v. Austria,* app. 40016/98, 38 Eur. H.R. Rep. 528 (2003); *SL v. Austria,* app. 45330/99, 37 Eur. H.R. Rep. (2003); *L and V v. Austria,* app. 39392/98 and 39829/98, 36 Eur. H.R. Rep. 1022 (2003); *ADT v. United Kingdom,* app. 35765/97, 31 Eur. H.R. Rep. 803 (2000); *Lustig-Prean v. United Kingdom,* app. 31417/96 and 32377/96, 29 Eur. H.R. Rep. 548 (1999); *Smith and Grady v. United Kingdom,* app. 33985/96 and 33986/96, 29 Eur. H.R. Rep. 493 (1999); *Salgueiro da Silva Mouta v. Portugal,* app. 33290/96, 31 Eur. H.R. Rep. 1055 (1999).

22. International Covenant on Civil and Political Rights (ICCPR), U.N.T.S. 999: 171, December 16, 1966. In contrast to the European Convention, the United States is a party to the ICCPR. However, the United States ratified the ICCPR subject to a declaration that its operative provisions would not be self-executing, which effectively prevents an action from being brought under the ICCPR in U.S. courts until such time as implementing legislation is enacted. *Cong. Rec.* 138 (1992): 8068–8071.

In addition, the United States has not ratified the optional protocol to the ICCPR that would allow the committee to accept individual complaints concerning U.S. compliance with the ICCPR. See Optional Protocol to the International Covenant on Civil and Political Rights, U.N.T.S. 999: 302, 302 n.1, December 16, 1966 (entered into force on March 23, 1976); Office of the UN High Commissioner for Human Rights, "Status of Ratifications of the Principal International Human Rights Treaties," available at www.unhchr.ch/pdf/report.pdf.

23. *Toonen v. Australia,* UN Human Rights Commission, Communication 488/1992, Doc. CCPR/C/50/D/488/1992 §§8.3, 8.6, 9, April 4, 1994.

24. *Young v. Australia,* UN Human Rights Commission, Communication 941/2000, Doc. CCPR/C/78/D/941/2000 §11, September 18, 2003.

25. *Joslin v. New Zealand,* UN Human Rights Commission, Communication 902/1999, Doc. CCPR/C/75/D/902/1999 §8.3, July 30, 2002.

26. ICCPR, U.N.T.S. 999, art. 23(2).

27. *Joslin v. New Zealand,* §8.2.

28. Ibid., app. (citations and footnotes omitted).

29. Ibid.

30. The word "homophobia" was coined by the psychologist George Weinberg in the late 1960s. Gregory M. Herek, "The Psychology of Sexual Prejudice," *Current Directions in Psychol. Sci.* 9 (2000): 19. This term has proven to be an effective rhetorical device for lesbians and gay men because it stands "a central assumption of heterosexual society on its head by locating the 'problem' of homosexuality not in homosexual people, but in heterosexuals who were intolerant of gay men and lesbians." Gregory M. Herek, "Beyond 'Homophobia': Thinking about Sexual Prejudice and Stigma in the Twenty-first Century," *Sexuality Res. and Soc. Pol'y* 1, no. 2 (2004): 6, 8. Notwithstanding both its rhetorical power and its usefulness in drawing attention to antigay hostility, scholars and psychologists have criticized the term because of its imprecision and ability to mislead. Herek, "The Psychology of Sexual

Prejudice," 19; see also Colleen R. Logan, "Homophobia? No, Homoprejudice," *J. Homosexuality* 31 (1996): 31, 32; Tony White, "Homophobia: A Misnomer," *Transactional Analysis J.* 29 (1999): 77, 77–79. To remedy these problems, research psychologist Gregory Herek has broken antigay hostility down into three different categories: sexual stigma (i.e., "the shared knowledge of society's negative regard for any nonheterosexual behavior, identity, relationship, or community"), heterosexism (i.e., "the cultural ideology that perpetuates sexual stigma by denying and denigrating any nonheterosexual form of behavior, identity, relationship, or community"), and sexual prejudice (i.e., "heterosexuals' negative attitudes toward homosexual behavior; people who engage in homosexual behavior or who identify as gay, lesbian, or bisexual; and communities of gay, lesbian, and bisexual people"). Herek, "Beyond 'Homophobia,'" 15–17.

In view of this criticism of the term "homophobia," I will eschew its use in this book except where another author employs the term. In its place, I will use broad terms such as "antigay hostility," "antigay oppression," or one of Herek's more precise terms where appropriate.

31. For example, Anne M. Bowen and Martin J. Bourgeois, "Attitudes Toward Lesbian, Gay, and Bisexual College Students: The Contribution of Pluralistic Ignorance, Dynamic Social Impact, and Contact Theories," *J. Am. C. Health* 50 (2001): 91 (students at two residence halls of a single university); Gregory M. Herek and John P. Capitanio, "'Some of My Best Friends': Intergroup Contact, Concealable Stigma, and Heterosexuals' Attitudes Toward Gay Men and Lesbians," *Personality and Soc. Psychol. Bull.* 22 (1996): 412 (national telephone survey); Gregory M. Herek and Eric K. Glunt, "Interpersonal Contact and Heterosexuals' Attitudes Toward Gay Men: Results from a National Survey," *J. Sex Res.* 30 (1993): 239 (national telephone survey); Donald W. Hinrichs and Pamela J. Rosenberg, "Attitudes Toward Gay, Lesbian, and Bisexual Persons Among Heterosexual Liberal Arts College Students," *J. Homosexuality* 43 (2002): 61 (students at six liberal arts colleges in the Northeast and Midwest).

At this juncture, it is worth noting that women and people of color may experience coming out differently than do gay white men, and many have questioned the centrality of coming out to gay identity. Armstrong, *Forging Gay Identities*, 136–137, 150. This topic will be discussed further in the closing section of this chapter.

32. I have chosen to use the term "sympathy" rather than "empathy" because straight people generally do not identify with and understand the experiences of lesbians and gay men. Ingrained societal discomfort with homosexual sex makes it difficult for heterosexuals truly to put themselves in the place of lesbians and gay men. See, for example, Anthony C. Infanti, "The Internal Revenue Code as Sodomy Statute," *Santa Clara L. Rev.* 44 (2004): 763, 777, 783–784 (discussing the desexualized euphemisms employed by straight society to describe the members of a same-sex couple; for example, "friend," "special friend," "partner," or "significant other"). The correlation between contact with lesbians and gay men and positive attitudes toward us can most plausibly be explained as instances of straight sympathy (and not empathy). These individuals likely feel an affinity toward lesbians and gay men whom they know personally (as opposed to truly understanding what their lives are like); as a result, these individuals naturally deplore any unjustified ill treatment of their lesbian or gay family and friends.

33. Nathaniel Persily, Patrick Egan, and Kevin Wallsten, "Gay Marriage, Public Opinion, and the Courts," University of Pennsylvania Law School Public Law and Legal Theory Research Paper Series 06-17, 2006, 11 (footnote omitted).

34. Herek and Capitanio, "'Some of My Best Friends.'"

35. Available at www.etymonline.com.

36. Byrne Fone, *Homophobia: A History* (New York: Picador, 2000), 7.

37. Ibid., 17.

38. Ibid., 26–27.

39. Ibid., 62.

40. Ibid., 114–115.

41. Ibid., 131 (footnote omitted).

42. Ibid., 174–175.

43. Ibid., 180.

44. Ibid., 214.

45. Ibid., 266.

46. William N. Eskridge, Jr., "Law and the Construction of the Closet: American Regulation of Same-Sex Intimacy, 1880–1946," *Iowa L. Rev.* 82 (1997): 1007; William N. Eskridge, Jr., "Privacy Jurisprudence and the Apartheid of the Closet, 1946–1961," *Fla. St. U. L. Rev.* 24 (1997): 703; William N. Eskridge, Jr., "Challenging the Apartheid of the Closet: Establishing Conditions for Lesbian and Gay Intimacy, Nomos, and Citizenship, 1961–1981," *Hofstra L. Rev.* 25 (1997): 817.

47. Eskridge, "Law and the Construction of the Closet," 1068–1069 (footnote omitted).

48. Ibid., 1054.

49. Ibid.

50. Ibid., 1069.

51. See Richard Delgado and Jean Stefancic, "Images of the Outsider in American Law and Culture: Can Free Expression Remedy Systemic Social Ills?" *Cornell L. Rev.* 77 (1992): 1258, 1280; Richard Delgado and Jean Stefancic, "The Racial Double Helix: Watson, Crick, and *Brown v. Board of Education* (Our No-Bell Prize Award Speech)," *How. L.J.* 47 (2004): 473, 487.

52. Diane Helene Miller, *Freedom to Differ: The Shaping of the Gay and Lesbian Struggle for Civil Rights* (New York: New York University Press, 1998), 140.

53. See, for example, Patricia A. Cain, *Rainbow Rights: The Role of Lawyers and Courts in the Lesbian and Gay Civil Rights Movement* (Boulder, CO: Westview Press, 2000), 5–9; Miller, *Freedom to Differ*, 145–148; Toni M. Massaro, "Gay Rights, Thick and Thin," *Stan. L. Rev.* 49 (1996): 45, 53; Jane S. Schacter, "Sexual Orientation, Social Change, and the Courts," *Drake L. Rev.* 54 (2006): 861.

54. See Cain, *Rainbow Rights*, 233–241; William B. Rubenstein, "The Myth of Superiority," *Const. Comment.* 16 (1999): 599.

55. Daniel R. Pinello, *Gay Rights and American Law* (Cambridge: Cambridge University Press, 2003), 105–117, 145–146. For a critique of this study, see Nan D. Hunter, "Federal Courts, State Courts, and Civil Rights: Judicial Power and Politics," *Geo. L.J.* 92 (2004): 941 (reviewing Pinello, *Gay Rights and American Law*).

56. Hunter, "Federal Courts, State Courts, and Civil Rights," 942.

57. See Todd Brower, "Multistable Figures: Sexual Orientation Visibility and Its Effects on the Experiences of Sexual Minorities in the Courts," *Pace L. Rev.* 27

(2007): 141, 165–181; Drury Sherrod and Peter M. Nardi, "Homophobia in the Courtroom: An Assessment of Biases Against Gay Men and Lesbians in a Multiethnic Sample of Potential Jurors," in Gregory M. Herek, ed., *Stigma and Sexual Orientation: Understanding Prejudice Against Lesbians, Gay Men, and Bisexuals* (Thousand Oaks, CA: Sage Publications, 1998), 24.

58. Delgado and Stefancic, "The Racial Double Helix," 474; see also Miller, *Freedom to Differ*, 142–145; Massaro, "Gay Rights, Thick and Thin," 55.

59. For example, Ellen Ann Andersen, *Out of the Closets and into the Courts* (Ann Arbor: University of Michigan Press, 2005), 85–86, 128–129, 186–187; Devon W. Carbado, "Black Rights, Gay Rights, Civil Rights," *UCLA L. Rev.* 47: 1467, 1505–1517; Anthony C. Infanti, "*Homo Sacer,* Homosexual: Some Thoughts on Waging Tax Guerrilla Warfare," *Unbound: Harv. J. of the Legal Left* 2 (2006): 27, 44–45 and n.87. But see Suzanne B. Goldberg, "On Making Anti-Essentialist and Social Constructionist Arguments in Court," *Or. L. Rev.* 81 (2002): 629, 661 n.117 (indicating that during her time at Lambda Legal an effort was made to obtain a diverse group of plaintiffs).

60. Andersen, *Out of the Closets and into the Courts,* 140–142, 199–202, 210–213; see also Tonja Jacobi, "Sharing the Love: The Political Power of Remedial Delay in Same-Sex Marriage Cases," *Tul. J.L. and Sexuality* 15 (2006): 11, 28–38; Persily et al., "Gay Marriage, Public Opinion, and the Courts," 43–44.

61. For those unfamiliar with the organization, "ACT UP is a diverse, nonpartisan group of individuals united in anger and committed to direct action to end the AIDS crisis. We advise and inform. We demonstrate. WE ARE NOT SILENT." ACT UP: AIDS Coalition to Unleash Power, available at www.actupny.org.

62. For a description of the ways in which an individual's story may be told better in court, see Goldberg, "On Making Anti-Essentialist and Social Constructionist Arguments," 661.

63. Miller, *Freedom to Differ,* 152 (quoting Urvashi Vaid, "After Identity," *New Republic* [May 10, 1993]: 28).

64. For example, Beverly Greene, ed., *Ethnic and Cultural Diversity Among Lesbians and Gay Men* (Thousand Oaks, CA: Sage Publications, 1997); Susan Raffo, ed., *Queerly Classed* (Boston: South End Press, 1997); William B. Rubenstein, R. Bradley Sears, and Robert J. Sockloskie, "Some Demographic Characteristics of the Gay Community in the United States" (2003), 16, available at www.law.ucla.edu/williamsinstitute/publications/GayDemographics.pdf.

65. Massaro, "Gay Rights, Thick and Thin," 105.

66. See Beverly Greene, "Ethnic Minority Lesbians and Gay Men: Mental Health and Treatment Issues," in Greene, ed., *Ethnic and Cultural Diversity,* 216, 233, 234; Althea Smith, "Cultural Diversity and the Coming-Out Process: Implications for Clinical Practice," in Greene, ed., *Ethnic and Cultural Diversity,* 279, 288; Nancy Ehrenreich, "Subordination and Symbiosis: Mechanisms of Mutual Support Between Subordinating Systems," *UMKC L. Rev.* 71 (2002): 251, 283–285.

67. See Kate Kendall, "Race, Same-Sex Marriage, and White Privilege: The Problem with Civil Rights Analogies," *Yale J.L. and Feminism* 17 (2005): 133, 137.

68. See Ian Ayres and Jennifer Gerarda Brown, *Straightforward: How to Mobilize Heterosexual Support for Gay Rights* (Princeton, NJ: Princeton University Press, 2005); Devon W. Carbado, "Straight out of the Closet," *Berkeley Women's L.J.* 15 (2000): 76, 108–124.

2

Public Accommodations and Bias Crimes

One Sunday morning, Michael and I decided to go out for breakfast. I was still in law school, and we were early in our relationship. We were spending all of our time together, absorbing as much as we could of, and about, each other.

When we arrived, the restaurant was rather busy—a normal state of affairs for a breakfast place on the weekend. We were seated by the hostess, who gave us two menus and told us that our waitress would be with us shortly. It didn't take long to decide what we wanted, and we closed our menus. But it seemed that the waitress kept forgetting to take our order. She was busily attending to all the patrons around us but didn't appear to remember that we were there. After we noticed that she was taking orders from patrons who had been seated well after we had been, we finally flagged her down and asked her to take our order.

Eventually our food made it to us, and we began to eat. I quickly drank the cup of coffee that the waitress had poured me when she had brought our food; however, she never stopped by our table to refill my cup, even though she made regular rounds to refill cups at the surrounding tables. In the end, I practically had to tackle her to get a refill.

By this time, our conversation had turned from talking about each other to talking about how rudely our waitress was acting. She was clearly unhappy about having to serve us, and we were wondering why. The only thing that distinguished us from the tables around us was that we were two young men dining together. All of the other tables had families or different-sex couples seated at them. Although I have never thought of myself—and certainly not of Michael—as being stereotypically gay, we couldn't help but wonder whether the waitress had correctly guessed that we were gay men based on our looks, mannerisms, and conversation. Or was it that Michael is Hispanic, or that we were a mixed-race couple? Or was something else triggering her behavior? Or were we just reading too much into the situation?

In any event, we were both completely annoyed by the time we had finished eating. Our waitress had succeeded in ruining a perfectly nice breakfast—and, it turned out, the rest of an otherwise nice day. Nevertheless, instead of confronting her or her manager about the poor service in the middle of a crowded restaurant based on mere suspicion, we decided to make our displeasure known by leaving a single penny on the table, which we felt to be more insulting than leaving no tip at all.

Sadly, this is neither an isolated nor a unique experience. Indeed, studies have demonstrated that sexual prejudice manifests itself in discriminatory behavior. In a study that focused on the treatment of same-sex and different-sex couples in retail stores, it was found that, "by virtue of their perceived status as homosexuals, the same individuals received poorer, less friendly, and more uncharitable service by sales associates."[1] In another study that focused on hotels, it was found that hotels contacted by mail granted fewer reservation requests from same-sex couples than from different-sex couples, with the disparity being greater in small hotels than in large hotels.[2]

The results of a recent study of lesbians' and gay men's expectations for interactions with heterosexuals are even more troubling.[3] Faced with a hypothetical situation, 38 percent of the self-identifying lesbian and gay respondents reported that they would fear physical or verbal abuse in interactions with unfamiliar people who had just learned about their sexual orientation. And when asked to more specifically describe the reactions that they expected to experience when a person with a high level of sexual prejudice learned about their sexual orientation, 63 percent of respondents actually volunteered that, in the past, high-prejudice people had harassed them after discovering their sexual orientation. Thirty-eight percent of respondents also reported experiencing hostile or contemptuous looks from high-prejudice people, and 26 percent perceived anxiety or tension in high-prejudice people. The most commonly reported response to situations like the hypothetical one was split evenly between (1) leaving the situation and (2) confronting the high-prejudice individual about his or her sexual prejudice. As you might expect, other studies have found a correlation between suffering harassment, abuse, or discrimination and harmful mental health effects,[4] with one study "finding that gay and lesbian survivors of antigay crimes were more likely than other respondents to regard the world as unsafe, to view people as malevolent, to exhibit a relatively low sense of personal mastery, and to attribute their personal setbacks to sexual prejudice."[5]

In this chapter, I explore the unpredictable manifestations of sexual prejudice that lesbians and gay men are forced to endure—or that they live in fear of enduring—in their everyday encounters. The chapter is split into two parts: In the first part, I discuss sexual prejudice encountered in interactions with staff at hotels, restaurants, retail stores, and other places of public accommodation; in the second part, I discuss some of the gravest manifestations of sexual prejudice—bias crimes. I conclude the chapter with a brief discussion of the relationship between everyday discrimination and violence against lesbians and gay men.

Public Accommodations

With the exception of innkeepers and common carriers (e.g., airlines and railroads), privately operated establishments are free to "exclude individuals arbitrarily unless a statute specifically prohibits the discriminatory conduct."[6] This general rule has its roots in racism, as it formed part of the legal groundwork that was laid in the latter part of the nineteenth century for the Jim Crow system of segregation.[7] Despite its checkered past, this general rule continues to reflect the prevailing legal norm of implicitly sanctioning discrimination. Thus, absent explicit legislative action, privately operated establishments are free to act on any or all of their owners' prejudices, including sexual prejudice.

Statutory Protection Against Discrimination

As of this writing, Congress has not yet extended the protection of federal public accommodations laws to lesbians and gay men. Eighteen states and the District of Columbia have, however, extended the protection of their public accommodations laws to lesbians and gay men.[8] The eighteen states are California, Connecticut, Hawaii, Illinois, Iowa, Maine, Maryland, Massachusetts, Minnesota, New Hampshire, New Jersey, New Mexico, New York, Oregon, Rhode Island, Vermont, Washington, and Wisconsin. A subgroup of these jurisdictions—California, Connecticut, the District of Columbia, New Hampshire, New Jersey, Oregon, and Vermont—also affords same-sex couples who have entered into a civil union or registered as domestic partners the same protections against discrimination on the basis of marital status in access to public accommodations as are afforded to married different-sex couples.[9] In addition, many cities and counties in other states have enacted local ordinances that protect lesbians and gay men from discrimination in public accommodations.

Naturally, the wording—and, hence, the coverage—of these laws varies from jurisdiction to jurisdiction. They range from the most terse in style to the most verbose. California, for example, protects against discrimination "in all business establishments of every kind whatsoever."[10] New Jersey, on the other hand, protects against discrimination in "any place of public accommodation,"[11] which it then goes on to define to include, but not to be limited to:

any tavern, roadhouse, hotel, motel, trailer camp, summer camp, day camp, or resort camp, whether for entertainment of transient guests or accommodation of those seeking health, recreation or rest; any producer, manufacturer, wholesaler, distributor, retail shop, store, establishment, or concession dealing with goods or services of any kind; any restaurant, eating house, or place where food is sold for consumption on the premises; any place maintained for the sale of ice cream, ice and fruit preparations or their derivatives, soda water or confections, or where any beverages of any kind are retailed for consumption on the premises; any garage, any public conveyance operated on land or water, or in the air, any stations and terminals thereof; any bathhouse, boardwalk, or seashore accommodation; any auditorium, meeting place, or hall; any theatre, motion-picture house, music hall, roof garden, skating rink, swimming pool, amusement and recreation park, fair, bowling alley, gymnasium, shooting gallery, billiard and pool parlor, or other place of amusement; any comfort station; any dispensary, clinic or hospital; any public library; any kindergarten, primary and secondary school, trade or business school, high school, academy, college and university, or any educational institution under the supervision of the State Board of Education, or the Commissioner of Education of the State of New Jersey.[12]

These differences in wording have, of course, led to differences in interpretation. For instance, the states have diverged on the application of public accommodations laws to medical offices. The Illinois courts have found that the state's public accommodations law does not apply to medical offices,[13] whereas the California courts have interpreted that state's public accommodations law to cover medical offices.[14] Indeed, as of this writing, a lawsuit is pending before the California Supreme Court in which a lesbian is claiming that her physician violated the state public accommodations law by refusing to provide her fertility treatment on the ground that the treatment conflicted with the physician's fundamentalist Christian religious beliefs.[15] In a state that more narrowly construes its public accommodations law, it simply would not be possible to bring such a suit against a discriminating physician.

Nearer the cutting edge of the law of public accommodations is the application of nondiscrimination requirements to membership organizations such as the Boy Scouts of America (BSA). The California Supreme Court held in 1998 that the BSA, which excludes "avowed" homosexuals, is not a "business establishment" and, therefore, is not subject to the state's public accommodations law. Consequently, the BSA was free to deny a gay man's application to become an assistant scoutmaster based solely on his sexual orientation.[16] In contrast, the New Jersey Supreme Court held in 1999 that the BSA, because of its broad public solicitation of members and its close relationships with government and other public accommodations, is itself a public accommodation under the state's law against discrimination.[17] As a result, the court held that the BSA's expulsion of an assistant scoutmaster because of his sexual orientation violated New Jersey's public accommodations law. As described in detail later, the New Jersey Supreme Court did not, however, have the last word in that dispute.

Even closer to the cutting edge of the law of public accommodations is the application of nondiscrimination requirements to newspapers' refusal to publish same-sex union announcements. As of August 2004, only about one-third of all daily newspapers had published, or had expressed a willingness to publish, these announcements.[18] A commentator has argued that certain public accommodations laws that cover sexual orientation might be used to compel reluctant newspapers to publish same-sex union announcements without violating the newspaper's constitutional right to freedom of speech.[19] But, whether voluntary or involuntary, a newspaper's publication of same-sex union announcements is bound to engender controversy. In fact, in June 2004, an uproar ensued when a same-sex marriage announcement ran in two daily newspapers in the small town of Oil City, Pennsylvania, located just outside Pittsburgh. There was, however, a silver lining in the Oil City situation—the letters to the newspapers were evenly split between those for and those against the announcement. This split surprised the newspapers' managing editor because he had expected opinion in the conservative town to be strongly against the announcement.

Federal Limitations on State Public Accommodations Laws

The scope of each state's public accommodations law thus depends both on the language used by the legislature in drafting the law and on the interpretation of that language by the courts. But whatever a state's choice about the breadth of its public accommodations law, the U.S. Supreme Court has significantly circumscribed the application of those laws in the case of discrimination on the basis of sexual orientation. In two notable decisions, the Court enjoined the application of state public accommodations laws on the ground that enforcing those laws would violate the constitutional rights to freedom of speech and association of those engaging in the discriminatory behavior.

In 1995, the Supreme Court unanimously held in *Hurley v. Irish-American Gay, Lesbian and Bisexual Group of Boston, Inc.* that Massachusetts could not apply its public accommodations law to require the organizers of Boston's Saint Patrick's Day–Evacuation Day Parade to include the Irish American Gay, Lesbian, and Bisexual Group of Boston (GLIB).[20] The Court found that a parade—defined as a group of marchers who are collectively attempting to make some point through their procession—is a form of expression protected by the First Amendment. Indicating that few processions would fail to meet this test, the Court had no difficulty holding the Boston parade to be a constitutionally protected form of speech.

Interestingly, however, the Court never actually described the point that the Boston parade's organizers sought to make through their procession; to the contrary, the Court implied that the organizers had no considered point

at all in mind when choosing marchers, as evidenced by their general le-
niency in admitting just about anyone (other than GLIB, of course) as a participant. But if the Boston parade lacked a discernible message, how, then,
could it qualify as a constitutionally protected form of speech? In the end, it
was enough for the Court that the organizers did not want to be seen as endorsing GLIB's message; thus, lacking any message of their own to be protected, the organizers' bare desire to exclude GLIB became their constitutionally protected speech. In closing its opinion, the Court bewilderingly
stated that its holding rested "not on any particular view about the Council's message but on the Nation's commitment to protect freedom of speech.
Disapproval of a private speaker's statement does not legitimize use of
[Massachusetts's] power to compel the speaker to alter the message by including one more acceptable to others."[21]

In 2000, reviewing the New Jersey Supreme Court's decision that the Boy
Scouts of America was a public accommodation (as discussed earlier), a
closely divided U.S. Supreme Court held in *Boy Scouts of America v. Dale*
that applying the public accommodations law to require the BSA to accept
an openly gay scoutmaster violated the organization's First Amendment
right of expressive association.[22] Because the general mission of the BSA is to
have its scoutmasters instill values in young people, the majority found that
it engages in expressive activity protected by the First Amendment. The majority then found that forcing the BSA to accept an openly gay scoutmaster
would significantly impair its ability to engage in expressive activity—that is,
in articulating its opposition to homosexuality—even though that opposition
had not been included among the BSA's publicly declared values prior to the
expulsion of the scoutmaster who had brought this case.

The majority's decision was harshly criticized by the dissenting justices
on the ground that it was devoid of analysis. Faced with the BSA's utter failure to take a clear public position on the relationship between scouting and
homosexuality, the majority had merely accepted at face value the BSA's
claims in its legal briefs that it did not wish to promote homosexuality and
that forcing it to accept an openly gay assistant scoutmaster would impair its
ability to express this view. As the dissenting justices pointed out, such deference effectively guts civil rights laws because it renders impossible the task
of distinguishing "between genuine exercises of the right to associate . . . and
sham claims that are simply attempts to insulate nonexpressive private discrimination."[23] Taking this trenchant criticism even further in a statement
that could, in its broad strokes, also be applied to the *Hurley* case, law professors Erwin Chemerinsky and Catherine Fisk remarked that:

> *Boy Scouts of America v. Dale* is a ruling in favor of discrimination and intol-
> erance that is wrapped in the rhetoric of freedom of association. Those who
> want to discriminate can always invoke freedom of association; all enforce-
> ment of antidiscrimination laws forces some degree of unwanted association.

It was not surprising that the five most conservative Justices on the Court favored the Boy Scouts and its condemnation of homosexuality. This, though, does not make it any more right than other decisions throughout history that have upheld bigotry and discrimination. Someday, *Boy Scouts of America v. Dale* will be repudiated by the Court like other rulings that denied equality to victims of discrimination.[24]

Until that day arrives, these decisions will embolden others to claim that their First Amendment rights trump the state's interest in ensuring that public accommodations are open to all in a nondiscriminatory fashion. Recall, for example, the California case mentioned earlier in which a physician—whose office is a public accommodation that must normally be open to all regardless of sexual orientation—is claiming that his First Amendment right to refuse to provide fertility treatments to a lesbian on religious grounds prevails over the state's public accommodations law.

Other Forms of Legal Redress

If you are the victim of discriminatory behavior in a jurisdiction without a public accommodations law that covers sexual orientation, a legal remedy may still be available. For instance, innkeepers and common carriers have historically been exempted from the general rule that permits establishments to choose their customers. If the perpetrator of the discrimination falls into either of these categories, you may have a cause of action under state judicial decisions, even if not under the public accommodations law.

Alternatively, if the perpetrator of discrimination is the government or a representative of the government, you may be able to allege a violation of your constitutional rights. A distressing case of sexual prejudice infecting the actions of a government official who was supposed to be "serving the public" took place in Minersville, Pennsylvania, in 1997.[25] In April of that year, two teenaged boys, Marcus Wayman and a friend, were in a car parked in the lot of a beer distributor. The beer distributor's building had been burglarized in the past, and a police officer who observed the car was suspicious because the headlights were out. The police officer called for backup; when the other officer arrived, the two approached the car and questioned the boys. The boys had apparently been drinking alcohol and were evasive when asked why they were in the parking lot. After a search uncovered two condoms, one of the police officers asked the boys if they were there to have sex. The officer claimed that the two admitted to being gay and to being in the parking lot to have sex, but there was some dispute about whether the boys actually made such an admission.

The officers arrested the boys for underage drinking and took them to the local police station. One of the officers then lectured the boys about homosexuality, telling them that it was condemned by the Bible. The officer warned Marcus to tell his grandfather that he was gay or the officer would do it himself. After receiving this warning, Marcus told his friend he was going to commit suicide. When Marcus was released from police custody that night, he went home and wrote a short suicide note to his grandfather. He then took a revolver from the family gun cabinet and shot himself in the face.[26]

Marcus's mother filed a federal civil rights lawsuit against the two police officers, the chief of police, and the Borough of Minersville. The lawsuit alleged that the police had violated her son's constitutional rights to privacy and equal protection of the law. In an early appeal before the case went to trial, the U.S. Court of Appeals for the Third Circuit ruled that the suit could proceed against the police officers because Marcus's right to keep his personal information (including his sexual orientation) private was well settled. At trial, the jury found for the police officers and the borough, but the federal magistrate judge set this verdict aside because it was against the weight of the evidence. Before a new trial was held, Marcus's mother settled her claim for $100,000.

Other Ways to Take Action

In some situations, you may wish to pursue legal redress for discrimination suffered in a public setting—if for no other reason than to obtain an official acknowledgment that society disapproves of the discriminatory behavior. In Marcus Wayman's case, the manifestation of prejudice was so clear, and the consequences were so tragic, that the officer's actions seemed to cry out for legal condemnation. If you wish to pursue legal redress, it would be wise to consult a lawyer to determine whether the discrimination that you suffered is actionable in the jurisdiction where it occurred, especially given the legal norm of discrimination and the patchwork of state and local exceptions, which are of varying scope and size.

In other situations, you may not wish to pursue legal redress. For example, in the case of the restaurant experience that opened this chapter, our right to legal redress under the California public accommodations law was less than clear. We had a couple of points in our favor. First, California law requires "equal treatment of patrons in all aspects of the business"[27] and does not apply merely to outright exclusion from a public accommodation. In addition, the discriminatory behavior need not be a routine occurrence or a policy of the business, so our single incident of differential treatment could have been actionable.[28] But the California courts have interpreted the state's public accommodations law to require that the victim prove *intentional* discrimination on a prohibited basis (e.g., sexual orientation),[29] which we were in no position to do. We had no proof that our waitress was treating us differently based on our sexual orientation, only suspicions that she was doing so. In any event, neither of us had a desire to press—and potentially escalate—this unpleasant matter any further.

In these situations, you also have at your disposal nonlegal means of taking action that protests or resists discriminatory behavior. To combat discrimination, you can take economic or political action in lieu of—or in addition to—legal action. In fact, that was exactly what Michael and I chose to do when we left our waitress a tip of a single penny. We made sure that our waitress suffered economically because of the way she had treated us. And we chose to leave the single penny to be sure that she could not be confused about our motivations. If we had left no tip, she simply might have thought us a couple of cheapskates, or she might have thought that we had simply forgotten to leave a tip. By leaving a single penny, there could be no question that we had thought about her tip and had decided to leave the most inconsequential amount possible.

If we had been more convinced of our waitress's motivations, we could have asked to speak with her supervisor. A discussion with someone in a position of authority can reveal whether an instance of discrimination is an isolated incident or part of a larger pattern of differential treatment that is approved of, or tolerated by, the establishment. A problem that extends beyond one employee acting on her own may warrant more serious action.

Where more serious action is appropriate, you can begin by relating your experience to family and friends and discouraging them from patronizing the establishment. On a larger scale, you might attempt to organize a boycott of the offending business. The lesbian and gay community is no stranger to boycotts; in the past, the community and its straight allies have taken action against Coors, Cracker Barrel Old Style Restaurants, the Boy Scouts of America, and the States of Colorado and Virginia. Boycotts can, however, be "difficult to pull off, because individual decisionmakers must coordinate their activities,"[30] and, unless the offending business capitulates quickly, a significant commitment of resources will be necessary to maintain the requisite level of coordination among the participants.[31]

Moreover, the economic effectiveness of boycotts is uncertain. Other business factors may mask the impact of the boycott, or people who support discrimination against lesbians and gay men may patronize the business to show their approval of the discriminatory behavior and to replace any lost dollars.[32] When boycotts have resulted in change, it has been unclear whether it was the economic impact of the boycott or the accompanying bad public relations (or a combination of the two) that caused the change.[33]

Rather than punishing those who discriminate, some commentators have advocated the more positive approach of rewarding those who treat lesbians and gay men fairly by engaging in what they term "buycotts" or "gaycotts."[34] In their book *Straightforward: How to Mobilize Heterosexual Support for Gay Rights,* Ian Ayres and Jennifer Gerarda Brown propose a "Vacation Pledge for Equal Marriage Rights, through which people would promise to vacation in the first state where either the *legislature* or the *electorate* itself votes to extend marriage rights to same-sex couples."[35] The purpose of the pledge is to provide a financial incentive for a state to take democratic action to legalize same-sex marriage. They argue that action by a state's voters or legislature would make it impossible for those who advocate a constitutional ban on same-sex marriage to attribute legalization to activist judges. Ayres and Brown have created a web site (www.vacation-pledge.org) where you can go to sign the pledge and join their "buycott."

In a related fashion, you can seek out establishments that welcome lesbians and gay men when your sexual orientation will be germane to your interaction with that establishment. Health care is a notable example of an area in which sexual orientation can negatively affect the treatment that you receive:

> A patient's sexual orientation may influence a physician's clinical judgment not only by making the physician less willing to pursue aggressive treatment on the patient's behalf, but also by leading the physician to focus inappropriately on the patient's sexuality, thus interpreting the patient's problems in sexual terms rather than considering the full range of diagnoses.
>
> Out of concern for the perceived likelihood of disapproval and substandard treatment, many lesbians and gay men are reluctant to disclose their sexual orientation to their physicians. . . . While . . . silence may prevent a physician from inappropriately considering the patient's sexuality in exercising medical judgment, it also precludes the physician from considering the patient's sexual orientation in an appropriate (i.e., a medical-needs-related) fashion. Gay men and lesbians do have certain health needs that differ from those of the heterosexual population.[36]

To avoid the adverse effects of these biases, you can choose a physician who welcomes lesbians and gay men and is sensitive to the impact of sexual orientation on your health needs. In fact, the Gay & Lesbian Medical Association (www.glma.org) maintains a health care referrals directory of friendly providers for just this purpose.

It bears repeating, however, that this advice is not confined to the context of health care but applies to *any* situation in which your sexual orientation may be relevant to the interaction with the business. Listings of businesses that reach out to lesbians and gay men can usually be found in the various yellow pages publications that cater to the lesbian and gay community as well as in advertisements in local lesbian and gay newspapers.[37]

Yet another option is to take political action with the aim of effecting legal—and, incidentally, social—change. If your locality has a public accommodations law that does not cover sexual orientation, you can lobby your local legislative body to add sexual orientation to the law's existing list of covered traits or characteristics, or, if no such law currently exists, you can lobby for the enactment of a public accommodations law that includes sexual orientation. As mentioned earlier, nondiscrimination laws send an important message; namely, that the community does not tolerate discrimination on the basis of sexual orientation. In addition, "the very existence of the law forces the potential discriminator to consider the point of view of the gay [or] lesbian . . . person against whom he or she intends to discriminate. Will they file a claim? Will there be publicity? Will they win? Is it worth it? While such a law clearly has deterrence value, more importantly, it encourages consideration of the individual."[38]

A successful lobbying campaign will require significant coordination and communication among and within community groups. Nevertheless, all of this hard work can have positive effects that last well beyond the lobbying campaign. Regardless of the campaign's success or failure, the efforts at coordination will lay the groundwork for future lobbying efforts. For instance, eventual success at the local level can ease the way for success at the state level because a state legislator from a district that has already enacted a nondiscrimination law that covers sexual orientation may be more apt to vote for such a law when it comes before the state legislature.[39]

To break down stereotypes and preconceptions, the organizers of the lobbying effort will need to deploy the stories of lesbians and gay men who have suffered discrimination to sensitize heterosexuals in the community to the emotional, psychological, and other effects that discrimination can have on an individual. The organizers may also wish to highlight the benefits to the community of enacting a nondiscrimination law that includes sexual orientation. For example, some communities have found including sexual orientation in their nondiscrimination laws to be a way of signaling their openness to diversity, which can help to attract businesses to the area.[40] By fostering understanding and working toward a culture of acceptance, the organizers will also produce benefits that extend beyond the lobbying process by fostering empathy for lesbians and gay men and promoting their unqualified acceptance by heterosexual society.[41]

Naturally, this discussion of the substantial work that a successful lobbying effort entails—as well as the significant benefits that can be derived from any lobbying effort—applies equally to suggestions of lobbying for political change in later chapters of this book.

Bias Crimes

Bob Gravel's Story

I am Bob Gravel from Lewiston, ME, and I am here to tell you about my ordeal as a gay man.

My ordeal started in March 1985 and lasted for 8 months. My tormentors followed me, threw objects at me. I went to the police department on 15 occasions and went to the court system, had papers served on these people. Nothing stopped them.

These people decided on November 1, 1985, to get me. They had earlier said they would "kill this faggot." What I did, I borrowed a gun. I never used a gun before, but I knew in my heart that these people were going to kill me.

Everyday Law for Gays and Lesbians

So, on November 3, 2 days after the severe attack, they came, surrounded my house, and started to kick the door in. I called the police. Apparently they were busy.

I informed them "I will take care of it myself." I figure by saying that, the police would get here in a hurry. I live a minute and a half from the police station.

The kicking continued. I grabbed the gun. I called the police again. I ran to the front of my apartment where I have another exit, and there were people out front. Then I decided, "There is no way I can get out of this apartment except to jump from a third floor window." I decided to face the men who were kicking in my door. These guys ran down the stairs before I got to the door. At first I thought, perhaps they are setting the building on fire to flush me out.

I went downstairs. I opened the door that enters into the building. One of them saw me and he said, "He is out here." Then they proceeded to come after me.

I fired in the air. It didn't stop them. Then I brought the gun down, and due to the fact that I never shot a gun, one of the men was hit. He fell to the ground. And then I shot at the other man, but toward his feet, toward the ground, and what happened, the bullet hit the man I had hit the first time again.

I recall that I was picked up, brought to the police station, but never arrested. In Maine, when there is a shooting and someone dies, the State police take over. And the State police saw the complaints I had, the court order for these people to stay away from me, and nothing was done.

This had a lot to do with my not being put in jail.

Three weeks after the shooting, I went to the man's grave who had decided he wanted to kill me. I knelt in prayer, put my hand over his grave, and I told him I forgave him for his hatred and wanting to kill me.

Five weeks later I was brought in front of a grand jury, and after hearing my testimony they decided not to indict me because they found me innocent by self-defense.[42]

Unfortunately, Bob Gravel's story is no less relevant today than it was when he told it to Congress more than twenty years ago. As described in Chapter 1, antigay violence persists at alarming levels. The National Coalition of Anti-Violence Programs (NCAVP) despairingly described 2003 and 2004 as "a period in which anti-LGBT violence has moved 'back to the future,' to a period in which such violence seemed expected, common and constant."[43] Indeed, the NCAVP's reports continue to be sprinkled with stories as distressing as Mr. Gravel's.

Criminal Punishment
Federal Level. Although laws addressing bias crimes "have been on the books for well over a century," no federal law directly punishes bias-motivated violence.[44] The federal sentencing guidelines do, however, authorize an increased

sentence for a defendant who "intentionally selected any victim or any property as the object of the offense of conviction because of the actual or perceived . . . sexual orientation of any person."[45] This penalty enhancement is limited in its application because it applies only where the victim is selected as a result of the perpetrator's antigay animus or hatred and to perpetrators who have been found guilty of a federal crime (most bias crimes are not punishable under federal law).[46] To fill these gaps, legislation that would criminalize sexual orientation–motivated violence has been proposed in both houses of Congress.[47] As of this writing, the House of Representatives has passed this legislation and it is pending in the Senate; however, even if the measure does pass the Senate, President Bush has vowed to veto it.[48]

State Level. The District of Columbia and a majority of the states have enacted laws that specifically address sexual orientation–motivated bias crimes. These laws generally provide some form of penalty enhancement in cases where the perpetrator of a crime chose his victim based on sexual orientation.[49] The required link between the victim's sexual orientation and the crime varies from state to state: Some states require a showing of malice or animus;[50] others require the act to demonstrate or evidence prejudice;[51] but most require only that the crime be "motivated by" or be committed "because of" or "by reason of" the victim's sexual orientation.[52]

States with bias-crime laws that cover sexual orientation are listed in the first column of Table 2.1. The remaining states are listed in the subsequent columns of the table and are broken down into three groups: (1) those with bias-crime laws that do not cover sexual orientation–motivated crimes, (2) those with bias-crime laws that do not contain specified categories of prohibited bias, and (3) those without bias-crime laws.

Civil Remedies and Victims' Rights

A number of the jurisdictions listed in the first column of Table 2.1 have also enacted laws that permit the victims of bias crimes to institute civil actions to recover compensatory and, in some cases, punitive damages and attorney's fees from the perpetrator. Although victims might be able to bring suit without the benefit of these laws, their "enactment . . . is significant in making the cause of action explicit and in making available to the plaintiff a wide array of remedies that might not [otherwise] be available."[53] The jurisdictions that have enacted such laws include California, Colorado, Connecticut, the District of Columbia, Florida, Illinois, Iowa, Maine, Massachusetts, Minnesota, Nebraska, Nevada, New Jersey, Oregon, Pennsylvania, Vermont, and Washington.[54]

In addition, every state and the District of Columbia have created crime victim compensation funds to provide financial assistance to the victims of violent crimes with respect to a limited amount of losses or expenses that are

Table 2.1   D.C. and State Bias-Crime Laws

Covering Crimes Motivated by Sexual Orientation	Not Covering Crimes Motivated by Sexual Orientation	No Categories of Prohibited Bias	No Bias-Crime Law
Arizona	Alabama	Utah	Arkansas
California	Alaska		Georgia[b]
Colorado	Idaho		Indiana
Connecticut	Michigan		South Carolina
Delaware	Mississippi		Wyoming
District of Columbia	Montana		
Florida	North Carolina		
Hawaii	North Dakota		
Illinois	Ohio[a]		
Iowa	Oklahoma		
Kansas	South Dakota		
Kentucky	Virginia		
Louisiana	West Virginia		
Maine			
Maryland			
Massachusetts			
Minnesota			
Missouri			
Nebraska			
Nevada			
New Hampshire			
New Jersey			
New Mexico			
New York			
Oregon			
Pennsylvania			
Rhode Island			
Tennessee			
Texas			
Vermont			
Washington			
Wisconsin			

[a]However, in determining whether an offender's conduct is more serious than the conduct that normally constitutes the offense, Ohio does permit a sentencing judge to take into account the fact that the offender was motivated by prejudice based on sexual orientation when he committed the offense. Ohio Rev. Code §2929.12 (2006).

[b]Georgia's bias-crimes law, which specified no prohibited categories of bias or prejudice, was held to be unconstitutionally vague by the Georgia Supreme Court in October 2004. *Botts v. State*, 604 S.E.2d 512 (Ga. 2004). As of this writing, the Georgia legislature has failed to enact a new bias-crime law.

not covered by insurance.[55] Likewise, every state and the District of Columbia have enacted victims' rights laws, with a majority of the states also having added victims' rights amendments to their constitutions.[56] The precise nature of the rights granted to crime victims varies from state to state, but they often include the right to attend and/or participate in the criminal case, the right to confer or discuss the case with the prosecutor, and the right to make a victim impact statement at sentencing or a parole hearing.[57]

Another important resource for bias-crime victims can be found on the Human Rights Campaign's (HRC's) web site (www.hrc.org). HRC maintains a list of organizations that document bias crimes based on sexual orientation and provide assistance to victims. This list can be located by searching for "LGBT Anti-Violence Programs" on the HRC web site.

Fighting Bias Crimes

When a bias crime is committed, the perpetrator may be punished criminally with an enhanced sentence and may be held accountable through a civil suit for the damage caused to the victim. But these are not the only actions that can (or should) be taken when a community is faced with a bias crime. The Southern Poverty Law Center (SPLC), which monitors hate groups and tracks extremists throughout the United States,[58] has published a helpful pamphlet for those interested in fighting bias. The pamphlet, *Ten Ways to Fight Hate: A Community Response Guide*, contains a series of suggestions—some reactive and others proactive—that are briefly summarized below.

Reactive Suggestions. When a bias crime has already been committed, SPLC recommends that:

1. We act, because the failure to act may be interpreted as approval.
2. We unite together to form a diverse coalition that includes as many individuals and groups as possible, including law enforcement and the media.
3. We provide the victim of the bias crime with necessary support—and SPLC further recommends that all bias crimes be reported.
4. We do our homework and determine whether an organized hate group is involved in the incident, because such research can help to improve the effectiveness of our response.

Proactive Suggestions. To combat bias more generally, SPLC recommends that:

1. We not attend demonstrations that promote antigay bias or prejudice to protest what is being said; instead, we should organize alternative, positive events at the same time, but at some distance away, so that

media and community attention will be drawn away from bias and prejudice and toward tolerance.

2. We speak up to denounce antigay hostility and bias crimes in "church bulletins, door-to-door fliers, web sites, local cable TV bulletin boards, letters to the editor, and print advertisements." In the same vein, we should work with and educate the media about antigay hostility and bias crimes, and we should not be afraid to criticize the media when they fall short in their coverage of bias-related issues.

3. We lobby and educate our public officials, the police, and community leaders about the effects of antigay hostility and bias crimes so that they can become allies in the fight against bias. By the same token, when public officials, the police, and community leaders are making biased statements or if they fail to take action when faced with the biased statements of others, we should not hesitate to hold them accountable for their statements or to put pressure on them to act to fight bias. And, in states with no bias-crime law or a bias-crime law that does not cover sexual orientation, lobbying and educational activity might fruitfully be aimed at the passage of a law that covers sexual orientation–motivated bias crimes.

4. We "look long range" by regularly bringing people from different backgrounds, including straights and gays, together in one place where they can meet and interact with each other—and come to better understand each other. As research psychologist Dr. Gregory Herek has stated, "coming out to heterosexuals is perhaps the most powerful strategy that lesbians and gay men have for overcoming psychological heterosexism and anti-gay violence."[59]

5. We teach tolerance to children and young adults by modeling inclusive language and behavior and ensuring that the local schools are doing the same (for more on the topic of education, see Chapter 3).

6. We all look inside and confront the prejudices that we harbor in an effort to overcome them.[60]

Critiquing Bias-Crime Laws

Questioning Their Existence. Enhancing the penalty for bias-motivated offenses has engendered a considerable amount of controversy.[61] Significantly, there had been some concern that bias-crime laws might run afoul of the federal constitutional right to freedom of speech because the penalty enhancement is based on the speech or ideas of the perpetrator.[62] However, in 1993, the U.S. Supreme Court dispelled this concern when it unanimously upheld Wisconsin's penalty enhancement statute.[63] The Wisconsin statute enhanced the penalty for the underlying offense when the offender intentionally selected the victim "because of" her sexual orientation (or other protected characteristic).[64] In reaching its decision, the Court accepted Wisconsin's justification for penalty enhancement:

The Wisconsin statute singles out for enhancement bias-inspired conduct because this conduct is thought to inflict greater individual and societal harm. For example, according to the State and its *amici,* bias-motivated crimes are more likely to provoke retaliatory crimes, inflict distinct emotional harms on their victims, and incite community unrest. The State's desire to redress these perceived harms provides an adequate explanation for its penalty-enhancement provision over and above mere disagreement with offenders' beliefs or biases. As Blackstone said long ago, "it is but reasonable that among crimes of different natures those should be most severely punished, which are the most destructive of the public safety and happiness."[65]

Since the Court's decision in *Wisconsin v. Mitchell,* state bias-crime laws have been challenged on a variety of other constitutional grounds, but these challenges have been largely unsuccessful.[66]

Apart from these constitutional concerns, opponents of bias-crime legislation have questioned the deterrent effect of penalty enhancement, and they have made the related argument that penalty enhancement actually has no more than a symbolic effect—by "arguably (although not demonstrably) mak[ing] it slightly less politically correct to express bigotry."[67] Bias-crime laws have also been criticized out of concern that members of minority groups will be "more likely to be arrested, convicted, and punished as bias-criminals" than members of majority groups because bias-crime laws make no distinction between majority-group and minority-group perpetrators.[68] In a similar vein, bias-crime laws have been criticized on the ground that they transfer too much power to the prosecutor (even more than other cases) because the prosecutor will not only be able to circumscribe the judge's power over sentencing through her choice of charges but will also be able to use penalty enhancement as a powerful chip in plea bargaining with the alleged offender.[69] The validity of these (and other) critiques of bias-crime laws is, unsurprisingly, the subject of serious scholarly debate.

Questioning Their Scope. From the perspective of this project, however, a more trenchant critique of bias-crime laws—one that concerns the scope of their application and not their very existence—deserves our attention. In a series of articles, law professor Lu-in Wang has challenged our preconceptions about the types of criminal conduct that should be classified as bias crimes.[70]

Bias crimes are commonly referred to as "hate" crimes, a label that evokes a certain set of images. When someone mentions a hate crime, we generally picture "a stranger-on-stranger crime, usually involving multiple perpetrators who target an individual victim who represents a hated social group, inflict on that person extreme, gratuitous violence, and appear to have no goal other than to terrorize, injure, or kill."[71] Bob Gravel's story, reproduced at the beginning of this section, fits snugly into this prototypical view of bias crimes as "hate" crimes.

The prototypical view of bias crimes has found favor with Congress,[72] some state legislators,[73] and commentators.[74] Yet, even when a state legislature has adopted a broadly worded statute that does not specifically require a showing of antigay animus or prejudice (e.g., when the law requires only that the crime have been committed "because of" or "by reason of" the victim's sexual orientation), the prototypical view may nonetheless influence the police and prosecutors when they choose which acts to charge and prosecute as bias crimes.[75] For example, when a gay man was both robbed *and* murdered by two men in Colorado, the district attorney declined to charge the perpetrators under the state's bias-crime law because the motive for the crime was "ambiguous" (i.e., was it hate or profit?), even though witnesses indicated that one of the perpetrators had stated that he wanted to beat up the victim for making sexual advances and the other perpetrator then suggested robbing him as well.[76] When making such choices, police and prosecutors only further solidify the popular conception of bias crimes that led to their choice in the first place.

But, according to Wang, the prototypical view represents an unduly narrow conception of bias crimes; indeed, she asserts, "the term 'hate crime' [itself] reflects and reinforces an oversimplification of the phenomenon it seeks to describe."[77] As Wang goes on to explain, "the term attributes the commission of bias crimes solely to the perpetrator's deviant personal attitudes toward, and desire to inflict harm upon, the targeted social group. It fails to account for the possibility of more mundane, opportunistic motivations, such as the desire to obtain material rewards."[78] In this regard, consider the following story from the New York *Daily News,* which was reported in October 2005:

> Two men were shot and robbed by a gunman clad in dark clothes early yesterday morning in a gay meeting spot in Prospect Park, police said.
>
> The gunman shot a 29-year-old in the thigh about 5:30 A.M., then pumped a slug into the chest of his 28-year-old companion and swiped a gold chain from his neck, police said.
>
> The men were engaged in a sex act when the trigger-happy thug pounced on them in the wooded Vale of Cashmere, a gay hangout dubbed Boys' Town, police sources said.
>
> "Any place that gay people congregate is a hotbed for attacks," said Basil Lucas, spokesman for the Gay and Lesbian Anti-Violence Project. "People assume that these men are easy targets because they don't think they're going to report it."
>
> Lucas said he knows of other victims robbed and attacked at the Vale of Cashmere within the past year who are too afraid to go to cops.[79]

On the face of this story, the perpetrator appears to have selected his victims because of their sexual orientation, but not necessarily due to a hatred of lesbians and gay men. It is quite possible that the perpetrator is merely a "calculating discriminator"; that is, someone who selects his victims "on the basis of their social group membership, not because he consciously bears any ill will toward that group, but because he seeks to maximize the 'benefits' relative to the 'costs' of criminal conduct in which he already was planning to engage."[80] This "calculating discriminator" may simply have exploited the victims' vulnerability—they were two gay men engaged in a sex act in a public place—to his advantage. And, as Basil Lucas points out, perpetrators assume that gay men in cruising spots will be less likely to report crimes for fear that they will be outed to the police, their employers, or their family and friends.

Next, consider the following story from the *Los Angeles Times*, reported in September 2003:

> Three Inland Empire gang members have pleaded guilty to involuntary manslaughter for their roles in the June 2002 stabbing death of a gay man outside a bar in downtown Riverside. Under the terms of the plea agreement, the three will not have to testify against the fellow gang member charged with the stabbing death of 40-year-old Jeffrey Owens of Moreno Valley outside the Menagerie nightclub. Owens and a friend were allegedly attacked to enhance the street gang's reputation, a prosecutor said. Viviano Cruz Marin, 26, and David Leal Martinez, 29, agreed to plead guilty to involuntary manslaughter for their roles in the murder.[81]

Earlier coverage had explained that the victim received multiple stab wounds outside a gay nightclub when he came to the aid of a friend who was punched and stabbed by the perpetrators.[82] Again, the perpetrators apparently selected the victim because of his sexual orientation, but not necessarily due to their hatred of lesbians and gay men. The gang members were likely "violent show-offs"; that is, they selected their victim "to impress [their] peers or to evoke a strong reaction from observers."[83] The gang members chose to attack a gay man—someone whom society has designated as a "suitable target"[84]—because it would impress others and enhance their reputation.

Wang argues that enhanced punishment should apply not only to prototypical "hate" crimes but also to the robbery reported in the *Daily News* and the stabbing reported in the *Los Angeles Times*. In making this argument, Wang looks to the peculiar psychological and social harms caused by bias crimes because they are relied upon by supporters of enhanced punishment both to justify penalty enhancement and to fend off arguments that bias-crime laws do no more than punish offensive thought. Wang maintains that penalty enhancement ought to apply to all three categories of bias crimes (i.e., the prototypical "hate" crime, the crime committed by the calculating discriminator, and the crime committed by the violent show-off) because they all have the same harmful effects upon the victim (and, vicariously, upon the broader lesbian and gay community)—and, at the same time, provide the same benefits to members of the heterosexual majority:

> All three produce a victim who explains the crime to herself by attributing it to her social group status, an aspect of her identity or "character" that she cannot change. Having attributed the crime to such a factor, the victim both feels stigmatized and comes to believe that she cannot prevent victimization in the future without drastically limiting her activities. As a result, the victim is likely to withdraw from interactions with other people and from activities that require her to be "visible," thus depriving herself of potentially rewarding social and financial opportunities. These are predictable responses to victimization in cases where the victim cannot make "sense" of the crime without attributing it to her group-based identity.
>
> Observers, too, will explain the crime as being attributable to the victim's group identity. For those observers who share this identity with her, the explanation can have much the same effect as if they themselves were victims of the crime. Members of the "target group" will view themselves as especially vulnerable to victimization and, like the victim herself, may feel that the best way to avoid victimization is to avoid activities that make them visible or require them to interact with others. Target group members also might feel compelled to make themselves less visible by acting in an "expected," stereotyped fashion that further impedes their ability to take advantage of potentially rewarding opportunities.
>
> These greater harms to the victim and target group members stand in sharp contrast to the "benefits" that non-target-group members can derive from the explanation for the crime. The fact that they can distinguish themselves from the target group allows these observers to feel that they are protected from harm and have greater control over their lives. Moreover, the way the crime is explained can actually serve to increase the social distance between groups, for non-target-group members who need to feel that they "deserve" their invulnerable position may come to view their social group status as rendering target group members "deserving" victims. This kind of social distancing is well documented, even among individuals who do not view it as a morally desirable way to preserve their own feelings of security.[85]

Clearly, then, the peculiar harms associated with bias crimes can be caused even when the perpetrator's actions are not motivated purely by antigay animus.[86] The prototypical view of "hate" crimes thus paints an incomplete picture because it fails to acknowledge the reality that a perpetrator's actions may result from the convergence of "a variety of social, psychological, and situational forces."[87] As explained by Dr. Herek, the common denominator of these crimes is not the perpetrator's state of mind but the perpetrator's embrace and affirmation of the sexual prejudice that is ubiquitous in American society:

Whereas psychological heterosexism [i.e., the manifestation of heterosexism in an individual's actions and attitudes][88] may not always be the principal reason for an anti-gay attack (e.g., a gang might well have selected another type of "outsider" as a suitable victim), the importance of cultural heterosexism [i.e., the manifestation of heterosexism in societal customs and institutions][89] cannot be underestimated. For it is cultural heterosexism that defines gay people as suitable targets that can be "used" for meeting a variety of psychological needs. And anti-gay attacks, regardless of the perpetrator's motivation, reinforce cultural heterosexism. Thus, when a teenage gang member attacks a gay man on the street, it is a hate crime *not* because hate necessarily was the attacker's primary motive (it may or may not have been) but because the attack expresses cultural hostility, condemnation, and disgust toward gay people and because it has the effect of terrorizing the individual victim as well as the entire lesbian and gay community. The attack in effect punishes the gay person for daring to be visible.[90]

In addition to inviting us to question our preconceived notions about the type of conduct that constitutes a bias crime, these insights draw attention to the high cost of leaving heterosexual privilege unchallenged. In particular, Dr. Herek's remark about bias-crime perpetrators' "use" of lesbians and gay men to meet their own needs is quite disturbing. Pervasive antigay hostility in American society has the effect of dehumanizing lesbians and gay men. It paints a target upon each of us and creates an atmosphere in which violence can be inflicted upon us with little fear of legal repercussions.[91] As discussed in Chapter 1, it paralyzes us to the point where we would often prefer to suffer in silence rather than risk being outed or further harassed at the hands of police. And even when crimes are reported, it tacitly assures that the police will often refuse to designate the crime as a bias crime; that advocacy groups will have to press for the investigation of complaints; and that, despite these efforts, a staggering number of complaints will still not result in arrests. It does nothing less than rob us of our dignity as human beings and, when acted upon, turns us into no more than a disposable tool or toy to be used by heterosexuals to meet their own needs—whether to reaffirm their masculinity and heterosexuality, to impress their friends and feel more positive about themselves, or to relieve their boredom and get a thrill.[92]

Coping with "Minority Stress"

In this vein, Wang has described the "feedback loop" that exists between the everyday discrimination described in the first part of this chapter (as well as in later chapters) and the bias crimes described in the latter part of this chapter. Everyday discrimination against lesbians and gay men marks them as an appropriate target for inferior treatment, which contributes to the perception that they are likewise appropriate targets for violence, which, when such violence occurs, then further reinforces the notion that lesbians and gay men are appropriate targets for everyday discrimination.[93] Some psychologists view the sexual stigma that feeds and is fed by this loop as creating an atmosphere of chronic stress for lesbians and gay men as they confront, live in fear of, or hide in the closet from the effects of everyday discrimination and bias-crime victimization.[94] This chronic stress, which is in addition to the general stresses of life and is "socially based—that is, it stems from social processes, institutions, and structures beyond the individual,"[95] is referred to as "minority stress."[96] Minority stress is associated with adverse health effects (e.g., psychological distress) among lesbians and gay men.[97]

Although this book surely does not fall into the genre of psychology, I thought it useful to point out that the prevalence of heterosexism is not only vexing but also potentially bad for your health. From this perspective, challenging and attempting to overturn the privileging of heterosexuality in our society becomes an important step in breaking the feedback loop that helps to nourish sexual stigma and, in turn, to foster an atmosphere in which minority stress thrives. While minority stress persists, I would note that the psychological literature suggests that tapping into the resources provided by formal and informal social support networks (e.g., family, friends, and the lesbian and gay community) can help you to cope with that stress.[98]

Notes

1. Andrew S. Walters and Maria-Cristina Curran, "'Excuse Me, Sir? May I Help You and Your Boyfriend?' Salespersons' Differential Treatment of Homosexual and Straight Customers," in Daniel L. Wardlow, ed., *Gays, Lesbians, and Consumer Behavior: Theory, Practice, and Research Issues in Marketing* (New York: Harrington Park Press, 1996), 135, 148.

2. David A. Jones, "Discrimination Against Same-Sex Couples in Hotel Reservation Policies," in *Gays, Lesbians, and Consumer Behavior,* 153, 155–156.

3. Terri D. Conley, Patricia G. Devine, Jerome Rabow, and Sophia R. Evett, "Gay Men and Lesbians' Experiences in and Expectations for Interactions with Heterosexuals," *J. Homosexuality* 44 (2002): 83.

4. For example, Anthony R. D'Augelli and Arnold H. Grossman, "Disclosure of Sexual Orientation, Victimization, and Mental Health Among Lesbian, Gay, and Bisexual Older Adults," *J. Interpersonal Violence* 16 (2001): 1008; David M. Huebner, Gregory M. Rebchook, and Susan M. Kegeles, "Experiences of Harassment, Discrimination, and Physical Violence Among Young Gay and Bisexual Men," *Am. J. Pub. Health* 94 (2004): 1200; Vickie M. Mays and Susan D. Cochran, "Mental Health Correlates of Perceived Discrimination Among Lesbian, Gay, and Bisexual Adults in the United States," *Am J. Pub. Health* 91 (2001): 1869; Melanie D. Otis and William F. Skinner, "The Prevalence of Victimization and Its Effect on Mental Well-Being Among Lesbian and Gay People," *J. Homosexuality* 30 (1996): 93.

5. Gregory M. Herek, J. Roy Gillis, and Jeanine C. Cogan, "Psychological Sequelae of Hate-Crime Victimization Among Lesbian, Gay, and Bisexual Adults," *J. Consulting and Clinical Psychol.* 67 (1999): 945, 949.

6. Joseph William Singer, "No Right to Exclude: Public Accommodations and Private Property," *Nw. U. L. Rev.* 90 (1996): 1283, 1290.

7. Ibid., 1303–1412.

8. Cal. Civ. Code §51 (2007); Conn. Gen. Stat. §46a-81d (2007); D.C. Code §2-1402.31 (2007); Haw. Rev. Stat. §489-3 (2006); 775 Ill. Comp. Stat. 5/1-102(A), -103(Q), 5/5-102 (2006); Iowa Code §216.7 (2007); Me. Rev. Stat. tit. 5, §§4591–4592 (2006); Md. Code art. 49B, §5 (2006); Mass. Gen. Laws ch. 272, §§92A, 98 (2007); Minn. Stat. §363A.11 (2006); N.H. Rev. Stat. §354-A:16 (2006); N.J. Rev. Stat. §10:5-4 (2007); N.M. Stat. §28-1-7(F) (2006); N.Y. Exec. Law §296(2)(a) (2007); R.I. Gen. Laws §11-24-2 (2006); Vt. Stat. tit. 9, §4502 (2006); Wash. Rev. Code §§49.60.030(1)(b), .040(10), .215 (2007); Wis. Stat. §106.52 (2006); Act of May 9, 2007, ch. 100, §5, 2007 Ore. SB 2 (Lexis) (to be codified at Or. Rev. Stat. §659A.403; see the discussion of Oregon's domestic partnership regime in Chapter 6 for an explanation of the effective date of this provision).

Although the Nevada Equal Rights Commission now has the power to investigate complaints of discrimination on the basis of sexual orientation in public accommodations, such discrimination is not currently prohibited by state law. Nev. Rev. Stat. §§233.150(1)(a), 651.070 (2005).

9. Cal. Fam. Code §297.5(f) (2007); Conn. Gen. Stat. §§46a-64(a), 46b-38nn, -38oo (2007); D.C. Code §2-1401.02(17) (2007); N.J. Rev. Stat. §37:1-32(g) (2007); Vt. Stat. tit. 15, §1204(e)(7) (2006); Act of June 4, 2007, §1, 2007 N.H. Adv. Legis. Serv. ch. 58 (to be codified at N.H. Rev. Stat. §457-A:6 effective January 1, 2008); Act of May 9, 2007, ch. 99, §9(1), 2007 Ore. HB 2007 (Lexis) (see the discussion of Oregon's domestic partnership regime in Chapter 6 for an explanation of the effective date of this provision).

10. Cal. Civ. Code §51(b) (2007).

11. N.J. Rev. Stat. §10:5-4 (2007).

12. Ibid., §10:5-5(l).

13. *Baksh v. Human Rights Commission,* 711 N.E.2d 416 (Ill. App. Ct. 1999).

14. *Washington v. Blampin,* 38 Cal. Rptr. 235 (Cal. Ct. App. 1964).

15. *N. Coast Women's Care Med. Group, Inc. v. Super. Ct.,* 46 Cal. Rptr. 3d 605 (Cal. 2006) (petition for review granted).

16. *Curran v. Mount Diablo Council of the Boy Scouts of Am.,* 952 P.2d 218 (Cal. 1998).

17. *Dale v. Boy Scouts of Am.,* 734 A.2d 1196 (N.J. 1999).

18. Compare Gay and Lesbian Alliance Against Defamation (GLAAD), "Newspapers That Publish Same-Sex Union Announcements" (2004), available at www.glaad.org/action/campaigns_detail.php?id=3297 (including 504 newspapers on this list), with U.S. Census Bureau, Statistical Abstract of the United States (2006), p. 738, table 1120 (indicating that there were 1,456 daily newspapers in the United States in 2004).

19. James M. Donovan, "Same-Sex Union Announcements: Whether Newspapers Must Publish Them, and Why We Should Care," *Brook. L. Rev.* 68 (2003): 721.

20. *Hurley v. Irish-American Gay, Lesbian and Bisexual Group of Boston, Inc.,* 515 U.S. 557 (1995).

21. Ibid., 581.

22. *Boy Scouts of America v. Dale,* 530 U.S. 640 (2000).

23. Ibid., 687.

24. Erwin Chemerinsky and Catherine Fisk, "The Expressive Interest of Associations," *Wm. and Mary Bill Rts. J.* 9 (2001): 595, 596–597.

25. *Sterling v. Borough of Minersville*, 232 F.3d 190, 192–193 (3d Cir. 2000).

26. Brad S. Weinstein, "A Right with No Remedy: Forced Disclosure of Sexual Orientation and Public 'Outing' Under 42 U.S.C. §1983," *Cornell L. Rev.* 90 (2005): 811, 812–813.

27. *Koire v. Metro Car Wash*, 707 P.2d 195, 197 (Cal. 1985).

28. *Jackson v. Super. Ct.*, 36 Cal. Rptr. 2d 207, 209 (Cal. Ct. App. 1994).

29. *Harris v. Capital Growth Investors XIV*, 805 P.2d 873, 891, 893 (Cal. 1991).

30. Ian Ayres and Jennifer Gerarda Brown, *Straightforward: How to Mobilize Heterosexual Support for Gay Rights* (Princeton, NJ: Princeton University Press, 2005), 146.

31. M. V. Lee Badgett, *Money, Myths, and Change: The Economic Lives of Lesbians and Gay Men* (Chicago: University of Chicago Press, 2001), 236.

32. Ibid., 235; Ayres and Brown, *Straightforward*, 73–76.

33. Badgett, *Money, Myths, and Change*, 235–236.

34. Ayres and Brown, *Straightforward*, 64–67; Badgett, *Money, Myths, and Change*, 225.

35. Ayres and Brown, *Straightforward*, 64.

36. Mary Crossley, "Infected Judgment: Legal Responses to Physician Bias," *Vill. L. Rev.* 48 (2003): 195, 233–234 (footnotes omitted).

37. For listings of lesbian and gay newspapers, visit www.gaydata.com or www.bglad.com (click on "News and Media").

38. Kristine Shaw, "Local Sexual Orientation Non-Discrimination Laws: A Means of Community Empowerment," *Cornell J.L. and Pub. Pol'y* 10 (2001): 385, 393.

39. Ibid., 395.

40. For example, David Crowder, "City's Lifestyle for Gays Kept Gap Away, Official Says," *El Paso Times*, April 16, 2001, 1A; "The Right Thing," *Orlando Sentinel Tribune*, November 17, 2002, G2; Howard Troxler, "A Grown-up Subject, Met with Maturity," *St. Petersburg Times*, November 16, 2001, 1B; Charles K. Wilson, "City Amends Ordinance on Discrimination," *El Paso Times*, April 9, 2003, 1A.

41. Shaw, "Local Sexual Orientation Non-Discrimination Laws," 394.

42. Reprinted from hearing before the Subcommittee on Criminal Justice of the Committee on the Judiciary H.R. on Anti-Gay Violence, 99th Cong. (1986), 154–155 (testimony of Robert Gravel).

43. National Coalition of Anti-Violence Programs, *Anti-Lesbian, Gay, Bisexual, and Transgender Violence in 2004* (New York: NCAVP, 2005), 20.

44. Lu-in Wang, "The Transforming Power of 'Hate': Social Cognition Theory and the Harms of Bias-Related Crime," *S. Cal. L. Rev.* 71 (1997): 47, 61; see also Donald Altschiller, *Hate Crimes: A Reference Handbook*, 2d ed. (Santa Barbara, CA: ABC-CLIO, 2005), 3; Lu-in Wang, "Recognizing Opportunistic Bias Crimes," *B.U. L. Rev.* 80 (2000): 1399, 1401; Taron K. Murakami, "Constitutional Law Chapter: Hate Crimes," *Geo. J. Gender and L.* 5 (2004): 63.

45. *U.S. Sentencing Guidelines Manual*, §3A1.1(a) (2006).

46. H.R. Rep. 103-244 (1993), 5; Wang, "Recognizing Opportunistic Bias Crimes," 1404.

47. Local Law Enforcement Hate Crimes Prevention Act of 2007, H.R. 1592, 110th Cong. §6; Matthew Shepard Local Law Enforcement Hate Crimes Prevention Act of 2007, S. 1105, 110th Cong. §7.

48. David Stout, "House Votes to Expand Hate-Crime Protection," *New York Times*, May 4, 2007, A17.

49. Lu-in Wang, "The Complexities of Hate," *Ohio St. L.J.* 60 (1999): 799, 808.

50. Ariz. Rev. Stat. §13-702(C)(15) (2006); Conn. Gen. Stat. §§53a-181j to -181l (2007); Haw. Rev. Stat. §706-662(6) (2006); 18 Pa. Cons. Stat. §2710 (2006); R.I. Gen. Laws §12-19-38 (2006); Vt. Stat. tit. 13, §1455 (2006); Wash. Rev. Code §9A.36.080 (2007).

51. D.C. Code §22-3701 (2007); Fla. Stat. §775.085 (2007); Tex. Code Crim. Proc., art. 42.014 (2006).

52. Cal. Penal Code §422.55 (2007); Colo. Rev. Stat. §18-9-121 (2006); Del. Code tit. 11, §1304 (2007); 720 Ill. Comp. Stat. 5/12-7.1 (2006); Iowa Code §729A.2 (2006); Kan. Stat. §21-4716(c)(2)(C) (2005); Ky. Rev. Stat. §532.031 (2006); La. Rev. Stat. §14:107.2 (2006); Me. Rev. Stat. tit. 17-A, §1151 (2006); Md. Code, Crim. Law §10-304 (2006); Mass. Gen. Laws, ch. 265, §39 (2007); Minn. Stat. §§609.595, .749, .2231 (2006); Mo. Rev. Stat. §557.035 (2006); Neb. Rev. Stat. §28-111 (2006); Nev. Rev. Stat. §193.1675 (2005); N.H. Rev. Stat. §651:6 (2006); N.J. Rev. Stat. §2C:16-1 (2007); N.M. Stat. §§31-18B-2 to -3 (2006); N.Y. Penal Law §485.05 (2007); Or. Rev. Stat. §§166.155, .165 (2005); Tenn. Code §40-35-114 (2006); Wis. Stat. §939.645 (2006).

53. Thomson and West, *Hate Crimes Law* (Eagan, MN: Thomson/West, 2005), 394.

54. Cal. Civ. Code §§51.7, 52 (2007); Colo. Rev. Stat. §13-21-106.5 (2006); Conn. Gen. Stat. §52-571c (2007); D.C. Code §22-3704 (2007); Fla. Stat. §775.085(2) (2007); 720 Ill. Comp. Stat. 5/12-7.1(c) (2006); Iowa Code §729A.5 (2006); Me. Rev. Stat. tit. 5, §§4682, 4684-A (2006); Mass. Gen. Laws, ch. 12, §11I (2007); Minn. Stat. §611A.79 (2006); Neb. Rev. Stat. §28-113 (2006); Nev. Rev. Stat. §41.690 (2005); N.J. Rev. Stat. §2A:53A-21 (2007); Or. Rev. Stat. §30.198 (2005); 42 Pa. Cons. Stat. §8309 (2006); Vt. Stat. tit. 13, §1457 (2006); Wash. Rev. Code §9A.36.083 (2007).

55. National Association of Crime Victim Compensation Boards, "Crime Victim Compensation: Resources for Recovery," available at www.nacvcb.org/documents/Fact%20sheet.doc.

56. D.C. Code §23-1901 (2007); see Victoria Schwartz, "The Victims' Rights Amendment," *Harv J. on Legis.* 42 (2005): 525, 526–527, and nn.13–14 (citing the state statutes and constitutional provisions).

57. National Center for Victims of Crime, "Rights of Crime Victims," available at www.ncvc.org/ncvc/main.aspx?dbName=DocumentViewerandDocumentID=32512.

58. Southern Poverty Law Center, "About the Center," available at www.splcenter.org/center/about.jsp.

59. Gregory M. Herek, "Psychological Heterosexism and Anti-Gay Violence: The Social Psychology of Bigotry and Bashing," in Gregory M. Herek and Kevin T. Berrill, eds., *Hate Crimes: Confronting Violence Against Lesbians and Gay Men* (Newbury Park, CA: Sage Publications, 1992): 149, 166.

60. Southern Poverty Law Center, "Ten Ways to Fight Hate: A Community Response Guide," available at www.tolerance.org/pdf/ten_ways.pdf.

61. See, for example, "Symposium: Hate Speech and Hate Crimes," *Harv. J. on Legis.* 41 (2004): 389.

62. Wang, "The Transforming Power of 'Hate,'" 53–54 (footnotes omitted).

63. *Wisconsin v. Mitchell*, 508 U.S. 476 (1993).

64. Ibid., 480.

65. Ibid., 487–488 (citations omitted).

66. Thomson and West, *Hate Crimes Law*, 293–306.

67. Susan B. Gellman and Frederick M. Lawrence, "Agreeing to Agree: A Proponent and Opponent of Hate Crime Laws Reach for Common Ground," *Harv. J. on Legis.* 41 (2004): 421, 428–433.

68. Frederick M. Lawrence, "Enforcing Bias-Crime Laws Without Bias: Evaluating the Disproportionate-Enforcement Critique," *Law and Contemp. Probs.* 66 (2003): 49, 52–55.

69. David Goldberger, "The Inherent Unfairness of Hate Crimes Statutes," *Harv. J. on Legis.* 41 (2004): 449.

70. Wang, "The Complexities of Hate"; Wang, "Recognizing Opportunistic Bias Crimes"; Wang, "The Transforming Power of 'Hate.'"

71. Lu-in Wang, "Hate Crime and Everyday Discrimination: Influences of and on the Social Context," *Rutgers Race and L. Rev.* 4 (2002): 1, 4.

72. See note 46 and accompanying text.

73. See note 50 and accompanying text.

74. Wang, "The Complexities of Hate," 813.

75. Ibid., 814, 825–829; see also Jeannine Bell, "Deciding When Hate Is a Crime: The First Amendment, Police Detectives, and the Identification of Hate Crime," *Rutgers Race and L. Rev.* 4 (2002): 33, 53–71 (describing the conservative application of bias-crime laws by the members of a police antibias task force in a large U.S. city).

76. Nancy Lofholm, "Motive Unclear in Death of Montrose Gay Man," *Denver Post,* August 9, 2005, A1; Nancy Lofholm, "Strangling Suspect Pleads," *Denver Post,* June 14, 2006, B3; Ellen Miller, "Plea Deal in Gay's Death," *Rocky Mountain News,* March 31, 2006, 24A.

77. Wang, "The Complexities of Hate," 801; see also Howard J. Ehrlich, "The Ecology of Anti-Gay Violence," in Herek and Berrill, eds., *Hate Crimes,* 105, 108; Herek, "Psychological Heterosexism and Anti-Gay Violence," 164. It is for this reason that I have assiduously avoided use of the term "hate crime" in this chapter, opting instead for "bias crime."

78. Wang, "The Complexities of Hate," 801.

79. Scott Michels, Tony Sclafani, and Carrie Melago, "2 Gays Shot in Prospect Park Attack," *New York Daily News,* October 7, 2005, 30.

80. Wang, "The Transforming Power of 'Hate,'" 57.

81. Lance Pugmire, "3 Gang Members Plead Guilty in Fatal Stabbing," *Los Angeles Times,* September 25, 2003, B3.

82. Janet Wilson, "4 Held in Killing of Man Stabbed at Club," *Los Angeles Times,* June 21, 2002, 7.

83. Wang, "The Transforming Power of 'Hate,'" 57.

84. Herek, "Psychological Heterosexism and Anti-Gay Violence," 164.

85. Wang, "The Transforming Power of 'Hate,'" 129–130.

86. Wang, "The Complexities of Hate," 870–871.

87. Karen Franklin, "Unassuming Motivations: Contextualizing the Narratives of Antigay Assailants," in Gregory M. Herek, ed., *Stigma and Sexual Orientation: Understanding Prejudice Against Lesbians, Gay Men, and Bisexuals* (Thousand Oaks,

CA: Sage Publications, 1998), 1, 2; see also Herek, "Psychological Heterosexism and Anti-Gay Violence," 158–164; Wang, "The Complexities of Hate," 870–900.

88. Herek, "Psychological Heterosexism and Anti-Gay Violence," 151.

89. Gregory M. Herek, "The Social Context of Hate Crimes: Notes on Cultural Heterosexism," in Herek and Berrill, eds., *Hate Crimes*, 89.

90. Herek, "Psychological Heterosexism and Anti-Gay Violence," 164; see also Franklin, "Unassuming Motivations," 20.

91. Anthony C. Infanti, *"Homo Sacer,* Homosexual: Some Thoughts on Waging Tax Guerrilla Warfare," *Unbound: Harv. J. of the Legal Left* 2 (2006): 27, 39–40.

92. Herek, "Psychological Heterosexism and Anti-Gay Violence," 158–163; Franklin, "Unassuming Motivations," 7–19.

93. See Wang, "Hate Crime and Everyday Discrimination," 16–17.

94. For example, Joanne DiPlacido, "Minority Stress Among Lesbians, Gay Men, and Bisexuals: A Consequence of Heterosexism, Homophobia, and Stigmatization," in Herek, ed., *Stigma and Sexual Orientation,* 138, 138–139; Ilan H. Meyer, "Minority Stress and Mental Health in Gay Men," *J. Health and Soc. Behav.* 36 (1995): 38, 40–42.

95. Ilan H. Meyer, "Prejudice, Social Stress, and Mental Health in Lesbian, Gay, and Bisexual Populations: Conceptual Issues and Research Evidence," *Psychol. Bull.* 129 (2003): 674, 676.

96. Meyer, "Minority Stress and Mental Health in Gay Men," 38.

97. Ibid., 45–52; Robin J. Lewis, Valerian J. Derlega, Jessica L. Griffin, and Alison C. Krowinski, "Stressors for Gay Men and Lesbians: Life Stress, Gay-Related Stress, Stigma Consciousness, and Depressive Symptoms," *J. Soc. and Clinical Psychol.* 22 (2003): 716, 717–718, 725–726; Ilan H. Meyer and Laura Dean, "Internalized Homophobia, Intimacy, and Sexual Behavior Among Gay and Bisexual Men," in Herek, ed., *Stigma and Sexual Orientation,* 160, 178–183.

98. DiPlacido, "Minority Stress Among Lesbians, Gay Men, and Bisexuals," 144–146; Meyer, "Prejudice, Social Stress, and Mental Health," 677; Meyer and Dean, "Internalized Homophobia, Intimacy, and Sexual Behavior," 175.

3
Education

For as long as I can remember, I've known that I'm gay. In retrospect, even some of my early childhood memories bespoke the existence of this difference. At recess in the early years of elementary school, the kids in my class usually broke into gendered groups: The boys played with the boys and the girls with the girls. I proved the exception to this rule, spending every recess playing hopscotch and other games with the girls. Even at such a young age, one of my classmates recognized both the norm and my variation from it. She tried a number of times to persuade me that I should be playing with the boys instead of the girls, going so far as to bring me over to introduce me to some of the boys in an attempt to get me to start playing with them. But her efforts were to no avail. I never ended up playing with the boys, and the girls ended up accepting me as I was. At the end of that year, one of the girls in the class held a birthday party to which she invited all the other girls—and me.

Nevertheless, the potential for continued acceptance of my difference quickly faded away. I vividly recall the torture visited upon one of my classmates near the end of elementary school (which was sixth grade where I grew up), simply because his father had gone on a business trip to San Francisco. This may not seem like an event that would warrant, or could even give rise to, torture, yet the other boys relentlessly taunted him over a period of several days. They kept calling his father a faggot and saying that he had gone to San Francisco to be with the other fags (why else would he have gone there?). They teased him that it wasn't a business trip at all, just an opportunity for his father to go visit his boyfriend. All of the accusations and insinuations clearly hurt and upset this boy. He quickly went on the defensive, asserting that his father wasn't a fag at all—he was just in San Francisco for work.

Plainly, these elementary school boys had already learned that calling someone a "faggot" is an insult and had further ascertained that, in the hierarchy of insults, questioning a man's heterosexuality is one of the more potent forms of attack. Somehow they had also learned that San Francisco is a gay mecca, which was the crucial piece of knowledge that had furnished the connection between the ostensibly innocuous business trip and the sustained, malicious taunting.

What amazes me most about this incident is that these boys had absorbed several important pieces of information about sexual orientation years before they would understand what sex is or what it involves. At the time of the incident, they probably didn't fully understand what being gay means or what gay sex is or represents. In any case, the finer points of homosexuality were irrelevant because all they really needed to know for their attack to be successful was that being a fag is bad and that many fags live in San Francisco. Society had obviously armed them with these weapons at an early age.

When I was growing up, these events formed part of an atmosphere of rejection and hostility toward homosexuality. They were accompanied by an endless parade of fag jokes, derogatory remarks, and whispers about someone's sexual orientation (because such a discussion was not a topic for polite conversation). The Catholic Church (to which my family belonged) seemed to be the grand marshal of this parade with its focus on the traditional family and its loud condemnation of homosexuality. My fifth grade catechism teacher epitomized this pious self-righteousness. She was a frustrated, would-be nun who liked to regale us with stories of how she prayed the rosary while driving (and you thought cell phones were a hazard) and who seemed to derive great enjoyment from telling us that we would burn in hell for the least infraction of religious law. When I was young, the clear message from all quarters was that being gay is abnormal, wrong, and a ticket straight to hell.

Faced with this level of disapprobation, I found the closet to be a necessity once I realized that this scorn was appropriately directed at me. I began to deny my sexual orientation to myself and to others in the idle hope that I could simply wish away being gay and not have to spend eternity in blazes. Interestingly, though, denial became both a means of defending myself from attack and a proxy for those attacks. Through denial, I tried to fend off attacks from others, but at the same time I began to attack myself—questioning what was wrong with me, why I was different, why I couldn't change and be normal like everyone else. By high school, society had so successfully ingrained in me its hostility toward lesbians and gay men that, even when defending myself from its attacks, I was still being attacked. I had simply traded one oppressor (society at large) for another (myself). To cope with the anguish created by this self-loathing, I redirected my energy and attention toward studying. Schoolwork helped to lessen the constant pain and anguish and brought the added bonus of serving as a convenient excuse for not dating.

Things didn't improve in college. Not many people at school were out of the closet, and the environment wasn't particularly welcoming for the few who were. I learned this within a week of arriving at school. I had been assigned to an all-male dormitory that year, which, you would think, would be a dream come true for any young gay man. But in reality, it was more like a nightmare. The testosterone level in the dorm ran high, and the antigay remarks and fag jokes were more pervasive and biting than any I had experienced before (or, for that matter, since). During that first week, when everyone feels vulnerable, nervous, and anxious about being away from home, I had a negative encounter with two upper-class students. I had just passed them in the stairwell when they started spitting "queer" and "fag" at me in a tone that oozed venom and with a physical presence that can only be described as menacing. I couldn't understand why they had targeted me. Was it that obvious? Whether it was or not, they had made it abundantly clear that being open about my sexual orientation at college would likely culminate in hospitalization. After that episode, I became all the more firmly ensconced in the closet because I was not about to risk having to come out to my parents from a hospital bed.

Then, in the more open atmosphere of a law school in northern California and at a time when I was becoming more self-sufficient (and, concomitantly, somewhat less vulnerable), I eventually came to the realization that this was no way to live and slowly began to make my way out of the closet.

Sadly, children and adolescents are particularly susceptible to the adverse effects of sexual stigma and the feedback loop between everyday discrimination and antigay violence described at the close of Chapter 2. One study reporting on the adverse effects suffered by lesbian and gay adolescents in schools in cities across the country noted that

> for lesbian, gay, and bisexual youth, life at school is . . . compromised by victimization. Approximately one quarter of the youth have experienced anti-lesbian/gay abuse from other students. Over 1 in 20 report abuse from teachers. Safety fears, discomfort with disclosure, and concealment of sexual orientation were prevalent. Approximately half of all respondents have hidden their sexual orientation from other students and from teachers; the same proportion have lost at least one friend after their sexual orientation became known. Not surprisingly, more than three quarters acknowledge discomfort with the prospect of future disclosure in school. One third link their reduced openness about their sexual orientation to fears of verbal abuse.[1]

A more recent study of sexual orientation victimization in high school indicated that 59 percent of the lesbian, gay, and bisexual youth surveyed had directly "experienced verbal abuse in high school, 24 percent were threatened with violence, 11 percent had objects thrown at them, 11 percent had been physically attacked, 2 percent were threatened with weapons, 5 percent were sexually assaulted, and 20 percent had been threatened with the disclosure of their sexual orientation."[2] Although the parents and families of children in other marginalized groups usually serve as a support network in the face of such victimization or discrimination, the parents and families of lesbian and gay youth may not be supportive; indeed, parents and family may become a further source of victimization and discrimination rather than the social support that is needed for coping.[3]

But lesbian and gay youth are more than just the victims of sexual stigma. They, along with the children of lesbian and gay parents, are also pawns in the reactionary right's "culture war." In its zeal for quashing any mention of homosexuality, the reactionary right has recently: (1) attacked a video featuring the cartoon character SpongeBob SquarePants, which was sent to schools in an effort to teach children tolerance of different family structures; (2) succeeded in getting PBS to pull an episode of *Postcards from Buster* that featured children with lesbian parents; and (3) succeeded in getting Montgomery County, Maryland, to revise a sex education curriculum that would have mentioned homosexuality for the first time (and, as of this writing, opponents continue to talk about fighting the revised curriculum, which has now been approved by the Maryland State Board of Education, because it still addresses homosexuality).

As law professor Ruthann Robson has forcefully argued, in this environment, it is incumbent upon each of us to do what we can to protect lesbian and gay youth and the children of lesbian and gay parents from harm.[4] In the following discussion, I focus on three broad areas in which we can take action to protect children from the harms associated with antigay hostility and oppression in the educational context: (1) access to education, (2) censorship, and (3) fostering a safe environment at school. As the chapter proceeds, I provide advice tailored to each of these specific areas on the steps that we can take to improve children's educational experiences.

Access to Education

After the fall 2003 semester, a gay Baylor University seminary student was forced to leave school for financial reasons—the university had revoked his scholarship after he had refused to answer administrators' questions about his sexual orientation but did express support for gay rights and same-sex marriage. In December 2004, a private religious high school in Texas forced out an honor student when it discovered that he was gay and that he had established a web site where lesbian and gay teens could chat and post pictures. In September 2005, a private religious high school in California expelled a fourteen-year-old girl because her parents are lesbians.

In *Brown v. Board of Education,* the U.S. Supreme Court stated: "In these days, it is doubtful that any child may reasonably be expected to succeed in life if he is denied the opportunity of an education."[5] Yet, despite the acknowledged importance of education, the Court has held that the U.S. Constitution does *not* grant individuals a right to an education.[6] In contrast, most states avow the importance of education, either by recognizing a right to education, providing that their primary and secondary schools should be open to all, or affirming the state's duty to educate all of its children. Nonetheless, only a small number of these jurisdictions have enacted laws that expressly prohibit discrimination on the basis of sexual orientation in access to education, with the precise coverage varying from state to state (e.g., not all of these prohibitions apply to private schools, and even those that do may not apply to private religious schools).[7]

Legislative Change

To combat the discrimination described at the beginning of this section, we can press for the passage of laws that explicitly prohibit discrimination on the basis of sexual orientation at all levels of public and private education, including in religious schools. This argument will require us to walk into a constitutional thicket, and it is unlikely that we will emerge unscathed. But some have already ventured down this path and made some progress. For example, the California courts recently refused to summarily dismiss a claim that a religious school had violated two students' rights under the state's public accommodations law when their principal expelled them because he believed they were lesbians.[8]

Academic commentators hold divergent opinions concerning the constitutionality of applying nondiscrimination provisions to private (and, more particularly, religious) schools.[9] Yet, even after *Boy Scouts of America v. Dale* (discussed in Chapter 2), an argument can be made that the state has a compelling interest in eradicating discrimination in education that overrides any federal constitutional right of association possessed by private schools. And, following the U.S. Supreme Court's decision in *Employment Division v. Smith*,[10] if the state has the power to ban discrimination in private schools, a law that applies to religious and nonreligious schools equally should not offend the right to free exercise of religion. Until the Supreme Court clears away the constitutional underbrush, we have a responsibility to argue that the federal constitution does not sanction schools that are involuntarily segregated along sexual-orientation lines.

If that position is unavailing, we can argue that nondiscrimination requirements should, at the very least, be imposed on schools that receive financial assistance from the government. Opportunely, the validity of nondiscrimination requirements tied to government funding promises to be an important topic in the ongoing debate over school voucher programs. For instance, to be eligible for the Colorado voucher program (before it was struck down by the state's Supreme Court), a private school could not "teach hatred of a person or group."[11] In a controversial move, the Denver and Jefferson County school boards refused to approve the participation of a private religious school in the voucher program because that school treated homosexuality as a ground for automatic expulsion and, therefore, could be seen as teaching hatred of lesbians and gay men. To gain approval for participation in the voucher program, the private school rewrote its policies to eliminate homosexuality as a ground for expulsion.

Several other school voucher programs contain nondiscrimination requirements; however, none of them covers sexual orientation. For instance, in Florida, where the nondiscrimination requirement covers only race, color, and national origin, a voucher student was expelled from a private religious school for being gay.[12] We would, therefore, do well to interject ourselves into debates over school financing and school choice to engage the community in a conversation about the propriety of using public money to fund discrimination. Prohibiting discrimination on the basis of sexual orientation may prove to be more politically palatable and less constitutionally problematic when imposed as a condition for receiving aid from the government.[13]

Grassroots Change

Activism can also begin at home. You can ask your local school, college, or university for a copy of its nondiscrimination policy (or search the school's web site for a copy). If the school has no policy or if the existing policy does not cover sexual orientation, then you can advocate for the adoption of a nondiscrimination policy that covers sexual orientation. Some helpful suggestions to enhance your potential for success include: (1) obtaining information about the process for changing the nondiscrimination policy; (2) identifying the individuals who will make the key decisions at each step in the process; (3) determining how best to educate these decision-makers about the need to include sexual orientation in the policy; (4) involving as many lesbian and gay students, faculty, staff, and allies as possible in the lobbying effort; and (5) doing your homework (i.e., reach out to individuals at other schools who have successfully lobbied for change so that you can anticipate problems and questions and identify strategies to emulate).[14]

Where the passage of statewide nondiscrimination laws appears politically impracticable, these grassroots efforts may be an effective alternative (or precursor) to statewide action.

Fighting Censorship

For a variety of reasons, reactionary efforts to banish homosexuality back to the invisibility of the closet are often at their fiercest in educational settings. Censorship of the discussion of homosexuality can take a number of different forms, ranging from the blatant to the subtle. In this section, I discuss several examples and suggest strategies for battling censorship. Nonetheless, you should bear in mind that censorship can take other forms, and I encourage you to combat censorship whatever its form.

As a prelude to this discussion, a brief overview of freedom-of-speech protections is in order. The First Amendment to the U.S. Constitution provides that "Congress shall make no law . . . abridging the freedom of speech." The U.S. Supreme Court has held that the Fourteenth Amendment's Due Process Clause incorporates the same restriction and applies it to the states.[15] In either case, the federal constitution protects freedom of speech from infringement only by the government (whether federal, state, or local) and not by purely private actors. Thus, the guarantee of freedom of speech generally applies in public schools; however, in private schools, it will apply only if state action is involved.[16]

In some cases, state constitutional or statutory provisions provide broader protections than the federal constitution.[17] In addition, private school students may find that their student handbook and school regulations contain freedom-of-speech protections; a school's failure to observe its own rules and regulations may form the basis for the student to sue the school for breach of contract.[18]

With this background, we can now turn to specific examples of censorship in the educational context, which will facilitate a more concrete discussion of these protections.

T-shirts and Newspapers

T-shirts. In 2005, the American Civil Liberties Union (ACLU) challenged the actions of two schools in Ohio and Missouri that punished students for wearing T-shirts with messages in support of lesbian and gay rights. In both cases, the schools singled out progay messages for suppression, having at times permitted other students to wear T-shirts expressing antigay messages and proreligious messages. The ACLU filed suit in the Missouri case and, in the Ohio case, sent a letter to the school explaining how it had violated the students' right to freedom of speech.[19] As the ACLU explained in that letter, the U.S. Supreme Court has held that students do not "shed their constitutional rights to freedom of speech or expression at the schoolhouse gate."[20]

In *Tinker v. Des Moines Independent Community School District,* a case in which students were suspended for silently wearing armbands in protest of the Vietnam War, the Supreme Court held that

> in order for the State in the person of school officials to justify prohibition of a particular expression of opinion, it must be able to show that its action was caused by something more than a mere desire to avoid the discomfort and unpleasantness that always accompany an unpopular viewpoint. Certainly where there is no finding and no showing that engaging in the forbidden conduct would "materially and substantially interfere with the requirements of appropriate discipline in the operation of the school," the prohibition cannot be sustained.[21]

The Court went on to clarify that a student's right to freedom of speech applies during the entire school day, both inside and outside the classroom. A student's right to freedom of speech may be infringed only when the student engages in conduct that "materially disrupts classwork or involves substantial disorder or invasion of the rights of others" or when school authorities "might reasonably . . . forecast substantial disruption of or material interference with school activities."[22] The Court has likewise applied *Tinker* to restrictions on the freedom of speech at the college and university level.[23]

In a later case, *Bethel School District No. 403 v. Fraser*,[24] the Supreme Court qualified its broadly protective statements in *Tinker* when it upheld a school's disciplinary action against a student who had made a speech at a school assembly. In *Fraser*, the school took disciplinary action not because of the viewpoint that the student expressed in the speech (he was endorsing another student in a run for student government) but because he had filled that speech with sexual innuendo. In upholding the school's action, the Court indicated that "the constitutional rights of students in public school are not automatically coextensive with the rights of adults in other settings."[25] The Court ultimately held that, taking into account the age and maturity of students, a school may prohibit vulgar, lewd, and indecent speech.

Against this background, once challenged by the ACLU, both the Ohio and Missouri schools reversed their positions and allowed students to wear T-shirts communicating progay messages.

More recently, in *Morse v. Frederick*, the Supreme Court further circumscribed its decision in *Tinker* by clearly stating that the "substantial disruption" standard employed in that case "does not set out the only ground on which in-school student speech may be regulated."[26] In *Morse*, the Court upheld a school principal's disciplinary action against a student who, "at a school-sanctioned and school-supervised event, . . . unfurl[ed] a large banner conveying a message [the principal] reasonably regarded as promoting illegal drug use."[27] In doing so, the Court carved out a further area in which schools may restrict student speech by holding "that schools may take steps to safeguard those entrusted to their care from speech that can reasonably be regarded as encouraging illegal drug use."[28]

Newspapers. Also in 2005, the ACLU challenged a California high school's suppression of the student-edited school newspaper's "Focus on Homosexuality." This series was to include articles on: (1) lesbian, gay, bisexual, and transgender students and their experiences; (2) whether sexual orientation is biologically determined; (3) parents of lesbian, gay, bisexual, and transgender students; and (4) religious opposition to homosexuality, featuring a community pastor and a student from a religious school. When they learned of the series, school administrators first ordered the names of the lesbian, gay, bisexual, and transgender students—but not the names of the individuals featured in the article discussing religious opposition to homosexuality—stricken from the articles as a condition of publication. School administrators later wholly suppressed the articles based on an unsubstantiated threat to the students who had been interviewed, even though all the students were already out on campus, and, in the case of students under eighteen, their parents had granted permission to include them in the articles. Notably, the school administrators had not objected a few months earlier when the school newspaper had published articles on teen rape and teen virginity, which concerned the sexuality of the straight students at the school. The ACLU filed suit against the school, asking the court to order the school to allow publication of the articles.[29]

In *Hazelwood School District v. Kuhlmeier*,[30] the U.S. Supreme Court upheld a school's censorship of two articles, one on teen pregnancy and the other on divorce, that were to appear in the school newspaper. In that case, the newspaper was written and edited by students enrolled in a journalism course, but the school principal reviewed each issue of the paper before publication, and the school largely covered the costs of publication. The Court distinguished this situation, which it viewed as involving school-sponsored speech in a nonpublic forum,[31] from the situation in *Tinker* and granted schools wider latitude to restrict speech that bears their imprimatur. The Court held that schools can exercise "editorial control over the style and content of student speech in school-sponsored expressive activities so long as their actions are reasonably related to legitimate pedagogical concerns."[32] In a footnote, the Court left open the question of what level of "deference is appropriate with respect to school-sponsored expressive activities at the college and university level."[33]

Lower courts have split on whether *Hazelwood* permits schools to discriminate based on a speaker's viewpoint when imposing restrictions on school-sponsored speech.[34] The courts similarly differ on the appropriate standard to apply to extracurricular newspapers (i.e., newspapers not written and edited as part of the students' coursework).[35] Moreover, with the question expressly left open by the Supreme Court, the lower courts differ on whether *Hazelwood* applies at the college and university level.[36] It is also worth noting that a few states, including California, have mitigated some of this uncertainty by passing statutes that afford greater freedom-of-speech protections to school newspapers than those afforded by the federal constitution.[37]

Again, once challenged by the ACLU, the California school reversed its position and allowed the "Focus on Homosexuality" series to be published by the school newspaper in November 2005. However, the lawsuit continued even after publication because the school asserted that it might censor students for the same reasons in the future.[38]

Students who perceive an infringement of their freedom of speech should contact an attorney to discuss how to resolve and redress any infringement.

Classroom and Library Materials

Classroom Materials. Attempts to eradicate the mention of homosexuality from classroom materials most naturally arise in the context of sex education courses. Recent examples include not only the Maryland case mentioned at the beginning of this chapter but also Texas's successful attempt to pressure a textbook publisher to define marriage as the union of one man and one woman in its health textbooks and to change any language in the textbooks that might be construed as a coded reference to same-sex relationships. Challenges surface in other areas of the curriculum as well, especially when teachers use materials that foster respect for lesbians and gay men. For example, when an Iowa teacher used stories that included lesbian and gay characters in her middle school class on fairy tales, parents lodged formal complaints challenging her use of those materials.

The U.S. Supreme Court has not, however, directly addressed the appropriate standard for determining whether a school's decisions concerning classroom materials violate the First Amendment. In the absence of guidance, the lower courts have taken different approaches to these First Amendment claims. Some courts treat the selection of teaching materials as speech by the government itself in a nonpublic forum, which frees the school to discriminate between different viewpoints in choosing the message that it wishes to send. For example, one court found that a public high school did not violate a teacher's freedom of speech when it ordered the removal of antigay materials posted outside his classroom. The teacher had posted the materials to counter a school-sponsored bulletin board presentation that conveyed a message of respect and tolerance during "Gay and Lesbian Awareness Month." The court permitted the school to remove the teacher's materials because they were inconsistent with the message that the school wished to send.[39] Other courts apply the *Hazelwood* standard and require the school's actions to be "reasonably related to legitimate pedagogical concerns"; thus, one court found that the First Amendment did not prevent a school board from removing an anthology with two sexually explicit stories from the curriculum because the action was reasonably related to legitimate pedagogical concerns.[40]

Whichever approach they choose, the federal courts have largely deferred to schools' decisions concerning the choice of classroom materials. Nonetheless, this deference may not be completely unbounded. The Supreme Court has "long recognized certain constitutional limits upon the power of the State to control even the curriculum and the classroom."[41] The Court has stated on occasion that the "First Amendment . . . does not tolerate laws that cast a pall of orthodoxy over the classroom."[42] It has gone on to state that "the classroom is peculiarly the 'marketplace of ideas.' The Nation's future depends upon leaders trained through wide exposure to that robust exchange of ideas which discovers truth 'out of a multitude of tongues, [rather] than through any kind of authoritative selection.'"[43] In this vein, the Court has struck down laws that flatly prohibit schools from teaching the theory of evolution or that condition the teaching of that theory on the presentation of religious viewpoints that reject evolution.[44] Accordingly, some commentators assert that the right of students to receive information (and, correlatively, to be free from indoctrination)—a right that has yet to be firmly established by the Court—may need to be balanced against the general deference to schools' decisions in selecting teaching materials.[45]

In the rare situation when schools exceed the outer boundaries of their discretion in making decisions regarding classroom materials, legal recourse will be appropriate. More commonly, schools will remain within the wide latitude granted them by the courts, and legal recourse will be unavailable. But that does not mean that you are powerless to effect change when schools censor classroom materials that mention lesbians and gay men. Taking a page from the playbook of the reactionary right, you can employ local political action to address negative curricular decisions when they occur. To reverse negative decisions, you can (1) speak with and educate members of the local school board and the school superintendent about the need to incorporate age-appropriate discussions of lesbian and gay issues in classroom materials; (2) attend school board meetings and testify; (3) vote in school board elections for candidates who are sympathetic to lesbian and gay issues (or, better yet, run for a seat yourself!); (4) become active in the parent-teacher association to educate parents and promote understanding of lesbian and gay issues; and (5) build networks of allies and encourage them to take these same steps.[46]

However, you can be even more effective in producing change if you take these steps before a decision is made. By laying the necessary groundwork in advance, you can use the courts' deference to your advantage and essentially insulate favorable decisions from legal attack (recall, for example, the bulletin-board case mentioned above). In this context, the political process is more efficient than a purely legal approach in fostering discussion of sexual orientation and family composition in the classroom.

Library Materials. In 2005, the Oklahoma House of Representatives passed a resolution urging libraries to confine access to "homosexually themed books" to adults only.[47] In 2006, Oklahoma legislators went a step further and introduced bills in both chambers that would have withheld state funding from libraries that fail to restrict access to materials with lesbian and gay themes—the Republican-led House actually passed its bill, but the Democrat-controlled Senate killed that chamber's bill in committee.[48] Similar efforts have been undertaken in other states, but, as of this writing, none has succeeded. Reactionaries also engage in more conventional attacks on books with lesbian and gay themes; in fact, according to the American Library Association, in 2004, three of the ten most frequently challenged books (i.e., books with respect to which a formal complaint was filed requesting removal of the book) were challenged due to homosexual themes.[49]

Dealing with conventional censorship. The Supreme Court addressed this latter form of censorship in *Board of Education v. Pico*[50] more than two decades ago. The *Pico* case concerned the First Amendment implications of a school's removal of books from its library. The Court was sharply divided in its decision, with a majority agreeing on the result but differing on how to reach that result (producing a "plurality"[51] opinion of three justices and two concurring opinions) and a minority strenuously objecting both to the result and to the plurality opinion.

At the outset, the plurality limited the scope of its opinion by confining it to the removal of library books only. Within this circumscribed sphere, the plurality recognized a right to receive information as being implicit in the First Amendment guarantee of freedom of speech and of the press. Although it indicated that schools "rightly possess significant discretion to determine the content of their school libraries,"[52] the plurality significantly restricted schools' discretion to remove books by holding "that local school boards may not remove books from school library shelves simply because they dislike the ideas contained in those books and seek by their removal to 'prescribe what shall be orthodox in politics, nationalism, religion, or other matters of opinion.'"[53] The plurality returned the case to the lower court for a determination of the motive for removing the books—largely because of suspicions raised by the school board's failure to make its decision pursuant to "established, regular, and facially unbiased procedures for the review of controversial materials."[54]

The dissenting justices each rejected the plurality's idea of a right to receive information, and they each would have afforded schools substantial discretion in deciding which books to acquire for, or remove from, their libraries. Furthermore, notwithstanding the plurality's repeated statements that its decision did not concern the acquisition of library books, each of the dissenting justices (and even one of the concurring justices) expressed doubt that the plurality's reasoning could be confined to the removal of books. For instance, Justice Blackmun argued in his concurring opinion that just as it is impermissible for a school to remove books from its library to suppress an entire point of view (e.g., by removing *all* books espousing a progay message), so must it be impermissible for a school to refuse to add books for the same purpose (e.g., by including *only* books espousing an antigay message).

Despite both the murky precedential value of plurality opinions and subsequent Supreme Court decisions that have moved in the direction taken by the dissenters, the plurality opinion in *Pico* has had "substantial impact in the lower courts," which have interpreted that opinion harmoniously with the subsequent case law and have applied it to school and public libraries.[55] In view of the opinion's continuing influence, you may be able to rely on the plurality's focus on the irregularity of the decision-making process in that case to encourage schools and public libraries to develop detailed, written policies and procedures for selecting and removing library materials.[56] Such policies and procedures should ensure some transparency and accountability in selection and removal decisions.

Once these policies and procedures are in place, you can take advantage of opportunities to suggest materials for inclusion in the library and comment on suggestions made by others. You will also need to keep watch for possible instances of censorship and avail yourself of any opportunity provided by the policies and procedures to voice concerns about them. Where censorship nonetheless occurs, departures from the established policies and procedures should bolster any legal claim that officials acted with constitutionally improper motives when making their decision.

Government funding conditioned on censorship. A more recent U.S. Supreme Court decision addresses the constitutionality of government funding conditioned on the censorship of library materials—the burgeoning approach to censorship of lesbian and gay materials recently considered by the Oklahoma legislature. In *United States v. American Library Association,*[57] the Court took up a First Amendment challenge to a law that conditioned public libraries' receipt of federal funding for Internet access on their installation of software that blocks access to online pornography. The justices generally agreed that the government's purpose in imposing the restriction—to protect minors from exposure to pornography—was legitimate. They split, however, on whether the available filtering software was a constitutionally adequate means for achieving that purpose because the software both "overblocked" and "underblocked" (i.e., it blocked some web sites that did not contain harmful material and failed to block others that did).

A six-justice majority of the Court agreed that the condition did not, on its face, violate the First Amendment. But, as in *Pico,* the justices differed in their reasons for reaching that decision. On the question of whether installing the software would cause libraries to violate the First Amendment, a four-justice plurality, seeing this as a case about the acquisition of library materials, would afford libraries broad discretion in making decisions about the content of their collections and find no violation. The plurality also dismissed the claim that the filtering software's "overblocking" created constitutional difficulties, citing the ease with which a patron could ask a librarian to disable the software. In addition, the plurality rejected the argument that Congress had imposed an unconstitutional condition on its financial assistance. Here, the plurality saw nothing more than Congress's ability to create a program and limit funding to authorized purposes: Congress did not penalize libraries for failing to install the software; it merely refused to subsidize a decision to provide library patrons with unfiltered Internet access.

The three dissenting justices found the overblocking problem to present constitutional difficulties, both because less restrictive alternatives were available and because it was unclear that disabling the software would be as effective a solution as the other justices asserted. Two of the dissenting justices also pointedly rejected the plurality's analogy of installing filtering software to a library's acquisition decisions, contending instead that installing the software was akin to the removal of materials from the library collection—a decision that should be subject to strict scrutiny.

In practice, dealing with this extortionary form of censorship will be difficult. Even though the justices agreed in *American Library Association* on the importance of shielding minors from pornography, they sharply divided on the constitutional propriety of the means employed to achieve that goal. If faced with a challenge to legislation similar to that considered in Oklahoma, there is a significant possibility that the Court would sharply divide on the question of whether shielding minors from materials with lesbian and gay themes is a legitimate legislative goal and on the question of whether limiting those materials to "adults only" is a constitutionally proper means of achieving that end. The success of a legal challenge is, therefore, far from certain. If anything, the Court's recent decision in *Rumsfeld v. Forum for Academic and Institutional Rights, Inc.*[58] renders the likelihood of success even less certain. In that case, a number of law schools and law professors challenged the constitutionality of a law that conditioned federal funding to universities on their granting military recruiters equal access to their facilities. For the law schools, granting such access would violate established policies against granting any access to school facilities to employers (such as the military; see Chapter 4) who discriminate on the basis of sexual orientation and would inhibit their ability to disassociate themselves from the message that discrimination on the basis of sexual orientation is acceptable. Nonetheless, the Court unanimously found this law to be a proper exercise of Congress's power to place conditions on government funding.

In view of this uncertain legal terrain, a better approach would involve a political strategy to prevent the enactment of such legislation in the first place. When a bill is introduced that ties library funding to the censorship of materials with lesbian and gay themes, you can call your state legislators to voice concern, urge your friends and neighbors to do the same, and contact interested organizations that can bring their lobbying experience and resources to bear in an effort to defeat the bill. A good place to start searching for organizations that can help with lobbying is the web site of the American Library Association's Office of Intellectual Freedom, which maintains a long list of "First Amendment advocates."[59] In addition, national, state, and local lesbian and gay rights organizations (e.g., the Human Rights Campaign and the National Gay and Lesbian Task Force) would likely be interested and helpful in organizing opposition to antigay legislation.

Self-Censorship

A more insidious, but no less coerced, form of censorship occurs when we allow the discussion of homosexuality in the classroom to be placed out of bounds. The uncertain state of the law regarding teachers' First Amendment rights with respect to classroom speech (often referred to as "academic freedom") can have a chilling effect on that speech. The U.S. Supreme Court has not provided a clear framework for determining whether (and, if so, how) freedom of speech protections apply to teachers' classroom speech.[60] In the absence of guidance, the lower courts have produced a body of case law that leaves the "constitutional contours of academic freedom in public schools and universities . . . unclear and controversial."[61] Faced with this uncertainty, teachers who wish to alleviate the impact of a negative school climate on lesbian and gay students or who simply wish to raise awareness of issues relating to sexual orientation may hold their tongues rather than risk their jobs.[62]

Any discussion of lesbian and gay issues, no matter how relevant to a course, can give rise to fear and trepidation in a teacher, especially in the current environment where conservatives are pushing for widespread enactment of an "academic bill of rights" that could be used to silence liberal voices at colleges and universities. In the tax classes that I teach, I periodically discuss the tax repercussions of the federal government's refusal to recognize same-sex relationships. For example, in the context of discussing the taxation of fringe benefits, I explain how my partner, who works for an airline, must pay tax on the value of any "free" flights that I take, while those same flights would be tax-free if provided to the husband or wife of his married coworkers. And later, in the context of discussing the taxation of married couples, I explain how my sister and her partner pay more tax than a similarly situated married couple because only one of them works outside the home and they are unable to file a joint federal income tax return splitting income between them. Before raising these issues, I always experience a moment of hesitation because I never know when one of my students will decide to complain to the university administration about "inappropriate" (any?) class discussion of lesbian and gay issues. Unfortunately, university professors have little choice but to grapple with this trepidation when engaging in educationally appropriate discussions of lesbian and gay issues.

To resolve this dilemma for elementary and secondary school teachers, however, commentators have suggested that schools adopt "clear, detailed, and thorough statements of curriculum and pedagogical parameters."[63] They further suggest that schools adopt a formal process for vetting proposed programs and materials concerning controversial subjects. They argue that implementing these additional controls over the curriculum would actually protect teachers' freedom of speech because they "are designed to avoid . . . the chilling of teacher speech."[64] By going through the formal vetting procedures, teachers could avoid being sandbagged by a supervisor who gives them oral approval to proceed with a program and then, once parents lodge complaints about it, denies having approved the program or claims that she did not receive an adequate description of it. Once a program has been formally approved by the school, it becomes difficult for the school to use that program as a basis for disciplining the teacher.

The issue of self-censorship is no less relevant for lesbian and gay parents of schoolchildren. Parents may not wish to reveal their sexual orientation, to protect themselves or their children. But parents should be as open as possible about their sexual orientation. After all, "school personnel cannot be supportive about family situations about which they have no knowledge."[65] The best avenue to acceptance is participation in school activities (e.g., join the local parent-teacher association; volunteer for work on committees, in classrooms, or on class trips; or go to potlucks).[66] In short, let people get to know you and your family rather than allowing them to make judgments based on stereotypes.[67]

Fostering a Safe School Environment

As amply demonstrated by my own experience, self-censorship is not confined to adults. Students, whether gay or straight, may refrain from asking a question or making a comment in class for fear of being labeled lesbian or gay by their peers or being censured by a teacher.[68] A lesbian or gay student may also fear the repercussions of bringing a same-sex date to the prom.[69] A child may evade questions about his family if his parents are lesbian or gay. For students, the stakes of speaking out in these situations can be high, entailing the potential for abuse from other students or even teachers. But, rather than advocating that students keep silent, this chapter closes with an exploration of ways in which we—and our heterosexual allies—can work to make the school environment safe for students to freely think, question, express themselves—and learn.

Protecting Lesbian and Gay Students from Their Peers

The Nature of the Problem. In elementary and secondary schools, where students are essentially held captive by compulsory attendance laws, harassment based on actual or perceived sexual orientation is a serious issue.[70] As one commentator has pointed out, "many LGBT students face a fundamental conflict of choice between safety and an education."[71] In 1985, the Hetrick-Martin Institute, in collaboration with New York City's Department of Education, responded to this problem by creating the Harvey Milk High School (HMHS).[72] HMHS "focus[es] on the educational needs of children who are in crisis or at risk of physical violence and/or emotional harm in a traditional educational environment."[73] And, far from being a relic of the past, HMHS, which began as a place for "displaced youths to earn a GED degree," recently expanded "into an accredited, four-year, diploma-granting high school."[74]

The paradigmatic case of the type of harassment that led to the creation of HMHS happened to Jamie Nabozny.[75] For years, Nabozny's classmates harassed him: They called him "faggot" and "queer"; they spat on and struck him; they pelted him with steel nuts and bolts; they subjected him to a mock rape in front of twenty other students in a science classroom; they knocked him into a urinal in the boys' bathroom and urinated on him; and, culminating this abominable behavior, one boy kicked him in the stomach for five to ten minutes in front of a group of laughing students, hurting him so badly that he later collapsed from internal bleeding. The abuse was so bad that Nabozny twice attempted suicide, ran away from home, and was finally diagnosed with post-traumatic stress disorder after dropping out of school in the eleventh grade. Yet, despite repeated complaints, school officials took no meaningful action to protect Nabozny; instead, they told him that "boys will be boys"; that he could expect such treatment if he was "going to be so openly gay"; and, indeed, that he deserved it.

Adopting an Antiharassment Policy. A first step toward creating a safe school environment is the adoption of an antiharassment policy. As of this writing, only a little more than half of the states have laws that require local school boards to adopt antiharassment policies and/or to take steps to prevent harassment.[76] Where such legislation is in place, you can ask for a copy of your school's policy and review it to determine whether it adequately addresses the problem. In the absence of such legislation (or while lobbying for its passage), you can ask your local school board whether it has voluntarily adopted an antiharassment policy: If it has, then you should review the policy for its adequacy; if not, then you can press the school to adopt a policy. Guidance on the drafting of antiharassment policies, including model policies, can be obtained from a number of sources.[77]

A common refrain in this guidance is that, at a minimum, school policies — and the legislation upon which they are based — should specifically mention sexual orientation as a prohibited ground for harassment.[78] In this way, there will be absolutely no question that antigay harassment is covered by the policy, and teachers will feel secure when intervening to stop the harassment of a lesbian or gay student (or a student who is perceived to be lesbian or gay).[79] Unfortunately, as of this writing, only three states have laws that specifically prohibit harassment on the basis of sexual orientation.[80]

First Amendment Concerns. Although antiharassment policies adopted by public colleges and universities have been vulnerable to First Amendment challenges,[81] commentators did not expect policies adopted by public primary and secondary schools to be vulnerable to such challenges because of the acknowledged "goal of public education in our nation . . . to inculcate basic values of our democracy, such as civility and respect for others with different backgrounds and beliefs."[82] A pair of recent decisions by the U.S. Court of Appeals for the Third Circuit has, however, shaken that expectation somewhat.

In *Saxe v. State College Area School District*[83] and *Sypniewski v. Warren Hills Regional Board of Education*,[84] the Third Circuit considered First Amendment challenges to a general antiharassment policy and a racial harassment policy, respectively. Employing the *Tinker* "substantial disruption" standard (discussed earlier in this chapter), the Third Circuit struck down the antiharassment policy in *Saxe* on the ground that it was unconstitutionally overbroad: The policy both prohibited constitutionally protected speech (e.g., remarks about another's "values") and covered speech that did not realistically threaten to substantially disrupt school activities or invade the rights of other students. In contrast, the Third Circuit generally upheld the racial harassment policy in *Sypniewski*, which had been implemented after a series of racial incidents had actually disrupted educational activities at the school.

Although the Third Circuit did not close the door on antiharassment policies in these two cases, it remains to be seen whether its restrictive view of the First Amendment will be followed or whether a more lenient reasonableness or balancing standard, which takes into account the Supreme Court's limiting of *Tinker* in its subsequent *Fraser* and *Hazelwood* decisions, will prevail.[85] In any event, the *Saxe* and *Sypniewski* decisions highlight the constitutional tension that exists between advocating for the right to freely speak about homosexuality and seeking to restrict the rights of others to use their speech to harass on the basis of sexual orientation.

Civil Liability as Motivating Force. These decisions also highlight the tension between the school's need, on the one hand, to observe the constitutional boundaries on its ability to restrict student speech and its desire, on the other, to avoid legal liability for student-on-student harassment.[86]

In the Nabozny case, the U.S. Court of Appeals for the Seventh Circuit ruled that Nabozny could proceed to trial with his claim that the public school district and school administrators had violated his federal constitutional right to equal protection under the law by treating his harassment complaints differently (i.e., by failing to take action against his harassers) either because of his gender or because of his sexual orientation. The day after a jury found for Nabozny on his claim against the school administrators (but not against the school district itself), the claim was settled for $900,000. Other courts have likewise allowed students' equal protection claims to proceed to trial in cases where complaints of harassment based on sexual orientation were treated differently (i.e., usually ignored or dismissed) by public school administrators.[87]

Courts have also permitted students to press claims under Title IX, which is a federal statute that provides that "no person . . . shall, on the basis of sex, be excluded from participation in, be denied the benefits of, or be subjected to discrimination under any education program or activity receiving Federal financial assistance."[88] Title IX's prohibitions have been construed to cover a school's inadequate response to harassment perpetrated by students (as well as teachers and staff).[89] Yet, despite the "interlocking and inseparable" nature of sex-based and sexual orientation–based harassment,[90] Title IX has been construed to prohibit *only* discrimination on the basis of sex—and *not* on the basis of sexual orientation.[91]

As a result, successful Title IX claims have largely depended on a show-ing that the harassment was due to sex-role stereotyping (e.g., that a male student was harassed because he departed from the general expectations of how a boy should act)[92] or was of a sexual nature (e.g., "if a male student or a group of male students target a gay student for physical sexual ad-vances").[93] Moreover, the Supreme Court has set a high standard for liabil-ity under Title IX: An action for damages will lie under Title IX "only where [school officials] are deliberately indifferent to sexual harassment, of which they have actual knowledge, that is so severe, pervasive, and objec-tively offensive that it can be said to deprive the victims of access to the ed-ucational opportunities or benefits provided by the school."[94] Because the standard has been set so high, commentators have remarked that "although plaintiffs have been successful in bringing peer-on-peer harassment claims under Title IX, victories occur only in the most egregious circumstances."[95]

State law may also provide a basis for imposing liability. For example, the New Jersey Supreme Court has held that a school district may be found li-able under the state's public accommodations law (discussed in Chapter 2) "for student-on-student sexual orientation harassment that creates a hostile educational environment when the school district knew or should have known of the harassment, but failed to take action reasonably calculated to end the harassment."[96] To meet this standard, "an aggrieved student must al-lege discriminatory conduct that would not have occurred 'but for' the stu-dent's [sexual orientation], that a reasonable student of the same age, matu-rity level, and [sexual orientation] would consider sufficiently severe or pervasive enough to create an intimidating, hostile, or offensive school envi-ronment, and that the school district failed to reasonably address such con-duct."[97] The New Jersey Supreme Court explicitly refused to adopt the strict Title IX standard for imposing liability, opting instead for what it de-scribed as a less "burdensome" standard.[98]

Of course, the goal is to create a safe environment that obviates the need to file a lawsuit. In that regard, the specter of civil liability may serve as a powerful motivating force for school officials to adopt, publicize, and cred-ibly enforce antiharassment policies.[99] School officials can also implement preventive programs that have been shown to reduce bullying and aggres-sion.[100] Indeed, as part of the ACLU's settlement of a recent case, the school district was required to amend its policies to specifically prohibit harass-ment and discrimination on the basis of sexual orientation and was further required to implement mandatory training on addressing and preventing antigay harassment for administrators, teachers, counselors, and all seventh and ninth grade students.[101]

Protecting Students from School Staff
At times, teachers and administrators may either exacerbate or actively con-tribute to the problem. As in the Nabozny case, they may fail to intervene

when one student is harassing another. Or they may themselves harass students who are perceived to be lesbian or gay.

For instance, the principal at a California high school suspended Charlene Nguon for being openly affectionate with her girlfriend (when similar behavior between different-sex couples was ignored), revealed Nguon's sexual orientation to her parents, and pressured Nguon to transfer to another high school in order to separate the couple. Nguon filed suit against the school district and several school officials. In an early test of her claims, Nguon's federal constitutional claims and her parallel state law claims generally survived the defendants' motion to dismiss.[102] As of this writing, a decision is still pending following the December 2006 trial of Nguon's case.

Nguon's case underscores the need for unambiguous legal prohibitions of discrimination on the basis of sexual orientation in schools. But her case also makes clear that a legal prohibition, by itself, is not enough; in fact, California already had such a prohibition in place when Nguon was singled out for punishment because of her sexual orientation. To be effective, legal prohibitions must be coupled with training on nondiscrimination and anti-harassment policies as well as diversity training that sensitizes teachers and administrators to the special needs of lesbian and gay youth.[103] Again, the prospect of legal liability is most effectively used to pressure schools to take these actions to prevent discrimination and harassment.

Creating Safe Havens at School

Student Clubs. Student clubs—often named "gay-straight alliances" (GSAs) when formed in secondary schools—are an important part of any strategy to create a safe and welcoming environment for lesbian and gay students.[104] GSAs provide a safe space in which lesbian and gay students can meet "to provide each other with peer support, seek information about issues related to sexual orientation . . . and ensure that schools respect their rights."[105] GSAs also provide an opportunity to foster understanding of lesbian and gay issues among straight students.

Many GSAs participate in the annual Day of Silence, when students across the country take a vow of silence to protest the harassment—"in effect the silencing"—of lesbian and gay students in schools.[106] In 2006, the Gay, Lesbian and Straight Education Network (GLSEN) estimated that 500,000 students at 4,000 schools participated in the Day of Silence.[107] The effectiveness of the Day of Silence was demonstrated by press coverage in newspapers across the country and by the organization of a counterprotest (the so-called Day of Truth) to argue for the right of Christians to speak out against homosexuality.

Anyone interested in creating a GSA can turn to GLSEN's web site (www.glsen.org), which has a wealth of information and ideas on its "Students Resource" page. Students who wish to form a GSA should, however, be prepared to encounter significant resistance from school officials and/or members of the community.[108] Indeed, in an effort to make the formation of GSAs as difficult as possible, Utah recently passed legislation that (1) requires all students to obtain written parental consent before joining a club, (2) requires all clubs to "maintain the boundaries of socially appropriate behavior," and (3) restricts clubs from making the discussion of human sexuality— including the "advocacy of homosexuality"—a "substantial, material, or significant part" of their activities.[109]

In the event of such resistance, the federal Equal Access Act (EAA) may protect students' right to form a GSA. The EAA provides that if a federally funded public secondary school creates a "limited open forum," then the school may not "deny equal access or a fair opportunity to, or discriminate against, any students who wish to conduct a meeting within that limited open forum on the basis of the religious, political, philosophical, or other content of the speech at such meetings."[110] A school creates a "limited open forum" when it "grants an offering to or opportunity for one or more noncurriculum related student groups to meet on school premises during noninstructional time."[111] A school may, therefore, avoid application of the EAA if it denies *all* noncurricular student groups the opportunity to meet on school premises. But if even one such group is actually permitted to meet on school premises, then the requirements of the EAA will be triggered.[112]

The First Amendment may also protect the right of public school students to form a lesbian and gay student group.[113] In *Rosenberger v. Rector and Visitors of the University of Virginia*,[114] the Supreme Court addressed the application of the First Amendment to the funding of student groups by public colleges and universities. The Court held that a student activities fund, which was used to provide financial support to extracurricular activities related to the university's educational purposes, constituted a "limited public forum." Once the university had created such a forum, the First Amendment operated to prohibit the university from discriminating between student groups based on the viewpoint that they expressed on topics that were within the ambit of that forum.

A few years later, the U.S. Court of Appeals for the Eleventh Circuit relied on *Rosenberger* when it invalidated an Alabama statute that prohibited colleges and universities from using public funds or public facilities "to, directly or indirectly, sanction, recognize, or support the activities or existence of any organization or group that fosters or promotes a lifestyle or actions prohibited by the sodomy and sexual misconduct laws of" Alabama.[115] This statute had been cited in denying funding to the Gay Lesbian Bisexual Alliance at the University of South Alabama. The Eleventh Circuit held that the university's system for funding student groups created a limited public forum, just as in *Rosenberger*. The court then struck down the Alabama statute because it discriminated based on the student group's viewpoint (i.e., it prohibited funding a group that fostered violation of Alabama's sodomy law but would permit funding a group that fostered compliance with that law).

Once again, state or local laws may provide additional protection. In *Gay Rights Coalition of Georgetown University Law Center v. Georgetown University*,[116] a fractured District of Columbia Court of Appeals considered the application of DC's Human Rights Act to Georgetown's refusal to accord "University Recognition" to a lesbian and gay student group. The court's lead opinion construed the act so as not to require the university to grant "recognition" to (and, therefore, to "endorse") the student group. However, balancing the university's right to freely exercise its religion against DC's compelling interest in eradicating discrimination on the basis of sexual orientation, the lead opinion went on to find that the act did require the university to provide the group equal access to the facilities and services that would normally accompany "University Recognition" of a student group. Unhappy with this result, Congress, in an exercise of its exclusive power over the District of Columbia,[117] promptly amended the Human Rights Act to provide an exception that would cover Georgetown's refusal to grant recognition to lesbian and gay student groups.[118]

Safe Zones. Heterosexual allies can also work with us to create a safe and welcoming environment for lesbian and gay students by helping to implement or participating in a "safe-zone" program. These programs train participating faculty and staff to sensitize them to the unique issues faced by lesbian and gay youth. Participating faculty and staff then post a sign or a sticker (e.g., a pink triangle or other recognizable lesbian and gay symbol) on their door to signal to students that their office is a place where they can feel safe to seek support with regard to issues relating to sexual orientation. Safe-zone programs have been implemented in secondary schools and at colleges and universities. The best place to find information on starting a safe-zone program is the Internet. A number of schools have posted information on their safe-zone programs, and the National Consortium of Directors of LGBT Resources in Higher Education maintains a list of colleges and universities that have safe-zone programs.[119] Even if they have not posted information about their programs online, schools are often willing to share information. In fact, when a committee here at the University of Pittsburgh began to explore the idea of implementing a safe-zone program, we contacted our neighbor, Carnegie Mellon University; its staff provided us with information and invited us to attend its training program to help us develop one of our own.

Notes

1. Neil W. Pilkington and Anthony R. D'Augelli, "Victimization of Lesbian, Gay, and Bisexual Youth in Community Settings," *J. Community Psychol.* 23 (1995): 34, 54.

2. Anthony R. D'Augelli, Neil W. Pilkington, and Scott L. Hershberger, "Incidence and Mental Health Impact of Sexual Orientation Victimization of Lesbian, Gay, and Bisexual Youths in High School," *Sch. Psychol. Q.* 17 (2002): 148, 156.

3. See, for example, Anthony R. D'Augelli and Gregory M. Herek, "Developmental Implications of Victimization of Lesbian, Gay, and Bisexual Youths," in *Stigma and Sexual Orientation: Understanding Prejudice Against Lesbians, Gay Men, and Bisexuals* (Thousand Oaks, CA: Sage Publications, 1998): 187, 194–195; Craig R. Waldo, Matthew S. Hesson-McInnis, and Anthony R. D'Augelli, "Antecedents and Consequences of Victimization of Lesbian, Gay, and Bisexual Young People: A Structural Model Comparing Rural University and Urban Samples," *Am. J. Community Psychol.* 26 (1998): 307, 309.

4. Ruthann Robson, "Our Children: Kids of Queer Parents and Kids Who Are Queer—Looking at Sexual Minority Rights from a Different Perspective," *Alb. L. Rev.* 64 (2001): 915.

5. *Brown v. Bd. of Educ.*, 347 U.S. 483, 493 (1954).

6. *San Antonio Indep. Sch. Dist. v. Rodriguez*, 411 U.S. 1, 29–39 (1973).

7. Cal. Educ. Code §§200, 220 (2007); Cal. Gov't Code §11,135 (2007); Conn. Gen. Stat. §10-15c (2007); D.C. Code §§2-1401.02(8), 2-1402.41 (2007); Iowa Code §216.9 (2007); Me. Rev. Stat. tit. 5, §§4601, 4602(4) (2006); Mass. Gen. Laws, ch. 76, §5 (2007); Minn. Stat. §§363A.03(14), .13, .26(2) (2006); N.J. Rev. Stat. §§10:5-4, -5(l) (2007); N.Y. Educ. Law §313 (2006); N.Y. Exec. Law §§291(2), 296(4), (11) (2007); Vt. Stat. tit. 9, §§4501(1), 4502 (2006); Wash. Rev. Code §§49.60.030(1)(b), .040(10), .215 (2007); Wis. Stat. §118.13 (2006); Act of May 9, 2007, ch. 100, §§23, 29, 2007 Ore. SB 2 (Lexis) (to be codified at Or. Rev. Stat. §§338.125, 659.850; see the discussion of Oregon's domestic partnership regime in Chapter 6 for an explanation of the effective date of this provision).

8. Bob Egelko, "Girls' Suit Allowed to Proceed," *San Francisco Chronicle*, June 29, 2006, B2.

9. Compare Ira C. Lupu and Robert W. Tuttle, "Zelman's Future: Vouchers, Sectarian Providers, and the Next Round of Constitutional Battles," *Notre Dame L. Rev.* 78 (2003): 917, 975–982, with Mark Tushnet, "Vouchers After Zelman," *Sup. Ct. Rev.* (2002): 1, 22–29.

10. *Employment Div. v. Smith*, 494 U.S. 872 (1990).

11. Colo. Rev. Stat. §22-56-106(1)(b)–(c) (2004); see *Owens v. Colo. Cong. of Parents, Teachers, and Students*, 92 P.3d 933 (Colo. 2004) (striking down the voucher program).

12. A recent Florida Supreme Court decision has cast a cloud over the constitutionality of the state's voucher programs. See *Bush v. Holmes*, 919 So. 2d 392 (Fla. 2006).

13. See Lupu and Tuttle, "Zelman's Future," 976–978.

14. Brett Beemyn and Luke Jensen, "Suggestions for How to Have 'Sexual Orientation/Gender Identity or Expression' Included in Nondiscrimination Policies," available at www.lgbtcampus.org/faq/nondis.pdf.

15. *Young v. American Mini Theatres, Inc.*, 427 U.S. 50, 52 n.1 (1976).

16. *W. Va. Bd. of Educ. v. Barnette*, 319 U.S. 624, 637 (1943); Vanessa Ann Countryman, "School Choice Programs Do Not Render Participant Private Schools 'State Actors,'" *U. Chi. Legal F.* (2004): 525, 531–540.

17. For example, Cal. Educ. Code §§48,907, 48,950 (2007).

18. See Michael Zolandz, "Storming the Ivory Tower: Renewing the Breach of Contract Claim by Students Against Universities," *Geo. Wash. L. Rev.* 69 (2000): 91.

19. Complaint, *Myers v. Thornsberry*, 05-5042 (W. D. Mo. Apr. 6, 2005); letter from Legal Director of American Civil Liberties Union of Ohio Jeffrey M. Gamso to Superintendent Linda Fenner, Dublin City Schools, April 6, 2005.

20. *Tinker v. Des Moines Indep. Cmty. Sch. Dist.*, 393 U.S. 503, 506 (1969).

21. Ibid., 509 (quoting *Burnside v. Byars*, 363 F.2d 744, 749 [5th Cir. 1966]).

22. Ibid., 513, 514.

23. *Healy v. James*, 408 U.S. 169, 180, 189–191 (1972).

24. *Bethel Sch. Dist. No. 403 v. Fraser*, 478 U.S. 675 (1986).

25. Ibid., 682.

26. *Morse v. Frederick*, No. 06-278, 2007 U.S. Lexis 8514, *52 (U.S. June 25, 2007) (Alito, J., concurring).

27. Ibid., *7.

28. Ibid., *8.

29. Petition for Writ of Mandate and Complaint, *Paramo v. Kern High Sch. Dist.*, S1500-CV-255519 (Cal. Super. Ct. July 29, 2005).

30. *Hazelwood Sch. Dist. v. Kuhlmeier*, 484 U.S. 260 (1988).

31. A nonpublic forum is "government property . . . that has not traditionally been open to public discourse and that the government has chosen not to throw open to public discourse. Examples of a nonpublic forum would include a public school classroom when class is in session." John E. Nowak and Ronald D. Rotunda, *Constitutional Law*, 7th ed. (St. Paul, MN: Thomson/West, 2004), §16.1, 1141.

32. *Hazelwood*, 273.

33. Ibid., 273 n.7.

34. *Peck v. Baldwinsville Cent. Sch. Dist.*, 426 F.3d 617, 631–633 (2d Cir. 2005).

35. Compare *Romano v. Harrington*, 725 F. Supp. 687 (E.D.N.Y. 1989), with *Desilets v. Clearview Reg'l Bd. of Educ.*, 647 A.2d 150 (N.J. 1994).

36. *Hosty v. Carter*, 412 F.3d 731, 738–739 (7th Cir. 2005) (en banc).

37. Cal. Educ. Code §48,907 (2007); see also Colo. Rev. Stat. §22-1-120 (2006); Iowa Code §280.22 (2006); Kan. Stat. §72-1506 (2005); Mass. Gen. Laws, ch. 71, §82 (2007).

38. Second Amended Petition for Writ of Mandate §40, *Paramo v. Kern High Sch. Dist.*, S1500-CV-255519 (Cal. Super. Ct. January 25, 2006).

39. *Downs v. Los Angeles Unified Sch. Dist.*, 228 F.3d 1003 (9th Cir. 2000).

40. *Virgil v. Sch. Bd.*, 862 F.2d 1517, 1520–1525 (11th Cir. 1989).

41. *Bd. of Educ. v. Pico*, 457 U.S. 853, 861 (1982) (plurality).

42. *Keyishian v. Bd. of Regents*, 385 U.S. 589, 603 (1967); for example, *Hazelwood*, 286.

43. *Keyishian*, 603 (quoting *United States v. Associated Press*, 52 F. Supp. 362, 372 [S.D.N.Y. 1943]).

44. *Edwards v. Aguillard*, 482 U.S. 578, 596–597 (1987); *Epperson v. Arkansas*, 393 U.S. 97, 107 (1968).

45. See, for example, Lisa Shaw Roy, "Inculcation, Bias, and Viewpoint Discrimination in Public Schools," *Pepp. L. Rev.* 32 (2005): 647; Jamie Kennedy, "The Right to Receive Information: The Current State of the Doctrine and the Best Application for the Future," *Seton Hall L. Rev.* 35 (2005): 789.

46. Allison F. Bauer and Nancy Goldstein, report for Family Pride Coalition, "Opening More Doors: Creating Policy Change to Include Our Families" (2003).

47. H. Res. 1039, 50th Leg., first sess. (Okla. 2005).

48. H. 2158, 50th Leg., second sess. (Okla. 2006); S. 1777, 50th Leg., second sess. (Okla. 2006).

49. American Library Association, "The Chocolate War," *Top 2004 Most Challenged Books List* (2005), available at www.ala.org/ala/pressreleases2005/februarya/2004mostchallengedbook.htm.

50. *Bd. of Educ. v. Pico,* 457 U.S. 853 (1982).

51. For a discussion of plurality opinions, see Linda Novak, "The Precedential Value of Supreme Court Plurality Decisions," *Colum. L. Rev.* 80 (1980): 756.

52. *Bd. of Educ. v. Pico,* 870.

53. Ibid., 872 (quoting *W. Va. Bd. of Educ. v. Barnette,* 319 U.S. 624, 642 [1943]).

54. Ibid., 872–875.

55. Richard J. Peltz, "Pieces of *Pico:* Saving Intellectual Freedom in the Public School Library," *BYU Educ. and L.J.* 103 (2005): 103–104, 136–145.

56. See Kristin Huston, "Silent Censorship: The School Library and the Insidious Book Selection Censor," *UMKC L. Rev.* 72 (2003): 241, 250–254.

57. *United States v. Am. Library Ass'n,* 539 U.S. 194 (2003).

58. *Rumsfeld v. Forum for Academic and Inst. Rights, Inc.,* 126 S. Ct. 1297 (2006).

59. American Library Association, "Intellectual Freedom: First Amendment Advocates," available at www.ala.org/ala/oif/firstamendment/advocates/advocates.htm#advocates.

60. For example, Karen C. Daly, "Balancing Act: Teachers' Classroom Speech and the First Amendment," *J. L. and Educ.* 30 (2001): 1, 4–7; Jennifer Elrod, "Academics, Public Employee Speech, and the Public University," *Buff. Pub. Int. L. J.* 22 (2003–2004): 1, 32, 35–36; see also *Garcetti v. Ceballos,* 126 S. Ct. 1951 (2006) (holding that there is no First Amendment protection for speech of public employees pursuant to their official duties but refusing to decide whether that standard should be applied to academic scholarship or classroom teaching).

61. Vikram Amar and Alan Brownstein, "Academic Freedom," *Green Bag* 9 (2005): 17, 18.

62. Compare *Weaver v. Nebo Sch. Dist.,* 29 F. Supp. 2d 1279 (D. Utah 1998) (teacher reinstated), with *Rowland v. Mad River Local Sch. Dist.,* 730 F.2d 444 (6th Cir. 1984) (teacher fired).

63. Amar and Brownstein, "Academic Freedom," 24.

64. Ibid.

65. Aimee Gelnaw, Margie Brickley, Hilary Marsh, and Daniel Ryan, report for Family Pride Coalition, "Opening Doors: Lesbian and Gay Parents and Schools" (1999), 7.

66. Ibid.

67. Ibid.

68. *McLaughlin v. Bd. of Educ.,* 296 F. Supp. 2d 960 (E.D. Ark. 2003).

69. *Fricke v. Lynch,* 491 F. Supp. 381 (D.R.I. 1980).

70. Gay, Lesbian, and Straight Education Network (GLSEN), *From Teasing to Torment: School Climate in America—A Survey of Students and Teachers* (New York: GLSEN, 2005); Human Rights Watch, *Hatred in the Hallways: Violence and*

Discrimination Against Lesbian, Gay, Bisexual, and Transgender Students in U.S. Schools (New York: Human Rights Watch, 2001).

71. Maurice R. Dyson, "Safe Rules or Gays' Schools? The Dilemma of Sexual Orientation Segregation in Public Education," *U. Pa. J. Const. L. 7* (2004): 183, 190.

72. Hetrick-Martin Institute, "FAQ's: About HMI," available at www.hmi.org.

73. Hetrick-Martin Institute, "FAQ's: What People Are Asking About HMHS," available at www.hmi.org.

74. John Colapinto, "'The Harvey Milk School Has No Right to Exist': Discuss," *New York* magazine (February 7, 2005): 32, 34–35.

75. *Nabozny v. Podlesny,* 92 F.3d 446 (7th Cir. 1996).

76. Ariz. Rev. Stat. §15-341(A)(40) (2006); Ark. Code §6-18-514 (2007); Cal. Educ. Code §§201, 32,282(a)(2)(E) (2007); Colo. Rev. Stat. §22-32-109.1(2)(a)(X) (2006); Conn. Gen. Stat. §10-222d (2006); Ga. Code §§20-2-145, -751.4 (2006); 105 Ill. Comp. Stat. 5/10-20.14(d) (2006); Ind. Code §20-33-8-13.5 (2006); Iowa Code §280.28 (2007); Act of May 11, 2007, §4, ch. 2007-185, 2007 Kan. SB 68 (Lexis); La. Rev. Stat. §17:416.13(b) (2006); Me. Rev. Stat. tit. 20-A, §1001(15)(H) (2006); Minn. Stat. §§120B.22, 121A.03, .0695 (2006); Miss. Code §37-11-54 (2007); Nev. Rev. Stat. §388.139 (2007); N.H. Rev. Stat. §193-F:3 (2006); N.J. Rev. Stat. §18A:37-15 (2007); N.Y. Educ. Law §2801-a(2)(j) (2007); Okla. Stat. tit. 70, §24-100.4(A) (2006); Or. Rev. Stat. §339.356 (2005); R.I. Gen. Laws §16-21-26 (2006); Tenn. Code §49-6-1016 (2006); Tex. Educ. Code §37.001(a)(7) (2006); Vt. Stat. tit. 16, §§165, 565 (2006); Va. Code §§22.1-208.01(A), -279.6(B) (2006); Wash. Rev. Code §28A.300.285 (2007); W. Va. Code §§18-2C-3, -5 (2007).

77. For example, Susan Hanley Kosse and Robert H. Wright, "How Best to Confront the Bully: Should Title IX or Antibullying Statutes Be the Answer?" *Duke J. Gender L. and Pol'y* 12 (2005): 53, 71–74; Thomas A. Mayes, "Confronting Same-Sex, Student-to-Student Sexual Harassment: Recommendations for Educators and Policy Makers," *Fordham Urb. L. J.* 29 (2001): 641, 665–681.

78. For example, Human Rights Watch, *Hatred in the Hallways,* 10; Kosse and Wright, "How Best to Confront the Bully," 71–72; Mayes, "Confronting Same-Sex, Student-to-Student Sexual Harassment," 671.

79. Bauer and Goldstein, *Opening More Doors,* 5.

80. N.J. Rev. Stat. §18A:37-14 (2007); Vt. Stat. tit. 16, §11(a)(26) (2006); Wash. Rev. Code §28A.300.285 (2007).

81. For example, *Dambrot v. Cent. Mich. Univ.,* 55 F.3d 1177, 1182–1185 (6th Cir. 1995).

82. Martha McCarthy, "Antiharassment Policies in Public Schools: How Vulnerable Are They?" *J. L. and Educ.* 31 (2002): 52, 55.

83. *Saxe v. State Coll. Area Sch. Dist.,* 240 F.3d 200 (3d Cir. 2001).

84. *Sypniewski v. Warren Hills Reg'l Bd. of Educ.,* 307 F.3d 243 (3d Cir. 2002).

85. McCarthy, "Antiharassment Policies in Public Schools," 52, 66; for example, *Denno ex rel. Denno v. Sch. Bd.,* 218 F.3d 1267, 1273–1274 (11th Cir. 2000).

86. Kathleen Hart, "Sticks and Stones and Shotguns at School: The Ineffectiveness of Constitutional Antibullying Legislation as a Response to School Violence," *Ga. L. Rev.* 39 (2005): 1109, 1142.

87. For example, *Flores v. Morgan Hill Unified Sch. Dist.,* 324 F.3d 1130 (9th Cir. 2003). For a critique of the equal protection analysis in *Nabozny,* see Deborah

Brake, "The Cruelest of the Gender Police: Student-to-Student Sexual Harassment and Anti-Gay Peer Harassment under Title IX," *Geo. J. Gender and L.* 1 (1999): 37, 66–68.

88. 20 U.S.C. §1681 (2007).

89. Office for Civil Rights, U.S. Department of Education, "Revised Sexual Harassment Guidance: Harassment of Students by School Employees, Other Students, or Third Parties" (2001), 3.

90. Brake, "The Cruelest of the Gender Police," 60–68, 81.

91. Office for Civil Rights, "Revised Sexual Harassment Guidance," 3.

92. Ibid.

93. Ibid.

94. *Davis v. Monroe County Bd. of Educ.*, 526 U.S. 629, 650 (1999).

95. Kosse and Wright, "How Best to Confront the Bully," 60.

96. *L.W. v. Toms River Reg'l Schs. Bd. of Educ.*, 915 A.2d 535, 550 (N.J. 2007).

97. Ibid., 547.

98. Ibid., 549.

99. For example, Bauer and Goldstein, *Opening More Doors*, 13.

100. For example, American Civil Liberties Union, "Making Schools Safe: Anti-Harassment Training Program," 2d ed. (2002).

101. American Civil Liberties Union, "Settlement Fact Sheet: *Flores v. Morgan Hill Unified School District*" (2004), available at www.aclu.org/lgbt/youth/11946res20040106.html.

102. *Nguon v. Wolf*, SACV 05–868 JVS (MLGx) (C.D. Cal. filed November 28, 2005).

103. For example, Bauer and Goldstein, *Opening More Doors*, 11, 13; Mayes, "Confronting Same-Sex, Student-to-Student Sexual Harassment," 674.

104. For example, Bauer and Goldstein, *Opening More Doors*, 12; Human Rights Watch, *Hatred in the Hallways*, 110–112.

105. Human Rights Watch, *Hatred in the Hallways*, 110.

106. GLSEN, "Thousands of Schools Participate in GLSEN's 10th Annual Day of Silence," April 26, 2006, available at www.glsen.org/cgi-bin/iowa/all/news/record/1926.html.

107. Ibid.

108. For example, *Caudillo v. Lubbock Indep. Sch. Dist.*, 311 F. Supp. 2d 550 (N.D. Tex. 2004); *Boyd County High Sch. Gay Straight Alliance v. Bd. of Educ.*, 258 F. Supp. 2d 667 (E.D. Ky. 2003); see also Carolyn Pratt, "Protecting the Marketplace of Ideas in the Classroom: Why the Equal Access Act and the First Amendment Require the Recognition of Gay/Straight Alliances in America's Public Schools," *First Amend. L. Rev.* 5 (2007), 370, 370–374.

109. Utah Code §§53A-11-1202(8)(A) (incorporating by reference Utah Code §53A-13-101, which prohibits local school boards from adopting materials that include "instruction in . . . the advocacy of homosexuality"), -1206(1)(A)(V) (on "maintaining the boundaries of appropriate social behavior"), -1206(1)(B)(III) (limiting activities "involving human sexuality"), -1209(1) (parental consent), -1210 (same) (2007); see also Kirk Johnson, "Utah Sets Rigorous Rules for School Clubs, and Gay Ones May Be Target," *New York Times*, March 17, 2007, A10.

110. 20 U.S.C. §4071(a) (2007).

111. Ibid., §4071(b).

112. *Boyd County High Sch. Gay Straight Alliance v. Bd. of Educ.,* 687–688. Those wishing to avoid application of the EAA have also attempted to rely on 20 U.S.C. §4071(f) (2007), which provides that the EAA does *not* limit the authority of the school "to maintain order and discipline on school premises, to protect the well-being of students and faculty, and to assure that attendance of students at meetings is voluntary." This strategy has met with mixed success. Compare *Caudillo,* 565–571, with *Boyd County,* 688–691; see also Pratt, "Protecting the Marketplace of Ideas in the Classroom," 380. Another tactic is to argue that GSAs are "curriculum-related" (and, therefore, exempt from the requirements of the EAA) because they discuss sex, a subject treated in sexual education courses at the school. See 20 U.S.C. §4072(3) (2007) ("meeting" is defined to include only activities "not directly related to the school curriculum"); Pratt, "Protecting the Marketplace of Ideas in the Classroom," 386–388. This strategy has likewise met with mixed success. Ibid., 388–393.

113. *Boyd County,* 691; *E. High Gay/Straight Alliance v. Bd. of Educ.,* 81 F. Supp. 2d 1166, 1186–1196 (D. Utah 1999); see also Pratt, "Protecting the Marketplace of Ideas in the Classroom," 393–398.

114. *Rosenberger v. Rector and Visitors of Univ. of Va.,* 515 U.S. 819 (1995).

115. Ala. Code §16-1-28 (1997); *Gay Lesbian Bisexual Alliance v. Pryor,* 110 F.3d 1543, 1546 (11th Cir. 1997).

116. *Gay Rights Coal. of Georgetown Univ. Law Ctr. v. Georgetown Univ.,* 536 A.2d 1, 5 (D.C. App. 1987).

117. U.S. Const. art. I, §8, cl. 17; see also D.C. Code §1-206.01 (2007).

118. D.C. Code §2-1402.41(3) (2007).

119. See, for example, GLSEN, "Safe Zone Programs" (2003), available at www .glsen.org/binary-data/GLSEN_ATTACHMENTS/file/245-1.pdf; National Consortium of Directors of LGBT Resources in Higher Education, "Safe Zone/Allies Programs" (2006), available at www.lgbtcampus.org/faq/safe_zone_roster.html.

4
The Military

Lacy's Story

When I was in seventh grade, I found an advertisement in a magazine for the U.S. Marines. It had a picture of a female marine officer on it, and stated, "We're looking for a few good men and women." From that moment on, I knew I wanted to be an officer in the United States Armed Forces. I knew even then that I didn't want to be a marine. I wanted to be an officer in the United States Air Force. Despite the fact that the picture in the advertisement was of a female marine, I ripped out that picture and taped it on my mirror in my bedroom. That picture stayed up until I went off to college in the fall of 1990. I knew I wanted to be in a career that held honor, integrity, and service to others above all else. Sounds cheesy, but those attributes meant (and still mean) a lot to me.

Even though I wanted to be in the air force, I didn't sign up for ROTC immediately when I arrived at college. Starting in late high school, I came to the realization that I was gay. I was in Arkansas, so I remained in the closet, and only came out to a few close friends. I knew there was a ban against gays serving in the military, and I had heard stories of witch hunts in the military—spies planted on female softball teams in the military to determine who was gay. I knew that those servicemembers who were kicked out received dishonorable discharges, and I didn't want to have that happen to me. I didn't want to always explain why I received a dishonorable discharge to potential future employers. For these reasons, I didn't sign up with the military during my first two years of college.

In the spring semester of my junior year, in 1993, however, I finally took the step to begin the military career I had always wanted. President Clinton had recently pushed through the "don't ask, don't tell" policy, and I knew that it would be safe for me to sign up for the military. I went to the AFROTC Detachment at the University of Arkansas and began the application process. When I signed up for the ROTC, the question "Are you now or have you ever been a homosexual?" was crossed out with a black marker. It was a relief to not have to deal with that question. I consider myself an extremely honest person, and I didn't think I could start a career that touted honesty and honor if I had to lie in order to begin that career. Having said that, I remained in the closet to everyone in the Air Force ROTC program, and I was only out to a few people. I was still very frightened that someone would out me and jeopardize my career with the Air Force.

That summer I went to boot camp, or field training, at Sheppard Air Force Base in Wichita Falls, Texas. It was a six-week program designed for cadets who had not gone through the first two years of AFROTC. Unfortunately for me, every cadet there had gone through at least one year of AFROTC classes and fitness training. After a steep learning curve, however, by the end of those six weeks, my cadet training officer ranked me as the third-highest cadet in my flight. Those were the best six weeks of my life. I learned how to be a leader, and that I could do more than I thought I could.

I returned to the University of Arkansas's AFROTC Detachment that fall with a great sense of energy and hope. I had received an ROTC scholarship because my grades were so high. To receive this scholarship, I had to become an inactive reserve member of the U.S. Air Force. I raised my hand and repeated the oath to protect and defend, and I felt such pride and honor to finally be a member of the United States Air Force. That fall, I was a flight commander (I was in charge of a group of ten first- and second-year cadets) and my flight was the top-ranked flight for the entire semester. I took the pilot's test in late fall, and several weeks later I learned I was one of 213 cadets across the country chosen to receive a pilot slot. I was going to be a pilot in the United States Air Force. That had been a secret dream of mine for years, but I didn't want to voice it aloud in case I didn't get the slot. The competition was fierce to win a pilot slot. I went on joint AFROTC/Civil Air Patrol missions and flew little twin-engine Cessnas all over Northwest Arkansas. Also, that spring, I was petitioned and received the slot of cadet corps commander for the next year. This is the highest-ranking cadet position in the detachment. I was going to be cadet colonel, in charge of over eighty cadets in the U of A's cadet program. Needless to say, I was very happy that things were going so well and that the military was such a great fit for me.

However, all of this came to a stop in the fall of 1994. One day in early September, during AFROTC Leadership Lab class, the captain passed around a sheet of paper for each of us to sign. He said it had come down from AFROTC headquarters in Maxwell Air Base. The piece of paper stated, "I, the undersigned, do solemnly swear that I am not now, nor have I ever been a homosexual, and I have not had homosexual relations with another person." (I'm not sure if these are truly the exact words, but those are the words that have always stuck with me.) I remember the other cadets snickering and cracking jokes with each other about how they shouldn't sign because they knew that they were secretly gay. I remember I stared at that piece of paper for a long time. Everyone else had just signed it and turned it in. I'm ashamed to admit that I signed the piece of paper. Maybe it's the one time in my life when peer pressure got to me. But I think I signed it because I was dumbstruck and didn't know what else to do.

That night, I didn't sleep at all. I just kept turning over in my mind whether I needed to get out of the Air Force or whether I could just keep myself closeted and keep serving my country in the Air Force. In the end, I knew that I had to retain my own honor and integrity. So the next morning, I went to the commandant of cadets and disenrolled from the AFROTC program. The colonel allowed me a moment to tell my fellow cadets during Leadership Lab class. I just said that I was getting out and that I wished them the best of luck in the future. I still remember the stunned looks on their faces.

After I disenrolled, I went through a really rough period of time. I had to pay back the $2,000 scholarship because I failed to fulfill my obligations to the Air Force after I received that money. Evidently that money was given to me on the condition that I serve four years in the Air Force upon completion of college. I also had to come up with lame excuses to offer my parents for why I got out of the Air Force. The one thing I had dreamed of doing since I was a kid in seventh grade. I still don't know if they bought my excuses of why I got out. I spent the next several years working at low-paying waitressing jobs and at bookstores because my career goal had disappeared. I didn't know what to do. I don't think I wanted to do much of anything.

Luckily, after several years and one master's degree in French, I finally figured out my new goal. I was going to go to law school. And hopefully, I could make sure that the discrimination that happened to me would not happen to anyone else. It's a lofty goal, and probably not attainable, but it's a goal I can be proud of. I've finally found another career path that involves honor and integrity and service to others.[1]

Early in the 1992 presidential campaign, when Lacy had just entered her sophomore year at the University of Arkansas, Bill Clinton became the first candidate to promise that, if elected, he would lift the long-standing ban on lesbians and gay men serving in the military.[2] In the weeks before the election, the brutal murder of Seaman Allen Schindler drove home the importance of lifting the ban and addressing antigay hostility in the military.[3] Because Schindler was gay, two of his shipmates beat him to death in a public restroom near the naval base where they were stationed in Japan. Schindler's shipmates beat him so severely that his mother had to identify his body by his tattoos, and the pathologist who performed Schindler's autopsy compared the damage to what might be seen when someone died in a high-speed car crash or was trampled by a horse.

As evidenced by Lacy's story, Clinton's initial, unqualified promise to lift the ban—and even his subsequent "Don't Ask, Don't Tell" compromise with supporters of the ban—raised the expectation that lesbians and gay men would be able to serve in the military without fear of expulsion solely because of their sexual orientation. But, as we will see, well-entrenched prejudices, no matter how wrong or damaging, don't give way quite so easily.[4]

Given the prolonged national debate over "gays in the military," my goal in this chapter is twofold: first, to cut through the rhetoric, dispel some of the misconceptions about the current policy, and explain how harmful the policy really is to lesbians and gay men; and second, to explore some of the ways in which we all can challenge and work to overturn the ban on lesbians and gay men serving in the military.

"Don't Ask, Don't Tell"

A Short History

Pre-Clinton Policy. Although lesbians and gay men had served in—and been drummed out of—the U.S. military since the Revolutionary War,[5] the military did not formally criminalize sodomy until World War I.[6] Following World War I, with the help of the psychiatric profession, the military began the move from criminalizing same-sex sexual conduct to excluding persons with a homosexual orientation.[7] By the end of World War II, the army had adopted regulations differentiating between homosexual and "normal" individuals, and the navy had indicated that persons with homosexual "tendencies" (even if they had not engaged in same-sex sexual activity) were to be excluded from military service.[8]

The military policy toward lesbians and gay men was unified in 1949, when the Department of Defense issued a memorandum stating: "Homosexual personnel, irrespective of sex, should not be permitted to serve in any branch of the Armed Services in any capacity, and prompt separation of known homosexuals from the Armed Services be made mandatory."[9] Then, in 1950, Congress enacted the Uniform Code of Military Justice (UCMJ), in which it codified the criminalization of sodomy.[10] Even though this criminal prohibition applies to same-sex and different-sex conduct alike, it has nonetheless "been used as justification for the prohibition on homosexual service."[11]

The Department of Defense revised the rules governing discharge from the military for homosexuality in 1959 and 1965.[12] After liberalizing the rules in 1965 to allow military personnel "to present their cases before administrative discharge boards and to be represented by counsel,"[13] the department tightened the rules in the waning days of the Carter administration by eliminating the discretion that had previously been vested in individual commanders to retain lesbian and gay service personnel.[14] The department also generally made discharge mandatory for personnel who, either before or after entering the military, (1) had engaged in, attempted to engage in, or solicited another to engage in a homosexual act; (2) had stated that they are homosexual or bisexual; or (3) had married or attempted to marry a person of the same sex.[15] These changes were made "in response to court rulings that had questioned inconsistencies in the way the prior policy had been implemented."[16]

Changes During the Clinton Administration. Shortly after being elected president, Bill Clinton reaffirmed his intention to lift the ban on lesbians and gay men in the military. However, recognizing that there would be opposition from within the military, Clinton abandoned his initial promise to

unqualifiedly lift the ban and decided instead to focus on the distinction between status and conduct; in other words, lesbians and gay men would be
permitted to serve openly in the military so long as their conduct did not
"conflict with the good order and efficiency of the military."[17]

Before Clinton took office, invoking the precedent set by President Tru-
man when he desegregated the armed forces by issuing an executive order,[18]
"pro-gay constituencies . . . urged the new president to exercise his unilateral powers as commander-in-chief to rewrite military policy 'with the
stroke of a pen.'"[19] But such an expeditious lifting of the ban was not to be.
Within days of taking office, Clinton encountered resistance not only from
the Joint Chiefs of Staff, who had earlier threatened to resign in protest if
the ban were lifted, but also from Congress, which was adamantly opposed
to lifting the ban and threatened to pass legislation codifying the ban and
overriding any executive order issued by Clinton.[20]

On January 29, 1993, President Clinton outlined an interim policy and directed his secretary of defense, Les Aspin, to submit a draft executive order
ending discrimination on the basis of sexual orientation in the military for his
review no later than July 15, 1993.[21] The draft executive order was to represent a compromise that Aspin was expected to hammer out between the
White House, the Joint Chiefs of Staff, and Congress.[22] Within days, however,
Congress had effectively shifted the playing field by including a provision in
the Family and Medical Leave Act that required Aspin to review the existing
policy on lesbians and gay men in the military and to submit any recommended changes to both the president *and* Congress by July 15, 1993.[23] The
legislation further required the Senate Armed Services Committee to conduct
hearings on the policy as well as oversight hearings on Aspin's recommended
changes once issued.[24] In effect, Congress had situated itself "as a possible but
not necessary final decision maker,"[25] dangling the threat of legislation before
the administration as it negotiated changes to the existing policy.

On July 19, 1993, President Clinton announced the new policy, which
was dubbed "Don't Ask, Don't Tell, Don't Pursue" (DADT). Clinton characterized and summarized the new policy in the following terms:

> We now have a policy that is a substantial advance over the one in place when
> I took office. I have ordered Secretary Aspin to issue a directive consisting of
> these essential elements: One, service men and women will be judged based on
> their conduct, not their sexual orientation. Two, therefore the practice, now 6
> months old, of not asking about sexual orientation in the enlistment procedure
> will continue. Three, an open statement by a service member that he or she is a
> homosexual will create a rebuttable presumption that he or she intends to en-
> gage in prohibited conduct, but the service member will be given an opportu-
> nity to refute that presumption; in other words, to demonstrate that he or she
> intends to live by the rules of conduct that apply in the military service. And
> four, all provisions of the Uniform Code of Military Justice will be enforced in
> an even-handed manner as regards both heterosexuals and homosexuals.[26]

Whether this new policy truly represented a marked improvement over the old policy was open to debate.[27] But any debate over the merits of Clinton's policy soon became moot.

The ink on the directive that embodied DADT[28] had barely dried when Congress intervened in November 1993 and, for the first time in history, exercised legislative control over lesbians and gay men in the military.[29] By enacting its "Policy Concerning Homosexuality in the Armed Forces" as a statute, Congress effectively wrested control over this issue from President Clinton—and any future president who might be inclined to rescind the ban on lesbians and gay men in the military.[30] Once the policy had been codified by Congress, unilateral action by the president as commander-in-chief of the military was no longer possible. The ban could not be eliminated (or, for that matter, changed in any particular) unless a future Congress acquiesced in the action by passing legislation codifying the elimination (or alteration) of the ban.

Under the statutory policy enacted by Congress, a service member is to be discharged from the military if, in accordance with procedures prescribed in regulations promulgated by the secretary of defense, any one (or more) of the following three findings is made with respect to that service member:

(1) That the member has engaged in, attempted to engage in, or solicited another to engage in a homosexual act or acts unless there are further findings . . . that the member has demonstrated that—
   (A) such conduct is a departure from the member's usual and customary behavior;
   (B) such conduct, under all the circumstances, is unlikely to recur;
   (C) such conduct was not accomplished by use of force, coercion, or intimidation;
   (D) under the particular circumstances of the case, the member's continued presence in the armed forces is consistent with the interests of the armed forces in proper discipline, good order, and morale; and
   (E) the member does not have a propensity or intent to engage in homosexual acts.
(2) That the member has stated that he or she is a homosexual or bisexual, or words to that effect, unless there is a further finding . . . that the member has demonstrated that he or she is not a person who engages in, attempts to engage in, has a propensity to engage in, or intends to engage in homosexual acts.
(3) That the member has married or attempted to marry a person known to be of the same biological sex.[31]

What the Policy Means in Theory

After the enactment of this policy, the Clinton administration claimed that the statute passed by Congress had not changed the policy that President Clinton had announced a few months before; it "merely restated and codified" that policy.[32] This characterization of the statute, along with the earlier claims that Clinton's new policy was a "substantial advance" over the ban that was in place when he took office, has led to a general belief among the public that, at least in theory, Clinton had managed to put in place a new policy that was "more lenient toward gay men and lesbians in uniform, less antigay, and less homophobic."[33] Unfortunately, as law professor Janet Halley has so cogently demonstrated in her book *Don't: A Reader's Guide to the Military's Anti-Gay Policy*, this belief is utterly false.

A Rhetorical Circle. The circular flow of the rhetoric surrounding the policy on lesbians and gay men in the military traces the Clinton administration's failure to effect meaningful change to the ban. The 1981 version of the ban, which was in force when Clinton took office, was based on a simple, yet wholly groundless, premise: "Homosexuality is incompatible with military service."[34] The policy went on to explain:

> The presence in the military environment of persons who engage in homosexual conduct or who, by their statements, demonstrate a propensity to engage in homosexual conduct, seriously impairs the accomplishment of the military mission. The presence of such members adversely affects the ability of the Military Services to maintain discipline, good order, and morale; to foster mutual trust and confidence among servicemembers; to ensure the integrity of the system of rank and command; to facilitate assignment and worldwide deployment of servicemembers who frequently must live and work under close conditions affording minimal privacy; to recruit and retain members of the Military Services; to maintain the public acceptability of military service; and to prevent breaches of security.[35]

What all of these justifications have in common is that they have absolutely nothing to do with the fitness or ability of lesbians and gay men to serve in the military. Instead, each of these justifications is premised upon the inability of heterosexual service members to cope with the presence of openly lesbian and gay service members. Thus, the opening sentence of the policy might more appropriately have been phrased: "Our fragile heterosexuality is incompatible with the military service of homosexuals."

When President Clinton announced his interim policy in January 1993, he staked out a position that was in stark contrast to the language of the old policy, which represented the favored position of the then Joint Chiefs of Staff:[36]

> The issue is not whether there should be homosexuals in the military. Everyone concedes that there are. The issue is whether men and women, who can and have served with real distinction, should be excluded from military service solely on the basis of their status. And I believe they should not.

The principle on which I base this position is this: I believe that American citizens who want to serve their country should be able to do so unless their conduct disqualifies them from doing so.[37]

In this statement, Clinton rejected the stigmatizing premise of the ban and affirmed the existence of the many lesbians and gay men who, like Lacy, wished to serve in the military and had done so in an exemplary fashion. Clinton also reiterated the distinction between status (which he did not believe should be regulated) and conduct (which he believed was an appropriate subject of regulation) that he had made shortly after the 1992 presidential election.

However, by the time Secretary of Defense Aspin issued the directive implementing the new policy in July 1993, the original ban's stigmatizing language had, consistent with the wishes of the Joint Chiefs of Staff,[38] resurfaced in the directive with only the barest of caveats acknowledging the service of lesbians and gay men in the military: "The Department of Defense has long held that, as a general rule, homosexuality is incompatible with military service because it interferes with the factors critical to combat effectiveness, including unit morale, unit cohesion and individual privacy. Nevertheless, the Department of Defense also recognizes that individuals with a homosexual orientation have served with distinction in the armed services of the United States."[39]

Congress closed the rhetorical circle when it enacted the statutory policy on lesbians and gay men in the military. Congress eliminated the caveat that had appeared in Aspin's directive and retained only the stigmatizing essence of the ban that was in force when President Clinton took office: "The prohibition against homosexual conduct is a longstanding element of military law that continues to be necessary in the unique circumstances of military service. . . . The presence in the armed forces of persons who demonstrate a propensity or intent to engage in homosexual acts would create an unacceptable risk to the high standards of morale, good order and discipline, and unit cohesion that are the essence of military capability."[40]

In view of the congressional rejection of the premise upon which President Clinton's changes to the ban were based and its overt hostility to lesbian and gay service members, it should come as no surprise that Congress also rejected the few changes that the administration had managed to preserve in its negotiations with the Joint Chiefs of Staff and Congress during the spring and summer of 1993.

Effacing the Procedural Improvements. As part of his attempt to introduce a status-conduct distinction into the policy on lesbians and gay men in the military, President Clinton advocated two procedural changes to the policy: (1) a prohibition on asking recruits or service members about their sexual orientation (i.e., the "don't ask" portion of the new policy's moniker) and

(2) a requirement that violations of the UCMJ be investigated in an even-handed manner (i.e., without regard to whether the alleged conduct occurred between persons of the same or different sexes).[41] Ultimately, however, Congress included neither of these changes in its statutory policy.

"Don't ask." In its statutory policy, Congress did not prohibit the military from asking recruits or service members about their sexual orientation. Indeed, a "Sense of Congress" statement accompanying the statutory policy indicated that "the Secretary of Defense may reinstate that questioning with such questions or such revised questions as he considers appropriate if the Secretary determines that it is necessary to do so in order to effectuate the policy."[42] In the guidelines implementing the statutory policy, the Department of Defense has, in fact, continued the suspension of questioning recruits and service members about their sexual orientation but has nonetheless made it clear that an individual service member has absolutely *no* right *not* to be asked about her sexual orientation and, if she is asked, has *no* recourse for a violation of the implementing regulations.[43] Thus, as Lacy learned all too painfully when she was asked to sign a statement concerning her (homo)sexual orientation, "don't ask" is both "more ephemeral and less meaningful than it may initially appear."[44]

Even-handed enforcement. Likewise, in its statutory policy, Congress did not require the military to investigate violations of the UCMJ in an even-handed manner. As mentioned before, the UCMJ provision criminalizing sodomy is neutral on its face, applying equally to same-sex and different-sex conduct. Yet the military has disproportionately targeted same-sex sodomy for criminal prosecution under this provision.[45] The government even obtained a court ruling in the early 1980s that sanctioned its discriminatory enforcement of the UCMJ sodomy prohibition.[46]

Nevertheless, in the course of implementing the statutory policy, the Department of Defense issued revised guidelines for criminal investigations in early 1994 that did include a policy of even-handed enforcement.[47] But in the absence of a mandate from Congress, the department has remained free to—and, in fact, recently did—remove that policy from the guidelines and eliminate any formal requirement of even-handed enforcement.[48] But even before it was formally removed from the guidelines, the policy of even-handed enforcement, like "don't ask," was far less meaningful than it appeared to be.[49]

At its inception, the policy of even-handed enforcement was rendered nearly meaningless by changes to the procedures for conducting criminal investigations. Prior to 1994, military law enforcement organizations were neither required nor permitted to ask the commander of the accused service member for authorization to conduct a criminal investigation—that decision lay with military law enforcement alone.[50] In the course of implementing the statutory policy, the department issued guidelines reversing this position and normally requiring military law enforcement to refer allegations of adult private sexual misconduct to the commander of the accused service member.[51] Punishment is now ordinarily left to the discretion of the service member's commander, who may choose to impose less serious sanctions than criminal punishment.[52]

However, a commander's discretion to impose the lesser punishment of discharge from the military depends on whether the sexual misconduct occurred between members of the same or different sexes. If it occurred between persons of different sexes, then a commander "may," but is not required to, discharge the service member who engaged in the sexual misconduct.[53] If it occurred between persons of the same sex, then the commander is left with no discretion—the service member "shall" be discharged from the military if she has engaged in "homosexual conduct."[54] As a result, "participants in cross-sex sodomy can hope for—and (let's be realistic) will often obtain—an indulgence that is legally withheld from participants in the same act committed with people of the same sex. Referring sodomy allegations to commanders will saddle some servicemembers with less-than-honorable discharges while reconfirming the military membership of others."[55]

From Bad to Worse: Status = Conduct = Status. It would be bad enough if Congress had taken a hostile stance toward lesbians and gay men in the military and erased any procedural improvements that the Clinton administration had attempted to include in the revised policy, and President Clinton had then sold Congress's statutory policy to the public as being no different from his DADT policy. You could look at it as just another example of straight limited sympathy for lesbians and gay men—and of how the boundaries of that sympathy vary from person to person. But the story actually manages to get worse.

President Clinton's consistent message during his time in office was that, under the new policy, lesbians and gay men could no longer be barred or discharged from military service solely based on their sexual orientation. Rather, they could be barred or discharged based only on their conduct— the same type of conduct that was punishable (and now would be punished) if engaged in by heterosexual service members. Yet, contrary to this message, under both Clinton's DADT policy and Congress's statutory policy, prohibited homosexual conduct includes more than conduct, and it includes more conduct than that which would be punished if engaged in by heterosexual service members.

The former ban, DADT, and the statutory policy all contain the same general categories of prohibited homosexual conduct, including (1) a homosexual act, (2) a statement that the service member is a homosexual or bisexual, and (3) a same-sex marriage (or attempted same-sex marriage). Let's consider each of these categories of prohibited "conduct" in turn.

Homosexual acts. For purposes of DADT and the statutory policy, a "homosexual act" is defined as "any bodily contact, actively undertaken or passively permitted, between members of the same sex for the purpose of satisfying sexual desires."[56] This definition of "homosexual act" goes well beyond the oral and anal sex that is covered by the sodomy provision of the UCMJ. As one commentator has noted, this definition is so broad that it appears to impose "a wholesale ban on any bodily contact that might satisfy human needs for intimacy."[57] Clearly, many of these acts would not be cause for punishment or discharge if they were performed by heterosexual service members.[58] When the same type of conduct is treated differently based on whether the persons engaging in the conduct are of the same or different sexes, the conduct itself cannot be said to be targeted—it is the participants' presumed status (i.e., heterosexual or homosexual) that determines their treatment.[59]

The targeting of status is underscored by DADT's and the statutory policy's expansion of the former ban's definition of "homosexual act." In addition to the more conventional definition described earlier, that term is further defined by DADT and the statutory policy to include "any bodily contact which a reasonable person would understand to demonstrate a propensity or intent to engage in" same-sex erotic contact.[60] The military's guidelines for applying this provision indicate that a "propensity" to engage in same-sex erotic contact "means more than an abstract preference or desire to engage in homosexual acts; it indicates a likelihood that a person engages in or will engage in homosexual acts."[61] The guidelines further indicate that, in most circumstances, hand-holding or kissing would be sufficient to demonstrate a propensity to engage in same-sex erotic contact.[62] Again, it is status (in the guise of conduct) that is being targeted. Under this provision, a service member may be discharged not for having engaged in any same-sex sexual contact but merely because of others' perception that she might engage in such contact in the future—that is, because of who they think she is.[63]

The targeting of status is further underscored by the statutory policy's retention of what has been derisively referred to as the "queen-for-a-day exception."[64] Under this exception, a service member who has engaged in a "homosexual act" will not be discharged if she can prove that the conduct was consensual and a departure from her usual behavior, the conduct is unlikely to recur, the service member does not have a propensity or intent to engage in homosexual acts, and it is in the interests of the military to retain her.[65] Due to the resurfacing of the word "propensity" in the text of the exception, only heterosexual service members who engage in same-sex erotic contact will be able to take advantage of this exception.

In this respect, the statutory policy has moved beyond treating heterosexual and homosexual service members differently for engaging in the same *type* of conduct; it treats them differently for engaging in the *exact same* conduct. A homosexual man who performs oral sex on a heterosexual man will be discharged from the military (because he has a "propensity" to engage in homosexual acts and therefore cannot qualify for the "queen-for-a-day" exception), whereas the heterosexual man may be able to remain in the military under that exception (because he can show that he has no "propensity" to engage in homosexual acts). At this point, there can be no doubt that "homosexual acts" are no more than a proxy for "homosexual status."

"I am a lesbian." For purposes of DADT and the statutory policy, a service member who utters the words "I am a homosexual," "I am gay," "I am a lesbian," or any other phrase communicating their (homo)sexual orientation is presumed to engage in, attempt to engage in, or to have a propensity or intent to engage in homosexual acts.[66] It does not matter whether the statement is made publicly or privately, whether it is made to someone within or without the military (even a statement to friends or family can serve, and has served, as the basis for discharge), or whether it is made when on or off duty.[67] Once again, it is status (in the guise of conduct) that is being targeted. A service member may be discharged not for having engaged in any same-sex sexual contact but solely because her admission of her sexual orientation (i.e., her status) indicates the likelihood that she might have such contact in the future.[68]

Same-sex marriage. Actual or attempted same-sex marriage, although involving an act, is not any sort of sexual behavior, either of the type prohibited by the UCMJ sodomy provision or contemplated in the definition of "homosexual act" above.[69] It must be that same-sex marriage (which some have construed to also cover commitment ceremonies and civil unions)[70] is, like the statement "I am a lesbian," an expression of a propensity to engage in homosexual acts. If so, and in view of the fact that the military not only permits heterosexual service members to marry but encourages them to do so by providing benefits to their spouses,[71] it is again status (in the guise of conduct) that is being targeted.

Thus, once considered carefully, it becomes clear that neither DADT nor the statutory policy embodies a status-conduct distinction. In each case, either conduct is being imputed based on status or status is being imputed based on conduct. As a result, DADT and the statutory policy are really no improvement over the former ban, which unabashedly targeted status.[72] In reality, DADT and the statutory policy are worse than the former ban because they pretend to be something other than what they are and, as a result, create a trap for the unwary and uninformed.[73]

What the Policy Means in Practice

Number of Discharges. Though it has been possible to obfuscate the letter and intent of the statutory policy, it is impossible to hide the policy's practical impact on lesbians and gay men serving in the military. Numerous violations of the statutory policy have been documented since it took effect.[74] And far from being more lenient on lesbians and gay men in the military, the statutory policy has generally resulted in a significant worsening of the annual rate of discharges for homosexuality.

In 1994, when Department of Defense directives implementing the statutory policy went into effect, the rate of discharges was the same as it had been in the prior three years.[75] Then, with the exception of 1999, the annual rate of discharges increased significantly every year from 1995 through 2001.[76] Even in 1999, when the rate of discharges dipped slightly, the discharge rate was still "73% higher than when the policy went into effect."[77] Consistent with past trends,[78] the rate of discharges for homosexuality declined following the events of September 11, 2001, when the demand for service personnel increased.[79] From 2001 to 2004, discharges declined nearly 40 percent before they experienced their first annual increase in 2005—only to decline once again in 2006.[80] Moreover, throughout the history of the statutory policy, women have been disproportionately targeted for discharge—often as a form of "lesbian-baiting," which occurs when a female service member is accused of being a lesbian (regardless of her actual or perceived sexual orientation) in retaliation for spurned sexual advances, a report of sexual harassment, or poor performance evaluations or unpopular orders.[81]

Character of the Discharge. The character of an administrative discharge for homosexuality will either be (1) honorable, (2) general (under honorable conditions), or (3) other than honorable.[82] Whether a discharge is characterized as honorable or general (under honorable conditions) will depend on the quality of the service member's conduct and performance of her duties.[83] When the sole basis for discharge is homosexuality, a discharge may be characterized as other than honorable only if the service member attempted, solicited, or committed a homosexual act "by using force, coercion, or intimidation; with a person under 16 years of age; with a subordinate in circumstances that violate customary military superior-subordinate relationships; openly in public view; for compensation; aboard a military vessel or aircraft; [or] in another location subject to military control under aggravating circumstances that have an adverse impact on discipline, good order, or morale comparable to the impact of such activity aboard a vessel or aircraft."[84]

The character of a service member's discharge can affect the service member in a number of different ways. First, the character of a discharge may affect Veterans Administration (VA) benefits. Most VA benefits require an "other than dishonorable" discharge.[85] Most honorable and general discharges will meet this requirement.[86] The VA must review others to determine whether the discharge was made under dishonorable conditions, which would result in the denial of most VA benefits.[87] Notably, to receive Montgomery G.I. Bill education benefits, a service member must receive an honorable discharge; thus, either a general *or* an other-than-honorable discharge will serve as a bar to obtaining these education benefits.[88]

Second, the character and circumstances of a discharge may determine whether the government seeks recoupment of scholarships, bonuses, or special pay when the service member is discharged before completing her service obligation. For amounts that the federal government became obligated to pay prior to April 2006, the terms of some programs require repayment whenever the service member fails to complete the required period of active duty (subject, in some cases, to waiver by the military), whereas other programs authorize the military to require repayment only if the service member fails to complete the required period of active duty either "voluntarily or because of misconduct."[89] These distinctions have now been replaced by a uniform repayment provision that requires repayment of any unearned portion of a bonus, special pay, or educational benefit whenever the service member ceases to satisfy the eligibility requirements for the bonus or similar benefit (subject to waiver by the military in specified circumstances).[90]

The Department of Defense has issued guidance concerning the application of the "voluntarily or because of misconduct" standard in cases of discharge for homosexuality.[91] Under this guidance, homosexual conduct will serve as a basis for recoupment if the conduct could either (1) serve as the basis for an other-than-honorable discharge (whatever the actual character of the discharge) or (2) be punished under the sexual misconduct provisions of the UCMJ (whether or not a conviction is actually obtained). Merely revealing one's sexual orientation is not, however, a basis for recoupment, unless it is determined that the service member revealed her sexual orientation "for the purpose of seeking separation" (i.e., if she "voluntarily" failed to complete the active-duty requirement). As Lacy learned, the U.S. Air Force has been particularly aggressive in seeking recoupment from those who make "coming-out" statements.[92]

Finally, the character of a discharge may affect the service member's ability to obtain civilian employment after discharge. A general discharge "may raise some questions among some civilian employers about a veteran's performance," and an other-than-honorable discharge will cause the service member to "face substantial prejudice in civilian employment."[93] An other-than-honorable discharge will also prevent the service member from collecting unemployment compensation benefits following discharge.[94] Furthermore, whatever the character of the discharge, the long form of the service member's discharge papers (Copy 4 of DD Form 214) will contain a narrative description of the reason for separation and, as a result, will reflect the fact that a discharge was for homosexual conduct—effectively outing the service member to a civilian employer (or anyone else) who asks to see it.[95]

A Bit of Important Advice. Although I advocate throughout this book that lesbians and gay men should be open about their sexual orientation and the peculiar obstacles that they face as lesbians and gay men, I do *not* advise lesbians and gay men who are in the military to speak out about their sexual orientation, sexual conduct, or activities to anyone, even a chaplain, doctor, or psychiatrist[96] — at least not before consulting an attorney. Speaking out without legal advice may endanger a service member's well-being on a number of different levels. Due to the breadth, complexities, and vagueness of the statutory policy, which have led to divergences between its application in theory and its application in practice,[97] speaking out without appropriate legal advice can have unpredictable (and sometimes rather unfavorable) results. More alarmingly, even after the highly publicized murder of Private First Class Barry Winchell in 1999 and the spotlight that it shone on antigay harassment in the military, such harassment continues today, and an admission of homosexuality may put a service member in grave physical danger.[98]

If a service member is contemplating "telling" the military about her sexual orientation as a means of being released from her service commitment, consultation with an attorney who is familiar with military law can help to ensure that (1) the risk of a court-martial for violating the sexual misconduct provisions of the UCMJ is minimized; (2) the character of the discharge is not adversely affected or inappropriately lowered in retaliation for coming out; and (3) the military's grounds for recouping scholarships, bonuses, and special pay are circumscribed or eliminated.[99] An attorney can also help prepare the service member for the possibility that she may not be discharged as a result of coming out and for any subsequent investigation of her personal life that her command may initiate following her statement.[100]

If a service member is the subject of an investigation into her sexual activities, she should refuse to answer questions or sign any documents, and she should request the assistance of counsel. A service member who is under investigation has the right to refuse to incriminate herself or to make a statement regarding the offense of which she is accused.[101] A service member also has the right to consult an attorney if she is in custody or is significantly deprived of her freedom of action or if questioning takes place after the preferral of charges.[102] In this situation, a service member has the right to consult a military defense attorney (and, before beginning to speak, should pointedly ask the military attorney to confirm that he is a defense attorney *and* that their conversation will remain confidential)[103] as well as a civilian attorney (at her own expense — but note that the Servicemembers Legal Defense Network provides free, confidential legal help to service members affected by the statutory policy).[104] Once the right to remain silent or the right to counsel has been invoked, all questioning should cease.[105] A service member should always invoke her right to remain silent, whether or not she is advised of it, and should ask to speak with an attorney before answering any questions.[106]

Looking Forward: The Prospects for Change

In the Courts

Although the validity of the statutory policy has been upheld by the courts,[107] the U.S. Supreme Court's decision in *Lawrence v. Texas,*[108] which struck down Texas's sodomy law as a violation of the constitutional right to liberty, appears to have opened the door to renewed attacks on the constitutionality of the policy.[109] Indeed, as of this writing, three separate challenges to the statutory policy have been filed by or with the support of the Servicemembers Legal Defense Network, the Log Cabin Republicans, and the American Civil Liberties Union.[110]

The constitutionality of the UCMJ sodomy provision, which underpins the statutory policy, has also been attacked using the *Lawrence* decision. However, in two cases, the U.S. Court of Appeals for the Armed Forces (CAAF) upheld the constitutionality of the UCMJ sodomy provision as applied to the specific facts of those cases. In *United States v. Marcum*,[111] the CAAF read *Lawrence* more generously than other courts have, holding that it requires "searching constitutional inquiry" and not simply the usual, highly deferential "any rational basis" review of a challenged law. Acknowledging the applicability of *Lawrence,* the CAAF nonetheless found it necessary to adapt *Lawrence* to the military context. To this end, the CAAF articulated a three-pronged analysis to be applied to constitutional challenges under *Lawrence* to the enforcement of the UCMJ sodomy provision: (1) The court must determine whether the conduct at issue is protected by *Lawrence* (i.e., was it private, consensual sexual activity); (2) the court must determine whether the conduct implicates the limits imposed by the Supreme Court on its holding in *Lawrence* (e.g., did the conduct involve minors); and (3) the court must determine whether any factors relevant solely to the military context will affect the nature or reach of the holding in *Lawrence.*

Although the CAAF found that the conduct in *Marcum* was of a type generally protected by *Lawrence* (i.e., it was private and consensual), the court found that the conduct implicated the limits articulated by the Supreme Court on its holding in *Lawrence*. In particular, the court felt that it might have been difficult for the defendant's sexual partner to refuse consent to engage in sodomy in that case because the defendant was his supervisor. Because the Supreme Court in *Lawrence* had specifically distinguished situations where "consent might not easily be refused,"[112] the CAAF felt that the defendant's conduct "fell outside of the liberty interest identified in *Lawrence.*"[113]

A month later, in *Stirewalt v. United States*,[114] the CAAF upheld the constitutionality of the UCMJ sodomy provision as applied to the converse of the *Marcum* situation (i.e., to a defendant who was the subordinate of a supervisor with whom he engaged in sodomy). In that situation, even assuming that the conduct was both protected by *Lawrence* and did not involve any of the limits on the holding in that case, the CAAF felt that the conduct implicated the third prong of the *Marcum* analysis, which requires consideration of factors unique to the military. Military regulations prohibit relationships between supervisors and subordinates because even the perception of unfairness may undermine leadership and discipline. The military's need for discipline and order was, therefore, found to limit the sphere of conduct protected by *Lawrence* in *Stirewalt* and served as the basis for upholding the constitutionality of the application of the UCMJ sodomy provision in that case.

In both *Marcum* and *Stirewalt*, the court left open the possibility of a successful challenge to the UCMJ sodomy provision where the conduct is protected by *Lawrence* and no factors unique to the military justify the contraction of *Lawrence*'s protective sphere. Even more promisingly, however, the office of the general counsel at the Pentagon in 2005 proposed repealing the UCMJ prohibition of consensual sodomy between adults—but that recommendation was quickly withdrawn "under pressure from the antigay right."[115]

In the Court of Public Opinion

Since September 11, 2001, public opinion has begun to swing in favor of repealing the statutory policy. Many Americans question the wisdom of a policy that results, for example, in the discharge of Arabic, Chinese, Farsi, and Korean linguists when the military desperately needs individuals with their skills. Amazingly, this shift in public opinion has begun to influence Congress. In March 2005, Representative Martin Meehan introduced a bill in the House of Representatives to repeal the statutory policy and put in its place a policy of nondiscrimination on the basis of sexual orientation.[116] By October 2006, this bill had 122 cosponsors. In February 2007, after the new Congress had convened, Representative Meehan reintroduced the bill in the House of Representatives and had 126 cosponsors by June 2007.[117]

Interestingly, this shift in public opinion has also had some influence on the 2008 presidential race. In March 2007, when General Peter Pace, then chairman of the Joint Chiefs of Staff, declared homosexuality "immoral," both Barack Obama and Hillary Clinton were criticized for waffling and sidestepping any sort of critical reaction to his remarks for fear of using the words "moral" and "homosexuality" in the same sentence. However, in a June 2007 debate in New Hampshire, *all* of the Democratic candidates for president expressed their support for repealing the statutory policy.[118] (It is worth noting, however, that later in the same week all of the Republican candidates expressed their opposition to repealing the statutory policy.)[119]

To capitalize on this shift, and even though we can only inadequately tell their stories, it is incumbent upon each of us in the civilian population (and particularly those who have previously served in the military) to lend our voices to silenced active-duty service members so that we can reveal the true nature of the statutory policy and its effects on lesbians and gay men serving in the military. This duty applies regardless of personal politics or feelings about the military because, as indicated by the discussion of the "feedback loop" between discrimination and antigay violence at the end of Chapter 2, what hurts some of us in the lesbian and gay community affects all of us—particularly when what hurts us is our own federal government unabashedly discriminating on the basis of sexual orientation.

Attacking the Justifications

At the same time, we should attack the government's justifications for the statutory policy. As was the case with similar justifications used to exclude racial minorities and women from the military in the past,[120] these justifications have nothing to do with the fitness of lesbians and gay men to serve in the military and everything to do with coddling and encouraging prejudice. Tellingly, the justifications that the military has used to exclude lesbians and gay men have been refuted by a series of its own reports over a span of decades beginning in the mid-1950s.[121]

Privacy. We can explain that the privacy argument, which justifies the statutory policy on the ground that it is necessary to protect heterosexual service members from leering gay stares when they find themselves naked in a common shower or living quarters, falls under its own weight. This argument is based on the bigoted stereotype of lesbians and gay men as sexual predators. Moreover, it does not actually protect heterosexual service members' privacy. By forcing lesbians and gay men ever deeper into the closet but leaving them in the military, the policy does no more than allow heterosexual service members to believe an untruth: that there are no lesbians and gay men in the military to leer at them. The statutory policy does not, therefore, protect privacy; rather, it creates a fictional space in which heterosexual service members can allow their sexual prejudices to run free.[122]

Unit Cohesion. We can explain that the unit-cohesion argument is not supported in fact.[123] "Unit cohesion," according to Congress, refers to "the bonds of trust among individual service members that make the combat effectiveness of a military unit greater than the sum of the combat effectiveness of the individual unit members."[124] Proponents of the statutory policy argue that if lesbians and gay men are permitted to serve openly, then heterosexual service members' dislike for them will undermine the bonds of trust and impede the functioning of the military. Yet every time the military has entered into combat (e.g., World War II, the Vietnam War, and the Persian Gulf War), the ban on lesbians and gay men has been relaxed and the number of discharges for homosexuality has dropped. If lesbians and gay men are a threat to unit cohesion, why is it that in times of combat, when unit cohesion is needed most, the military has tolerated open homosexuality and homosexual conduct? The military's pattern of actions clearly contradicts its own argument in favor of the statutory policy.[125] Furthermore, if lesbians and gay men are a threat to unit cohesion, why is it that the nearly two dozen countries that now allow lesbians and gay men to serve openly in the military have not experienced unit cohesion problems?[126]

Articulating the Costs

Rounding out this strategy, we must explain the costs of the statutory policy in order to help people understand that the policy has an impact on all of us, not just on lesbians and gay men serving in the military. According to a Government Accountability Office report, the financial cost of training replacements for individuals in the army, navy, and air force who were discharged under the statutory policy from 1994 through 2003 was approximately $95.1 million.[127] But this figure accounts for only a portion of the costs of the policy: It understates the true cost of training replacements because the marine corps was unable to calculate that cost. In addition, it does not include the costs of "investigations and inquiries, counseling and pastoral care, processing separations from military service, and the review of such separations by service boards," which are not susceptible to estimation.[128] Finally, it does not reflect the burdens imposed on heterosexual service members—particularly women—who have found it necessary to conform more closely to gender stereotypes (e.g., attempting to appear more feminine) or to engage in unwanted sexual relationships in order to avoid potential accusations of homosexuality.[129]

A University of California Blue Ribbon Commission conducted a more sophisticated analysis of the financial costs of the statutory policy during this period and estimated a far higher cost of at least $363.8 million.[130] The commission further maintained that, in all likelihood, even this staggering figure probably underestimates the true costs of the policy.

Creating Empathy

In short, we must draw attention to the lack of empathy for the plight of lesbians and gay men that is evinced by those who persist in supporting or acquiescing in the statutory policy. It is astounding that anyone could argue that the statutory policy is designed to make life more bearable for lesbians and gay men serving in the military. How many straight people would consider being constrained from uttering a single word that could be interpreted as revealing their (hetero)sexual orientation, being barred from marriage, and being banished to a life of celibacy an improvement in treatment? It is only by dispelling the myths of the statutory policy and articulating its costs to all of society that we can hope to foster the empathy that is so sorely lacking and solidify the groundswell of support for repealing the statutory policy. If this support were solidified, judges and legislators could rest assured that invalidating or repealing the statutory policy would not be met with a backlash, and the right thing to do would quickly become the easy thing to do.

Notes

1. Used with the permission of Lacy Wilber.
2. National Defense Research Institute, RAND Corp., Pub. MR-323-OSD, *Sexual Orientation and U.S. Military Personnel Policy: Options and Assessment* (1993), 9.
3. Randy Shilts, *Conduct Unbecoming: Lesbians and Gays in the U.S. Military* (New York: St. Martin's Press, 1993), 132–138, 359–360.

4. See generally Allan J. Futernick, "Sexual Orientation and the Armed Forces: Lifting the Ban with Caution," in Wilbur J. Scott and Sandra Carson Stanley, eds., *Gays and Lesbians in the Military: Issues, Concerns, and Contrasts* (New York: Aldine de Gruyter, 1994), 231.

5. Shilts, *Conduct Unbecoming*, 3–18.

6. Ibid., 15–16; see also National Defense Research Institute, *Sexual Orientation and U.S. Military Personnel Policy*, 3–4; R. L. Evans, "U.S. Military Policies Concerning Homosexuals: Development, Implementation, and Outcomes," *Tul. J.L. and Sexuality* 11 (2002), 113, 117.

7. Evans, "U.S. Military Policies Concerning Homosexuals," 118–119.

8. Allan Bérubé, *Coming Out Under Fire: The History of Gay Men and Women in World War II* (New York: Free Press, 1990), 142–148; Shilts, *Conduct Unbecoming*, 16–17; Evans, "U.S. Military Policies Concerning Homosexuals," 119–121.

9. Quoted in National Defense Research Institute, *Sexual Orientation and U.S. Military Personnel Policy*, 6.

10. Uniform Code of Military Justice, Pub. L. 81-506, ch. 169, art. 125, 64 Stat. 107, 141 (1950) (codified at 10 U.S.C. §925 [2007]). The statutory language actually speaks in terms of "unnatural carnal copulation"; however, the *Manual for Courts-Martial* makes clear that this language includes oral and anal sex. *Manual for Courts-Martial*, pt. IV, §51(c) (2005). Punishment includes dishonorable discharge, forfeiture of all pay and allowances, and imprisonment for five years. Ibid., §51(e)(4).

11. Evans, "U.S. Military Policies Concerning Homosexuals," 122; see also National Defense Research Institute, *Sexual Orientation and U.S. Military Personnel Policy*, 9.

12. National Defense Research Institute, *Sexual Orientation and U.S. Military Personnel Policy*, 6–7.

13. Ibid., 7.

14. Evans, "U.S. Military Policies Concerning Homosexuals," 123.

15. 32 C.F.R., ch. 1, pt. 41, app. A, pt. 1, §H(1)(c) (1982).

16. Evans, "U.S. Military Policies Concerning Homosexuals," 123.

17. Melissa Healy, "Clinton to Stress Conduct as Key for Gays in Military," *Los Angeles Times*, November 13, 1992, A1.

18. Executive Order 9981, *Federal Register* 13 (July 28, 1948): 4313.

19. Janet E. Halley, *Don't: A Reader's Guide to the Military's Anti-Gay Policy* (Durham, NC: Duke University Press, 1999), 20 (quoting Melissa Healy, "Clinton Aides Urge Quick End to Military Ban on Gays," *Los Angeles Times*, January 8, 1993, A1).

20. Ibid., 20–21; David M. Rayside, "The Perils of Congressional Politics," in Craig A. Rimmerman, ed., *Gay Rights, Military Wrongs: Political Perspectives on Lesbians and Gays in the Military* (New York: Garland Publishing, 1996), 147.

21. President's News Conference: Gays in the Military, *Weekly Comp. Pres. Doc.* 29 (January 29, 1993): 108–112.

22. Halley, *Don't*, 21–22.

23. Family and Medical Leave Act of 1993, Pub. L. 103-3, §601, 107 Stat. 6, 28–29; see also Halley, *Don't*, 22–23.

24. Family and Medical Leave Act §601; see also Halley, *Don't*, 22–23.

25. Halley, *Don't*, 23.

26. "Remarks Announcing the New Policy on Gays and Lesbians in the Military," *Weekly Comp. Pres. Doc.* 29 (July 19, 1993): 1369, 1372.

27. For example, Francisco Valdes, "Sexual Minorities in the Military: Charting the Constitutional Frontiers of Status and Conduct," *Creighton L. Rev.* 27 (1994): 381, 465–474.

28. Memorandum from Secretary of Defense Les Aspin to the secretaries of the army, navy, and air force and the chairman, Joint Chiefs of Staff, "Policy on Homosexual Conduct in the Armed Forces," July 19, 1993.

29. Halley, *Don't*, 19; see National Defense Authorization Act for Fiscal Year 1994, Pub. L. 103–160, §571, 107 Stat. 1547, 1670.

30. Halley, *Don't*, 20, 23.

31. 10 U.S.C. §654(b) (2007).

32. Halley, *Don't*, 28.

33. Ibid., 1.

34. 32 C.F.R., ch. 1, pt. 41, app. A, pt. 1, §H(1)(a) (1982).

35. Ibid.

36. Halley, *Don't*, 33.

37. President's News Conference: Gays in the Military, 109.

38. Halley, *Don't*, 33–34.

39. Aspin memorandum, 1.

40. 10 U.S.C. §654(a)(13), (15) (2007).

41. Halley, *Don't*, 35, 48; President's News Conference: Gays in the Military, 109; Aspin memorandum, 2.

42. National Defense Authorization Act for Fiscal Year 1994, Pub. L. 103-160, §571(d), 107 Stat. 1547, 1670.

43. U.S. Department of Defense (DOD), Directive 1332.14: Enlisted Administrative Separations §§E3.A4.4.3, -A4.5 (as amended March 4, 1994); U.S. DOD, Instruction 1304.26: Qualification Standards for Enlistment, Appointment, and Induction §E2.2.8.1 (2005); U.S. DOD, Instruction 1332.40: Separation Procedures for Regular and Reserve Commissioned Officers, §§E8.4.3, E8.5 (1997).

44. Halley, *Don't*, 49.

45. Ibid., 36; Shilts, *Conduct Unbecoming*, 229, 243.

46. *Hatheway v. Sec'y of the Army*, 641 F.2d 1376 (9th Cir. 1981).

47. U.S. DOD, Instruction 5505.8: Investigations of Sexual Misconduct by the Defense Criminal Investigative Organizations and Other DOD Law Enforcement Organizations §D.3 (1994).

48. U.S. DOD, Instruction 5505.8: Defense Criminal Investigative Organizations and Other DOD Law Enforcement Organizations Investigations of Sexual Misconduct (2005).

49. See Halley, *Don't*, 35–39.

50. U.S. DOD, Instruction 5505.3: Initiation of Investigations by Military Criminal Investigative Organizations §D.1 (1986).

51. U.S. DOD, Instruction 5505.8, §6.1; U.S. DOD, Instruction 5505.3: Initiation of Investigations by Military Criminal Investigative Organizations §6.6 (2002).

52. See Halley, *Don't*, 37.

53. U.S. DOD, Instruction 1332.40, §E2.2; U.S. DOD, Directive 1332.14, §E3.A3.1.11; see Halley, *Don't*, 37–38.

54. U.S. DOD, Instruction 1332.40, §E2.3; U.S. DOD, Directive 1332.14, §E3.A1.1.8.1.2; see Halley, *Don't*, 37–38.

55. Halley, *Don't*, 38.

56. 10 U.S.C. §654(f)(3)(A) (2007); see also Aspin memorandum, 2.

57. Valdes, "Sexual Minorities in the Military," 467.

58. Compare *United States v. McGinty*, 38 M.J. 131 (C.M.A. 1993), with *United States v. Stocks*, 35 M.J. 366 (C.M.A. 1992).

59. Valdes, "Sexual Minorities in the Military," 468; Halley, *Don't*, 38–39.

60. 10 U.S.C. §654(f)(3)(B) (2007); see also Aspin memorandum, 2.

61. U.S. DOD, Directive 1332.14, §E3.A4.2.4.4; see also U.S. DOD, Instruction 1332.40, §E1.1.17.

62. U.S. DOD Directive 1332.14, §E3.A4.1.2.4.1.

63. Valdes, "Sexual Minorities in the Military," 468–469.

64. Shilts, *Conduct Unbecoming*, 199; Servicemembers Legal Defense Network (SLDN), "Survival Guide," 4th ed. (2003), 43–44, available at www.sldn.org.

65. 10 U.S.C. §654(b)(1)(A)–(E) (2007).

66. Ibid. §654(b)(2); U.S. DOD, Directive 1332.14, §§E3.A4.2.4.2, -4.5; U.S. DOD, Instruction 1332.40, §§E1.1.23, E2.3.1.2; Aspin memorandum, 2.

67. 10 U.S.C. §654(a)(9)–(11) (2007); Halley, *Don't*, 51–52; SLDN, *Survival Guide*, 5, 6–7; Tobias Barrington Wolff, "Political Representation and Accountability Under Don't Ask, Don't Tell," *Iowa L. Rev.* 89 (2004): 1633, 1645–1650.

68. Valdes, "Sexual Minorities in the Military," 469.

69. Ibid., 469–470.

70. SLDN, *Survival Guide*, 7.

71. David F. Burrelli, "An Overview of the Debate on Homosexuals in the U.S. Military," in Scott and Stanley, eds., *Gays and Lesbians in the Military*, 17, 23–24.

72. Sharon E. Debbage Alexander, "A Ban by Any Other Name: Ten Years of 'Don't Ask, Don't Tell,'" *Hofstra Lab. and Emp. L.J.* 21 (2004): 403, 410; Lawrence Korb, "Evolving Perspectives on the Military's Policy on Homosexuals: A Personal Note," in Scott and Stanley, eds., *Gays and Lesbians in the Military*, 219, 228.

73. Halley, *Don't*, 2.

74. For example, SLDN, "Conduct Unbecoming: Tenth Annual Report on 'Don't Ask, Don't Tell, Don't Pursue, Don't Harass'" (2004), 14; SLDN, "Conduct Unbecoming: Second Annual Report on 'Don't Ask, Don't Tell, Don't Pursue'" (1996), i–ii, 1–27.

75. SLDN, "Conduct Unbecoming Continues: The First Year Under 'Don't Ask, Don't Tell, Don't Pursue'" (1995), iii.

76. SLDN, "Conduct Unbecoming: Tenth Annual Report," 1.

77. SLDN, "Conduct Unbecoming: The Sixth Annual Report on 'Don't Ask, Don't Tell, Don't Pursue, Don't Harass'" (2000), iv.

78. The military has consistently relaxed the ban whenever there has been an increased demand for service personnel (e.g., World War II, the Vietnam War, and the Persian Gulf War). Bérubé, *Coming Out Under Fire*, 262–263; Shilts, *Conduct Unbecoming*, 65. Notwithstanding the Pentagon's consistent denial that this trend represents military policy, "the first evidence of written military regulations that specifically call for retaining openly gay soldiers" who have been mobilized for active duty recently surfaced. Patrick Letellier, "Gays OK in Wartime," *Advocate* (September 27, 2005): 36.

79. SLDN, "Conduct Unbecoming: Tenth Annual Report," 1.

80. SLDN, "'Don't Ask, Don't Tell' Dismissals Decline to Record Low," March 13, 2007, available at www.sldn.org/templates/press/record.html?record=3656; SLDN, "Select Military Bases See Spike in 'Don't Ask, Don't Tell' Dismissals," August 14, 2006, available at www.sldn.org/templates/press/record.html?record=3133.

81. SLDN, "Conduct Unbecoming: Tenth Annual Report," 18–19; SLDN, *Survival Guide*, 40; Michelle M. Benecke and Kirstin S. Dodge, "Military Women: Casualties of the Armed Forces' War on Lesbians and Gay Men," in Rimmerman, ed., *Gay Rights, Military Wrongs*, 71.

82. U.S. DOD, Directive 1332.14, §§E3.A1.1.8.3, -A2.1.3.1; see also U.S. DOD, Instruction 1332.40, §E7.2.2.2.

83. U.S. DOD, Directive 1332.14, §E3.A2.1.3.2.1; U.S. DOD, Instruction 1332.40, §E7.2.1.

84. U.S. DOD, Directive 1332.14, §E3.A1.1.8.3; U.S. DOD, Instruction 1332.40, §E7.2.2.2.

85. U.S. Department of Veterans Affairs, Pamphlet 80-07-01, *Federal Benefits for Veterans and Dependents* (2007), vi; Barton F. Stichman and Ronald B. Abrams, eds., *Veterans Benefits Manual* (Charlottesville, VA: Lexis Law Publishing, 2006), §2.2.1, 26–29; Samuel W. Morris, "A Survey of Military Retirement Benefits," *Mil. L. Rev.* 177 (2003), 133, 139.

86. Stichman and Abrams, *Veterans Benefits Manual*, §2.2.1, 26; Morris, "A Survey of Military Retirement Benefits," 140.

87. Stichman and Abrams, *Veterans Benefits Manual*, §2.2.1, 26–28; Morris, "A Survey of Military Retirement Benefits," 140.

88. U.S. Department of Veterans Affairs, *Federal Benefits*, 30; Stichman and Abrams, *Veterans Benefits Manual*, §11.2.3, 809; Morris, "A Survey of Military Retirement Benefits," 156–157.

89. Compare, for example, 37 U.S.C. §§301b(g), 312(b), 315(c)(1) (2006), with 10 U.S.C. §2005, and 37 U.S.C. §308(d)(1). See National Defense Authorization Act for Fiscal Year 2006, Pub. L. 109-163, §687, 119 Stat. 3136, 3326–3336 (enacting the uniform repayment provision).

90. 37 U.S.C. §303a(e) (2007).

91. Memorandum from Secretary of Defense John M. Deutch to secretaries of the military departments, May 17, 1994; see *Hensala v. Department of the Air Force*, 343 F.3d 951 (2003) (upholding this guidance on several grounds but allowing freedom-of-speech and equal-protection challenges to proceed).

92. SLDN, *Survival Guide*, 45; Alexander, "A Ban by Any Other Name," 427–428.

93. SLDN, *Survival Guide*, 25.

94. 5 U.S.C. §8521(a)(1)(A) (2007); see also SLDN, *Survival Guide*, 25.

95. U.S. DOD, Instruction 1336.1: Certificate of Release or Discharge from Active Duty (DD Form 214/5 Series) §3.2.1.1.1 (as amended in 2003); SLDN, *Survival Guide*, 25–26.

96. Under the Military Rules of Evidence, which apply to investigative hearings and all other proceedings authorized under the Uniform Code of Military Justice or the *Manual for Courts-Martial*, there is no doctor-patient privilege, a limited clergy-penitent privilege that applies only to communications made "as a formal act of religion or as a matter of conscience," and a limited psychotherapist-patient privilege

that does not apply to administrative separation hearings. There is, however, an attorney-client privilege. *Mil. R. Evid.* §§501(d), 502, 503(a), 513, 1101(d).

97. SLDN, *Survival Guide.*

98. Ibid., 21–22; Alexander, "A Ban by Any Other Name," 429–431.

99. SLDN, *Survival Guide,* 16–19, 24.

100. Ibid., 17–18.

101. 10 U.S.C. §§831(a)–(b), 838(b) (2007); see also U.S. DOD, Directive 1332.14, §E3.A4.4.3; U.S. DOD, Instruction 1332.40, §E8.4.3.

102. *Mil. R. Evid.* 305(d)(1); SLDN, *Survival Guide,* 2, 40.

103. SLDN, *Survival Guide,* 12.

104. *Mil. R. Evid.,* §305(d)(2).

105. Ibid., §305(f)(1)–(2).

106. SLDN, *Survival Guide,* 39–40.

107. *Able v. United States,* 155 F.3d 628 (2d Cir. 1998); *Holmes v. Cal. Army Nat'l Guard,* 124 F.3d 1126 (9th Cir. 1997); *Philips v. Perry,* 106 F.3d 1420 (9th Cir. 1997); *Richenberg v. Perry,* 97 F.3d 256 (8th Cir. 1996); *Able v. United States,* 88 F.3d 1280 (2d Cir. 1996); *Thomasson v. Perry,* 80 F.3d 915 (4th Cir. 1996).

108. *Lawrence v. Texas,* 539 U.S. 558 (2003).

109. Shannon Gilreath, "Sexually Speaking: 'Don't Ask, Don't Tell' and the First Amendment After *Lawrence v. Texas,*" *Duke J. Gender L. & Pol'y* 14 (2007), 953; Diane H. Mazur, "Is 'Don't Ask, Don't Tell' Unconstitutional After *Lawrence?* What It Will Take to Overturn the Policy," *J.L. and Pub. Pol'y* 15 (2004): 423; Jeffrey S. Dietz, "Getting Beyond Sodomy: *Lawrence* and 'Don't Ask, Don't Tell,'" *Stan. J. C.R. and C.L.* 2 (2005): 63.

110. *Log Cabin Republicans v. United States,* CV04-8425 (C.D. Cal. filed October 12, 2004) (refiled in May 2006 to comply with the district court's order requiring the organization to name members injured by the statutory policy in order to satisfy standing requirements; see Log Cabin Republicans, "Log Cabin Republicans Re-File Federal Challenge to 'Don't Ask, Don't Tell' Policy," May 2, 2006, available at http://online.logcabin.org/news_views/reading-room-back-up/log-cabin-republicans-re-file.html; as of this writing, the trial court's decision on the government's motion to dismiss is pending; see Log Cabin Republicans, "Judge Hears Oral Arguments on Log Cabin's 'Don't Ask, Don't Tell' Lawsuit," June 19, 2007, available at http://online.logcabin.org/news_views/reading-room-back-up/judge-hears-oral-arguments-on.html); *Cook v. Rumsfeld,* 429 F. Supp. 2d 385 (D. Mass. 2006) (currently on appeal to the U.S. First Circuit Court of Appeals); *Witt v. U.S. Department of the Air Force,* 444 F. Supp. 2d 1138 (W.D. Wash. 2006) (currently on appeal to the U.S. Ninth Circuit Court of Appeals).

111. *United States v. Marcum,* 60 M.J. 198 (C.A.A.F. 2004).

112. *Lawrence v. Texas,* 578.

113. *United States v. Marcum,* 208.

114. *Stirewalt v. United States,* 60 M.J. 297 (C.A.A.F. 2004).

115. Chad Graham, "Fit to Serve," *Advocate* (May 24, 2005): 43, 46.

116. Military Readiness Enhancement Act of 2005, H.R. 1059, 109th Cong., first sess. (2005).

117. Military Readiness Enhancement Act of 2007, H.R. 1246, 110th Cong., first sess. (2007).

118. Robin Toner and Thom Shanker, "For 'Don't Ask, Don't Tell,' Split on Party Lines," *New York Times*, June 8, 2007, A1.

119. Ibid.

120. David Ari Bianco, "Echoes of Prejudice: The Debates over Race and Sexuality in the Armed Forces," in Rimmerman, ed., *Gay Rights, Military Wrongs*, 47; see also Francine D'Amico, "Race-ing and Gendering the Military Closet," in Rimmerman, ed., *Gay Rights, Military Wrongs*, 3, 23–27.

121. Gary L. Lehring, "Constructing the 'Other' Soldier: Gay Identity's Military Threat," in Rimmerman, ed., *Gay Rights, Military Wrongs*, 269, 272–274.

122. See Aaron Belkin and Geoffrey Bateman, eds., *Don't Ask, Don't Tell: Debating the Gay Ban in the Military* (Boulder, CO: Lynne Rienner, 2003), 51–68.

123. See ibid., 69–102.

124. 10 U.S.C. §654(a)(7) (2007).

125. Evans, "U.S. Military Policies Concerning Homosexuals," 134.

126. See Belkin and Bateman, *Don't Ask, Don't Tell*, 103–138.

127. U.S. Government Accountability Office, GAO-05-299, *Military Personnel: Financial Costs and Loss of Critical Skills Due to DOD's Homosexual Conduct Policy Cannot Be Completely Estimated* (2005), 14–15.

128. Ibid., 15–16; see also Belkin and Bateman, *Don't Ask, Don't Tell*, 140–144.

129. Belkin and Bateman, *Don't Ask, Don't Tell*, 149–150.

130. Compare the University of California Blue Ribbon Commission Report, "Financial Analysis of 'Don't Ask, Don't Tell': How Much Does the Gay Ban Cost?" (2006), 23, with letter from U.S. Comptroller General David M. Walker to Senator Edward M. Kennedy, July 13, 2006, available at www.gao.gov/new.items/d06909r.pdf (rebuttal to the commission's report).

5

Employment and Housing

While I was in my second year of law school (and still firmly ensconced in the closet), I accepted a position as a law clerk to a federal judge in San Diego, California. Between the time that I accepted this position and when I began work after graduation, I slowly made my way out of the closet and met Michael. When the time came to move to San Diego, I asked Michael to move with me, and he agreed.

In San Diego, we soon became thoroughly acquainted with the everyday difficulties of being gay. It started with the deceptively simple task of searching for an apartment. All we could afford was a one-bedroom apartment. We started scouring newspaper advertisements and responded to several of them. I made sure each time to be clear that we would be sharing the apartment. When I explained this to one landlady, she responded that she could not conceive of why two men would want or need a one-bedroom apartment and then told me that she would not, under any circumstances, rent a one-bedroom apartment to us.

Eventually we contacted a property management company that helped us find an apartment in Hillcrest, a predominantly gay neighborhood located near downtown. By moving to Hillcrest, we were able to escape blatant housing discrimination; however, it seemed that finding a welcoming neighborhood came at the price of having a target painted on our backs. Hillcrest was located near a military installation, and while we lived there, military personnel routinely came through to taunt the "fags" and "dykes." Not long after we moved in, we attended a candlelight vigil for a youth who had been stabbed to death for appearing to be gay. It turned out that Hillcrest was a coin with two very different sides: For us, it was a safe haven—a space in which we could live our lives more openly and freely; for those who wished to commit bias crimes, it was a guaranteed source of victims—sort of like shooting fish in a barrel.

Because I had not been out of the closet when I interviewed for my clerkship, I decided to remain in the closet at work during my year in San Diego. In retrospect, this was probably a mistake. My judge was kind and understanding; yet, having agreed to work in close quarters (it was just I, the judge, and his secretary), I feared what might happen if the judge proved to be less understanding than he appeared. This necessitated an entire web of lies: Michael became my "roommate," our one-bedroom apartment became a two-bedroom that we shared to split the rent, and so on. Because both the judge and his secretary took a personal interest in me (as they did with all of the law clerks who came through the chambers), I found myself having to be on guard in every personal conversation that we had. In the end, one of the most pleasant working experiences of my life became the most tiring.

After my clerkship and before I began teaching law at the University of Pittsburgh, I spent about six years working as a lawyer in New York. During that time, I worked at three different law firms and was always out at work. At the last firm, I was put in an office that was situated between the office of a partner, Richard, and a conference room. Because of where I was located, Richard and I shared a secretary. Richard, one of the few partners who had not interviewed me before I had been hired, did not learn about my being gay until shortly after I began work. He called our secretary into his office and began to grill her about why I had been placed next to him, whether she knew that I was gay, and how the other partners could do this to him. She told him that she knew about my being gay but said she didn't understand why he was making such a fuss. Before he let her go back to work, Richard ordered my secretary not to answer my phone and not to do any work for me (an order that she refused to follow).

From that time on, Richard had a wholly irrational fear of me. Even though I saw him all the time because our offices were right next to each other, he refused to speak to me for the first two years that I worked at the firm. Seeing an opportunity to turn the tables for once, I exploited his discomfort by being sure to say hello every time I saw him, by holding the door open for him, and by asking him how his weekend had been when I saw him at our secretary's desk on Monday mornings. Any of these gestures would send him running.

Eventually Richard found himself in a situation where he had no choice but to give me an assignment. When this happened, I was called into the office of another partner, Sandy, with whom I regularly worked. The two were already seated and talking in Sandy's office when I arrived. Sandy was sitting behind his desk, and Richard was seated in a chair in front of the desk. The other chair in front of the desk was piled high with papers (which was the usual state of affairs in Sandy's office), and I had to sit on the sofa in the back of the room. During the ten or fifteen minutes that this meeting lasted, Richard never once turned to speak to me and, in fact, never addressed me directly.

After I had completed the assignment, Richard realized that, despite being gay, I could actually do my job. He began to give me assignments directly but, when doing so, never crossed the threshold into my office—he would stand in the doorway but never get any closer. I can only imagine why he did this; however, when I left the firm to start teaching, Richard did manage to overcome his fear long enough to shake my hand and wish me luck.

Girded by my experience with Richard, I was both far more comfortable with my sexual orientation and far more willing to confront a hostile employer by the time that I went on the teaching market. I was out in the hiring process and did not shy away from interviewing with law schools from conservative locales. During the interview process, I was told by the recruiters from a law school in Texas that I would be safe while I was on campus but that they could not guarantee my safety off campus. At a school in Kansas, I was told by a group of students that my mere presence at the school would "make waves" among the student body. Ultimately, I took a position with the University of Pittsburgh, where the law school was very welcoming but the broader university was not.

At the time that I accepted my position, the university was embroiled in a lawsuit over domestic-partner health benefits and was vigorously defending its decision to discriminate against its lesbian and gay employees. After the election of a governor who actively supported domestic-partner benefits, I worked with a colleague to draft a letter to the chancellor of the University of Pittsburgh, the president of Temple University, and the president of Penn State University. A majority of the law school faculty at each of the three universities signed the letter, which urged the universities to create a united front against the hostile Pennsylvania legislature on the issue of domestic-partner benefits. A few years later, the University of Pittsburgh relented and began to offer domestic-partner health insurance coverage. Nonetheless, even after the university's change of heart, a university committee (of which I was a member) actively monitored the administration of the new coverage and successfully worked with the university to relax its definition of "domestic partner," which had initially been so restrictive that couples who had been together for decades had trouble meeting the requirements and benefiting from the new coverage.

During our adult lives, the two places where we spend the vast majority of our time are home and work. As the story of my clerkship demonstrates, these two areas are often intertwined—we bring home our problems from work and bring to work our troubles from home. Or, as is becoming more common, we may work from home, resulting in an even deeper fusion of these two areas. This chapter addresses issues of discrimination in both of these important areas of our lives.

Work

As explored in Chapter 1, employment discrimination on the basis of sexual orientation is a serious problem. It can adversely affect your ability to get (or keep) a job that will allow you to pay for the basic necessities of life. And even those who do remain in the closet, as I did during my clerkship, may not be able to escape the adverse effects of employment discrimination. Indeed, I am sure that my dissembling during my clerkship sapped my productivity and affected my job performance.

Contrary to the myth of affluence, the studies cited in Chapter 1 found that gay men earn lower wages than other men—and significantly lower wages than married men. These studies also showed that lesbians earned higher wages than other women; however, the studies' authors were more tentative in drawing conclusions from these data because of the potential interaction between sexual orientation and gender in determining wages. In either case, as we will explore further in this chapter, partnered lesbians and gay men are often paid less than their heterosexual married counterparts for the same work due to the lack of—or sometimes even in the presence of—comparable benefits packages.

Legal Protection from Discrimination

As of this writing, there is no generally applicable federal civil rights law that prohibits employment discrimination on the basis of sexual orientation. A bill that would add such protections has been languishing in Congress since 1995.[1] In the absence of such a broad-based measure, a patchwork of protections under federal and state law has partially filled this civil rights void. Unfortunately, this patchwork overlaps in some areas, is threadbare in others, and provides absolutely no protection at all in many others.

Whether an individual lesbian or gay man is protected under this patchwork depends on both the identity of the employer (i.e., whether public or private) and the place of employment. Accordingly, I have divided the discussion of employment discrimination protections along both of these lines. First, I describe the legal protections afforded to lesbian and gay employees of the federal government, which do not vary based on the place of employment. Then, I describe the legal protections afforded to lesbian and gay employees of state and local governments, which do vary based on place of employment and are generally broader than those afforded to employees of private businesses. Finally, I describe the legal protections afforded to lesbian and gay employees of private businesses, which also vary based on place of employment and are generally the narrowest of the three groups. At the end of this section, I include a separate discussion of the limited extent to which these protections against discrimination apply to fringe benefits.

Federal Employees

With a notable exception for military personnel (see Chapter 4), discrimination on the basis of sexual orientation in federal employment is now prohibited by statute and presidential executive order. But the tide did not turn in favor of protecting lesbian and gay federal employees until a series of court decisions in the late 1960s and early 1970s limited the government's ability to discriminate.[2] Prior to that time, lesbians and gay men were excluded from federal employment under civil service regulations that permitted individuals to be disqualified because of "immoral" conduct.[3]

Protections. In 1978, codifying the limitations created by the courts, Congress amended the statute governing the Civil Service Commission to prohibit discrimination against "any employee or applicant for employment on the basis of conduct which does not adversely affect the performance of the employee or applicant or the performance of others."[4] The U.S. Office of Personnel Management, a successor to the Civil Service Commission, has long interpreted this provision to prohibit discrimination on the basis of sexual orientation.[5] In 1998, President Bill Clinton issued an executive order that explicitly prohibits discrimination in federal employment on the basis of sexual orientation,[6] and, as of this writing, President George W. Bush has permitted this executive order to remain in force.

With regard to the granting of federal security clearances, however, discrimination persisted until President Clinton issued an executive order in 1995 that prohibited discrimination on the basis of sexual orientation in the issuance of security clearances.[7] The executive order's prohibition against discrimination was incorporated into a guideline that specifically provided that "sexual orientation or preference *may not be used* as a basis for or a disqualifying factor in determining a person's eligibility for a security clearance."[8] This unequivocal prohibition ended in 2005, when the Bush administration revised the guideline to read: "No adverse inference concerning the standards in the Guideline may be raised *solely on the basis of* the sexual orientation of the individual."[9] Although the Bush administration contended that this revision did not reflect a change in policy, the revision clearly replaced a categorical prohibition against discrimination with language that now permits sexual orientation to be used as a basis for denying a security clearance—just so long as it is not the only basis for doing so. This change highlights the fragility of protections implemented through executive order: Such protections are subject to change or elimination whenever the occupant of the White House changes.

Enforceability. Federal employees possess only a limited ability to enforce these legal protections. With respect to security clearances, to the extent that any protection remains, the 1995 executive order provides that determinations concerning the need for access to classified information are discretionary, and it further asserts that, after internal appeals, the agency's decision is final. The U.S. Supreme Court has recognized the discretionary nature of these decisions and, citing national security concerns, has severely curtailed the potential for judicial review.[10] The Court left the door open to judicial review only in situations where an adverse decision is alleged to violate a constitutional right.[11]

With regard to other adverse personnel decisions, federal employees "may pursue administrative relief, with the possibility of ultimately obtaining judicial review in the courts."[12] The Office of Personnel Management has published a brochure on its web site that summarizes the labyrinthine avenues of administrative review for claims of discrimination on the basis of sexual orientation.[13] Given the importance of administrative remedies to lesbian and gay federal employees, it is worth noting that the Bush administration has, at times, been demonstrably less than enthusiastic about the idea of enforcing the prohibitions against sexual orientation discrimination in federal employment.[14]

Federal employees who would prefer not to be confined to administrative remedies will find that their options for filing suit have been significantly constrained. As amended, President Clinton's 1998 executive order does *not* permit lesbian and gay employees to file suit to force the federal government to honor its promise not to discriminate on the basis of sexual orientation in employment.[15] In addition, the federal courts have precluded federal employees who have civil service remedies at their disposal from filing separate, so-called *Bivens*[16] claims for money damages on the ground that the employment discrimination infringed their constitutional rights.[17]

Federal employees who wish to obtain legal redress for discrimination on the basis of sexual orientation outside the civil service system will often be confined to the remedies provided under Title VII, which prohibits discrimination "against any individual with respect to his compensation, terms, conditions, or privileges of employment, because of such individual's . . . sex."[18] Before delving into the substance of Title VII, it is worth noting that so-called mixed cases (i.e., cases where civil service remedies and Title VII relief are both available) have been described by one court as a "procedural morass."[19] A federal employee who believes that she has been the victim of sexual orientation discrimination should, therefore, consult a lawyer familiar with federal employment law both promptly (to avoid missing any procedural deadlines) and before taking action (to ensure that her claim is in no way prejudiced).

Turning now to substantive legal protections, the federal courts are in agreement that Title VII, like Title IX (discussed in Chapter 3), does *not* prohibit discrimination on the basis of sexual orientation.[20] However, as in the Title IX area, the U.S. Supreme Court has interpreted Title VII's prohibition against discrimination on the basis of sex to include sex-role stereotyping and same-sex sexual harassment.[21] Nevertheless, Title VII litigants have not fared as well as Title IX litigants when making such claims.[22]

In *Price Waterhouse v. Hopkins*,[23] a woman was passed over for partnership at an accounting firm in part because she was judged to be insufficiently feminine. One partner even went so far as to suggest that she could improve her chances for partnership if she were to "'walk more femininely, talk more femininely, dress more femininely, wear makeup, have her hair styled, and wear jewelry.'"[24] Faced with these and similar remarks by other Price Waterhouse partners, the U.S. Supreme Court construed Title VII to prohibit sex-role stereotyping, stating that "an employer who objects to aggressiveness in women but whose positions require this trait places women in an intolerable and impermissible catch 22: out of a job if they behave aggressively and out of a job if they do not. Title VII lifts women out of this bind."[25] In a later case, the U.S. Court of Appeals for the Ninth Circuit found that a gay man had stated a claim for sex-role stereotyping when his male coworkers "habitually called him sexually derogatory names, referred to him with the female gender, and taunted him for behaving like a woman."[26]

In *Oncale v. Sundowner Offshore Services*,[27] a man who worked on an oil platform in the Gulf of Mexico was harassed by his male coworkers. The man was threatened with rape, his coworkers forcibly pushed a bar of soap into his anus while he was showering at work, and, on two occasions, one of his coworkers restrained him while another placed his penis on him.[28] The U.S. Supreme Court held that such sexually harassing activity may violate Title VII, whether it is perpetrated by someone of the same or a different sex than the victim and regardless of whether it was motivated by sexual desire, so long as the conduct is "severe or pervasive enough to create an objectively hostile or abusive work environment."[29]

But to constitute a violation of Title VII, harassing conduct must have occurred "because of . . . sex." In *Oncale*, the Court did little to further understanding of how this requirement applies in same-sex sexual harassment cases.[30] However, the Court did give a few examples of situations where same-sex harassment may be shown to have occurred "because of . . . sex": (1) The perpetrator makes explicit or implicit proposals of sexual activity and there is credible evidence that the perpetrator is a lesbian or gay man (and, therefore, presumably chose the target because she or he is of the same sex), (2) the perpetrator is motivated by hostility to the general presence of one sex in the workplace, or (3) the perpetrator treats one sex differently than the other in a mixed-sex workplace.

Despite the Court's ostensibly narrow focus on "sex" as "gender" in these cases, sexual orientation has proved relevant in Title VII sex discrimination analysis—but, it turns out, only when it can serve to harm the interests of lesbians and gay men. Thus, in same-sex sexual harassment cases, sexual orientation is important whenever the accused perpetrator is—or credibly is believed to be—a lesbian or gay man. Recall from the previous paragraph that, according to the Court in *Oncale,* the (homo)sexual orientation of the perpetrator can be used to establish that harassment occurred "because of . . . sex." Indeed, *Oncale* creates the distinct possibility that Title VII might be used *against* lesbians and gay men in ways that both play on and solidify sexual prejudice and stereotypes about lesbians and gay men (e.g., the stereotype of the homosexual as sexual predator).[31]

Sexual orientation has also proved important when the victim of discrimination is a lesbian or gay man (or refuses to deny being a lesbian or gay man).[32] Because Title VII does not prohibit sexual orientation discrimination, lesbians and gay men often find it difficult to prove that discrimination occurred impermissibly because of their sex rather than permissibly because of their sexual orientation.[33] Interestingly, the same problem generally does *not* arise when the victim claims to be a heterosexual who was mistakenly perceived to be a lesbian or gay man, because then the discrimination is not thought to be based on sexual orientation.[34]

Accordingly, even in the limited situations when Title VII relief is theoretically available to lesbian and gay federal employees, it may be difficult for them to make a successful claim. Notwithstanding the limited nature of the judicial remedies that Title VII provides, lesbian and gay federal employees in positions covered by Title VII are foreclosed from pursuing other available judicial remedies. In *Brown v. General Services Administration,* the U.S. Supreme Court held that when Congress extended the protections of Title VII to federal employees in 1972, it intended Title VII to provide "the exclusive judicial remedy for claims of discrimination in federal employment."[35] The federal courts have interpreted this unqualified statement to bar employment discrimination claims made directly under the U.S. Constitution[36] as well as claims made under state nondiscrimination laws.[37]

Consequently, even though lesbian and gay federal employees appear, at first blush, to be the beneficiaries of significant legal protections against discrimination based on their sexual orientation, when it comes to enforcement, these protections appear to be more rhetoric than reality.

State and Local Employees

In the District of Columbia and thirty-one states, lesbian and gay employees of state governments are protected by a statute, executive order, or policy that prohibits employment discrimination on the basis of sexual orientation. Table 5.1 divides these jurisdictions into two categories: (1) those that provide such protection *only* to state employees[38] and (2) those that provide such protection to state employees *and* further extend protection to employees of local governments and some private businesses.[39]

Table 5.1   D.C. and State Laws, Executive Orders, and Policies Prohibiting Employment Discrimination

Covering State Employees Only	Covering Both State Employees and Employees of Private Businesses	No Laws, Executive Orders, or Policies
Alaska	California[a,b]	Alabama
Arizona	Colorado[a]	Arkansas
Delaware	Connecticut[a,b]	Florida
Indiana	District of Columbia[a]	Georgia
Kansas	Hawaii[a]	Idaho
Louisiana	Illinois[a,b]	Kentucky[d]
Michigan	Iowa[a,b]	Mississippi
Montana	Maine[a]	Missouri
Ohio[c]	Maryland[a,b]	Nebraska
Pennsylvania	Massachusetts[a,b]	North Carolina
Virginia	Minnesota[a]	North Dakota
	Nevada[a,b]	Oklahoma
	New Hampshire[a,b]	South Carolina
	New Jersey[a]	South Dakota
	New Mexico[a,b]	Tennessee
	New York[a,b]	Texas
	Oregon[a]	Utah
	Rhode Island[a,b]	West Virginia
	Vermont[a]	Wyoming
	Washington[a,b]	
	Wisconsin[a]	

[a] Exemption for religious organizations.

[b] Exemption for small businesses.

[c] In 1983, Governor Richard Celeste issued Executive Order No. 83-64 (Dec. 30, 1983), which prohibited discrimination on the basis of sexual orientation in public employment. In 1998, Governor George Voinovich issued Executive Order No. 98-42V (Dec. 31, 1998), which provided that Executive Order No. 83-64 would expire at the end of his term as governor. Then, in 1999, Governor Bob Taft issued Executive Order No. 99-25T (Aug. 16, 1999), which replaced expired Executive Order No. 83-64 and reversed the protection that it afforded by omitting any mention of sexual orientation in its text. Most recently, in May 2007, Governor Ted Strickland issued Executive Order No. 2007-10S (May 17, 2007), which prohibits discrimination on the basis of sexual orientation in public employment; however, by its own terms, this executive order expires on the last day of Governor Strickland's time in office.

[d] In 2006, the governor of Kentucky issued Executive Order No. 2006-402 (Apr. 11, 2006), which superseded Executive Order No. 2003-533 (May 29, 2003) and eliminated its prohibition against discrimination on the basis of sexual orientation in public employment.

A subgroup of these jurisdictions—California, Connecticut, the District of Columbia, New Hampshire, New Jersey, and Oregon—also affords same-sex couples who have entered into a civil union or registered as domestic partners the same protections against employment discrimination on the basis of marital status as are afforded to married different-sex couples.[40] In addition, many local governments have independently passed ordinances or adopted policies that prohibit discrimination on the basis of sexual orientation.

Naturally, enforcement of these protections will vary from jurisdiction to jurisdiction. The fragility of the protection afforded by executive order is only underscored by the experience at the state level. As indicated in Table 5.1, governors of Kentucky and Ohio have, with the stroke of a pen, reversed protections earlier afforded to lesbian and gay state employees.

Federal law may be an additional source of protection for state and local employees. State and local employees are entitled to file claims under Title VII in the same limited circumstances under which federal employees can file such claims.[41] And, in contrast to its treatment of federal employees, Congress has provided state and local employees with specific means for filing employment discrimination suits based upon alleged violations of their federal constitutional rights, usually under the First and/or Fourteenth Amendments.[42]

Following the U.S. Supreme Court's decision in *Romer v. Evans*,[43] the Fourteenth Amendment prohibits state governments from treating people differently based on their sexual orientation unless there is a rational basis for doing so. In *Romer*, the Court struck down the infamous "Amendment 2" to the Colorado constitution, which prohibited "all legislative, executive or judicial action at any level of state or local government designed to protect . . . gays and lesbians."[44] The Court found this provision to be "inexplicable by anything but animus toward" lesbians and gay men,[45] and it held that animus is *not* a rational basis for treating lesbians and gay men differently from others. Being no more than a codification of antigay animus, Amendment 2 therefore violated the Fourteenth Amendment's guarantee of equal protection of the law. Earlier, in *City of Cleburne v. Cleburne Living Center*,[46] the Court had similarly held that the negative attitudes and biases of others cannot serve as a rational basis for differential treatment. More recently, relying on both *Romer* and *City of Cleburne*, a federal district court faced with a police officer who claimed to have been "ridiculed, humiliated, abused, and singled out because of his sexual orientation" found that, apart from Title VII, "individuals have a constitutional right under the Equal Protection Clause to be free from sexual orientation discrimination causing a hostile work environment in public employment."[47]

State and local employees may be able to rely on the First Amendment for protection if they believe that they have been discriminated against because of speech concerning their sexual orientation. In *Pickering v. Board of Education*,[48] the U.S. Supreme Court affirmed the application of the First Amendment to public employees' speech commenting on matters of public concern. The Court recognized, however, that the government, as employer, may have a legitimate interest in regulating its employees' speech. The problem, according to the Court, lies in attempting "to arrive at a balance between the interests of the [employee], as a citizen, in commenting upon matters of public concern and the interest of the State, as an employer, in promoting the efficiency of the public services it performs through its employees."[49] The application of this balancing test depends on the particular facts and circumstances of each case.[50] Nonetheless, the Court did indicate that if an employee's speech on a matter of public concern affects neither the performance of his duties nor the functioning of his government employer, then the government's interest in regulating his speech "is not significantly greater than its interest in limiting a similar contribution by any member of the general public" and would, therefore, not be a permissible basis for dismissal.[51]

Given this ambiguous guidance, it should be no surprise that lower courts differ on whether disclosure of one's sexual orientation is a matter of public or private concern. For instance, in *Rowland v. Mad River Local School District*,[52] the dismissal of a school guidance counselor for disclosing her bisexuality to a coworker was upheld under *Pickering* on the ground that her sexual orientation was a matter of private concern—as evidenced by the fact that she had made the initial disclosure in confidence. The Supreme Court denied the guidance counselor's petition for review of this decision; however, two justices took the unusual step of filing a dissenting opinion in which they suggested that sexual orientation might be an issue "'inherently of public concern.'"[53] In *Weaver v. Nebo School District*,[54] a federal district court appeared to embrace this position when it found that a school had violated a teacher's First Amendment rights by (1) restricting her ability to discuss her sexual orientation and (2) removing her from her position as volleyball coach in retaliation for revealing her sexual orientation. But another federal district court has held that, absent identifiable speech or conduct expressing one's sexual orientation, merely being openly gay is *not* expression protected by the First Amendment.[55]

On the subject of constitutional protections, it is worth noting that, because the U.S. Supreme Court has struck down state sodomy laws on federal constitutional grounds, the criminalization of same-sex sexual contact may no longer serve as a basis for discriminating against lesbians and gay men in employment.[56] It is also worth noting that state constitutions may provide even broader protection against employment discrimination on the basis of sexual orientation than is found in the federal constitution. For example, in *Merrick v. Board of Higher Education*,[57] the Oregon Court of Appeals considered the validity of a state ballot measure that was designed to reverse employment protections afforded to lesbian and gay state employees through a governor's executive order. The court held that the ballot measure violated the free speech provision of the Oregon Constitution because it chilled constitutionally protected "free and open expression about sexual orientation" and discouraged state employees from engaging in the constitutionally protected activity of joining with others to advocate for lesbian and gay rights.[58]

Employees of Private Businesses

As indicated in Table 5.1, twenty states and the District of Columbia have enacted laws that prohibit private employers from discriminating on the basis of sexual orientation (and, as mentioned earlier, some of these jurisdictions also protect against civil union status or domestic partnership status discrimination in employment).[59] These jurisdictions normally prohibit discrimination in decisions about hiring; firing; promotion; salary; and any other terms, conditions, or privileges of employment.[60] However, all of these nondiscrimination laws contain some form of exemption for religious organizations, and most exempt small businesses from their purview. Again, many local governments have themselves passed ordinances that prohibit employment discrimination on the basis of sexual orientation.

Outside these jurisdictions, employers are generally free to discriminate on the basis of sexual orientation. Most employment relationships are "at will," meaning that the relationship may be terminated at any time and for any reason (or even for no reason at all).[61] Nonetheless, a number of state courts have read an exception into "at will" employment relationships: They prohibit an employee from being terminated on a ground that violates a significant, established public policy of the state.[62] But, without explicit, preexisting protection against discrimination, lesbians and gay men have found it difficult to show that termination because of their sexual orientation violated a significant, established public policy of the state.[63] Of course, once such affirmative protection exists—for example, when sexual orientation is added to the state nondiscrimination law—the need for the common law public policy claim largely disappears.

Where lesbians and gay men are covered by an employment contract, they may be able to rely on the provisions of that contract (e.g., a provision that allows an employee to be terminated only for "good cause") to contest an adverse employment decision stemming from discrimination on the basis of sexual orientation. Even absent a written employment contract, a court will sometimes treat an employer's nondiscrimination policy as an enforceable contractual promise made to the employee.[64]

Employees of private businesses can also bring suit under Title VII in the same limited circumstances as federal employees; however, like most state nondiscrimination laws, Title VII contains an exemption for religious organizations and small businesses.[65] Private employers' discrimination on the basis of sexual orientation will rarely violate the federal constitution, though it may violate state constitutional provisions that have been construed to apply to purely private action.[66]

Obtaining Legal Redress

Given the peculiar nature of government employment, if you believe that your government employer has discriminated against you on the basis of sexual orientation, you should contact an attorney for legal advice. Private-sector employees who suffer discrimination and who are located in a jurisdiction listed in Table 5.1 (or in a locality with a nondiscrimination law that covers sexual orientation) should contact the state or local agency that handles enforcement of the relevant fair employment practices law for guidance on the procedure for making a complaint. If you are not protected by a nondiscrimination law, you should contact an attorney who specializes in employment law to determine whether you have an actionable claim against your employer on some other ground (e.g., breach of contract).

Fringe Benefits

Once lesbians and gay men have obtained employment, receiving equal pay for equal work becomes a significant concern. As mentioned in Chapter 1, studies have shown that gay men are paid lower wages than other men (and significantly lower wages than married men), whereas lesbians earn more than other women (possibly due to the interaction between sexual orientation and gender stereotypes). But whether we receive equal pay for equal work cannot be judged by reference to our wages alone; for most workers, fringe benefits form a significant portion of their pay package. When the provision of fringe benefits is taken into account, the pay differential between gay and straight men can only be exacerbated, and any wage advantage afforded to lesbians as compared to straight women can only be eroded.

Whether an employer provides fringe benefits to its employees is a matter of choice.[67] In practice, employers provide a number of important fringe benefits to their employees, including health insurance; family, medical, and bereavement leave; retirement benefits; death benefits; life insurance; and employee discounts. Once an employer decides to provide fringe benefits to its employees, the employer is often free to discriminate on the basis of sexual orientation in the provision of those benefits, notwithstanding state nondiscrimination laws.

Take for example the provision of health insurance benefits to state employees: The District of Columbia and thirty states nominally protect their own employees against discrimination on the basis of sexual orientation. Yet only about half of these jurisdictions offer domestic-partner health insurance coverage to their employees.[68] Attempts at litigating equal access to benefits provided by government employers have had mixed success. In Alaska, Montana, and Oregon, courts found the failure to provide equal benefits to violate the state constitution, and, in New Hampshire, a trial court judge found the failure to provide equal benefits to violate the state's nondiscrimination law.[69] Courts in California, New Jersey, and Wisconsin have all, however, rejected efforts to attain equal access to benefits through litigation.[70] And the mere possibility of persuading governmental entities that extending benefits to their lesbian and gay employees is the correct thing to do—whether for reasons of social justice or as a means of attracting and retaining qualified employees—has been cast in doubt by broadly worded state legislation and constitutional amendments that prohibit same-sex couples from being afforded the rights and benefits of marriage (for more on so-called defense of marriage acts, see Chapter 6).[71]

In the case of private employers, persuasion is nearly the only means to obtain equal benefits. Federal law provides no basis for coercing private employers to extend benefits to the same-sex partners of lesbian and gay employees; in many cases, it actually goes a step further and effectively nullifies any *state* law basis for doing so. The federal Employee Retirement Income Security Act (ERISA) supersedes state laws affecting most private employers' plans that provide health, sickness, accident, disability, death, unemployment, vacation, or retirement benefits.[72] As a result, state nondiscrimination laws cannot be used as a ground for forcing private employers to extend benefits governed by ERISA to the same-sex partners of lesbian and gay employees.[73]

In an attempt to circumvent ERISA preemption, a handful of jurisdictions have enacted "equal benefits laws."[74] These laws require that, in order to be eligible to contract with the relevant state or local government, a business must offer equal benefits to all of its employees; for example, if the employer offers health insurance coverage to the spouses of married heterosexual employees, the law requires the employer to offer health insurance coverage to the domestic partners of lesbian and gay employees. The scope of these laws has, however, been significantly narrowed by court decisions. Recently, the New York Court of Appeals held that New York City's equal benefits law was preempted by the state's competitive bidding law and ERISA (to the extent that it applied to benefits governed by ERISA).[75] Earlier, the San Francisco equal benefits law was largely struck down because it violated the Commerce Clause of the U.S. Constitution (to the extent that it forced businesses to offer domestic-partner benefits to employees located outside California who were not working on city contracts) and was preempted by ERISA (to the extent that it applied to benefits governed by ERISA).[76]

In an interesting (though unsurprising)[77] turn that further underscores the importance of persuasion, ERISA preemption has been used defensively in Massachusetts—where same-sex couples are now permitted to marry and, therefore, should be able to qualify as "spouses" for purposes of benefit plans that define that term by reference to state law. Several of the largest employers in Massachusetts—including FedEx and General Dynamics—have relied on ERISA preemption to claim that they are not bound by Massachusetts's extension of the right to marry to same-sex couples.[78] Instead, these companies follow the federal definition of "marriage," which embraces "only a legal union between one man and one woman as husband and wife."[79] As a result, they refuse to extend health insurance coverage to the same-sex partners of their married lesbian and gay employees—despite the fact that ERISA would not prevent them from voluntarily offering such coverage.[80]

Even when employers do *offer* the same benefits packages to all of their employees regardless of sexual orientation, the benefits *received* by lesbian and gay employees are often less than what heterosexual employees receive. To illustrate the point, let's return to the health insurance example. For federal income tax purposes, the value of employer-provided health insurance coverage is not subject to tax when it is provided to an employee, the employee's spouse, or the employee's dependents.[81] For this purpose, "spouse" includes "only . . . a person of the opposite sex who is a husband or a wife."[82] A "dependent" is someone who, during a given taxable year, shares the same principal place of abode as the employee and more than half of whose support is provided by the employee.[83]

Thus, when an employer provides health insurance coverage to its married, heterosexual employees (as my employer, the University of Pittsburgh, does), the federal government allows the heterosexual employee to exclude the value of the health insurance coverage provided to him *and* his wife from the amount of his taxable wages. In other words, this valuable fringe benefit—for both spouses—is provided completely tax free. In contrast, if I were to enroll my current partner, Hien, in the University of Pittsburgh health plan (which I am now permitted to do), then the amount of my taxable wages would be increased by the value of the health insurance coverage provided by the university to Hien (less any amount contributed by me—after taxes—toward the cost of that coverage).[84] My taxable wages would increase because Hien qualifies neither as my "spouse" nor as my "dependent" for federal income tax purposes. Such an increase in taxable wages normally leads to a larger tax bill.

In effect, the federal government would step in to reinstate a lost heterosexual privilege by reducing my fringe benefits by an amount equal to the tax imposed but leaving those of my married, heterosexual colleagues untouched. The problem is only exacerbated in states that follow the federal lead and charge state income tax on the benefits as well. Notably, a few jurisdictions (e.g., California, Connecticut, the District of Columbia, Massachusetts, Oregon, and Vermont) do not impose state income tax on the value of these domestic-partner benefits.[85]

Housing

Discrimination in the Rental or Purchase of a Home

In affirming a landlord's ability to discriminate against lawyers when choosing the tenants for his building, one court nicely summarized the starting point for this discussion: "Absent a supervening statutory proscription, a landlord is free to do what he wishes with his property, and to rent or not to rent to any given person at his whim."[86] Therefore, as is the case with most public accommodations and most employment relationships, the general default rule is one that sanctions discrimination. Lesbians and gay men across the country feel the impact of this default rule every day. In fact, 34 percent of lesbians, gay men, and bisexuals responding to a nationwide survey in 2000 reported that they, or someone they knew, had experienced discrimination on the basis of sexual orientation when buying or renting a home.[87]

General Legal Protections. As of this writing, there is no generally applicable federal civil rights law that prohibits housing discrimination on the basis of sexual orientation. A bill that would add such protections has been languishing in the House of Representatives for more than a decade.[88] In the absence of such a broad-based measure, a small number of states and a larger number of localities have acted to fill the void. The District of Columbia and eighteen states have adopted laws that prohibit housing discrimination on the basis of sexual orientation. Table 5.2 identifies these states and summarizes both the coverage of their housing discrimination laws and the significant areas that they have carved out as exempt from coverage.[89]

As indicated in Table 5.2, subject to certain exceptions, these jurisdictions generally prohibit an owner or landlord of real property (as well as those acting on her behalf, including realtors) from discriminating on the basis of sexual orientation when selling or renting property. (It is worth noting that a subgroup of these jurisdictions—California, Connecticut, the District of Columbia, Massachusetts, New Hampshire, New Jersey, Oregon, and Vermont—also affords same-sex couples who have married, entered into a civil union, or registered as domestic partners the same protections against housing discrimination on the basis of marital status as are afforded to married different-sex couples.[90]) The precise coverage of the statutes varies; however, in this context, "discrimination" commonly includes refusing to rent or sell property (or to negotiate for the rental or sale of property), falsely stating that the property is unavailable, discouraging a prospective tenant or buyer from moving into the neighborhood by suggesting that she will not be safe or welcomed by neighbors, harassing a tenant based on sexual orientation, providing segregated housing, and/or providing housing under different terms or conditions (e.g., charging a higher rent or additional fees or not providing needed repairs that are provided to others). Each of these jurisdictions also prohibits discrimination on the basis of sexual orientation in applying for a loan in connection with the purchase, construction, improvement, or repair of a home.

Marital Status Protections. When a nondiscrimination law does not explicitly cover sexual orientation, lesbians and gay men may nonetheless be able to avail themselves of protections against discrimination on the basis of marital status. For instance, although the federal Equal Credit Opportunity Act provides no protection against discrimination on the basis of sexual orientation, it does prohibit discrimination on the basis of marital status.[91] Accordingly,

Table 5.2 Coverage of Nondiscrimination Laws Relating to Housing

	Coverage				Exemptions		
	Landlord	Seller	Realtors	Banks and Mortgage Companies	Religious Organizations	Landlord Living on Premises	Nondealer Sales of Single-Family Homes; No Realtor or Discriminatory Advertising
California	✓	✓	✓	✓	✓	✓a	
Connecticut	✓	✓	✓	✓	✓	✓b	✓e
District of Columbia	✓	✓	✓	✓	✓	✓b	
Hawaii	✓	✓	✓	✓	✓	✓b	
Illinois	✓	✓	✓	✓	✓	✓b	✓
Iowa	✓	✓	✓	✓	✓	✓b	
Maine	✓	✓	✓	✓	✓	✓b	✓e
Maryland	✓	✓	✓	✓	✓	✓c	✓e
Massachusetts	✓	✓	✓	✓	✓	✓b	
Minnesota	✓	✓	✓	✓	✓	✓b	✓e
New Hampshire	✓	✓	✓	✓	✓	✓b	
New Jersey	✓	✓	✓	✓	✓	✓b	
New Mexico	✓	✓	✓	✓	✓	✓b	✓e,f
New York	✓	✓	✓	✓	✓	✓b	
Oregon	✓	✓	✓	✓	✓	✓a	
Rhode Island	✓	✓	✓	✓	✓	✓b	
Vermont	✓	✓	✓	✓	✓	✓b	
Washington	✓	✓	✓	✓		✓a	
Wisconsin	✓	✓	✓	✓		✓d	

a Boarders only.
b Boarders and small multiunit dwellings.
c Small multiunit dwellings only.
d Roommates only.
e Also applies to rentals.
f No requirement that a Realtor not be used to facilitate the sale or rental.

under federal regulations, a creditor must evaluate married and unmarried applicants using the same standards, unless otherwise permitted by law.[92] Of particular importance to same-sex couples, these regulations go on to provide that "in evaluating joint applicants, a creditor shall not treat applicants differently based on the existence, absence, or likelihood of a marital relationship between the parties."[93]

Similarly, lesbians and gay men—particularly partnered lesbians and gay men—may be able to avail themselves of the nondiscrimination laws in the handful of states that do not prohibit housing discrimination on the basis of sexual orientation but that do prohibit housing discrimination on the basis of marital status.[94] The availability of these protections is most likely in states that have affirmatively indicated that the phrase "marital status" in their statutes protects both married and unmarried couples.[95] In the remaining states in this group, the availability of "marital status" protection to lesbians and gay men is uncertain because the state law either leaves unmarried couples (at least of different sexes) unprotected or is silent on what "marital status" means.[96]

In any event, these prohibitions against housing discrimination on the basis of marital status should interest lesbians and gay men for another reason. Notwithstanding the frequent exemption of religious *organizations* from their purview, nondiscrimination laws do not normally contain an exemption for individuals whose religious *beliefs* are in conflict with the requirements of the law. As a result, landlords have lodged federal and state constitutional challenges against the "marital status" provisions of nondiscrimination laws when allowing unmarried heterosexual couples to cohabitate would violate their religious beliefs. In response to these suits, courts have reached differing conclusions on the question of whether constitutional guarantees (particularly those relating to free exercise of religion) mandate an implicit exemption from state nondiscrimination laws.[97] Obviously, religious landlords could make similar arguments to circumvent nondiscrimination laws that cover sexual orientation.

Public and Subsidized Housing. Under federal regulations, public housing agencies are required to make tenant selection decisions for public (i.e., government-owned and -operated) housing for low-income individuals on an individual basis and without regard to attributes or behavior that "may be imputed to a particular group or category of persons of which an applicant may be a member."[98] This regulation should prohibit public housing agencies from making tenant selection decisions on the basis of stereotypes concerning an applicant's sexual orientation. In contrast, under the "Section 8," or "Housing Choice Voucher," program, which provides federal subsidies for the rental of privately owned and operated housing, the landlord generally screens and selects the tenants for a unit.[99] Though federal regulations do not subject private landlords to the same broad nondiscrimination requirement as public housing agencies, landlords are required to comply with applicable federal, state, and local nondiscrimination laws (e.g., those listed in Table 5.2).[100]

In order for a same-sex couple to qualify together for federally subsidized public housing or to participate in the Housing Choice Voucher program, the couple must qualify as a "family." Federal law and regulations provide some guidance on the definition of "family" but leave the definition open-ended so that local public housing agencies may flesh it out in accordance with local laws and policies.[101] This means that, in some areas, the public housing agency will take a narrow view of what constitutes a "family," as does the Oxford Housing Authority in Mississippi: "MEMBERS OF THE SAME HOUSEHOLD MUST BE RELATED BY BLOOD, MARRIAGE, OR LEGAL GUARDIAN-SHIP. BOYFRIEND(S) AND/OR GIRLFRIEND(S) MAY *NOT* LIVE WITH YOU. IF THEY DO, THEY WILL CAUSE YOU TO BE EVICTED."[102] In other areas, the public housing agency will take a more relaxed and inclusive view of what constitutes a "family," as does the New York City Housing Authority: "The term 'family' as used by the New York City Housing Authority includes the following: (1) Two or more persons related by blood, marriage, registered domestic partnership, adoption, guardianship or court awarded custody. (2) Two or more unrelated persons living together as a cohesive household group in a sharing relationship."[103] Accordingly, whether a same-sex couple may apply together for housing assistance will vary from locality to locality.

No Home Is a Sanctuary

Home Buyers. The purchase of a home does not necessarily end the possibility of housing discrimination for lesbians and gay men, particularly those who are partnered and live with children, parents, or others. For more than fifty years, municipalities throughout the country have engaged in exclusionary zoning practices by restricting the use of property to the construction of single-family homes and by further imposing limits on the number and the relationship of those who may occupy those homes.[104] These single-family zoning rules often severely limit the ability of individuals who are not related by blood, marriage, or adoption from living together—including same-sex couples outside the few states that legally recognize their relationships.[105] The rules serve a gatekeeping function by barring entry to those living in disfavored arrangements (e.g., non-"nuclear" families and the poor or immigrants who share the cost of housing in an expensive market), especially given that enforcement is driven by complaints from neighbors rather than systematic surveys of who is occupying a particular home.[106] Reactionaries have resisted attempts to relax single-family zoning rules for fear that any "redefinition" of what constitutes a "family" might be viewed as legitimizing households headed by same-sex couples.

In *Village of Belle Terre v. Boraas,*[107] the U.S. Supreme Court upheld the constitutionality of a single-family zoning ordinance that limited the number of unrelated individuals who could occupy a home together. The Court found that the restriction did not violate the Equal Protection Clause because it was rationally related to a permissible objective. In this regard, the Court noted that "the police power is not confined to elimination of filth, stench, and unhealthy places. It is ample to lay out zones where family values, youth values, and the blessings of quiet seclusion and clean air make the area a sanctuary for people."[108] Yet, when faced a few years later with a zoning ordinance that specifically defined which members of a family could occupy a home together, the Court found that the ordinance violated the property owner's right to liberty under the Fourteenth Amendment's Due Process Clause.[109]

Most states have followed the Court's lead and have upheld single-family zoning ordinances that restrict the occupancy of a home by unrelated persons.[110] A small number of states have, however, departed from the majority view and have struck down such ordinances on state constitutional grounds; these states include California, Illinois, Michigan, New Jersey, New York, and Pennsylvania.[111] One commentator maintains that *Lawrence v. Texas* gives new impetus to this trend because its extension of the constitutional right to liberty to intimate lesbian and gay relationships should apply with equal force to single-family zoning ordinances.[112]

Tenants. As mentioned earlier, the nondiscrimination laws listed in Table 5.2 protect lesbian and gay renters from discrimination during their tenancies. But many lesbians and gay men will not benefit from these protections, either because the property where they live is exempted from the application of the law or because the jurisdiction's nondiscrimination law does not cover sexual orientation. In these situations, a written lease or local law may provide some protection against a landlord's arbitrary actions.

For example, a landlord generally may not evict you before the end of your tenancy, if you have complied with your obligations under the lease.[113] Under New Jersey law, many landlords are prohibited from either evicting residential tenants or refusing to renew a residential tenant's lease except where they can show good cause (e.g., nonpayment of rent)—regardless of any contrary provision in the lease.[114] Similar "good cause" limitations apply to federally funded public and subsidized housing as well as to dwellings covered by state and local rent control laws.[115] In New York, these protections are even afforded to certain "family members" who live with the tenant of a rent-controlled apartment; they can succeed to the tenant's rights under the rent-control law when the tenant permanently vacates the premises (e.g., when the tenant passes away).[116] Following the New York Court of Appeals' decision in *Braschi v. Stahl Associates Co.*, broadly construing "family member" to include the same-sex partner of a deceased tenant,[117] the New York legislature passed a statute adopting a broad definition of "family member" that includes "any . . . person residing with the tenant in the housing accommodation as a primary residence who can prove emotional and financial commitment, and interdependence between such person and the tenant."[118]

Obtaining Legal Redress

If you believe that you have been the subject of prohibited discrimination on the basis of sexual orientation, you should contact your local fair-housing enforcement agency for guidance on the procedure for making a complaint, because the method for enforcing these statutory protections varies from state to state.[119] To help prospective buyers and renters report discrimination, the Leadership Conference on Civil Rights and the Leadership Conference on Civil Rights Education Fund maintain a list of enforcement agencies (with contact information) broken down by state on their helpful web site, www.fairhousinglaw.org; they also provide links to the relevant nondiscrimination laws of each state. If you live outside a jurisdiction with a nondiscrimination law that protects against discrimination on the basis of sexual orientation, you should contact an attorney who specializes in housing law or your local legal services organization (see www.lsc.gov for a list) to determine whether your rights under an agreement of sale, a lease, or local law have been violated by the seller of a home or a landlord.

Securing the Basic Necessities of Life

In the areas of housing and employment, where the ability to secure the basic necessities of life is at stake, the risks associated with challenging the privileging of heterosexuality in our society loom all the larger. Naturally, some lesbians and gay men will speak out and challenge that privileging whether or not the law protects them against discrimination; however, many others will accede to the pressure to remain silent for fear that they will be unable to provide food, clothing, or shelter for themselves or their loved ones. As one commentator has noted, "a shaming experience where one is most vulnerable—in her relationships with family and friends, work or home—may be particularly difficult due to the accompanying anxiety about the security of the future. If one landlord [or employer] can turn a person down because he is gay, he has no way of knowing that the next landlord [or employer] will see things differently, or the next, and that ultimately he will find a decent place to live [or work]."[120]

In polls, an overwhelming majority of the American public actually agrees on the need for laws banning discrimination on the basis of sexual orientation in housing and employment. Given the signal importance of housing and employment to all human beings, we should capitalize upon this wide support for nondiscrimination measures and lobby for laws prohibiting discrimination on the basis of sexual orientation in these areas. As described more fully in Chapter 2, these efforts are probably most fruitfully applied first at the local and then at the state and, ultimately, federal levels so that networks of allies can be built and local successes can be used as stepping-stones to state and federal successes. These lobbying efforts also provide an opportunity to break down stereotypes and preconceptions—to change people's minds about what it means to be a lesbian or gay man.

By working toward the establishment of popularly supported nondiscrimination protections, we can create a legal safety net that will ensure that those who do suffer discrimination have some form of legal recourse available to them. In this way, we can help to foster a safe space in which all lesbians and gay men can speak out without fear of retribution that may deprive them of food, clothing, and/or shelter. From this safe space, efforts to educate and effect further change can more easily be undertaken.

For example, in retrospect, I missed an educational opportunity when I allowed myself to be cowed by the landlady in San Diego who simply could not comprehend why two men would need to share a one-bedroom apartment. I should have stood firm and confronted her hostility by explaining my situation to her. At that point, if her prejudices were not deeply entrenched, she might have backed down and allowed Michael and me to see the apartment. If those prejudices were more deeply entrenched and she failed to back down, I could have filed a discrimination complaint against her with the California Department of Fair Employment and Housing to let her know that her actions were countenanced neither by me nor by the State of California. She would then have been forced to pay the price for the harm that she had caused us.

Although I might have missed my first educational opportunity due to youth and inexperience, that opportunity was certainly not the only one ever presented to me. Openly lesbian and gay individuals encounter daily opportunities—sometimes tacit, sometimes explicit—to break down stereotypes and preconceptions. Last year, my partner, Hien, and I consolidated houses: I sold my home and moved into Hien's home in a somewhat conservative suburb of Pittsburgh. Before that, we shuttled back and forth between our two homes for quite some time. During the long period of consolidation, Hien's neighbors saw a lot of me (and my dog, Kasha). At first, Hien was a bit concerned about the neighbors' reaction to my being around so much and to his mention that I would eventually be moving in with him. But he was pleasantly surprised when the neighbors made a point of coming over personally to invite both of us to the block party that they were organizing. The neighbors continue to be friendly, and I think that it can only be helpful that the three young children next door are growing up in a house next to a gay couple. For them, a gay couple will not be an oddity or something that they have only seen on television or in the movies—we will be the people next door whom they say hello to when they are playing outside and whose garbage cans they sometimes bring in just to be neighborly.

The workplace also presents an unending array of educational opportunities; indeed, I view the entire time that I worked next door to the (initially unabashedly homophobic) Richard as one long educational moment. If an organization has several lesbian and gay employees, which was not the case at the law firm where I worked, those employees can organize a formal or informal workplace group. Through such a group, they can provide each other with needed emotional and/or social support to cope with an unwelcoming environment.[121] Lambda Legal has published a helpful online guide, "Out at Work: A Guide for LGBT Employees,"[122] that provides advice about how to start such a workplace group, and the Human Rights Campaign (HRC) has published a similar online resource, "How to Start an Employee Network Group."[123]

Workplace groups can also serve as vehicles to take educational opportunities a step further by advocating for improvements in the work environment, such as reducing sexual prejudice (through diversity training or less formal encounters), adding sexual orientation to the company nondiscrimination policy, and obtaining domestic-partner benefits.[124] Lambda Legal, HRC, and the National Gay and Lesbian Task Force all have helpful online publications that provide guidance on how to advocate for change, particularly with regard to adding sexual orientation to company nondiscrimination policies and obtaining domestic-partnership benefits.[125] And, as mentioned in the narrative at the beginning of this chapter, it is important to monitor an employer's implementation of any new policies to ensure that what has been achieved is more than just a Pyrrhic victory.

Where positive changes in the workplace can be achieved, they will redound to the benefit of lesbian and gay employees and their employers. In fact, the few studies in this area have demonstrated both (1) a correlation between the existence of supportive organizational policies (i.e., written nondiscrimination policies and diversity training that expressly include sexual orientation—accompanied by management's backing of an open environment) and being out at work and (2) a correlation between being out at work and increased job satisfaction, increased commitment to the organization, and decreased conflict between work and home.[126] Clearly, more satisfied and committed employees are also likely to be more productive employees. Furthermore, by creating an atmosphere in which employees can feel safe to come out and be out, employers will allow closeted employees to redirect their energies from passing as straight in the workplace to performing their jobs and increasing their productivity.[127]

Even where a workplace group or an individual employee acting on her own does not achieve a specific goal (e.g., adding sexual orientation to a nondiscrimination policy or extending fringe benefits coverage to domestic partners), their efforts may nevertheless provide tangible benefits by improving the climate at work: "An ambitious education and lobbying *process* in the workplace can create progress as coalitions are formed, alliances are forged, and attitudes are changed, even if a specific institutional change is not achieved immediately."[128]

Notes

1. Arthur S. Leonard, "Sexual Minority Rights in the Workplace," *Brandeis L.J.* 43 (2004): 145, 146, 158.

2. See William N. Eskridge Jr., "Challenging the Apartheid of the Closet: Establishing Conditions for Lesbian and Gay Intimacy, Nomos, and Citizenship, 1961–1981," *Hofstra L. Rev.* 25 (1997): 817, 911–918.

3. *Scott v. Macy*, 249 F.2d 182, 183 n.2 (D.C. Cir. 1965).

4. Civil Service Reform Act of 1978, Pub. L. 95-454, §101(a), 92 Stat. 1111, 1117 (codified at 5 U.S.C. §2302(b)(10) [2007]).

5. See U.S. Office of Personnel Management, "Addressing Sexual Orientation Discrimination in Federal Civilian Employment: A Guide to Employee's Rights," available at www.opm.gov/er/address2/guide01.asp.

6. Executive Order 13,087, *Federal Register* 63 (June 2, 1998): 30,097.

7. Executive Order 12,968, §3.1(c)–(d), *Federal Register* 60 (August 7, 1995): 40,245, 40,250.

8. Adjudicative Guidelines for Determining Eligibility for Access to Classified Information, Guideline D: Sexual Behavior §12 (1997) (emphasis added).

9. Adjudicative Guidelines for Determining Eligibility for Access to Classified Information, Guideline D: Sexual Behavior §12 (2005) (emphasis added).

10. *Webster v. Doe*, 486 U.S. 592, 600–601 (1988); *U.S. Dep't of Navy v. Egan*, 484 U.S. 518, 526–530 (1988).

11. See *Webster*, 601–605; Lex K. Larson, *Employment Discrimination*, 2d ed. (New York: Matthew Bender, 2005), 10, §168.05; Christopher Scott Maravilla, "Judicial Review of Security Clearances for Homosexuals Post–*U.S. Department of the Navy v. Egan*," *St. Thomas L. Rev.* 13 (2001): 785.

12. Larson, *Employment Discrimination*, 10, §168.04[1].

13. U.S. Office of Personnel Management, "Addressing Sexual Orientation Discrimination."

14. Christopher Lee, "Groups Applaud Discrimination Ban," *Washington Post*, April 10, 2004, A3.

15. Executive Order 13,152, *Federal Register* 65 (May 4, 2000): 26,115.

16. This type of claim is named for *Bivens v. Six Unknown Named Agents*, 403 U.S. 388 (1971), in which the Supreme Court found an implied right of action under the Fourth Amendment.

17. For example, *Blade v. U.S. Bankr. Ct.*, 109 F. Supp. 2d 872, 875–878 (S.D. Ohio 2000), aff'd without opinion, 22 F. App'x 487 (6th Cir. 2001); *Rhyne v. Perry*, 91 CIV 8691 (LMM), 1995 U.S. Dist. Lexis 2129, *8–*16 (S.D.N.Y. February 24, 1995). But see *Hardison v. Cohen*, 375 F.3d 1262, 1266–1267 (11th Cir. 2004) (courts differ on whether federal employees are precluded from bringing a *Bivens* action seeking equitable relief, e.g., an injunction).

18. 42 U.S.C. §2000e-2(a)(1) (2007).

19. *Valentine-Johnson v. Roche*, 386 F.3d 800, 805 (6th Cir. 2004).

20. For example, *Medina v. Income Support Div.*, 413 F.3d 1131, 1135 (10th Cir. 2005); *Dawson v. Bumble and Bumble*, 398 F.3d 211, 217 (2d Cir. 2005).

21. 42 U.S.C. §2000e-16(a) (2007).

22. Courtney Weiner, "Sex Education: Recognizing Anti-Gay Harassment as Sex Discrimination under Title VII and Title IX," *Colum. Hum. Rts. L. Rev.* 37 (2005): 189, 227.

23. *Price Waterhouse v. Hopkins,* 490 U.S. 228 (1989).

24. Ibid., 235.

25. Ibid., 251 (plurality opinion).

26. *Nichols v. Azteca Rest. Enter., Inc.,* 256 F.3d 864, 872 (9th Cir. 2001).

27. *Oncale v. Sundowner Offshore Servs.,* 523 U.S. 75 (1998).

28. *Oncale v. Sundowner Offshore Servs.,* 83 F.3d 118, 118–119 (5th Cir. 1996).

29. *Oncale,* 79–81.

30. See Clare Diefenbach, "Same-Sex Sexual Harassment After *Oncale*: Meeting the 'Because of . . . Sex' Requirement," *Berkeley J. Gender L. & Just.* 22 (2007): 42, 44–48.

31. See Janet Halley, "Sexuality Harassment," in Catharine A. MacKinnon and Reva B. Siegel, eds., *Directions in Sexual Harassment Law* (New Haven, CT: Yale University Press, 2004), 182, 189–198; Diefenbach, "Same-Sex Sexual Harassment After *Oncale*," 56–57, 74. But see Marc S. Spindelman, "Sex Equality Panic," *Colum. J. Gender and L.* 13 (2004): 1.

32. See *Vickers v. Fairfield Med. Ctr.,* 453 F.3d 757 (6th Cir. 2006).

33. B. J. Chisholm, "The (Back)door of *Oncale v. Sundowner Offshore Services, Inc.*: 'Outing' Heterosexuality as a Gender-Based Stereotype," *Tul. J.L. and Sexuality* 10 (2001): 239, 240–241; Diefenbach, "Same-Sex Sexual Harassment After *Oncale*," 80–92; Keith J. Hilzendeger, "Walking Title VII's Tightrope: Advice for Gay and Lesbian Title VII Plaintiffs," *Tul. J.L. and Sexuality* 13 (2004): 705, 708–709, 715–725; Michael Sachs, "The Mystery of Title VII: The Various Interpretations of Title VII as Applied to Homosexual Plaintiffs," *Wis. Women's L.J.* 19 (2004): 359, 364–374; Weiner, "Sex Education," 208–216.

34. See Sachs, "The Mystery of Title VII," 371–374; Weiner, "Sex Education," 208–216.

35. *Brown v. Gen. Servs. Admin.,* 425 U.S. 820, 835 (1976).

36. For example, *Mlynczak v. Bodman,* 442 F.3d 1050, 1056–1057 (7th Cir. 2006); *Ford v. West,* 222 F.3d 767, 773 (10th Cir. 2000).

37. For example, *Rivera v. Heyman,* 157 F.3d 101, 105 (2d Cir. 1998); *Callanan v. Runyan,* 903 F. Supp. 1285, 1295–1296 (D. Minn. 1994), aff'd on other grounds, 75 F.3d 1293 (8th Cir. 1996).

38. Administrative Order 195 (Alaska March 5, 2002); Executive Order 2003-22 (Ariz. June 21, 2003); Executive Order 10 (Del. January 23, 2001); Governor's Policy Statement (Ind. April 26, 2005); Executive Order 07-24 (Kan. August 31, 2007); Executive Order. KBB 2004-54 (La. December 6, 2004); Executive Directive 2003-24 (Mich. December 23, 2003); Nondiscrimination–Equal Employment Opportunity Policy, Policy 3-0630 (in Montana Operations Manual §§2.21.4002, .4005, December 22, 2000); Executive Order No. 2007-10S (Ohio May 17, 2007); Executive Order 2003-10 (July 28, 2003), 33 Pa. Bull. 4063 (August 16, 2003); Executive Order 1 (Va. January 14, 2006).

39. Cal. Gov't Code §§12,926(d), 12,940 (2007); Act of May 25, 2007, ch. 295, §2, 2007 Colo. SB 25 (Lexis) (to be codified at Colo. Rev. Stat. §24-34-402; see §4 of the act for its effective date); Colo. Rev. Stat. §24-34-401(3) (2006); Executive Order D0035 90 (Colo. December 10, 1990); 4 Colo. Code Regs. §801, R. 9-3 (2006); Conn. Gen. Stat. §§46a–51(10), –81c, –81h, –81p (2007); D.C. Code §§2–1401.02(10), –1401.03(b), –1402.11 (2007); Haw. Rev. Stat. §§378–1, –2, –3(5) (2006); 775 Ill. Comp. Stat. 5/1–103(Q), 5/2–101(B), –102 (2006); Iowa Code §§216.2(7), .6 (2007); Me. Rev. Stat. tit. 5, §§4553(4), 4571–4572 (2006); Md. Code art. 49B, §§15(b), 16, 18

(2006); Executive Order 01.01.2007.09 (Md. May 15, 2007); Mass. Gen. Laws ch. 151B, §§1(5), 4(1)–(3) (2007); Minn. Stat. §§363A.03(16), (30), .08, .20(2), .26 (2006); Nev. Rev. Stat. §§281.370, 338.125, 613.310(2), .320, .330 (2005); N.H. Rev. Stat. §§354-A:2(VII), -A:7 (2006); N.J. Rev. Stat. §§10:5–5(e), –12(a)–(c) (2007); N.M. Stat. §§28–1–2(A)–(B), –7(A)–(E), –9(C) (2006); N.Y. Exec. Law §§292(5), 296(1)–(1-a), (11) (2007); Executive Order 33 (April 9, 1996), reprinted in N.Y. Comp. Codes R. and Regs. tit. 9, §5.33 (2006); Or. Rev. Stat. §659A.001(4), (9) (2005); Act of May 9, 2007, ch. 100, §§3–4, 2007 Ore. SB 2 (Lexis) (to be codified at Or. Rev. Stat. §§659A.006 and 659A.030; see the discussion of Oregon's domestic partnership regime in Chapter 6 for an explanation of the effective date of this provision); R.I. Gen. Laws §§28–5–6(7), –7 (2006); Vt. Stat, tit. 21, §§495, 495d(1) (2006); Wash. Rev. Code §§49.60.040(1), (3), .180–.200 (2007); Wis. Stat. §§111.32, .321–.325, .337, .36 (2006).

40. Cal. Fam. Code §297.5(f) (2007); Conn. Gen. Stat. §§46a-60, 46-38nn, -3800 (2007); D.C. Code §2-1401.02(17) (2007); Act of June 4, 2007, §1, 2007 N.H. Adv. Legis. Serv. ch. 58 (to be codified at N.H. Rev. Stat. §457-A:6 effective January 1, 2008); N.J. Rev. Stat. §37:1-32(g) (2007); Act of May 9, 2007, ch. 99, §9(1), 2007 Ore. HB 2007 (Lexis) (see the discussion of Oregon's domestic partnership regime in Chapter 6 for an explanation of the effective date of this provision).

41. 42 U.S.C. §2000e(a) (2007); *Fitzpatrick v. Bitzer,* 427 U.S. 445 (1976).

42. For example, 42 U.S.C. §§1983, 1985 (2007); see Larson, *Employment Discrimination,* 10, §168.03; John C. Jeffries Jr., "In Praise of the Eleventh Amendment and Section 1983," *Va. L. Rev.* 84 (1998): 47; Pamela S. Karlan, "The Irony of Immunity: The Eleventh Amendment, Irreparable Injury, and Section 1983," *Stan. L. Rev.* 53 (2001): 1311; Leonard, "Sexual Minority Rights in the Workplace," 147–148.

43. *Romer v. Evans,* 517 U.S. 620 (1996).

44. Ibid., 624.

45. Ibid., 632.

46. *City of Cleburne v. Cleburne Living Ctr.,* 473 U.S. 432 (1985).

47. *Quinn v. Nassau County Police Dep't,* 53 F. Supp. 2d 347, 350–351 (E.D.N.Y. 1999).

48. *Pickering v. Bd. of Educ.,* 391 U.S. 563, 568 (1968).

49. Ibid.

50. *Connick v. Meyers,* 461 U.S. 138, 150–151 (1983).

51. *Pickering,* 572–573.

52. *Rowland v. Mad River Local Sch. Dist.,* 730 F.2d 444, 449 (6th Cir. 1984).

53. *Rowland v. Mad River Local Sch. Dist.,* 470 U.S. 1009, 1012 (1985) (Brennan, J., dissenting).

54. *Weaver v. Nebo Sch. Dist.,* 29 F. Supp. 2d 1279, 1283–1286, 1290–1291 (D. Utah 1998).

55. *Tester v. City of New York,* 95 Civ. 7972 (LMM), 1997 U.S. Dist. Lexis 1937 (S.D.N.Y. Feb. 25, 1997).

56. *Lawrence v. Texas,* 539 U.S. 558 (2003); *Shahar v. Bowers,* 114 F.3d 1097, 1110 (11th Cir. 1997).

57. *Merrick v. Bd. of Higher Educ.,* 841 P.2d 646 (Or. Ct. App. 1992).

58. Ibid., 650.

59. See note 40.

60. Larson, *Employment Discrimination,* 6, §114.03[1].

61. Ibid., 10, §174.01.

62. Ibid., §§174.04, .06.

63. For example, *Hicks v. Arthur*, 843 F. Supp. 949, 956–957 (E.D. Pa. 1994); *Greenwood v. Taft, Stettinius, and Hollister*, 663 N.E.2d 1030, 1031–1034 (Ohio Ct. App. 1995); *Webb v. Puget Sound Broad. Co.*, 138 Lab. Cas. (CCH) 58,612 (Wash. Ct. App. 1998) (predating the enactment of the statutory protections listed in Table 5.1).

64. See, for example, *Torrez v. BEI Graphics Corp.*, 96-1436, 1998 U.S. App. Lexis 1203 (10th Cir. January 27, 1998). But see S.C. Code §41-1-110 (2006).

65. 42 U.S.C. §2000e(a)–(b), 2000e-1(a) (2007).

66. See, for example, *Peper v. Princeton Univ. Bd. of Trs.*, 389 A.2d 465, 476–478 (N.J. 1978); *Gay Law Students Ass'n v. Pac. Tel. and Tel. Co.*, 595 P.2d 592, 597–602 (Cal. 1979).

67. Maria O'Brien Hylton, Constance Hiatt, Shannon Minter, and Teresa S. Collett, "Same Sex Marriage and Its Implications for Employee Benefits: Proceedings of the 2005 Meeting of the Association of American Law Schools Sections on Employee Benefits, and Sexual Orientation and Gender Identity Issues," *Emp. Rts. & Emp. Pol'y J.* 9 (2005): 499, 501.

68. Cal. Fam. Code §297.5 (2007); Cal. Gov't Code §§22,775, 22,818, 22,830 (2007); Conn. Gen. Stat. §46b-38nn (2007); D.C. Code §§32-701(7), -706 (2007); N.J. Rev. Stat. §§37:1-32(e), -33, 52:14-17.26(d), -17.28 (2007); R.I. Gen. Laws §36-12-1(3) (2006); Vt. Stat. tit. 15, §1204 (2006); *Alaska Civil Liberties Union v. Alaska*, 122 P.3d (Alaska 2005), 781; Executive Order 2003-010 (N.M. April 9, 2003); Executive Order 28 (November 18, 1983), reprinted in N.Y. Comp. Codes R. and Regs. tit. 9, §4.28 (2006); Or. Admin. R. 101-015-0005(3) (2006); Wash. Admin. Code 182-12-260 (2006); Dep't Admin. Servs., State of Iowa, *Fact Sheet: Domestic Partner Benefits* (2007), available at http://das.hre.iowa.gov/benefits/benefit_documents/domestic_partner_fact_sheet.pdf; Human Res. Div., State of Mass., *Guidance on Same-Sex Spousal Benefits* (May 10, 2004); Employee Benefits Bureau, State of Mont., *Employee Benefits Annual Change Booklet* 13 (2005); Adriana Colindres, "AFSCME Members Ratify Contract," *State Journal-Register* (Springfield, Ill.), July 2, 2004, at 11; Press Release, Office of the Governor of Illinois, "Governor Blagojevich Extends Health Benefits to State Employee Domestic Partners" (May 8, 2006), available at www.illinois.gov/PressReleases/ShowPressRelease.cfm?SubjectID=1&RecNum=4837; Gary J. Remal, "Domestic Partners Win State Benefits," *Portland Press Herald*, March 9, 2001, 1A; see also *Alaska v. Alaska Civil Liberties Union*, 159 P.3d 513 (Alaska 2006) (approving regulations adopted by the state to comply with the court's 2005 decision and ordering the state to begin offering benefits no later than January 1, 2007).

69. *Alaska Civil Liberties Union*, 781; *Snetsinger v. Mont. Univ. Sys.*, 104 P.3d 445 (Mont. 2004); *Tanner v. Or. Health Sci. Univ.*, 971 P.2d 435, 444–448 (Or. Ct. App. 1998); Order, *Bedford v. N.H. Community Tech. College Sys.*, 04-E-229 and 04-E-230 (N.H. Super. Ct. May 3, 2006) (in May 2007, the State of New Hampshire dropped its appeal in this case, see Press Release, Gay and Lesbian Advocates and Defenders, "Victory for Gay New Hampshire Employees Seeking Family Benefits," available at www.glad.org/News_Room/press142-05-07-07.html).

70. *Hinman v. Dep't Pers. Admin.*, 213 Cal. Rptr. 410 (Cal. Ct. App. 1985); *Rutgers Council of AAUP Chapters v. Rutgers*, 689 A.2d 828 (N.J. Super. Ct. App. Div. 1997); *Phillips v. Wis. Pers. Comm'n*, 482 N.W.2d 121 (Wis. Ct. App. 1992).

71. See *Nat'l Pride at Work, Inc. v. Governor of Mich.*, 274 Mich. App. 147, 173 (Mich. Ct. App.), appeal granted, 731 N.W.2d 405 (Mich. 2007) (holding that

Michigan's "defense of marriage" constitutional amendment "prohibits public employers from recognizing same-sex unions for any purpose," including the provision of domestic-partner health insurance benefits); Op. Att'y Gen. 07-004, 2007 Ky. AG Lexis 4 (June 1, 2007) (concluding that the domestic partner benefits regimes adopted or under consideration by the University of Kentucky and the University of Louisville violated the "defense of marriage" provision in the Kentucky constitution). To circumvent these prohibitions, public employers in Kentucky and Michigan expanded their plans to cover individuals who live together in nonspousal relationships. P. J. Huffstutter, "A Clash over Gay Couples' Benefits," *Los Angeles Times,* July 8, 2007, 19; Art Jester, "Group Pushes for Legal Action on UK's Benefits Plan," *Lexington Herald-Leader,* June 30, 2007, 5. However, these efforts have only led to further political attacks; for example, in his call for a special session of the legislature in July 2007, the governor of Kentucky included the need for action on a ban on domestic partner benefits that would close this loophole left open in the attorney general's opinion. Megan Boehnke, "Including Partner Benefits Disputed," *Lexington Herald-Leader,* July 3, 2007, A8.

72. 29 U.S.C. §§1002, 1144(a) (2007).

73. *Shaw v. Delta Air Lines, Inc.,* 463 U.S. 85 (1983).

74. Human Rights Campaign (HRC) Foundation, *Workplace: Equal Benefits Ordinances* (2006), available at www.hrc.org/Template.cfm?Section=Get_Informed2&Template=/ContentManagement/ContentDisplay.cfm&ContentID=27323.

75. *In re Council of the City of New York v. Bloomberg,* 846 N.E.2d 433 (N.Y. 2006).

76. *Air Transp. Ass'n of Am. v. City and County of San Francisco,* 992 F. Supp. 1149, 1160–1180 (N.D. Cal. 1998); see also *Catholic Charities of Me., Inc. v. City of Portland,* 304 F. Supp. 2d 77 (D. Me. 2004).

77. See Catherine L. Fisk, "ERISA Preemption of State and Local Laws on Domestic Partnership and Sexual Orientation Discrimination in Employment," *UCLA Women's L.J.* 8 (1998), 283; Jeffrey G. Sherman, "Domestic Partnership and ERISA Preemption," *Tul. L. Rev.* 76 (2001): 373, 398.

78. Human Rights Campaign Foundation, *The State of the Workplace for Lesbian, Gay, Bisexual and Transgender Americans: 2004* (2005), 11; Kimberly Blanton, "Firms Block Gays' Benefits, Cite US Law," *Boston Globe,* December 18, 2004, A1.

79. 1 U.S.C. §7 (2007).

80. See Neal S. Schelberg and Carrie L. Mitnick, "Same-Sex Marriage: The Evolving Landscape for Employee Benefits," *Hofstra Lab. and Emp. L.J.* 22 (2004): 65, 74.

81. I.R.C. §§105(b), 106(a) (2007); Treas. Reg. §1.106-1 (1960).

82. 1 U.S.C. §7 (2007).

83. I.R.C. §§105(b), 152(d) (2007); Notice 2004-79, 2004-49 I.R.B. 898.

84. I.R.S. Priv. Ltr. Rul. 200339001 (June 13, 2003).

85. Cal. Rev. and Tax Code §17,021.7 (2007); Conn. Gen. Stat. §46b–38pp (2007); D.C. Code §47-1803.02(a)(2)(W) (2007); Vt. Stat. tit. 32, §5812 (2006); Mass. Dep't Rev., Tech. Info. Release 04-17, §D(1)(b)(i) (July 7, 2004); Act of May 9, 2007, ch. 99, §§9(8), 11, 2007 Ore. HB 2007 (Lexis) (see the discussion of Oregon's domestic partnership regime in Chapter 6 for an explanation of the effective date of this provision); Op. Att'y Gen. 8268, 49 Or. Op. Att'y Gen. 197 (May 25, 1999); Or. Admin. R. 150-316.007-(B) (2006).

Although New Jersey affords parties to a civil union the same tax treatment as married couples, New Jersey's exemptions for fringe benefits are in some ways narrower than the federal exemptions. See N.J. Rev. Stat. §§54A:5-1(a) (defining gross income to include salaries and wages, whether paid in cash or in property), :6-6 (exclusion for compensation for personal injuries or sickness but failing to mention premiums for health insurance), :6-24 (exclusion for certain cafeteria plans), 37:1-32(n) (affording the same tax treatment to parties to a civil union as is afforded to married couples) (2007); see also N.J. Div. Tax'n, Tech. Bull. TB-39(R) (March 3, 2003) (indicating that New Jersey has not adopted the federal tax treatment of cafeteria plans and has adopted a more limited exclusion).

86. *Kramarsky v. Stahl Mgm't*, 401 N.Y.S.2d 943, 945 (N.Y. Sup. Ct. 1977); see Richard R. Powell, *The Law of Real Property*, rev. ed., 2, §16B.09 (Newark, NJ: Matthew Bender, 2006).

87. Kaiser Family Foundation, "Inside-OUT: A Report on the Experiences of Lesbians, Gays and Bisexuals in America and the Public's Views on Issues and Policies Related to Sexual Orientation" (2001), chart 4.

88. Compare Civil Rights Amendments Act of 2005, H.R. 288, 109th Cong. §3 (2005), with Civil Rights Amendments Act of 1993, H.R. 423, 103d Cong. §3 (1993).

89. Cal. Gov't Code §§12,927, 12,955, 12,955.4 (2007); Conn. Gen. Stat. §§46a-64b, -81e, -81f, -81p (2007); D.C. Code §§2-1401.02(30), .03(d), -1402.21, .24 (2007); Haw. Rev. Stat. §§515-2 to -5, -8 (2006); 775 Ill. Comp. Stat. 5/1-103(Q), 5/3-101, -102, -106, 5/4-101 to -102 (2006); Iowa Code §§216.8, .8A, .12 (2007); Me. Rev. Stat. tit. 5, §§4553(6), 4582 (2006); Md. Code art. 49B, §§20–23 (2006); Mass. Gen. Laws ch. 151B, §§1, 4(3B)–(3C), (6)–(7), (7B), (14) (2007); Minn. Stat. §§363A.09, .21, .26 (2006); N.H. Rev. Stat. §§354-A:9, -A:10, -A:13 (2006); N.J. Rev. Stat. §§10:5-5(n), -12(g)–(l), (o) (2007); N.M. Stat. §§28-1-7(G)–(H), -9(A)–(D) (2006); N.Y. Exec. Law §§296(3-b), (5)(a)–(d), (11), 296-a (2007); R.I. Gen. Laws §§34-37-4, -4.2 to -4.4, -5.2, -5.4 (2006); Vt. Stat. tit. 8, §10,403 (2006); ibid., tit. 9, §§4503(a), 4504(2), (5); Wash. Rev. Code §§49.60.040, .175–.176, .222–.224 (2007); Wis. Stat. §§66.1201(2m), .1213(3), .1331(2m), 106.50 (2006); Act of May 9, 2007, ch. 100, §§3, 8, 2007 Ore. SB 2 (Lexis) (to be codified at Or. Rev. Stat. §§659A.006[3], .421; see the discussion of Oregon's domestic partnership regime in Chapter 6 for an explanation of the effective date of this provision).

90. Cal. Fam. Code §297.5(f) (2007); Conn. Gen. Stat. §§46a-64c, 46b-38nn, -38oo (2007); D.C. Code §2-1401.02(17) (2007); N.J. Rev. Stat. §37:1-32(g) (2007); Vt. Stat. tit. 15, §1204(e)(7) (2006); Act of June 4, 2007, §1, 2007 N.H. Adv. Legis. Serv. ch. 58 (to be codified at N.H. Rev. Stat. §457-A:6 effective January 1, 2008); Act of May 9, 2007, ch. 99, §9(1), 2007 Ore. HB 2007 (Lexis) (see the discussion of Oregon's domestic partnership regime in Chapter 6 for an explanation of the effective date of this provision); *Goodridge v. Dep't of Pub. Health*, 798 N.E.2d 941 (Mass. 2003).

91. 15 U.S.C. §1691 (2007).

92. 12 C.F.R. §202.6(b)(8) (2007); see Equal Credit Opportunity, *Federal Register* 68 (March 18, 2003): 13,144, 13,150.

93. 12 C.F.R. §202.6(b)(8) (2007).

94. E.g., Alaska Stat. §18.80.240 (2006); Colo. Rev. Stat. §24-34-502 (2006); Del. Code tit. 6, §4603 (2007); Mich. Comp. Laws Serv. §37.2502 (2007); Mont. Code §49-2-305 (2005); N.D. Cent. Code §14-02.5-02 (2005).

95. Del. Code tit. 6, §4602(17) (2007); *Swanner v. Anchorage Equal Rights Comm'n*, 874 P.2d 274, 278 (Alaska 1994); *McCready v. Hoffius*, 586 N.W.2d 723, 725–728 (Mich. 1998), vacated in part on other grounds, 593 N.W.2d 545 (Mich. 1999).

96. N.D. Cent. Code §14-02.5-02(4) (2005); *N. Dakota Fair Hous. Council, Inc. v. Peterson*, 625 N.W.2d 551 (N.D. 2001).

97. Compare *Thomas v. Anchorage Equal Rights Comm'n*, 102 P.3d 937 (Alaska 2004), and *Smith v. Fair Emp. and Housing Comm'n*, 913 P.2d 909 (Cal. 1996), with *McCready v. Hoffius*, 593 N.W.2d 545 (Mich. 1999), and *Minnesota ex rel. Cooper v. French*, 460 N.W.2d 2, 8–11 (Minn. 1990).

98. 24 C.F.R. §960.203(a) (2007).

99. Ibid., §§982.307, .452(b)(1); 42 U.S.C. §1437f(o)(6)(B) (2007).

100. 24 C.F.R. §982.452(b)(3) (2007); see ibid., §§982.301(b)(10), .307(a)(2)–(3); see also *Comm'n on Human Rights and Opportunities v. Sullivan Assocs.*, 739 A.2d 238, 245–246 (Conn. 1999); *Att'y Gen. v. Brown*, 511 N.E.2d 1103, 1105–1107 (Mass. 1987); *Franklin Tower One, L.L.C. v. N.M.*, 725 A.2d 1104 (N.J. 1999).

101. 42 U.S.C. §1437a(b)(3) (2007); 24 C.F.R. §§5.403, 960.201(a)(1), 982.4(b), .201(c)(3) (2007); see Definitions and Other General Requirements for Assistance Under the United States Housing Act of 1937, *Federal Register* 61 (February 13, 1996): 5662, 5663–5664.

102. Oxford Housing Authority, "Important Applicant Information," available at www.oxfordhousing.org/Application%20Information.htm.

103. N.Y.C. Housing Authority, "Applying for Public Housing," available at www.nyc.gov/html/nycha/html/assistance/app_for_pubhsg.shtml; N.Y.C. Housing Authority, "Guide to Section 8 Housing Assistance Program," available at www.nyc.gov/html/nycha/downloads/pdf/070213.pdf.

104. Powell, *The Law of Real Property*, 13, §79D.07(2)(e); Frank S. Alexander, "The Housing of America's Families: Control, Exclusion, and Privilege," *Emory L.J.* 54 (2005): 1231, 1260.

105. Alexander, "The Housing of America's Families," 1260, 1263.

106. Ibid., 1265.

107. *Village of Belle Terre v. Boraas*, 416 U.S. 1 (1974).

108. Ibid., 9.

109. *Moore v. City of E. Cleveland*, 431 U.S. 494 (1977) (plurality).

110. See Powell, *The Law of Real Property*, 13, §79D.07(2)(e); Alexander, "The Housing of America's Families," 1263.

111. *City of Santa Barbara v. Adamson*, 610 P.2d 436 (Cal. 1980); *City of Des Plaines v. Trottner*, 216 N.E.2d 116 (Ill. 1966); *Charter Township of Delta v. Dinolfo*, 351 N.W.2d 831 (Mich. 1984); *State v. Baker*, 405 A.2d 368 (N.J. 1979); *McMinn v. Town of Oyster Bay*, 488 N.E.2d 1240 (N.Y. 1985); *Hopkins v. Zoning Hearing Bd. of Abingdon Township*, 423 A.2d 1082 (Pa. Commw. Ct. 1980).

112. Sara L. Dunski, "Make Way for the New Kid on the Block: The Possible Zoning Implications of *Lawrence v. Texas*," *U. Ill. L. Rev.* (2005): 847.

113. *Restatement (Second) of the Law of Property: Landlord and Tenant* §6.1 (St. Paul, MN: American Law Institute Publishers, 1977); Powell, *The Law of Real Property*, 2, §16B.03.

114. N.J. Rev. Stat. §§2A:18-61.1, -61.3, -61.4 (2007); see *316 49 St. Assocs. Ltd. P'ship v. Galvez*, 635 A.2d 1013, 1016–1018 (N.J. Super. Ct. App. Div. 1994).

115. Powell, *The Law of Real Property*, 2, §§16A.02[6]–[7], 16B.05[2]; see, for example, 42 U.S.C. §§1437d(l), 1437f(d)(1)(B), (o)(7) (2007); I.R.C. §42(h)(6)(B)(i) (2007); 24 C.F.R. §§247.3, 966.4, 982.310 (2007); Rev. Rul. 2004-82, Q- and A-5, 2004-2 C.B. 350; Rev. Proc. 2005-37, 2005-28 I.R.B. 79; Berkeley, Cal., Rent Stabi-

lization and Eviction for Good Cause Ordinance §13.76.130 (2007); Los Angeles, Cal., Rent Stabilization Ordinance §151.09 (2007).

116. N.Y. Public Housing Law §14(4)(a) (2007).

117. *Braschi v. Stahl Assocs. Co.*, 543 N.E.2d 49 (N.Y. 1989) (plurality); see Paris R. Baldacci, "Pushing the Law to Encompass the Reality of Our Families: Protecting Lesbian and Gay Families from Eviction from Their Homes—*Braschi*'s Functional Definition of 'Family' and Beyond," *Fordham Urb. L.J.* 21 (1994): 973.

118. N.Y. Public Housing Law §14(4)(c) (2007).

119. Powell, *The Law of Real Property*, 2, §16B.09(2)(c).

120. Marie A. Failinger, "Remembering Mrs. Murphy: A Remedies Approach to the Conflict Between Gay/Lesbian Renters and Religious Landlords," *Cap. U. L. Rev.* 29 (2001): 383, 398.

121. M. V. Lee Badgett, *Money, Myths, and Change: The Economic Lives of Lesbians and Gay Men* (Chicago: University of Chicago Press, 2001), 241; Lambda Legal, "Out at Work: A Guide for LGBT Employees" (2004), 20, available at www.lambdalegal.org/take-action/tool-kits/out-at-work.

122. Lambda Legal, "Out at Work."

123. HRC, "How to Start an Employee Network Group," available at www.hrc.org/Template.cfm?Section=Resources1&Template=/ContentManagement/ContentDisplay.cfm&ContentID=27356

124. Badgett, *Money, Myths, and Change*, 241–245; Lambda Legal, "Out at Work," 20.

125. In addition to Lambda Legal's publication "Out at Work," mentioned earlier, HRC has published "Achieving a Non-Discrimination Policy that Includes Sexual Orientation," available at www.hrc.org/Template.cfm?Section=Resources1&Template=/ContentManagement/ContentDisplay.cfm&ContentID=11126, and "Steps to Achieve Domestic Partner Benefits in Your Workplace," available at www.hrc.org/Template.cfm?Section=Resources1&Template=/ContentManagement/ContentDisplay.cfm&ContentID=10910. The National Gay and Lesbian Task Force has published a comprehensive (albeit a bit dated) manual, "The Domestic Partnership Organizing Manual for Employee Benefits," available at www.thetaskforce.org/downloads/reports/reports/1999DomesticPartnershipOrganizingManual.pdf.

126. Nancy E. Day and Patricia Schoenrade, "The Relationship Among Reported Disclosure of Sexual Orientation, Anti-Discrimination Policies, Top Management Support and Work Attitudes of Gay and Lesbian Employees," *Pers. Rev.* 29 (2000): 346, 357–360; Kristin H. Griffith and Michelle R. Hebl, "The Disclosure Dilemma for Gay Men and Lesbians: 'Coming Out' at Work," *J. Applied Psychol.* 87 (2002): 1191, 1192–1196; Sharon S. Rostosky and Ellen D. B. Riggle, "'Out' at Work: The Relation of Actor and Partner Workplace Policy and Internalized Homophobia to Disclosure Status," *J. Couns. Psychol.* 49 (2002): 411, 416.

127. W. E. Douglas Creed and Maureen A. Scully, "Songs of Ourselves: Employees' Deployment of Social Identity in Workplace Encounters," *J. Mgm't Inquiry* 9 (2000): 391, 392.

128. Badgett, *Money, Myths, and Change*, 246.

6

Marriage and
Its Alternatives

Elyse and Cindy's Story

We had been together for two years and were fully committed to spending the rest of our lives together. We'd bought a house together and had begun talking about getting a dog and having children. But there was something missing—a wedding. We should be married, we thought (after all, you really shouldn't have kids before you get married, right?). But how? It felt like the most logical next step, though we didn't know where to start. We didn't know any other gay couples who had done it—not even in the form of a commitment ceremony, which is all we were afforded under the law anyway. But we went ahead and started planning the very big (very "hetero") wedding—the largest and most extravagant either of our families had seen.

So, "why get married?" we thought and were quite often asked (even out loud, on occasion). It's not that we thought it would "solidify" our relationship in any way and we weren't looking to make a statement. We were rock solid and stable as a couple and not quite what you would call politically active. But still, it was so strong a desire for us. Strangely, living outside societal norms had done nothing to diminish our desire to do what all those straight people were doing to "validate" their love and commitment for each other. Validation for us, however, was not linked to the recognition of our "marriage" by strangers. Rather, it was committing ourselves to each other in front of God and our friends and families. Our marriage was thus recognized and celebrated by all the people we loved and who loved us. In the toast, Cindy's brother hit the nail on the head: "It is not the church, nor the state that gives validity to today's events, but rather the solemn vow that Cindy and Elyse have made to each other, and we are going to celebrate that today."

Neither of us thought it would, but getting married made us feel different. Though it's still hard to describe, there is an overwhelming sense of peace in being married. An unspoken promise that neither of you will just leave, that you will fight with everything to keep it all together. It is a feeling to take comfort in every day.

Then the big announcement came—domestic partnership is coming to New Jersey! Looking back, I thought we would have been more excited than we were. Two years had passed and we were living the American dream. We had a beautiful house in the suburbs, a dog and a baby on the way. I guess we just thought that we had everything we needed and any further validation was gratuitous at best. (Or it could have been that I was pregnant and we were more excited about the baby coming than anything else on this Earth.) On July 10, 2004, there were elaborate celebrations planned for several towns across the state. Maplewood, a town just a few miles away, hosted the big event for our part of the state. It was a steamy, hot and humid day and I was due in two weeks, and really not in the mood, but we went. What kind of lesbians would we be if we didn't join in the celebration of what may likely be the most important legislation that we will see in our lifetimes? Hundreds of couples stood in line for hours to get their domestic-partnership certificates. We did not. We decided to wait until the baby was born and then go to our town hall and file there.

A few weeks later, baby in tow, we walked into the county clerk's office with several documents proving we were more than roommates and stood proudly, and nervously, before the clerk and uttered, "We are here to file for our domestic partnership." Little did we realize that we would be the first couple in Cranford to file and the county clerk would be more nervous than us about the whole thing. After a nervous giggle, introductions, a few questions about the baby, and hearty and sincere congratulations, she pulled out her guide to filing domestic partnerships, cracked it open, and diligently followed each step as outlined in the crisp new pages of her reference book, so as to ensure it was done properly. After a very long hour of questions and paperwork, it was done. She smiled proudly, shook our hands and asked if we would send a picture for the wall. We smiled back, thanked her graciously and assured her we would send a picture shortly. We left there as state-recognized domestic partners. We did send a picture and found through a stranger that recognized Cindy on the bus that it still hangs there today.

Sadly, it felt nice, but that was all. It seemed too little. Domestic partnership in New Jersey just doesn't seem to mean enough. Perhaps that's just the cynic in me, because after all, we'd already had all our ducks in a row. We had our lawyer draw up all the legal documents we needed (wills, medical and financial powers of attorney, and advance directives) to protect us financially and to afford us the rights automatically given spouses. But we had done it. And I am glad. I think lately, I have begun to look at it differently. I think it is our responsibility to take advantage of what we do have—every little crumb we are thrown (there goes the cynic again). Every legal step is a big one and I have slowly come to appreciate that.

As far as the state and country still have to go, it has been our very pleasant experience that the people in our community have been nothing but friendly and welcoming, though curious. But we see ourselves as educators. We take every opportunity to smile and to welcome and encourage people to ask us questions about our relationship and our family. We are the people next door, the ones at the table next to you in your favorite restaurant and in the pew behind you in church.

We look forward to the state and the country making great strides toward complete equality and eager acceptance in our lifetime; for gay marriage to be not only legally recognized, but sincerely celebrated and honored. Until then, however, we remain the dedicated, loving family we have always been.[1]

In many ways, same-sex couples—like my sister Elyse and her partner, Cindy, or my partner, Hien, and I—are similar to our heterosexual counterparts. When we enter a committed relationship, we often feel the need to make our commitment publicly known to ensure that it is acknowledged and honored by others. To this end, each couple determines the correct mixture of social and legal recognition for their relationship. Will the public affirmation of their commitment take place in a church, at city hall, in a park, or at a friend's home? Will the ceremony be religious or secular? Will many or only a few people be present? Will legal recognition of the relationship be sought from the state or arranged through private contracts, agreements, and other legal documents?

To decide among these alternatives can be difficult for any couple, gay or straight. But for same-sex couples the decision is further complicated by the fact that same-sex marriage has proved to be a lightning-rod issue. It has galvanized the reactionary right, which has made same-sex marriage a defining issue in its "culture war." Evidence of the right's success is not hard to come by—just consider the number of states (and the federal government) that prohibit legal recognition of same-sex relationships and the number of religions that have been riven by debates over blessing same-sex marriages and the ordination of openly lesbian or gay clergy.

Naturally, lesbians and gay men and their straight allies have protested these reactionary measures, even going so far as to engage in acts of civil disobedience. In early 2004, the City of San Francisco issued wedding licenses to a deluge of same-sex couples despite California's prohibition against same-sex marriage. A week later, the clerk of Sandoval County, New Mexico, issued marriage licenses to same-sex couples for less than a day before being told by the state attorney general to desist. And, reacting to President Bush's announcement of support for a federal constitutional ban on same-sex marriage, a number of municipalities in New Jersey, New York, and Oregon began issuing marriage licenses to same-sex couples; ministers in New York solemnized same-sex marriages in the face of criminal charges; and one municipality even stopped issuing marriage licenses at all (i.e., both to same- and different-sex couples) until its state supreme court issued a decision resolving the question of whether same-sex couples are permitted to marry.

Although the issue of same-sex marriage has at times united each side, it divided the lesbian and gay community and its straight allies following the 2004 presidential election, when lesbians and gay men were blamed for the

Democrats' losses. This was not, however, the first time that controversy surfaced over the community's pursuit of the right to marry.

The Debate over Same-Sex Marriage

The debate over same-sex marriage first raged in the early 1970s, when legal challenges to state marriage laws were flourishing. That debate quieted after a series of resounding defeats in the courts. Intermittent challenges to state marriage laws persisted, but the issue generally remained dormant until the late 1980s. Since that time, the debate has taken a triangular shape: At one point of the triangle, you have the proponents of same-sex marriage; at the other two, you have the heterosexual and the lesbian and gay opponents of same-sex marriage, who oppose same-sex marriage for different reasons.

The Proponents' Arguments

Proponents take the denial of access to marriage to be "the most public affront possible to . . . civil equality."[2] In American society, marriage "is a social and public recognition of a private commitment"[3] that represents "the centerpiece of our entire social structure, the core of the traditional notion of 'family.'"[4] Denying same-sex couples this "essential affirmation" relegates them to second-class status, even though their relationships may be as strong as (and, in some cases, stronger than) heterosexual relationships.[5]

Moreover, same-sex couples already voluntarily assume many of the responsibilities associated with marriage (e.g., providing emotional and financial support to each other and to their children). Yet, in denying same-sex couples the right to marry, society deprives them of access to the many benefits that are associated with marriage. The Massachusetts Supreme Judicial Court has provided the following laundry list of benefits that attach to a marital relationship:

> The benefits accessible only by way of a marriage license are enormous, touching nearly every aspect of life and death. . . . With no attempt to be comprehensive, we note that some of the statutory benefits conferred by the Legislature on those who enter into civil marriage include, as to property: joint Massachusetts income tax filing; tenancy by the entirety (a form of ownership that provides certain protections against creditors and allows for the automatic descent of property to the surviving spouse without probate); extension of the benefit of the homestead protection (securing up to $300,000 in equity from creditors) to one's spouse and children; automatic rights to inherit the property of a deceased spouse who does not leave a will; the rights of elective share and of dower (which allow surviving spouses certain property rights where the decedent spouse has not made adequate provision for the survivor in a will); entitlement to wages owed to a deceased employee; eligibility to continue certain businesses of a deceased spouse; the right to share the medical policy of one's spouse; thirty-nine week continuation of health coverage

for the spouse of a person who is laid off or dies; preferential options under the Commonwealth's pension system; preferential benefits in the Commonwealth's medical program . . . ; access to veterans' spousal benefits and preferences; financial protections for spouses of certain Commonwealth employees (fire fighters, police officers, prosecutors, among others) killed in the performance of duty; the equitable division of marital property on divorce; temporary and permanent alimony rights; the right to separate support on separation of the parties that does not result in divorce; and the right to bring claims for wrongful death and loss of consortium, and for funeral and burial expenses and punitive damages resulting from tort actions.

Exclusive marital benefits that are not directly tied to property rights include the presumptions of legitimacy and parentage of children born to a married couple; and evidentiary rights, such as the prohibition against spouses testifying against one another about their private conversations, applicable in both civil and criminal cases. Other statutory benefits of a personal nature available only to married individuals include qualification for bereavement or medical leave to care for individuals related by blood or marriage; an automatic "family member" preference to make medical decisions for an incompetent or disabled spouse who does not have a contrary health care proxy; the application of predictable rules of child custody, visitation, support, and removal out-of-State when married parents divorce; priority rights to administer the estate of a deceased spouse who dies without a will, and requirement that surviving spouse must consent to the appointment of any other person as administrator; and the right to interment in the lot or tomb owned by one's deceased spouse.

Where a married couple has children, their children are also directly or indirectly, but no less auspiciously, the recipients of the special legal and economic protections obtained by civil marriage. Notwithstanding the Commonwealth's strong public policy to abolish legal distinctions between marital and nonmarital children in providing for the support and care of minors, the fact remains that marital children reap a measure of family stability and economic security based on their parents' legally privileged status that is largely inaccessible, or not as readily accessible, to nonmarital children. Some of these benefits are social, such as the enhanced approval that still attends the status of being a marital child. Others are material, such as the greater ease of access to family-based State and Federal benefits that attend the presumptions of one's parentage.[6]

Some proponents argue that, despite the lack of universal support within the lesbian and gay community for pursuing marriage, the community should nonetheless pursue the right to marry because that right should exist for those who wish to avail themselves of it.[7] Other proponents further maintain that, while the institution of marriage has many disadvantages, expanding the institution to include same-sex couples may "transform it into something new."[8] For instance, "abolishing the traditional gender requirements of marriage can be one of the means, perhaps the principal one, through which the institution divests itself of the sexist trappings of the past."[9]

The Heterosexual Opposition

Outright Opponents. Some heterosexuals argue that the "law should encourage male-female marriage vows over homosexual attachments in the interests of physically, mentally, and psychologically healthy children."[10] They also fear that bestowing "the solemnity of legal marriage would wrongly send social cues that male-female marriages are not preferable."[11] Moreover, allowing same-sex couples to marry would create a slippery slope because the same reasoning would require us to allow bigamous and polygamous marriages, incestuous marriages, marriages between pedophiles and children, and marriages between people and animals.[12]

Opponents in Disguise. Other heterosexuals are not opposed to granting same-sex couples the protections and benefits of marriage; they simply oppose using the words "same-sex" and "marriage" together. They prefer terms such as "civil union" or "domestic partnership." These individuals are now usually viewed as occupying the middle ground between proponents and opponents of same-sex marriage.

But choosing a different label for the same store of rights and obligations is not a benign compromise. It serves only to visibly—and more permanently—relegate lesbians and gay men to the second-class status that they already inhabit, as witnessed by court decisions in Connecticut and New Jersey (described later in this chapter) that rely on the extension of all of the benefits and obligations of marriage to same-sex couples as a ground for insulating their relegation to a "separate, but equal" status from constitutional attack. A similar decision by the California Supreme Court seems to be a distinct possibility, as that court has asked the parties in a challenge to the constitutionality of that state's marriage laws to address several questions that suggest the court is "trying to determine whether the [California] domestic-partners law makes same-sex marriage necessary."[13] Yet, notwithstanding any legal sanction that may be granted to the idea that the word "marriage" does not matter, this "compromise" approach is really no more than a veiled means of denigrating same-sex relationships. As the Massachusetts Supreme Judicial Court so eloquently put it when rejecting the idea that civil unions could serve as a substitute for same-sex marriage: "The history of our nation has demonstrated that separate is seldom, if ever, equal."[14]

One need not look far for evidence of the truth of this proposition. Following the enactment of New Jersey's civil union regime, UPS drew an important distinction between its unionized employees who had entered into same-sex marriages in Massachusetts and those who had entered into civil unions in New Jersey: The Massachusetts unionized employees were allowed to add their spouses to their health coverage, but the New Jersey unionized employees were not allowed to do so.[15] According to UPS, the Massachusetts couples qualified for benefits because they were "married" and, therefore, legal "spouses" under the terms of the union contract; in contrast, the New Jersey couples did not qualify for benefits because they were merely parties to a civil union—even though a civil union is supposed to afford the couples the same rights and obligations as marriage, and New Jersey law specifies that any reference to "marriage" or "spouse" "in any law, rule, regulation, judicial or administrative proceeding or otherwise" includes a civil union.[16] This specious distinction, which UPS has not been alone in making and which it refused to disavow until the governor of New Jersey brought political pressure to bear on the company, belies the argument that the word "marriage" does not matter.

The Lesbian and Gay Opposition

Some lesbians and gay men argue that marriage has a history that should not be palatable to gay men—and certainly not to lesbians: "Steeped in a patriarchal system that looks to ownership, property, and dominance of men over women as its basis, the institution of marriage long has been the focus of radical feminist revulsion. Marriage defines certain relationships as more valid than all others. Lesbian and gay relationships . . . are always at the bottom of the heap of social acceptance and importance."[17]

Lesbians and gay opponents have further argued that gaining access to marriage "will not transform our society from one that makes narrow, but dramatic, distinctions between those who are married and those who are not married to one that respects and encourages choice of relationships and family diversity."[18] In lieu of seeking the right to marry, these opponents contend that we should seek to "bridge the economic and privilege gap between the married and the unmarried."[19] They would prefer to see other types of relationships recognized as being equally valuable and for marital conditions on access to government benefits (e.g., health care and Social Security) to be eliminated.[20]

These opponents also contend that to ape heterosexual marriage simply to gain the benefits that accompany it is to sell ourselves short. Rather than seek to be accepted because we are like heterosexuals, they argue that we should seek to be accepted "*despite* our differences from the dominant culture and the choices we make regarding our relationships."[21]

Coming to Grips with the Debate

At some point, each of us will be confronted with these arguments and will need to resolve our own feelings about the collective rush toward marriage. Speaking from my own experience, I must admit that the arguments made by the lesbian and gay opponents of same-sex marriage had a distinct appeal, and for a long time, I was rather skeptical about the idea of same-sex marriage. During the nine years that Michael and I were together, same-sex marriage was not in the realm of possibility. In any event, neither of us had any interest in a public celebration of our commitment. We simply held ourselves out as a couple and were accepted as such by our friends, families, and coworkers. After a few years, we began to wear rings as a symbol of our relationship. We always joked that we had had a commitment ceremony; it was just a small one—comprising the two of us and the woman who had sold us our wedding rings.

My sister and Cindy opted for a more traditional and public affair. The ceremony was held outdoors at a hotel near where we had grown up, which also happened to be located near Cindy's family. The ceremony took place at the end of an outdoor pier that extended over the river that ran behind the hotel. A minister officiated, and two of Cindy's nieces served as bridesmaids of a sort. Cindy's sister stood up for her, and I stood up for my sister. I also escorted my sister down the aisle because my father had passed away before the ceremony took place (my mother had passed away before my sister had even met Cindy). Cindy and Elyse exchanged vows, lit a unity candle, and released doves into the air at the end of the ceremony. It was all quite moving. The ceremony was followed by a wedding reception at the hotel.

My feelings about same-sex marriage changed drastically after I attended Elyse and Cindy's commitment ceremony. After the ceremony, the wedding party exited first and went back to the hotel lobby. The guests remained outside for a cocktail hour on the pier. While we were waiting to go out to the cocktail hour, Cindy's sister and I sat down in the hotel lobby and were chatting when two elderly women came up to ask us about the wedding. By our attire, they could tell that we were in the wedding party. They had been a bit confused when the first two people they had seen come back from the ceremony were two women. They had been watching the ceremony, which you could observe from inside the hotel; however, because the ceremony had taken place out on the edge of the pier, it had been difficult for them to see who was participating.

After exchanging pleasantries, they asked us why two women had come back from the ceremony first when they would have expected to see a bride and groom. Cindy's sister answered that two women had gotten married. "How nice," they replied. "Are they sisters?" Cindy's sister and I gave each other a knowing glance.

"No," Cindy's sister said, "two *women* got married."

"Oh, are they friends?"

"No, *two women* got married."

Finally it began to sink in. "*Ohhhhh,*" they said simultaneously with a tone of manifest disapproval and a complete lack of understanding or empathy. They then unceremoniously turned and walked away.

It had seemed as if Cindy and Elyse had done everything possible to replicate a heterosexual wedding, but the one thing that they could not do was change the fact that they are two women. This one detail, which I had thought had been buried in the overwhelmingly traditional trappings of the affair, wasn't buried at all. It clearly wasn't lost on these two women because it was the first and only thing that struck them. Seeing the ceremony from their perspective led me to rethink the value and desirability of same-sex marriage. This experience drove home for me how same-sex marriage, no matter how much it is disparaged as a drowning of our differences from the heterosexual majority, is a radical political act that defies and belies entrenched stereotypes and simultaneously demonstrates both our similarity to the heterosexual mainstream and our differences from it.

Following my sister's commitment ceremony, I came to agree with the proponents of same-sex marriage who argue that extending the right to marry to same-sex couples has the potential to "transform it into something new." There is still something quite subversive about two men or two women getting married. After all, President Bush only announced his support for a constitutional ban on same-sex marriage after the Massachusetts Supreme Judicial Court issued its decision legalizing same-sex marriage and the City of San Francisco began to issue marriage licenses to same-sex couples. Although Hien and I had discussed the idea of getting married before all of this occurred, these events only stiffened my resolve. On September 17, 2004, Hien and I were married in Toronto, Ontario, Canada, in a small, private ceremony at Toronto City Hall. The ceremony included only the two of us, an officiant (who, it turns out, was an Old Roman Catholic priest), and two witnesses (Hien's cousin and his partner). After the ceremony, we snapped a few photos near city hall and had a dinner party with a few close friends.

These experiences demonstrate the different forms of social recognition that we can seek for our relationships and the possibility that, over time, our attitudes may change. My sister and Cindy opted for a traditional religious commitment ceremony and a reception with many guests. I initially opted for no ceremony or reception at all, only tacitly seeking and receiving social recognition for my relationship. More recently, I changed my views about same-sex marriage and opted for a civil wedding ceremony followed by a small dinner party. The decision about the type and level of social recognition that we seek for our relationships is a personal one that will vary from couple to couple.

Intimately connected with this question of social recognition is the form, if any, of legal recognition that we seek for our relationships. Again, neither Cindy and Elyse nor Michael and I initially had any possibility of legal recognition for our relationships. With the advent of legal recognition, Elyse and Cindy entered first into a New Jersey domestic partnership and later into a Connecticut civil union. Hien and I, on the other hand, were legally married in Canada. The Massachusetts Supreme Judicial Court's extensive laundry list of benefits that turn on legal recognition (quoted earlier) demonstrates the importance of such recognition to our lives and the lives of our partners and families.

But whatever choices we ultimately make, the decision to acknowledge our relationships on a social or legal level will challenge stereotypes about lesbians and gay men and highlight the inequities created by privileging different-sex marital relationships above all others.

Legal Recognition of Same-Sex Relationships

The fight for legal recognition of same-sex relationships dates back to the early 1970s. The battles have mostly been waged at the state level and, during their first two decades, produced a string of resounding defeats. Courts in Alabama, the District of Columbia, Kentucky, Minnesota, New York, Ohio, Pennsylvania, Texas, and Washington all decided against the legality of same-sex marriage.[22] The attorneys general of Alabama, Colorado, Kansas, Maine, Mississippi, South Carolina, and Tennessee opined that same-sex marriage would not be permitted under their respective state marriage laws.[23] And the legislatures of a number of states, including California, Louisiana, Minnesota, Texas, and Virginia, took steps to ensure that same-sex marriage would be contrary to their laws.[24]

Nearly fifteen years ago, the logjam finally broke, and states began to recognize the inequity of excluding same-sex couples from the possibility of having their relationships legally recognized. The subsequent moves toward redressing this inequity have resulted in a dizzying, and sometimes rather fluid, array of types and levels of legal recognition for same-sex couples at the state and federal levels. In the next section, I sketch the important positive developments at the state level during this period.

Movement!

Hawaii. The logjam broke in 1993 when the Hawaii Supreme Court issued its decision in *Baehr v. Lewin*.[25] In that case, a plurality of the court found that Hawaii's marriage laws discriminated on the basis of sex by limiting the issuance of marriage licenses to different-sex couples. The court held this discrimination to be a presumptive violation of the Hawaii constitution—a presumption that the state could rebut only by showing that (1) the sex-based classification in the statute was justified by a compelling state interest and (2) "the statute is narrowly drawn to avoid unnecessary abridgments of . . . constitutional rights."[26] After a hearing, the trial court found that the state could not meet this heavy burden and held that Hawaii's marriage laws violated its constitution.[27] While an appeal was pending before the Hawaii Supreme Court, the state constitution was amended in 1998 to empower the state legislature to limit marriage to different-sex couples.[28] In December 1999, the Hawaii Supreme Court took judicial notice of this amendment and held that it validated Hawaii's marriage laws.[29]

Even though same-sex marriage was never legalized in Hawaii, the state legislature did pass a law in 1997 allowing any two persons legally prohibited from marrying (including, but not limited to, same-sex couples) to register as "reciprocal beneficiaries."[30] This status allows the pair to obtain only a limited number of benefits and obligations accorded to married couples under Hawaii law.[31] These benefits and obligations include the right to hospital visitation and to make health care decisions for each other, the ability to create a special form of joint ownership together, the right to a specified share of each other's estates upon death, and the right to sue for each other's wrongful death.[32] There is no requirement that either party to a reciprocal beneficiary relationship must be a Hawaii resident.[33]

Alaska. Similarly, an Alaska trial court held in 1998 that "marriage, i.e., the recognition of one's choice of a life partner, is a fundamental right."[34] In the court's view, limiting the issuance of marriage licenses to different-sex couples might, therefore, have violated rights guaranteed by the Alaska constitution. Accordingly, the trial court held that the state would be required to show a compelling interest justifying the abridgment of any constitutionally protected rights. However, before a hearing could be held to determine whether the state could make this showing, the Alaska constitution was amended to limit marriage to different-sex couples.[35]

Vermont. In 1999, the Vermont Supreme Court held that the exclusion of same-sex couples from the benefits and obligations of marriage violated the "common benefits clause" of the Vermont Constitution.[36] This clause provides "that government is, or ought to be, instituted for the common benefit, protection, and security of the people, nation, or community, and not for the particular emolument or advantage of any single person, family, or set of persons, who are a part only of that community."[37] Because the court held only that "plaintiffs are entitled under . . . the Vermont Constitution to obtain the same benefits and protections afforded by Vermont law to married opposite-sex couples," it left open to the state legislature the choice of affording same-sex couples either the right to marry or some other recognition of their relationships that would offer them the benefits and protections accorded to married couples.[38]

Later that year, the Vermont legislature chose to enact a "civil union" law that affords same-sex couples all of the benefits and protections associated with marriage under Vermont law but denies them the status of marriage.[39] There is no requirement that either party to a civil union must be a Vermont resident.[40]

California. The legal situation has been particularly fluid in California. In October 1999, California created a state domestic-partnership registry and afforded a limited number of benefits to same-sex couples.[41] A few months later, California voters approved Proposition 22, the California Defense of Marriage Act, which provides that "only marriage between a man and a woman is valid or recognized in California."[42] Nonetheless, in 2003, the state legislature extended nearly all of the benefits and obligations of marriage to

California domestic partners.[43] The legislature's extension of these additional benefits and obligations to domestic partners was challenged as inconsistent with Proposition 22; however, the California courts rejected this argument and upheld the validity of the revised domestic partnership law.[44] California has since enacted legislation that fills most of the remaining gaps between the benefits and obligations of marriage and those of domestic partnerships; however, California law continues to deny same-sex couples the status of marriage.[45] There is no requirement that either party to a domestic partnership must be a California resident, and California will recognize out-of-state legal unions of same-sex couples—other than marriages—that are equivalent to a California domestic partnership.[46]

In February and March 2004, the City of San Francisco issued marriage licenses to same-sex couples in defiance of Proposition 22 until it was ordered to cease issuing the licenses by the California Supreme Court. In the wake of the issuance of these marriage licenses, which were later nullified by the California Supreme Court, the city and a number of couples filed legal challenges to the constitutionality of the state's marriage laws. In March 2005, the trial court in these cases decided that California's restriction of the right to marry to different-sex couples violates the state constitution.[47] The court of appeals then reversed that decision,[48] and, as of this writing, the case is on appeal to the California Supreme Court.[49]

In September 2005, the California legislature became the first in the nation to pass a bill voluntarily extending the right to marry to same-sex couples. The bill was, however, quickly vetoed by the governor, who invoked Proposition 22 and argued that it should be overturned only by the courts or by another popular vote—and not by the legislature.[50]

District of Columbia. In 1992, the District of Columbia created a domestic-partner registry, extended hospital visitation rights to registered domestic partners, and extended certain employee benefits to the registered domestic partners of city employees.[51] This law did not, however, take effect until 2002 because, until that time, Congress prohibited the district from expending funds to implement the law.[52] Since 2002, D.C. has extended a number of additional benefits to registered domestic partners, including rights to make medical decisions, immunity from testifying against a domestic partner, inheritance rights, joint income tax filing, and exemptions from certain transfer taxes.[53]

Massachusetts. In late 2003, the Massachusetts Supreme Judicial Court held that excluding same-sex couples from access to civil marriage violates the Massachusetts Constitution.[54] As a remedy, the court reformulated "civil marriage to mean the voluntary union of two persons as spouses, to the exclusion of all others. This reformulation redresse[d] the plaintiffs' constitutional injury and further[ed] the aim of marriage to promote stable, exclusive relationships."[55] The court then stayed its judgment for 180 days to allow time for legislative action based on its opinion.

During this 180-day period, the Massachusetts Senate submitted a question to the court, asking whether the enactment of a law prohibiting same-sex couples from marrying but allowing them to form civil unions would satisfy the constitutional concerns raised in its opinion. The court answered that it would not: "The same defects of rationality evident in the marriage ban . . . are evident in, if not exaggerated by, [the civil unions bill]. . . . Because the proposed law by its express terms forbids same-sex couples entry into civil marriage, it continues to relegate same-sex couples to a different status. . . . Group classifications based on unsupportable distinctions, such as that embodied in the proposed bill, are invalid under the Massachusetts Constitution. The history of our nation has demonstrated that separate is seldom, if ever, equal."[56]

On May 17, 2004, the first same-sex couples legally married in Massachusetts, and more than five thousand same-sex couples married during the following twelve months. But same-sex couples who reside, and intend to continue to reside, outside Massachusetts are not permitted to marry there unless same-sex marriage is not prohibited in their state of residence.[57] Naturally, this latter exception has been of limited application. Thus far, only couples from New Mexico and Rhode Island have been cleared to marry in Massachusetts because their state laws do not expressly prohibit same-sex marriage.[58] It is also worth noting that the Massachusetts courts have affirmed the validity of same-sex marriages entered into by New York couples *before* July 6, 2006, when the New York Court of Appeals definitively interpreted that state's law to prohibit same-sex marriage.[59]

Following the Supreme Judicial Court's decisions, the state legislature began the lengthy process of amending the state constitution to ban same-sex marriage. That attempt failed when the amendment's backers lost a necessary vote by a wide margin. Anticipating the legislature's failure to amend the constitution, antigay forces began the process for a citizen-initiated amendment to the Massachusetts constitution, which would still require the legislature's approval but at a much lower level.[60] They gathered the requisite number of signatures to put the question before the legislature. To be placed on the ballot, the referendum had to garner the approval of at least 25 percent of the state's legislators in two consecutive sessions. In January 2007, at the very end of the 2005–2006 session of the Massachusetts legislature, the referendum passed by a margin of twelve votes. But in June 2007, near the beginning of the legislature's 2007–2008 session, the referendum came up five votes short and, as a result, will not appear on the ballot in 2008. Nonetheless, opponents of same-sex marriage in Massachusetts have made it clear that they are "not going away."[61] They are, of course, free to renew their efforts to get the legislature to place the constitutional amendment on the ballot in the future, and there is even talk of exploring the possibility of a legal challenge to the vote based on the inducements used to get several lawmakers to change their votes at the eleventh hour.

In any case, this episode underscores how precarious the legal position of lesbians and gay men remains in the United States today. After same-sex marriage became legal in Massachusetts, the conventional wisdom seemed to be that opposition would abate as time passed and opponents realized that the sky had not fallen. But the Massachusetts legislature's passage of the proposed referendum in January 2007 seriously undermined this idea. That the outcome of the June 2007 vote was not clear even a few hours before the vote was taken only further erodes support for the idea that time is on our side and that we can simply wait out our opponents.

New Jersey. Early in 2004, the New Jersey legislature passed a domestic partnership law.[62] A New Jersey domestic partnership did not provide the full panoply of benefits and obligations accorded to married couples in that state, but it did make available certain of those benefits and obligations, including protection against discrimination on the basis of domestic-partnership status, certain health-related visitation and decision-making rights, certain tax benefits, and certain health and pension benefits for domestic partners of state employees.[63] To register as domestic partners, a couple had to share a common residence and demonstrate a financial and emotional commitment to each other; if the couple did not live in New Jersey, then one of the partners had to be a member of the state-administered retirement system.[64]

At the same time, a lawsuit challenging the constitutionality of New Jersey's marriage laws was making its way through the state's courts. Both the trial court and the court of appeals turned back this challenge. In October 2006, the New Jersey Supreme Court reversed the lower court decisions and unanimously held that excluding same-sex couples from the full panoply of benefits and obligations associated with marriage violated the state constitution's guarantee of equal protection of the law.[65] The court thus ordered the state legislature to confer all of the benefits and obligations of marriage on same-sex couples within 180 days of its decision; however, the court sharply split on whether the legislature must apply the label "marriage" to the legal union of a same-sex couple.

The majority, which did not expressly rule on the question, expressed doubt that a difference in label would be an issue "of constitutional magnitude" once all of the benefits and obligations of marriage had been conferred on same-sex couples.[66] The dissenters, however, found the difference in label to be constitutionally significant because it sends the message that "what same-sex couples have is not as important or as significant as 'real' marriage, that such lesser relationships cannot have the name of marriage."[67] In the end, however, the court allowed the legislature to decide whether the label "marriage" or some other label would be applied to the legal union of same-sex couples, and it attached a presumption of constitutionality to whatever decision the legislature made.

Acting surprisingly quickly to comply with the court's order, the New Jersey legislature enacted a civil union regime in December 2006 that took effect on February 19, 2007.[68] Parties to a civil union are afforded "all of the same benefits, protections and responsibilities under law, whether they derive from statute, administrative or court rule, public policy, common law or any other source of civil law, as are granted to spouses in a marriage."[69] There is no requirement that either party to a civil union must be a New Jersey resident.[70] Following the effective date of the civil union regime, same-sex couples are no longer eligible to enter into domestic partnerships in New Jersey; however, then-existing domestic partnerships will continue to be honored and same-sex domestic partners will be offered the opportunity to enter into a civil union in place of their domestic partnership.[71]

New Jersey recognizes both civil unions and domestic partnerships entered into in other jurisdictions.[72] The attorney general of New Jersey has opined that the following relationships will be recognized as the equivalent of a New Jersey civil union: same-sex marriages celebrated in Massachusetts, Canada, the Netherlands, Belgium, South Africa, and Spain; Vermont and Connecticut civil unions; California domestic partnerships; and civil partnerships entered into in Great Britain, Sweden, New Zealand, and Iceland.[73] Similarly, the attorney general has opined that District of Columbia and Maine domestic partnerships, Hawaiian reciprocal beneficiary relationships, and same-sex relationships recognized by foreign countries "that provide a set of rights and obligations fewer in number and scope than those afforded to married couples will be valid in New Jersey and treated as domestic partnerships."[74]

Oregon. In March 2004, Multnomah County, which embraces Portland, Oregon, began issuing marriage licenses to same-sex couples. A few weeks later, the state attorney general told state agencies and urged other counties in Oregon to refuse to recognize same-sex marriages on the ground that Oregon law did not permit same-sex marriage. Defying the attorney general, Benton County announced a few days later that it would join Multnomah County in issuing marriage licenses to same-sex couples. Less than a week later, Benton County reversed course and decided that it would treat all couples equally—by refusing to issue marriage licenses to same-sex *and* different-sex couples until the question of whether same-sex couples could marry was definitively decided.

At the same time, it was agreed that a lawsuit would be brought in order that the state courts might resolve the legality of same-sex marriage in Oregon. In April 2004, the trial court ordered Multnomah County to cease issuing marriage licenses to same-sex couples but recognized as valid the marriage licenses that had already been issued. The court ordered the legislature to address the question of same-sex marriage in its next session but imposed a deadline for action: If the legislature did not act within ninety days of convening, then the judge would order Multnomah County to begin issuing marriage licenses to same-sex couples once again.

In November 2004, while an appeal of this decision to the Oregon Supreme Court was pending, Oregon voters passed Ballot Measure 36, an amendment to the state constitution that provides: "It is the policy of Oregon, and its political subdivisions, that only a marriage between one man and one woman shall be valid or legally recognized as a marriage."[75] In April 2005, the Supreme Court of Oregon ruled that the thousands of marriage licenses issued to same-sex couples before the passage of Measure 36 were void because they were issued in contravention of state marriage laws and further held that marriage in Oregon would be limited to different-sex couples beginning on the effective date of Measure 36.[76]

In May 2007, Oregon enacted a domestic partnership regime that, like California's, would afford all of the rights and obligations of marriage under Oregon law to same-sex couples but deny them the status of marriage.[77] To register as domestic partners, at least one member of a same-sex couple must be a resident of Oregon.[78] As of this writing, the domestic partnership regime is set to go into effect on January 1, 2008; however, a coalition of anti-gay forces is gathering signatures to place a referendum on the ballot in 2008 that would allow the state's voters to accept or reject both the law creating this domestic partnership regime and a contemporaneous law adding "sexual orientation" to the state's antidiscrimination laws.[79] If this effort proves successful, which will not be clear until after this book goes to press, then the effective date of both of these laws will be delayed until after the November 2008 general election, when they will be considered by the voters.

Maine. In April 2004, Maine passed a law creating a domestic-partnership registry.[80] Domestic partners are afforded only a limited number of the benefits and obligations associated with marriage, including inheritance rights, inclusion among the "next of kin" for purposes of making funeral and burial arrangements, and priority in the naming of a guardian for an incapacitated domestic partner.[81] To register as domestic partners, a same-sex couple must have been legally domiciled together in Maine for at least twelve months prior to registration.[82]

Washington. In August and September 2004, two Washington superior court judges ruled that prohibiting same-sex couples from marrying violates the state constitution.[83] In July 2006, a sharply divided Washington Supreme Court reversed these decisions. A majority of the court upheld the state's same-sex marriage ban against constitutional attack, despite the vigorous assertions of four dissenting judges that the ban was born of little more than antigay animus.[84]

In April 2007, Washington passed a law creating a domestic partnership registry, which went into effect on July 21, 2007.[85] Domestic partners are afforded only a limited number of the benefits and obligations associated with marriage, including hospital visitation rights, inheritance rights, and priority in being allowed to make medical decisions on behalf of an incapacitated partner who has not executed a durable power of attorney for health care.[86] To register as domestic partners, a same-sex couple must share a common residence.[87]

Before the creation of this domestic partner registry, a Washington appellate court recognized that same-sex relationships can qualify as "meretricious relationships" under Washington case law.[88] For this purpose, a meretricious relationship is a stable, "marital-like" relationship. The factors considered in determining whether a meretricious relationship exists between two individuals include, but are not limited to, "continuous cohabitation, duration of the relationship, purpose of the relationship, pooling of resources and services for joint projects, and the intent of the parties."[89] If a meretricious relationship is found to exist, the parties to that relationship may be entitled to certain property rights upon dissolution of the relationship or possibly upon the death of one of the partners. Significantly, however, this limited grant of quasi-marital rights applies only retrospectively; that is, a same-sex couple "cannot be confident of their status until it has been tested in court" after the termination of the relationship or the death of one of the partners.[90]

New York. In February 2005, a trial court in New York held that excluding same-sex couples from access to civil marriage violates the New York constitution; however, this decision was bookended by the contrary decisions of other trial courts in the state.[91] In July 2006, the New York Court of Appeals issued a ruling in a consolidated appeal of several of these cases.[92] In its decision, the court first held that the New York Domestic Relations Law limits marriage to different-sex couples. A majority of the court (in plurality and concurring opinions) then held that the Domestic Relations Law does not violate the New York constitution because there are rational grounds for limiting marriage to different-sex couples.

Interestingly, in justifying its decision, the plurality turned the usual stereotypes on their head to argue that a legislature could rationally decide that there is a greater need to encourage stable different-sex relationships than there is to encourage stable same-sex relationships. According to the plurality, because of their licentiousness and the propensity of their liaisons to result in pregnancy, heterosexuals are desperately in need of the stable framework provided by marriage in order to protect any children that might result from their sexual activity from being raised in "unstable homes." In contrast, lesbians and gay men cannot accidentally conceive children through their sexual activity; they can only form a family intentionally—either through adoption, artificial insemination, surrogacy, or other assistance—making them paragons of stability in no need of government encouragement to form stable families before rearing children.

Ultimately, the Court of Appeals put the question of whether to authorize same-sex marriage to the state legislature. The majority found that the New York constitution neither requires nor prohibits the extension of the right to marry to lesbians and gay men, effectively taking the question out of the hands of the courts (there being no constitutional right to same-sex marriage) and placing it squarely in those of the legislature (there being no impediment to statutorily created same-sex marriage). In her dissenting opinion, Chief Judge Kaye chided the majority of the court for shirking its duty to remedy what she perceived to be a clear violation of the constitutional rights of lesbians and gay men: "It is uniquely the function of the Judicial Branch to safeguard individual liberties guaranteed by the New York State Constitution, and to order redress for their violation. The Court's duty to protect constitutional rights is an imperative of the separation of powers, not its enemy. I am confident that future generations will look back on today's decision as an unfortunate misstep."

New York's newly elected governor, Eliot Spitzer, has taken up where the New York Court of Appeals left off. In April 2007, Governor Spitzer proposed legislation that would legalize same-sex marriage in New York.[93] In June 2007, the bill passed the State Assembly by a vote of 85-61, but it is not even expected to make it to the floor in the State Senate because the Senate majority leader opposes the bill.[94]

On the separate question of whether New York will recognize same-sex marriages (or their equivalent) contracted in other states, the New York attorney general's office has issued an informal opinion that "New York law presumptively requires that parties to such unions must be treated as spouses for purposes of New York law."[95] The New York courts have, however, thus far differed on whether the attorney general's interpretation of New York law is correct. In at least two cases, New York courts have refused to recognize a Vermont civil union and a Canadian same-sex marriage; yet, more recently, another New York court ruled that the Westchester County executive acted properly in ordering the county government to recognize out-of-state same-sex marriages.[96]

Connecticut. In April 2005, Connecticut enacted a civil union law that, like Vermont's, affords a same-sex couple all of the benefits and protections associated with marriage under Connecticut law but denies the couple the status of marriage.[97] There is no requirement that either party to a civil union must be a Connecticut resident.[98] In addition, the Connecticut attorney general has opined that out-of-state same-sex marriages will not be recognized in Connecticut but that out-of-state civil unions and other relationships that are the equivalent of Connecticut civil unions (e.g., a California domestic partnership) will be recognized by the state.[99]

In the process of enacting the civil union law, an amendment defining marriage "as the union of one man and one woman" was attached to the portion of the bill that established the benefits and obligations of the parties to a civil union.[100] To placate conservative legislators and the state's Republican governor, this amendment reaffirmed the existing interpretation of Connecticut's marriage laws as applying only to different-sex couples.

Connecticut's marriage laws (now including the amendment to the civil union bill) are the subject of a state constitutional challenge. In July 2006, a state trial court upheld the marriage laws against this attack. In contrast to the Massachusetts Supreme Judicial Court, the Connecticut trial court premised its decision on the notion that separate really can be equal; it found that lesbians and gay men suffered "no harm of constitutional magnitude" from being relegated to the separate, second-class status of civil unions.[101] As of this writing, the trial court's decision is on appeal.

Maryland. In early 2006, a Baltimore Circuit Court judge ruled that Maryland's statutory same-sex marriage ban violates the state constitution.[102] This decision was stayed pending appeal. Republican lawmakers then immediately began the process of amending the state constitution to ban same-sex marriage; however, these efforts ultimately proved unsuccessful. The Maryland Court of Appeals agreed to hear a direct appeal of the case, and that appeal was still pending at the time of this writing.

New Hampshire. In June 2007, New Hampshire passed a law establishing a civil union regime, which will take effect on January 1, 2008.[103] Like the civil union regimes in Connecticut, New Jersey, and Vermont, the New Hampshire regime affords a same-sex couple all the benefits and protections associated with marriage under New Hampshire law but denies the couple the status of marriage.[104] New Hampshire will recognize both civil unions and same-sex marriages entered into in other states as civil unions under New Hampshire law.[105]

Iowa. In August 2007, an Iowa District Court judge ruled that the Iowa "defense of marriage" act, which restricts marriage to different-sex couples, violates the state constitutional guarantees of due process and equal protection of the law.[106] The judge further ruled that Iowa's marriage laws "must be read and applied in a gender neutral manner so as to permit same-sex couples to enter into a civil marriage."[107] A single same-sex couple was actually able to marry before the judge issued a stay of his ruling pending an appeal to the Iowa Supreme Court.[108]

Backlash

The forward movement unleashed by the Hawaii Supreme Court has engendered a backlash from opponents of same-sex marriage. These opponents have lobbied for the passage of laws and constitutional amendments limiting marriage to different-sex couples. Sometimes they have gone further and attempted to erase *any* legal recognition of same-sex relationships.

Federal Level. While the *Baehr* case was still wending its way through the Hawaii courts, Congress decided to take action to limit the impact of any decision that might be favorable to same-sex couples.[109] To this end,

Congress enacted, and President Clinton signed, the Defense of Marriage Act (DOMA).[110] DOMA has two operative provisions: One addresses the treatment of same-sex marriages by the federal government and the other addresses interstate recognition of same-sex marriages.

The former provision defines the word "marriage" for purposes of federal law as "a legal union between one man and one woman as husband and wife."[111] This effectively ensures that, even if a state extends the right to marry to same-sex couples (as Massachusetts has done), its same-sex marriages will *not* be recognized by the federal government for any purpose. The impact of this provision should not be underestimated: The U.S. General Accounting Office has identified "1,138 federal statutory provisions . . . in which marital status is a factor in determining or receiving benefits, rights, and privileges."[112] This includes areas of frequent importance to same-sex couples such as tax and immigration law; in the latter case, a same-sex marriage, civil union, or domestic partnership may not only be denied recognition but may also serve as the basis for denying renewal of a visa or reentry into the country (because it may be construed as evidence of an intent to remain in the United States permanently).[113]

The federal government has even relied on DOMA to reject a lesbian's passport application.[114] The passport agency rejected the application on the ground that it would not recognize the married name listed on the application. As permitted under Massachusetts law, the woman had legally changed her name on her marriage certificate when she wedded her partner. Although the federal government accepts name changes on marriage certificates when effected by members of different-sex married couples, it has said that it will not honor such name changes when made by members of same-sex married couples. Instead, the federal government requires lesbians and gay men to go through the more cumbersome and expensive process of going to court to legally change their names.

The other provision of DOMA purports to be an application of congressional power under the U.S. Constitution's Full Faith and Credit Clause. This clause requires each state to give full faith and credit to the public acts, records, and judicial proceedings of other states and gives Congress the power to prescribe the manner in which those records are to be proved "and the Effect thereof."[115] Acting under the guise of this latter power,[116] DOMA allows each state to refuse to give effect to the public acts, records, or judicial proceedings of "any other State, territory, possession, or tribe respecting a relationship between persons of the same sex that is treated as a marriage under the laws of such other State, territory, possession, or tribe, or a right or claim arising from such relationship."[117]

Ever since its enactment, there has been a serious debate among academic commentators concerning the constitutionality of DOMA.[118] There is further disagreement over the extent to which DOMA's interstate-recognition provision would be affected by any judicial decision striking DOMA down on constitutional grounds. This latter disagreement arises from the uncertain scope of the states' ability, even before DOMA, to refuse to recognize marriages celebrated in other states. The uncertainty in this area is compounded by the fact that many of the academic contributions to this debate are "far from neutral,"[119] which portends similarly inconsistent, ideologically driven decisions from the courts.

Right-wing reactionaries have cited these uncertainties as a reason for amending the federal constitution to prohibit same-sex marriage. But the "federal marriage amendment" has not yet made it out of Congress: In 2004, it failed to garner the support of even a majority of the Senate. Nonetheless, following the presidential election that year, one of President Bush's key advisers indicated that there would be a renewed push from the White House for the amendment in Bush's second term—a push that materialized only when the Senate was to consider (but had no hope of passing) the amendment in an effort to shore up a disaffected Republican base in advance of the 2006 midterm elections.

State Level. Only a handful of states enacted laws prohibiting same-sex marriage prior to the *Baehr* decision. Following that decision and the passage of DOMA, the pace of the states' enactment of these so-called "mini-DOMAs" intensified. Table 6.1 documents the tangible results of this backlash on the state level. It breaks the state prohibitions against same-sex marriage down into four categories: (1) those that have only a statutory prohibition,[120] (2) those that have only a constitutional prohibition,[121] (3) those that have both a statutory and a constitutional prohibition,[122] and (4) those that have no express statutory or constitutional prohibition.

As indicated in Table 6.1, some states have adopted both statutory *and* constitutional prohibitions against same-sex marriage. The reason for this bootstrapping is quite simple: It narrows the legal grounds upon which the prohibition can be challenged. A statutory prohibition alone is subject to challenge on the ground that it violates the state constitution, the federal constitution, and/or federal law. Because state constitutional rights are often interpreted more broadly than federal constitutional rights, adopting a state constitutional prohibition removes a fertile ground of attack. The only grounds left are inconsistency with federal law, which, through DOMA, actually authorizes states to refuse to recognize same-sex marriages, or the federal constitution, which reactionaries are attempting to amend to include a nationwide prohibition against same-sex marriage.[123]

A Limited Choice

When different-sex couples think about whether to seek legal recognition for their relationships, the choice is generally clear-cut—either to purchase a marriage license and "make it legal" or simply to live together and arrange their affairs privately. For same-sex couples, there is often no choice—because legal recognition is plainly unavailable—and, even when it appears as if there is a choice, that choice is really no more than a false choice.

Table 6.1   D.C. and State Same-Sex Marriage Prohibitions

Statutory Prohibition Only	Constitutional Prohibition Only	Statutory and Constitutional Prohibitions	No Express Prohibition
Arizona[a]	Nebraska[b,e]	Alabama[b]	Dist. of Columbia[g]
California	Oregon	Alaska[b]	New Jersey[g]
Connecticut		Arkansas[b]	New Mexico
Delaware		Colorado	New York[g]
Florida[b]		Georgia[b,f]	Rhode Island
Hawaii[c]		Idaho[b]	
Illinois		Kansas[b]	
Indiana[d]		Kentucky[b]	
Iowa		Louisiana[b,f]	
Maine		Michigan[b]	
Maryland		Mississippi	
Minnesota		Missouri	
New Hampshire		Montana[b]	
North Carolina		Nevada	
Pennsylvania		North Dakota[b]	
Vermont		Ohio[b]	
Washington[d]		Oklahoma[b]	
West Virginia		South Carolina[b]	
Wyoming		South Dakota[b]	
		Tennessee	
		Texas[b]	
		Utah[b]	
		Virginia[b]	
		Wisconsin[b]	

[a] Upheld against state and federal constitutional challenges. *Standhardt v. Super. Ct.*, 77 P.3d 451 (Ariz. Ct. App. 2003). A ballot initiative that would have added a ban on same-sex marriage to the state constitution was defeated in November 2006.

[b] Also refuses to recognize statuses that are similar to marriage (e.g., civil union or domestic partnership). In the case of Alabama, the recent amendment to the state constitution does not mention statuses similar to marriage; however, the legislation that placed that amendment before the state's voters does contain language about refusing to recognize a domestic or foreign "union replicating marriage," which might be construed to cover civil unions and domestic partnerships. Pub. Act No. 35, 2005 Ala. Adv. Legis. Serv. 35.

[c] The Hawaii constitution puts the question whether to extend the right to marry to same-sex couples in the hands of the legislature but does not itself ban same-sex marriage. Haw. Const. art. I, §23.

[d] Upheld against a state constitutional challenge. *Morrison v. Sadler*, 821 N.E.2d 15 (Ind. Ct. App. 2005); *Andersen v. King County*, 138 P.3d 963 (Wash. 2006).

[e] Upheld against a federal constitutional challenge. *Citizens for Equal Prot., Inc. v. Bruning*, 455 F.3d 859 (8th Cir. 2006).

[f] Constitutional amendment upheld against a procedural challenge. *Perdue v. O'Kelley*, 632 S.E.2d 110 (Ga. 2006); *Forum for Equal. PAC v. McKeithen*, 893 So. 2d 715 (La. 2005).

[g] The courts have nonetheless construed the marriage laws in these jurisdictions to be limited to different-sex couples. *Dean v. Dist. of Columbia*, 653 A.2d 307 (D.C. 1995) (*per curiam*); *Lewis v. Harris*, 908 A.2d 196 (N.J. 2006); *Hernandez v. Robles*, 855 N.E.2d 1 (N.Y. 2006); see also N.J. Rev. Stat. §26:8A-2(e) (2006) (embracing the same construction).

No Choice. As of this writing, only Massachusetts legally recognizes same-sex marriages. California, Connecticut, New Jersey, and Vermont allow same-sex couples to enter legal relationships that are equivalent to marriage; in 2008, New Hampshire and, hopefully, Oregon will be added to this list. The District of Columbia, Hawaii, Maine, and Washington permit same-sex couples to enter into legal relationships that fall short (in some cases, far short) of marriage. Of the remaining forty states, thirty-eight either expressly prohibit same-sex marriage (and sometimes other forms of legal recognition) or their laws have been construed not to permit same-sex marriage.

Same-sex couples living in this group of thirty-eight states are presented with no choice: Their home states will not legally recognize their relationships. As described more fully in Chapters 7 and 8, couples in these states may nevertheless be able to attain a measure of legal recognition for their relationships. But they must do so on their own and, in contrast to different-sex couples who need pay only a nominal amount for a marriage license, at potentially considerable expense. Those who can afford the cost will need an attorney who is familiar with lesbian and gay legal issues to create the web of documents (e.g., contracts governing property ownership, the sharing of debts and expenses, and other aspects of your relationship; powers of attorney for health care and finances; and wills) that are necessary for the couple to replicate—at best, partially—the myriad of benefits and obligations attendant to marriage.

False Choice. In contrast, same-sex couples who live in California, Connecticut, the District of Columbia, Hawaii, Maine, Massachusetts, New Jersey, Washington, and Vermont—and, beginning in 2008, in New Hampshire and, hopefully, Oregon—seem to be presented with a choice similar to the one faced by different-sex couples: They can either choose to enter into a marriage, civil union, domestic partnership, or reciprocal beneficiary relationship or they can choose not to seek formal legal recognition of their relationships and instead construct their own contractual arrangements. But, in reality, DOMA and its surrounding cloud of uncertainty place these couples in the same situation as couples who live in states that afford same-sex couples no choice at all. Even if a couple's home state legally recognizes their relationship, most other states and the federal government will *not* do so.[124] Because it is difficult to avoid traveling across state lines, entering into transactions with out-of-state persons, or dealing with the federal government, these couples are forced to act as if the legal recognition of their relationships does not exist.

Again as described more fully in Chapters 7 and 8, these couples will need an attorney to draw up the same web of documents as couples who live in states that do not legally recognize same-sex relationships—just in case their relationship status becomes relevant in another state or with the federal government. For example, even after registering as domestic partners in

New Jersey, Elyse and Cindy still needed the wills, powers of attorney, and other documents that their lawyer had drawn up before New Jersey extended legal recognition to same-sex relationships. The geographically limited nature of the legal recognition afforded by Cindy and Elyse's New Jersey domestic partnership was underscored when they found it necessary to enter into a civil union in Connecticut to satisfy the requirements that Cindy's New York employer had established for its domestic-partner health insurance coverage.

To be clear, I am not contending that it is pointless to marry or to enter into a civil union or domestic partnership, if that is what you wish to do. The choice to enter into a legal relationship often depends on far more than a weighing of legal benefits and detriments. For instance, my decision to marry in Canada was motivated by, among other things, my desire to signal my commitment to Hien and to make a political statement; it certainly was not motivated by the prospect of any legal rights or obligations, because our home state of Pennsylvania flatly refuses to recognize our marriage. My point here is that these legal statuses are, for the most part, relevant only in the state where they were entered into and the few states that currently choose to recognize them.[125] The need to create a web of documents that replicates these legal protections (to the limited extent possible) is a duplicative and unnecessary cost that society imposes on same-sex couples but not on different-sex married couples. You might even reconceptualize this cost as a penalty tax—on the purchase of legal recognition for same-sex relationships—that is intended to reduce our—now "after-tax"—civil rights gains.

Shaping Change

To predict change in this area is to state the obvious. What becomes important, once change is a given, is shaping that change. Thus far, lesbians and gay men have been placed on the defensive in the debate over same-sex marriage. Either we are accused of plotting the destruction of marriage or the burden is placed on us to prove why we deserve access to marriage. There are a number of ways in which we all—coupled or uncoupled, in favor of or opposed to the idea of marriage—can act to shift the direction of this conversation, create empathy, and shape favorable heterosexual attitudes toward the social and legal recognition of same-sex relationships.

Despite being prohibited from marrying in most states, lesbians and gay men are routinely invited to attend weddings and to purchase gifts for different-sex couples. When faced with the prospect of attending yet another wedding, we are presented with an opportunity to turn the tables of the debate over same-sex marriage by drawing attention to, and subverting, the privileging of heterosexual marriage. If the wedding is celebrated anywhere other than Massachusetts, you could decline to attend and explain that you simply do not feel right attending a ceremony that you are legally barred from participating in.[126] If nothing else, you will have started the couple thinking about how their relationship is privileged over yours and the ways in which they profit from that privileging.

A supportive couple may then contact you to see how they can address your concerns. Or, if you don't feel comfortable with a boycott, you could simply contact the couple to explain your concerns. In either case, you could ask the couple to show sensitivity to their lesbian and gay guests. For example, friends of mine who married recently included an insert in their invitation explaining their support for same-sex marriage and asking that any gifts take the form of a donation to an organization that fights for same-sex marriage. Not all couples may be so giving and committed to advancing lesbian and gay rights, but, when approached in a nonconfrontational manner, a couple may at least be willing to acknowledge their support for same-sex marriage before, during, or after the ceremony or may even be willing to make a donation of a portion of their gifts to a lesbian and gay rights organization.[127] In any event, you will have drawn attention to and subverted the privileging of heterosexuality by placing heterosexuals on the defensive for once, effectively asking them to justify why *they* should be entitled to the benefits and obligations of marriage.

And you need not wait for a wedding invitation to increase sensitivity and foster empathy. As my sister and Cindy have experienced, once the subject is raised, heterosexuals are sometimes surprisingly curious about what it is like to be lesbian or gay. Each time that you confront a hurdle in your relationship that would not be faced by a heterosexual married couple—from difficulties in visiting a hospitalized partner to the inability to speak with school officials about a partner's child or to get the marriage discount on your car insurance—you should explain the situation to your heterosexual family, friends, and coworkers to sensitize them to the costs that are inexorably imposed on you when society chooses to privilege their relationships over yours.

If you support same-sex marriage and are inclined to be more public about the harms that you have suffered, you could go to Freedom to Marry's story center on the web (www.freedomtomarry.org) and submit your story for use by that organization (or its coalition partners) as they work for equal marriage rights. The impact that our stories can have is demonstrated by the instrumental role that they played in the passage of the Connecticut civil union law. Love Makes a Family laid the groundwork for this legislation by arranging "meet-and-greet" gatherings where legislators could interact with and listen to the personal stories of lesbian and gay families. None of us can expect heterosexuals to understand our position until they understand exactly how we are disadvantaged by our exclusion from the rights and obligations of marriage.

You can also take advantage of the social and legal recognition that is available to us to make a point, as Hien and I did. Public affirmation of our relationships is the most effective way to counter society's attempts to banish us to social and legal invisibility. This is true whether you choose to marry, to enter into a civil union or a domestic partnership, to have a commitment ceremony, or simply to exchange rings or hold yourselves out as a couple. Whichever path you choose, you might consider publishing an announcement of your commitment in your local newspaper to make a truly "public" statement. Holding yourself out as part of a couple invites questions about your partner and creates opportunities to dispel the presumption of heterosexuality as well as stereotypes about lesbians and gay men. It allows us to be seen; to become familiar; and, as my sister and Cindy learned, eventually to be recognized.

Notes

1. Used with the permission of Elyse Infanti and Cynthia Bonforte.

2. Andrew Sullivan, "The Politics of Homosexuality," *New Republic* (May 10, 1993): 37.

3. Ibid.

4. Thomas Stoddard, "Why Gay People Should Seek the Right to Marry," in William B. Rubenstein, ed., *Lesbians, Gay Men, and the Law* (New York: New Press, 1993), 398, 400.

5. Sullivan, "The Politics of Homosexuality," 37.

6. *Goodridge v. Dep't of Pub. Health,* 798 N.E.2d 941, 955–957 (Mass. 2003) (citations omitted).

7. Stoddard, "Why Gay People Should Seek the Right to Marry," 401.

8. Ibid.; see also Barbara J. Cox, "A (Personal) Essay on Same-Sex Marriage," in Robert M. Baird and Stuart E. Rosenbaum, eds., *Same-Sex Marriage: The Moral and Legal Debate* (Amherst, NY: Prometheus Books, 1997), 27–29.

9. Stoddard, "Why Gay People Should Seek the Right to Marry," 401; see also Chai R. Feldblum, "Gay Is Good: The Moral Case for Marriage Equality and More," *Yale J. L. and Feminism* 17 (2005): 139, 173.

10. Bruce Fein, "No: Reserve Marriage for Heterosexuals," *A.B.A. J.* (Jan. 1990): 43; see also Matthew Spalding, "A Defining Moment: Marriage, the Courts, and the Constitution," *Backgrounder* 2 (May 17, 2004): 1759, available at www.heritage.org.

11. Fein, "No: Reserve Marriage for Heterosexuals," 43; see also Stanley Kurtz, "The Libertarian Question: Incest, Homosexuality, and Adultery," *Nat'l Review* (April 30, 2003), available at www.nationalreview.com/kurtz/kurtz043003.asp; Spalding, "A Defining Moment," 4.

12. Hadley Arkes, "The Closet Straight," *Nat'l Review* (July 5, 1993): 44–45; Kurtz, "The Libertarian Question"; Dahlia Lithwick, "Slippery Slope: The Maddening 'Slippery Slope' Argument Against Gay Marriage," *Slate* (May 19, 2004), available at http://slate.msn.com/id/2100824.

13. Maura Dolan, "More Information Sought in Marriage Case," *Los Angeles Times,* June 21, 2007, B4.

14. Opinions of the Justices to the Senate, 802 N.E.2d 565, 569 (2004).

15. Letter from Plan Admin., UPS Health & Welfare Package, to Gabriael Brazier (May 31, 2007), available at http://data.lambdalegal.org/pdf/legal/brazier/ups-letter.pdf; Kareem Fahim, "U.P.S. Agrees to Benefits in New Jersey's Civil Unions," *New York Times,* July 31, 2007, B4.

16. N.J. Rev. Stat. §37:1-33 (2007).

17. See Paula Ettelbrick, "Since When Is Marriage a Path to Liberation?" in Rubenstein, ed., *Lesbians, Gay Men, and the Law,* 402.

18. Ibid.

19. Ibid., 405.

20. For example, "Beyond Same-Sex Marriage" (July 26, 2006), available at www.beyondmarriage.org.

21. Ettelbrick, "Since When Is Marriage a Path to Liberation?" 402.

22. *Weaver v. G.D. Searle and Co.,* 558 F. Supp. 720 (N.D. Ala. 1983) (applying Alabama law); *Dean v. Dist. of Columbia,* 653 A.2d 307 (D.C. 1995) (per curiam); *Jones v. Hallahan,* 501 S.W.2d 588 (Ky. Ct. App. 1973); *Baker v. Nelson,* 191 N.W.2d 185 (Minn. 1971), appeal dismissed 409 U.S. 810 (1972); *Anonymous v. Anonymous,* 325 N.Y.S.2d 499 (N.Y. Sup. Ct. 1971); *Gajovski v. Gajovski,* 610 N.E.2d 431 (Ohio Ct. App. 1991); *DeSanto v. Barnsley,* 476 A.2d 952 (Pa. Super. Ct. 1984); *Slayton v. State,* 633 S.W.2d 934 (Tex. Ct. App. 1982); *Singer v. Hara,* 522 P.2d 684 (Wash. Ct. App. 1974).

23. Op. Att'y Gen., 1983 Ala. AG Lexis 54 (March 1, 1983); Op. Att'y Gen., 1975 Colo. AG Lexis 38 (April 24, 1975); Op. Att'y Gen. 77-248, 1977 Kan. AG Lexis 150 (August 4, 1977); Op. Att'y Gen., 1984 Me. AG Lexis 1 (October 30, 1984); Op. Att'y Gen., 1978 Miss. AG Lexis 684 (July 10, 1978); Op. Att'y Gen., 1976 S.C. AG Lexis 423 (August 12, 1976); Op. Att'y Gen. 88-43, 1988 Tenn. AG Lexis 42 (February 29, 1988).

24. Cal. Civ. Code §4100 (1993); La. Civ. Code art. 89 (1993); Minn. Stat. §517.01 (1990); Tex. Fam. Code §1.01 (1993); Va. Code §20-45.2 (1993).

25. *Baehr v. Lewin,* 852 P.2d 44 (Haw. 1993).

26. Ibid., 67.

27. *Baehr v. Miike,* CIV 91-1394, 1996 WL 694235 (Haw. Cir. Ct. December 3, 1996).

28. Haw. Const. art. I, §23.

29. *Baehr v. Miike,* 1999 Haw. Lexis 391 (Haw. December 9, 1999).

30. Act Relating to Unmarried Couples, 1997 Haw. Sess. Laws 383.

31. Haw. Rev. Stat. §572C-6 (2006).

32. Ibid., §§323-2, 509-2, 560:2-102, -202, 663-3.

33. Ibid., §572C-4.

34. *Brause v. Bureau of Vital Statistics,* 1998 WL 88743, *1 (Alaska Super. Ct. February 27, 1998).

35. Alaska Const. art. I, §25.

36. *Baker v. Vermont,* 744 A.2d 864, 877–886 (Vt. 1999).

37. Vt. Const. ch. I, art. 7.

38. *Baker v. Vermont,* 886–887.

39. Act Relating to Civil Unions, §3, 2000 Vt. Acts and Resolves No. 91 (codified at Vt. Stat. tit. 15, §1204 [2006]).

40. Vt. Stat. tit. 18, §5160(a) (2006).

41. Act of October 10, 1999, 1999 Cal. Legis. Serv. (A.B. 26), ch. 588.

42. Cal. Fam. Code §308.5 (2007).

43. The California Domestic Partner Rights and Responsibilities Act of 2003, 2003 Cal. Legis. Serv. (A.B. 205), ch. 421.

44. *Knight v. Super. Ct.,* 26 Cal. Rptr. 3d 687 (Cal. Ct. App. 2005).

45. Act of September 30, 2006, 2006 Cal. Legis. Serv., ch. 802 (S.B. 1827).

46. Cal. Fam. Code §§297(b), 299.2 (2007).

47. *In re Marriage Cases,* JCCP 4365, slip op. at 3-23 (Cal. Super. Ct. March 14, 2005).

48. *In re Marriage Cases,* JCCP 4365, 2006 Cal. App. Lexis 1542 (Cal. Ct. App. October 5, 2006).

49. *In re Marriage Cases,* 149 P.3d 737 (2006) (petition for review granted).

50. For an argument that the governor was wrong to veto this legislation, see Jessica L. Blome, "The Religious Freedom and Civil Marriage Protection Act: How Governor Schwarzenegger Failed His Constituents," *J. Gender Race & Just.* 10 (2007): 481.

51. 1992 D.C. Code Adv. Leg. Serv. 114.

52. Compare Act of December 21, 2001, PL. 107-96, 115 Stat. 923, 950, with Act of October 5, 1992, PL 102-382, 106 Stat. 1422, 1422.

53. Domestic Partnerships Joint Filing Act of 2006, 54 D.C. Reg. 1080 (February 9, 2007); Domestic Partnership Equality Amendment Act of 2006, 53 D.C. Reg. 1035 (February 17, 2006); Domestic Partnership Protection Amendment Act of 2004, 52 D.C. Reg. 1718 (February 25, 2005); Department of Motor Vehicles Reform Amendment Act of 2004, §402, 52 D.C. Reg. 1700 (February 25, 2005); Deed Recordation Tax and Related Amendments Amendment Act of 2004, 51 D.C. Reg. 5707 (June 4, 2004); Health-Care Decisions Act of 2003, 50 D.C. Reg. 3387 (May 2, 2003).

54. *Goodridge v. Dep't of Pub. Health,* 798 N.E.2d 941, 960–968 (Mass. 2003).

55. Ibid., 969.

56. Opinions of the Justices to the Senate, 802 N.E.2d 565, 569 (Mass. 2004).

57. Mass. Gen. Laws ch. 207, §§11–12 (2007); *Cote-Whitacre v. Dep't of Pub. Health,* 844 N.E.2d 623 (Mass. 2006).

58. *Cote-Whitacre v. Dep't of Pub. Health,* 04-2656, 2006 WL 3011295 (Mass. Super. Ct. September 29, 2006); David Abel, "Same-Sex Couples from N.M. Allowed to Marry in Mass.," *Boston Globe,* July 27, 2007, 3B.

59. *Cote-Whitacre v. Dep't of Pub. Health,* 04-2656, 2007 Mass. Super. Lexis 149 (Mass. Super. Ct. May 10, 2007).

60. See *Doyle v. Sec'y of the Commonwealth,* 858 N.E.2d 1090 (Mass. 2006) (explaining the history of the proposed referendum as well as the constitutional provisions governing its placement before state voters); *Schulman v. Att'y Gen.,* 850 N.E.2d 505 (Mass. 2006) (turning back a procedural challenge to the voter-initiated referendum process and ruling that, should it pass all of the necessary steps for approval, this voter-initiated amendment to the state constitution could prospectively ban same-sex marriage); Pam Belluck, "State Legislators Let Same-Sex Marriage Vote Proceed," *New York Times,* January 3, 2007, A10 (reporting the circumstances and history of the referendum's passage on the first of the two votes in the state legislature).

61. Pam Belluck, "Massachusetts Gay Marriage Referendum Is Rejected," *New York Times,* June 15, 2007, A16.

62. New Jersey Domestic Partnership Act, 2003 N.J. Sess. Law Serv., ch. 246.

63. N.J. Rev. Stat. §26:8A-2(c) (2007).

64. Ibid., §§26:8A-3, -4.

65. *Lewis v. Harris,* 908 A.2d 196 (N.J. 2006).

66. Ibid., 221.

67. Ibid., 226–227.

68. Act of December 21, 2006, 2006 N.J. Laws 103.

69. N.J. Rev. Stat. §37:1–31(a) (2007).

70. Ibid., §37:1–30.

71. Ibid., §26:8A-4.1.

72. Ibid., §§26:8A-6(c), 37:1–34.

73. Op. Att'y Gen. 3-2007, 2007 N.J. AG Lexis 2, *2–*3 (February 16, 2007).

74. Ibid., *4.

75. Or. Const. art. XV, §5(a).

76. *Li v. Oregon*, 110 P.3d 91 (Or. 2005).

77. Act of May 9, 2007, ch. 99, 2007 Ore. HB 2007 (Lexis).

78. Ibid., §3(1).

79. Bill Graves, "Gay-Rights Opponents File for Statewide Vote," *The Oregonian* (Portland, OR), May 17, 2007, B2; see also Or. Const. art. IV, §1, cl. 3 (reserving the referendum power to the people of Oregon).

80. Act to Promote the Financial Security of Maine's Families and Children, 2003 Me. Legis. Serv., ch. 672 (H.P. 1152) (L.D. 1579).

81. Me. Rev. Stat. tit. 18-A, §§2-102, 5-311; ibid., tit. 22, §2843-A (2006).

82. Ibid., tit. 22, §2710(2)(b).

83. *Andersen v. King County*, 04-2-04964-4 SEA, slip op. (Wash. Super. Ct. August 4, 2004), rev'd, 138 P.3d 963 (Wash. 2006); *Castle v. Washington*, 04-2-00614-4, slip op. (Wash. Super. Ct. September 7, 2004), rev'd sub nom. *Andersen v. King County*, 138 P.3d 963 (Wash. 2006).

84. *Andersen v. King County*, 138 P.3d 963 (Wash. 2006).

85. Act of April 20, 2007, 2007 Wash. Adv. Legis. Serv. 156 (S.B. 5336).

86. Ibid., §§8, 11, 27.

87. Ibid., §4(1).

88. *Gormley v. Robertson*, 83 P.3d 1042, 1046 (Wash. Ct. App. 2004).

89. *Connell v. Francisco*, 898 P.2d 831, 834 (Wash. 1995).

90. Marsha Garrison, "Is Consent Necessary? An Evaluation of the Emerging Law of Cohabitant Obligation," *UCLA L. Rev.* 52 (2005): 815, 872.

91. Compare *Hernandez v. Robles*, 794 N.Y.S.2d 579 (N.Y. Sup. Ct. 2005), rev'd, 805 N.Y.S.2d 354 (N.Y. App. Div. 2005), aff'd, 855 N.E.2d 1 (N.Y. 2006), with *Seymour v. Holcomb*, 790 N.Y.S.2d 858 (N.Y. Sup. Ct. 2005), aff'd, 811 N.Y.S.2d 134 (N.Y. App. Div. 2006), aff'd sub nom. *Hernandez v. Robles*, 855 N.E.2d 1 (N.Y. 2006), and *In re Shields v. Madigan*, 783 N.Y.S.2d 270 (2004), and *Kane v. Marsolais*, 3473-04 (N.Y. Sup. Ct. Jan. 31, 2005), aff'd, 808 N.Y.S.2d 566 (N.Y. App. Div. 2006), aff'd sub nom. *Hernandez v. Robles*, 855 N.E.2d 1 (N.Y. 2006), and *Samuels v. Dep't of Pub. Health*, 1967-04 (N.Y. Sup. Ct. December 7, 2004), aff'd, 811 N.Y.S.2d 136 (N.Y. App. Div. 2006), aff'd sub nom. *Hernandez v. Robles*, 855 N.E.2d 1 (N.Y. 2006).

92. *Hernandez v. Robles*, 855 N.E.2d 1 (N.Y. 2006).

93. S.B. 5884, 2007–2008 Reg. Sess. (N.Y. 2007); A.B. 8590, 2007–2008 Reg. Sess. (N.Y. 2007).

94. Michael M. Grynbaum, "Gay Marriage, a Touchy Issue, Touches Legislators' Emotions," *New York Times,* June 21, 2007, B5.

95. Op. Att'y Gen. 2004-1, 2004 N.Y. AG Lexis 5 (March 3, 2004).

96. Compare *Langan v. St. Vincent's Hosp.*, 802 N.Y.S.2d 476 (N.Y. App. Div. 2005), and *Funderburke v. N.Y. State Dep't of Civil Serv.*, 13 Misc. 3d 284 (N.Y. Sup.

Ct. 2006), with *Godfrey v. Spano*, 16894/06, 2007 N.Y. Misc. Lexis 853 (N.Y. Sup. Ct. March 12, 2007).

97. Act Concerning Civil Unions, 2005 Conn. Legis. Serv. P.A. 05-10 (S.S.B. 963).

98. Conn. Gen. Stat. §§46b-38bb, -38cc (2007).

99. Opinion Att'y Gen. 2005-024, 2005 Conn. AG Lexis 23 (September 20, 2005).

100. Conn. Gen. Stat. §46b-38nn (2007).

101. *Kerrigan v. State*, NNH-CV-04-4001813-S, slip op. at 16 (Conn. Super. Ct. July 12, 2006).

102. *Deane v. Conaway*, 24-C-04-005390, 2006 WL 148145 (Baltimore City Cir. Ct. January 20, 2006).

103. Act of June 4, 2007, §1, 2007 N.H. Adv. Legis. Serv. ch. 58.

104. Ibid., §1 (to be codified at N.H. Rev. Stat. §457-A:6).

105. Ibid., §1 (to be codified at N.H. Rev. Stat. §457-A:8).

106. *Varnum v. Brien*, CV5965, slip op. at 43-61 (Iowa Dist. Ct. August 30, 2007).

107. Ibid., slip op. at 61.

108. Monica Davey, Patrick Healy, and Michael Cooper, "Iowa Permits Same-Sex Marriage, for 4 Hours, Anyway," *New York Times*, September 1, 2007, A9.

109. H.R. Rep. 104-664 (1996), 2, 4, reprinted in 1996 U.S.C.C.A.N. 2905, 2906, 2908.

110. Defense of Marriage Act, Pub. L. 104-199, 110 Stat. 2419, 2419 (1996).

111. 1 U.S.C. §7 (2007).

112. U.S. Gen. Accounting Office, GAO-04-353R, Defense of Marriage Act: Update to Prior Report 1 (2004).

113. Jill Schachner Chanen, "The Changing Face of Gay Legal Issues," *A.B.A. J.* 90 (2004): 46.

114. Dianne Williamson, "Gay Right Springs a Leak," *Sunday Telegram* (Worcester, MA), March 4, 2007, B1.

115. U.S. Const. art. IV, §1.

116. H.R. Rep. 104–664, 24–26, reprinted in 1996 U.S.C.C.A.N. 2905, 2929–2931.

117. 28 U.S.C. §1738C (2007).

118. Compare Mark Strasser, "*Baker* and Some Recipes for Disaster: On DOMA, Covenant Marriages, and Full Faith and Credit Jurisprudence," *Brook. L. Rev.* 64 (1998): 307; and Mark Strasser, "'Defending' Marriage in Light of the *Moreno-Cleburne-Romer-Lawrence* Jurisprudence: Why DOMA Cannot Pass Muster After *Lawrence*," *Creighton L. Rev.* 38 (2005): 421; and Mark Strasser, "Ex Post Facto Laws, Bills of Attainder, and the Definition of Punishment: On DOMA, the Hawaii Amendment, and Federal Constitutional Constraints," *Syracuse L. Rev.* 48 (1998): 227; and Mark Strasser, "*Loving* the *Romer* out for *Baehr*: On Acts in Defense of Marriage and the Constitution," *U. Pitt. L. Rev.* 58 (1997): 279; with Lynn D. Wardle, "Non-Recognition of Same-Sex Marriage Judgments Under DOMA and the Constitution," *Creighton L. Rev.* 38 (2005): 365; and Lynn D. Wardle, "*Williams v. North Carolina*, Divorce Recognition, and Same-Sex Marriage Recognition," *Creighton L. Rev.* 32 (1998): 187, 223–233.

Two lower courts have upheld DOMA against constitutional attack. *Wilson v. Ake*, 354 F. Supp. 2d 1298 (M.D. Fla. 2005); *In re Kandu*, 315 B.R. 123 (Bankr. W.D. Wash. 2004).

119. Linda Silberman, "Same-Sex Marriage: Refining the Conflict of Laws Analysis," *U. Pa. L. Rev.* 153 (2005): 2195, 2195; see also Ralph U. Whitten, "Full Faith and Credit for Dummies," *Creighton L. Rev.* 38 (2005): 465, 466 n.5.

120. Ariz. Rev. Stat. §§25-101(c), -112 (2006); Cal. Fam. Code §§299.2, 300, 308.5 (2007); Conn. Gen. Stat. §46b-38nn (2007); Del. Code tit. 13, §101(a), (d) (2007); Fla. Stat. §§741.04(1), .212 (2007); Haw. Const. art. I, §23; Haw. Rev. Stat. §§572-1, -3 (2006); 750 Ill. Comp. Stat. 5/212(a)(5), 5/213, 5/213.1 (2006); Ind. Code §31-11-1-1 (2006); Iowa Code §§595.2(1), .20 (2006); Me. Rev. Stat. tit. 19-A, §§650, 701 (2006); Md. Code, Fam. Law §2-201 (2006); Minn. Stat. §§517.01, .03 (2006); N.H. Rev. Stat. §§457:1–3 (2006); N.C. Gen. Stat. §§51-1, -1.2 (2006); 23 Pa. Cons. Stat. §§1102, 1704 (2006); Vt. Stat. tit. 15, §8 (2006); Wash. Rev. Code §§26.04.010–.020 (2007); W. Va. Code §§48-2-104, -603 (2007); Wyo. Stat. §20-1-101 (2006).

121. Neb. Const. art. I, §29; Or. Const. art. XV, §5a.

122. Ala. Const. amend. 774; Ala. Code §30-1-19 (2007); Alaska Const. art. 1, §25; Alaska Stat. §25.05.013 (2006); Ark. Const. amend. 83; Ark. Code §§9-11-107(b), -109, -208 (2006); Colo. Const. art. II, §31; Colo. Rev. Stat. §14-2-104(1)(b), (2) (2006); Ga. Const. art. I, §4, para. 1; Ga. Code §§19-3-3.1, -30 (2006); Idaho Const. art. III, §28; Idaho Code §§32-201, -209 (2006); Kan. Const. art. 15, §16; Kan. Stat. §§23-101, -115 (2005); Ky. Const. §233A; Ky. Rev. Stat. §§402.020(1)(d), .040, .045 (2006); La. Const. art. XII, §15; La. Civ. Code arts. 89, 96, 3520(b) (2006); Mich. Const. art I, §25; Mich. Comp. Laws §§551.1–.4, .271–.272 (2007); Miss. Const. art. 14, §263A; Miss. Code §93-1-1(2) (2006); Mo. Const. art. I, §33; Mo. Stat. §451.022 (2006); Mont. Const. art. XIII, §7; Mont. Code §40-1-401 (2005); Nev. Const. art. I, §21; Nev. Rev. Stat. §122.020 (2005); N.D. Const. art. XI, §28; N.D. Cent. Code §14-03-01, -08 (2005); Ohio Const. art. XV, §11; Ohio Rev. Code §3101.01 (2006); Okla. Const. art. II, §35; Okla. Stat. tit. 43, §§3–3.1 (2006); S.C. Const. art. XVII, §15; S.C. Code §§20-1-10, -15 (2006); S.D. Const. art. XXI, §9; S.D. Codified Laws §§25-1-1, -38 (2006); Tenn. Const. art. XI, §18; Tenn. Code §36-3-113 (2006); Tex. Const. art. I, §32; Tex. Fam. Code §§2.001, 6.204 (2006); Utah Const. art. I, §29; Utah Code §§30-1-2(5), -4, -4.1 (2006); Va. Const. art. I, §15-A; Va. Code §§20-45.2, -45.3 (2006); Wis. Const. art. XIII, §13; Wis. Stat. §§765.001, .01 (2006).

123. See Andrew Koppelman, "The Difference the Mini-DOMAs Make," *Loy. U. Chi. L.J.* 38 (2007): 265 (questioning the validity of the state mini-DOMAs under the federal constitution).

124. The attorney general of Rhode Island has opined that "Rhode Island will recognize same-sex marriages lawfully performed in Massachusetts as marriages in Rhode Island." Op. Att'y Gen. (February 20, 2007), available at www.glad.org/News_Room/RIAttorneyGeneral_Statement.pdf.

125. See notes 46, 72–74, 95–96, 99, 105, and 124 and accompanying text.

126. Ian Ayres and Jennifer Gerarda Brown, *Straightforward: How to Mobilize Heterosexual Support for Gay Rights* (Princeton, NJ: Princeton University Press, 2005), 173–175; Eric Rofes, "After California Votes to Limit Marriage: A Call for Direct Action and Civil Disobedience," *Soc. Pol'y* 30 (2000): 31, 32–33.

127. Ayres and Brown, *Straightforward*, 175–176; Ann Rostow, "Making Vows for Equality," *Advocate* (September 27, 2005): 42.

7

Medical, Financial, and Tax Planning

It was the day after classes had ended. My dog Kasha was soaking up some sun on a lovely spring afternoon as I sat in my yard grading papers while sipping tea and eating some banana bread that I'd made the night before. Then, all at once, I began to get sharp pains in my abdomen.

I took Kasha for a walk in the hope that the exercise would do me some good. But it didn't. When Hien arrived home a few hours later, I was still not feeling well, and the pains were coming more frequently. At Hien's urging, I called my doctor's office, and the doctor on duty advised me to go to the emergency room if the pains did not subside. The pain continued to worsen, and we were at the emergency room within a half hour. Soon after we arrived, I was in such pain that I couldn't sit up. The emergency room personnel were, of course, unmoved by the sight of me lying on the floor. Hien eventually found an empty room off the waiting area where I could lie down.

When the doctor finally examined me, she thought I might have appendicitis. I was sent for X-rays and a CT scan of my abdomen. After these tests, the doctor ruled out appendicitis, but she did see a blockage in my intestines—she just couldn't tell what was causing it. I was admitted to the hospital during the night and in the morning was sent for another X-ray, which indicated that the blockage was still there, but they still couldn't tell what was causing it. At that point, doctors seemed to come from every direction, and the surgeon came to speak with me. He asked if there were anyone he should speak with about my condition, and I told him that he should talk to Hien.

The doctor explained to the two of us that they wished to do exploratory surgery to see what was causing the intestinal blockage. Weak and a bit out of it, I was all for the surgery—or, for that matter, anything that promised to end the intense pain I experienced whenever my pain medication wore off. Hien, on the other hand, was rather nervous. He called my sister, Elyse, and my former partner, Michael, to tell them what was happening. Within a short time, I was wheeled into surgery. They quickly discovered why my intestines were blocked (a complication from a birth defect called Meckel's diverticulum), removed the affected area, and sewed me back up. After the surgery, the doctors went out to explain to Hien what they had found and what they had done to correct the problem. During the entire week that I was in the hospital, all of the doctors and nurses treated Hien respectfully, as they would the spouse of any patient.

Now fast-forward one year. Classes had again just ended, and I had already turned in my grades. Hien had to go to Denver on a business trip, and, free for the summer, I joined him. Hien's conference was not to start until Tuesday, so we flew out early and drove up to Boulder, where we spent the night. The next morning we drove to Estes Park, Colorado, which is just outside Rocky Mountain National Park. We drove around the park and later went on a four-hour hike on one of the trails in the park, which was still partially snow-covered. Hien was slipping and sliding on the snow and often had to grab on to the trees for support. All in all, it was a nice hike, followed by a picnic lunch in the park. We drove back to Denver that afternoon for the start of Hien's conference.

The following Sunday, Hien awoke with a 103-degree fever and a headache. We had to try several different over-the-counter medications before we finally succeeded in reducing the fever. Hien still wasn't feeling well on Monday morning, so we made an appointment with his doctor. The doctor wasn't sure what had caused the fever but told Hien to come back for a blood test if his condition didn't improve. On Monday night, an itchy rash broke out over Hien's torso, and the fever returned.

We spent the next several days managing the fever. With no improvement by the end of the week and no real help from his doctor, we went to the emergency room on Friday evening. It took four hours before the doctor came in, but it didn't take long to figure out what the problem was: Hien had contracted Rocky Mountain spotted fever while we were hiking in Colorado. They began to administer antibiotics immediately, admitted Hien to the hospital, and called in an infectious-disease specialist to confirm the diagnosis.

Hien began to respond to the antibiotics but was still weak the next day. The infectious-disease specialist stopped in while I was sitting with Hien in his hospital room. The doctor looked me up and down and then asked me to leave the room so that he could speak with Hien privately. Knowing that I had no legal right to be there and that Hien was feeling weak, I left. Up to that point, I had been present when he had been examined and treated by every one of the other doctors; indeed, I had often had to do the talking for Hien because he was weakened by days of fever, rashes, and persistent headaches. After the infectious-disease specialist left, I told Hien he had the right to tell the doctor that I could stay with him while he was being treated. Hien said not to worry because the doctor had just asked him to consent to an HIV test (because his white-cell count had been dropping at an alarming rate, and they wished to rule out HIV-related disease) and had asked him about his sexual orientation. When Hien had told the doctor that he is gay, the doctor had apparently put the pieces of the puzzle together and apologized for asking me to leave. Hien was released from the hospital a few days later, but somehow I never ran into that doctor again.

Lesbians and gay men may feel the government's failure to legally recognize their relationships most acutely when they are denied the benefits of marriage that aid them in fulfilling their (moral, if not legal) responsibility to care or provide for a partner or child. Everyone, whether gay or straight, must deal with the vicissitudes of life—accidental injury, unexpected illness, an untimely death. Yet many of us fail to plan for the occurrence of such events.[1] To fill these gaps, the states have created default rules that are designed to replicate the plans most people would make.[2] The problem for lesbians and gay men is that the states did not write these default rules with us in mind; rather, they were built on and around a presumption of heterosexuality.[3]

In practice, this means that our partners and families of choice are legally (and/or socially) ignored. When unexpected events occur, our partners and friends usually find themselves at the mercy of authority figures (e.g., a doctor or lawyer) or our relatives. Sometimes we are lucky, as I was when I was hospitalized. I was fortunate to be surrounded by doctors and nurses who unquestioningly treated Hien as my spouse and demonstrated the level of respect for our relationship that different-sex married couples take for granted. Other times, we are not quite so lucky, as when Hien was hospitalized. The infectious-disease specialist acted on the societal presumption of heterosexuality, assumed that Hien and I were unrelated, and asked me to leave so he could speak with Hien privately. I was treated as no more than a stranger to the man to whom I am married.

In life, we all face situations—both expected and unexpected—that could go more smoothly if only we did a bit of advance planning. For lesbians and gay men, planning is even more imperative because the safety net of default rules that exists for heterosexuals acts more like a snare when we become entangled in it. The purpose of this chapter is to show the location of some of the more dangerous traps for the unwary and to furnish some advice on how to avoid them. This chapter also builds on the discussion in Chapter 6 of the importance of achieving social and legal recognition for same-sex relationships by highlighting additional costs of allowing our relationships to be banished to social and legal invisibility.

Medical Planning

Medical Decisions

From a legal perspective, American notions of personal autonomy and bodily integrity are firmly entrenched in the requirement that a patient provide informed consent prior to medical treatment.[4] As the U.S. Supreme Court has recognized, a "logical corollary of the doctrine of informed consent is that the patient generally possesses the right not to consent, that is, to refuse treatment."[5] Thus, we each generally have the power to determine the medical treatments that we will, or will not, receive.

In *Cruzan v. Director, Missouri Department of Health,* a plurality of the Supreme Court found that "a competent person has a constitutionally protected liberty interest in refusing unwanted medical treatment."[6] Under the Fourteenth Amendment's Due Process Clause, a state may not deprive an individual of this liberty interest without due process of law. Thorny questions arise, however, when we are no longer able to refuse medical treatment ourselves and must rely upon others to do so for us. In *Cruzan,* the Court held that the State of Missouri did not violate a patient's right to refuse medical treatment when it required her parents (who were acting for her because she was in a persistent vegetative state) to show clear and convincing evidence of her intent, expressed while she was competent, to refuse the medical treatment at issue.

Advance Directives. Every state and the District of Columbia provide a mechanism for you to document your wishes, while still competent, concerning the provision—or withholding—of life-sustaining treatment. The terminology for this documentation varies from state to state. But whether the document is called an instruction; a directive; or, in keeping with common parlance, a living will, the purpose is the same: to provide those who must make medical decisions for you with concrete evidence of your wishes. To further this end, some form documents actually encourage you to think about a wide array of common life-sustaining treatments and prompt you to express your wishes concerning each form of treatment. For example, Pennsylvania's statutory form of living will contains a checklist of life-sustaining treatments that you can choose to accept or reject, including cardiac resuscitation, mechanical respiration, tube feeding or other artificial nutrition or hydration, blood or blood products, surgery, chemotherapy, radiation treatment, kidney dialysis, and treatment with antibiotics.

In addition, every state provides a mechanism to name another person to make medical decisions on your behalf. You can choose to make this grant of authority effective immediately, or you can have it "spring" into force only upon your incapacity.[7] States have likewise given this documentation a variety of names, including "health care proxy," "durable power of attorney for health care," "medical power of attorney," or "mandate." But again, despite the differing nomenclature, the purpose remains the same: to allow you to name someone whom you know and trust to make decisions on your behalf when you are unable to do so. In this way, you can not only ensure that medical decisions will comport with your wishes but also empower someone whom you trust to make decisions in the many situations not covered by your living will, which normally relates only to end-of-life treatment under very narrow circumstances. In her concurring opinion in *Cruzan*, Justice O'Connor went so far as to suggest that a state may be constitutionally required to give effect to decisions made by a patient's agent under a durable power of attorney for health care.

Collectively, these two documents are often referred to as "advance directives," and in many states both an expression of your wishes concerning end-of-life treatment and the appointment of a representative for making health care decisions may be made in a single, overall document. Indeed, given the limited scope of living wills, it is useful to view them as a single document because (1) you should always have both of them to ensure that you are fully protected, and (2) you should ensure that they are consistent (e.g., designations of agents should be consistent in both documents if your state requires separate documents). You should also speak with your agent about your wishes concerning medical treatment to make the agent aware of those wishes and to determine whether the agent will be comfortable making decisions in accordance with your wishes.

Given the ready availability of form documents, the actual preparation of an advance directive is a relatively simple task. What is difficult, however, is thinking through, either on your own or with the input of others, the life-sustaining treatments that you wish (or do not wish) to have and whom you can trust to make medical decisions for you. Nonetheless, you should be aware that the form and contents of these documents vary from state to state, and you will need to obtain the correct form document. Free advance directive forms for each state are readily accessible on the Internet; for example, Caring Connections, a program of the National Hospice and Palliative Care Organization, provides free forms and instructions for each state on its web site (www.caringinfo.org), along with a toll-free help line that you can call with questions. You may also be able to obtain advance directive forms from your local hospital or doctor.

Notwithstanding the accessibility of these documents, free advice on how properly to prepare them, and the national attention that is periodically brought to this issue (e.g., the Terri Schiavo case), most people still do not have an advance directive.

Surrogate Decision-Making Statutes and Guardianship. Most states have enacted "surrogate decision-making" or "family decision-making" statutes to address situations in which an individual is incapacitated and does not have an advance directive. To resolve the question of who possesses decision-making authority, surrogate decision-making statutes normally contain a list of individuals (e.g., spouse, parents, siblings, grandparents) who, in order of priority, may act on behalf of an incapacitated patient when medical decisions must be made.[8] In effect, these statutes give legal sanction to the common practice of looking to family members to make medical decisions when a patient is unable to do so herself. These statutes also "provide a means, short of cumbersome and possibly expensive guardianship proceedings [in court], for designating a surrogate decisionmaker when the patient has no close family members to act as a surrogate."[9] These statutes provide default rules that serve as a helpful safety net for heterosexuals without an advance directive.

For the most part, however, these default rules provide little protection to lesbians and gay men because they were not drafted with us in mind.[10] A number of surrogate decision-making statutes confine the list of potential surrogates to (legal) spouses and relatives. For lesbians and gay men, this means that neither a same-sex partner nor a close friend could ever be appointed a surrogate under one of these statutes. Many others do not confine the list of potential surrogates to (legal) spouses and relatives, but only California, Connecticut, the District of Columbia, Hawaii, Maine, New Mexico, Oregon, and Washington accord a same-sex partner the same priority as a legal spouse.[11] (Yet, reminiscent of the false choice described in Chapter 6, even if you live in one of these jurisdictions, you may fall ill while traveling in a state that does not give priority to same-sex partners and find that the safety net has been pulled out from under you.) In the remaining states, same-sex partners and close friends occupy the same spot in the priority list, which usually means that they may serve only as a surrogate of last resort (i.e., after every available relative of the patient who is listed in the statute has first been approached and declined to act). In states without a surrogate decision-making statute, the only available option in the absence of an advance directive is to request that a court adjudicate the patient incompetent and appoint a guardian for the patient.[12]

The well-known case of Sharon Kowalski amply demonstrates the substantial costs of pursuing guardianship proceedings. In 1983, Kowalski was in a car accident and suffered severe brain injuries that "left her in a wheelchair, impaired her ability to speak, and caused severe loss of short-term memory."[13] At the time of the accident (and unbeknown to her parents), Kowalski had been living with her lesbian partner, Karen Thompson, for four years. About six months after the accident, Kowalski's partner and her father cross-petitioned for guardianship. Thompson agreed to the appointment of Kowalski's father as guardian in the expectation that she would be allowed to visit Kowalski and to participate in medical decisions made by Kowalski's father. Kowalski's father, who "refused to believe that his daughter was homosexual,"[14] soon terminated Thompson's visits.

Nearly three years later, after court-ordered examinations of Kowalski and hearings on whether she wished Thompson to visit her, the court allowed Thompson to resume visiting Kowalski. Later that year, Kowalski's father asked to be removed as guardian for health reasons, and Thompson petitioned the court to be appointed as successor guardian. The trial court ignored overwhelming evidence of Thompson's suitability for appointment as guardian and denied her petition; however, that decision was reversed on appeal. So, after seven years of legal wrangling and more than $225,000 in litigation costs, Karen Thompson was finally appointed Sharon Kowalski's legal guardian.[15]

Importance of Advance Planning. Given the obvious lack of a reliable safety net for lesbians and gay men, advance directives take on far greater importance for us than they do for heterosexuals. If you wish your partner or a friend to make medical decisions for you when you are incapacitated, then you must execute an advance directive. In some states, you may also be able to nominate a guardian in the advance directive. Although these nominations are not binding, courts do take them into consideration.[16] It is also worth noting that, because of issues surrounding the "portability" of advance directives, you may wish to complete forms not only for your home state but also for any state to which you routinely travel.[17]

Once the advance directive is executed, you should keep the original document in a safe place and distribute copies to your physician, the person you have appointed to make decisions on your behalf, your family, your close friends, and anyone else who might become involved in your medical care. Some states have created registries for advance directives that are accessible to health care providers or allow you to indicate on your driver's license that you have an advance directive.[18] If hospitalized, you should bring a copy of the advance directive with you (or ask someone to bring it for you) because your agent may encounter resistance from the hospital staff and need to show the directive to them and insist that they honor it.[19] Failure to comply with an advance directive may be punishable by law (either through a civil, criminal, or disciplinary action).[20]

Durable Power of Attorney for Finances. When planning for incapacity, it is equally important to think about financial decisions. Every state and the District of Columbia now permit you to execute a durable power of attorney authorizing an agent to act on your behalf in financial matters. In many states, you can choose to make the power of attorney effective immediately, or you can have it "spring" into force only upon your incapacity.[21] Durable powers of attorney are designed to be an easy and inexpensive alternative to requesting a court to adjudicate the incapacitated individual incompetent and to appoint a conservator to handle her finances.[22] In the event that appointment of a conservator nonetheless proves necessary, you can nominate a conservator in the power of attorney; although these nominations are not binding, courts do take them into consideration.[23]

Due to differences in state law, you should have an attorney prepare this document for you. Before speaking with the attorney, you should contact any financial institutions that you do business with to learn about their policies on powers of attorney and to obtain copies of any special forms that they might require so that your attorney can complete them and be sure they do not conflict with your general power of attorney. You should also consider whom you would like to name as your agent, the powers that you wish to grant your agent, and whether you wish the grant to be effective immediately or only upon your incapacity. Your attorney can provide advice on these issues, and should caution you not to make decisions lightly because powers of attorney are easily susceptible to abuse. An attorney can also document your capacity when preparing and executing the power of attorney, in case it is later challenged on the ground that you lacked the mental capacity to execute it.[24]

Hospital Visitation

Unfortunately, lesbians and gay men are sometimes denied the opportunity to visit a hospitalized same-sex partner or close friend because we are not "family." A particularly heart-wrenching case took place in October 2000 when Robert Daniel, who had fallen seriously ill, was transferred from one Maryland hospital to another.[25] Daniel's partner, Bill Flanigan, whom Daniel had named as his agent in an advance directive, arrived at the hospital while the transfer was taking place and repeatedly asked to see Daniel and for information about his condition. The hospital staff refused to update Flanigan on Daniel's condition or to allow him to see Daniel because visitation was restricted to "family." It was not until Daniel's sister and mother arrived that the hospital released information about his condition and allowed them to visit him. By that time, Daniel had lost consciousness, and he died a few days later. Because the hospital staff employed an overly restrictive definition of "family"—apparently a result of the hospital's failure to train its staff properly—Flanigan was prevented from saying his last good-bye to Daniel.

If you are named as the agent in the advance directive of a hospitalized partner or friend, then you should be permitted to visit in order to make necessary medical decisions (although, as evidenced by Flanigan's situation, this does not always happen). Even so, this decision-making power—and hence the need for access—does not normally spring into force until the patient is incapacitated. Many times, a partner or friend is hospitalized when she is still able to make medical decisions for herself; that is, before the advance directive becomes effective. Alternatively, individuals may be hospitalized without having executed an advance directive. In either case, restrictive hospital visitation policies may make it difficult to gain access to an ill same-sex partner or friend.

In California, Connecticut, the District of Columbia, Hawaii, Massachusetts, New Jersey, Vermont, and Washington same-sex couples who have married, entered into a civil union, or registered as domestic partners or reciprocal beneficiaries are accorded the same hospital visitation rights enjoyed by different-sex married couples.[26] New York likewise guarantees equal hospital visitation rights to domestic partners.[27] Several states—including Illinois, Louisiana, Maine, Nebraska, Nevada, and Rhode Island—have enacted legislation that allows a hospitalized patient to designate individuals who must be allowed to visit.[28] A number of other states—including Michigan, Minnesota, New Hampshire, North Carolina, Virginia, and West Virginia—have enacted legislation that prohibits hospitals from restricting visits by nonrelatives.[29]

Outside these jurisdictions, hospitals set their own visitation policies. These policies usually follow social custom, which opens the door for the privileging of heterosexuality to influence their drafting and implementation. Counterbalancing this influence, the Joint Commission on Accreditation of Healthcare Organizations (JCAHO), a nonprofit organization that accredits hospitals nationwide, has promulgated a set of accreditation standards that requires hospitals to respect a patient's right to have visitors from outside the hospital.[30] For purposes of these standards, JCAHO defines "family" as "the person(s) who plays a significant role in an individual's life. This may include a person(s) not legally related to the individual."[31] This inclusive definition of "family" plainly embraces both same-sex partners and close friends.

Although many lesbian and gay rights organizations encourage the execution of documents authorizing a same-sex partner or a close friend to visit you in the hospital, these documents are of limited legal effect. In a number of states, these documents are unnecessary because the state either accords same-sex partners the same visitation rights as spouses or prohibits hospitals from restricting visits by nonrelatives. In states where you can designate individuals who must be allowed to visit, you should be careful to observe all of the required formalities to ensure that the designation will be legally enforceable. In places where hospitals are free to set their own visitation policies, hospital visitation authorizations are not legally binding on the hospital.

Despite these caveats, it may be wise to execute a hospital visitation authorization—no matter where you live—to memorialize your desire that your partner or a friend be allowed to visit you. Even if hospitals in your home state may not prevent your partner or a friend from visiting, you may fall ill when traveling out of state and end up in a hospital with a restrictive visitation policy. A hospital visitation authorization, which should be made to look as official as possible (e.g., it should be dated, witnessed, and, if possible, notarized), can be used to persuade the hospital to allow your partner or a friend to visit. It would also be wise to enlist the help of your doctor and the hospital's patient advocate when making a plea to ease visitation restrictions.

If you live in a state where hospitals are free to set their own visitation policies, you can lobby for the enactment of a law requiring hospitals to relax their visitation policies in one of the ways described above. On the grassroots level, you can call your local hospital and ask for a copy of its visitation policy. If the hospital does not permit visits by nonrelatives, you can contact the hospital's patient advocate or community relations office to ask that (1) the hospital visitation policy be revised in accordance with the JCAHO definition of "family" (described earlier), (2) sexual orientation be included in the nondiscrimination statement in the hospital's patient bill of rights, and (3) staff be trained in these policies so that difficulties do not arise in their implementation.

Financial Planning

Financial planning, when approached from a legal perspective, does not usually concern the choice of investments. After all, financial planners are in a far better position than most attorneys to provide advice on managing finances and meeting personal financial goals. Lawyers tend to focus instead on the most effective legal means of structuring the acquisition, holding, and transfer of property—after the initial choice of investment has been made. Maintaining that lawyerly focus, this section first addresses estate planning and then addresses the related topic of planning for the dissolution of a relationship.

Estate Planning

Estate planning—it sounds like something that only the elderly and the idle rich need to worry about. But don't be fooled. We all own things of monetary or sentimental value—whether clothing, jewelry, family photos, a stamp or record collection, a car, or a home—that we want certain people to have when we pass away. In this regard, estate planning is no different from medical planning: It is all about expressing our wishes while we still can. And again, for lesbians and gay men, estate planning takes on even greater importance than for heterosexuals because the default rules created for those who do not plan ahead were not drafted with us in mind.[32]

Intestate Succession. When someone dies without having planned ahead for the transfer of her property, she is said to have died wholly or partially "intestate." To the extent that an individual dies intestate, the relevant state intestacy laws (also called laws of descent and distribution) determine who inherits her property. Each state has its own statutory scheme for intestate succession, developed with a number of different purposes in mind. However, the central focus of these laws is on distributing the decedent's property in a way that (1) reflects her likely intentions, (2) will be perceived as fair by those who inherit the property, and (3) promotes the nuclear family.[33]

Given the last of these three concerns, it should come as little surprise that intestacy laws have generally been drafted with only heterosexuals in mind.[34] In fact, the intestacy laws of all but a handful of states provide that the decedent's property shall pass to the surviving (legal) spouse and relatives (no matter how estranged) in a prescribed order of priority. If there is no surviving spouse or relatives, then the government takes the property. Most intestacy laws *make no provision whatsoever* for a surviving same-sex partner or other legally unrelated person. Consequently, these default rules in many cases produce results that are clearly at odds with the way that many lesbians and gay men would prefer their property to be distributed upon death (e.g., many would prefer distribution to a same-sex partner rather than to estranged relatives or the government).[35]

It is only in jurisdictions that legally recognize same-sex relationships (i.e., California, Connecticut, the District of Columbia, Hawaii, Maine, Massachusetts, New Hampshire, New Jersey, Oregon, Washington, and Vermont) that a surviving same-sex partner is entitled to claim a share of the decedent's property. In each of these jurisdictions, a surviving, legally recognized partner is entitled to the same intestate share of a decedent's property as would be a surviving different-sex spouse.[36] And, except in Maine and Washington, the surviving legal partner is protected against disinheritance in each of these jurisdictions by being provided the same statutory share of the decedent's estate as would be provided to a surviving different-sex spouse.[37]

The State of Washington may also afford some legal protection to a surviving partner outside a registered domestic partnership. As mentioned in Chapter 6, a state appellate court has recognized that same-sex relationships can qualify as "meretricious relationships" under Washington law, which affords the parties to such a relationship certain property rights when they separate. When a meretricious relationship instead ends by reason of the death of one of the partners, it has been argued that the surviving partner should similarly be entitled to a share of the deceased partner's property acquired during the relationship.[38] If so, the surviving same-sex partner would be entitled to a share of the decedent's property, albeit a lesser share than that of a surviving spouse or registered domestic partner taking by intestate succession (who would be entitled to a share of both property acquired during the relationship and any property separately belonging to the decedent).[39]

These protections may disappear, however, if the decedent owned property outside one of these jurisdictions. To illustrate the point, let's explore a hypothetical example involving my sister, Elyse, and her partner, Cindy, whose relationship is legally recognized by the State of New Jersey. If Cindy were to pass away intestate, then, under New Jersey law, Elyse would be entitled to the same intestate share of Cindy's property as a surviving spouse. But what if Cindy owned real property (e.g., land) and personal property (e.g., a car) in Ohio at the time of her death? Which state's law should apply to this property—New Jersey's (as the state of Cindy's residence at death) or Ohio's (as the state where the property was physically located at her death)?

Generally speaking, if someone dies owning property in more than one state, then: (1) in the case of real property, the intestacy laws of the state where the property is located determine who shall inherit the property, and (2) in the case of personal property, the intestacy laws of the decedent's home state at the time of death determine who shall inherit the property.[40] Thus, in the case of nonresident decedents, Ohio's intestacy laws determine who inherits real property located in Ohio, and the intestacy laws of the decedent's home state (here, New Jersey) determine who inherits personal property located in Ohio.[41] Under a straightforward application of these rules, Cindy's land in Ohio would not pass to Elyse, regardless of Cindy's wishes, because Ohio is one of the many states whose intestacy laws ignore same-sex relationships.[42]

You might expect, however, that Elyse would fare better with respect to Cindy's car in Ohio because New Jersey's intestacy laws should determine who inherits that property. But Ohio reserves the right to apply its own intestacy laws to personal property if application of the law of the decedent's home state (here, New Jersey) would produce a result that is contrary to Ohio public policy.[43] In this regard, Ohio law plainly states that "the recognition or extension by the state of the specific statutory benefits of a legal marriage to nonmarital relationships between persons of the same sex or different sexes is against the strong public policy of this state."[44] Even absent the public policy exception and this clear statement of Ohio public policy, the Ohio Constitution currently provides that "only a union between one man and one woman may be a marriage valid in or recognized by this state and its political subdivisions. This state and its political subdivisions shall not create or recognize a legal status for relationships of unmarried individuals that intends to approximate the design, qualities, significance or effect of marriage."[45] Accordingly, Cindy's personal property in Ohio also would not pass to Elyse because their legal relationship, however valid in New Jersey, is of no legal effect at all in Ohio.

Alternatives for Planning Ahead. There are a variety of ways to avoid these default rules if they would produce a distribution of property inconsistent with your wishes. Some of the more common methods include execution of a last will and testament, the creation of a living trust, taking title to property as joint tenants with right of survivorship, and investing in property that passes through a beneficiary designation (e.g., life insurance and retirement accounts). I provide a brief description of each of these methods in this section; nevertheless, it would be wise to consult an attorney for advice in developing an appropriate estate plan.

Last will and testament. A last will and testament is a document that directs the distribution of your property upon your death. To be honored as a valid will, a document must satisfy the formal requirements prescribed by state law. Usually, a will must be made by someone who is both competent and over a minimum age, reduced to writing, signed by the decedent, and attested by a designated number of witnesses in a specified manner.[46] Moreover, the operative provisions of a will must be carefully drafted to avoid ambiguity and "to pre-empt litigation that will drain the estate's assets."[47] To make certain that your will is properly drafted and executed, it is best to hire an attorney to perform this task.

Before meeting with an attorney about preparing your will, there are a few matters that you need to consider. Obviously, you must decide how you wish your property to be distributed when you pass away: Are there specific items that you would like certain individuals to receive? Who should get the remainder of your property? Who would you like to get these items if the first person you name predeceases you? Next, you must name an "executor" (i.e., the person whom you trust to carry out the directions in your will), along with an alternate in case your first choice is unable or unwilling to serve. And, if you have minor children, you should consider whom you would like to serve as their guardian after your death (e.g., you could name your partner if you are not both legal parents) because a will is often an appropriate place to nominate a guardian. Keep in mind that, as circumstances in your life change, you should revisit these decisions and consider whether you need to make corresponding changes to your will, which you are free to modify or revoke at any time.

If properly drafted and executed, a will can be an effective device for distributing property. Yet wills do have certain disadvantages. Depending on the state, the probate and administration process—that is, proving the validity of a will and then inventorying the decedent's property, paying her debts, and distributing the remaining property according to the provisions of the will—can be costly and time-consuming. (To address this disadvantage, states have taken steps to streamline the probate and administration process for small estates.[48]) In addition, wills are open to public inspection because they are filed in court in connection with probate.[49] For lesbians and gay men, keeping the extent of one's assets private can be an important means of avoiding a will contest by a disgruntled or hostile family member.[50]

To defeat a transfer to a same-sex partner or a close friend, a family member may challenge the validity of the will on one or more grounds, including failure to comply with the formalities required by state law in the execution of a will, lack of mental competence, undue influence, duress, or fraud.[51] Having an attorney prepare a will can reduce the possibility of a successful challenge because an experienced attorney is less likely to make a mistake in observing the formalities of execution, and an attorney can take steps to document the decedent's competence at the time that the will is prepared and executed.[52] Furthermore, if each member of a same-sex couple is separately represented (i.e., if each hires her own attorney to engage in estate planning), the couple can similarly reduce the possibility of a challenge on the common ground of undue influence.[53]

Living trust. A "living" trust is an alternative means for directing the distribution of property at death while retaining control over it during life. Typically, a living trust involves the transfer of a portion of a person's property in trust. The transferor retains the income from the trust during her life and directs the property to be distributed to specified individuals at her death—in much the same way that she would in a will. The transferor retains day-to-day control over the transferred property by naming herself trustee (and she usually names her partner or a trusted friend or family member as cotrustee or successor trustee in case she is unable to act).[54] Rounding out her control over the property, the transferor retains the right to revoke or amend the trust during her life.

The primary advantage of a living trust is that assets in the trust avoid the probate and administration process.[55] Although living trusts can be challenged on grounds of lack of mental capacity or undue influence in the same way that wills can,[56] they are thought to be less susceptible to attack because they are more difficult to detect—unlike wills, they are not open to public inspection—and, if established well in advance of death, because the transferor "can be shown to have exercised dominion and control and an awareness of the trust's terms."[57] An additional benefit of living trusts is the ability of a cotrustee or successor trustee to easily take over the management of the property if the transferor becomes incapacitated.[58]

Balanced against these advantages are the costs and limitations of a trust arrangement. The primary costs involved in a living trust are the attorney's fees for preparation of the trust instrument and the costs involved in transferring title to the assets to the trust.[59] Furthermore, a living trust cannot serve as a complete substitute for a will. Execution of a will is necessary to ensure that any property not transferred to the trust passes according to the decedent's wishes (rather than by intestate succession), and a will may be the only appropriate vehicle for nominating a guardian for minor children.[60] Finally, it is worth noting that a living trust provides no federal tax advantages over a will: During life, the trust property will continue to be treated as if you owned it yourself for federal income tax purposes,[61] and, at death, the trust property will be subject to federal estate tax in your hands.[62]

Joint tenancy with right of survivorship. In most states, there are two primary forms of co-ownership of property available to lesbians and gay men: "tenancy in common" and "joint tenancy with right of survivorship."[63] The principal difference between them lies in the effect of death on ownership of the property. Upon the death of a co-owner of property held as tenants in common, the deceased co-owner's share of the property passes under her will or state intestacy laws to her beneficiaries or heirs, making the property subject to the probate and administration process. In contrast, upon the death of a co-owner of property held as joint tenants with right of survivorship, the deceased co-owner's share of the property automatically passes to the surviving co-owner(s) by operation of law, avoiding the probate and administration process. Because of the automatic nature of this transfer, joint tenancies are another alternative for directing the distribution of property at death.

Joint tenancies have the added advantage of being essentially free and relatively easy to create—all that is necessary is inclusion in the deed or title of the phrasing required by state law to create the right of survivorship.[64] Like living trusts, joint tenancies are thought to be less susceptible to attack on grounds of undue influence.[65] Weighed against these advantages, however, are potential federal tax disadvantages: For lesbians and gay men (but not different-sex married couples), the creation of the joint tenancy may have federal gift tax consequences, and the property may also be subject to federal estate tax at the death of a co-owner.[66]

Beneficiary designations. As part of your financial planning, you may participate in a 401(k) retirement plan at work; open an individual retirement account (IRA) (e.g., a traditional or Roth IRA); purchase life insurance, stocks, or bonds; or open a bank or brokerage account. In many cases, you can designate the person who will receive this property on your death simply by filling out the appropriate form (and, through additional paperwork, can later change beneficiaries). Bank accounts with such beneficiary designations may be called "POD" ("payable on death") accounts, and designating a beneficiary for your securities may be called "TOD" ("transfer on death") registration. A few states even allow TOD registration of a motor vehicle.[67] By taking advantage of these opportunities to designate a beneficiary for your property, you can avoid state intestacy laws as well as the probate and administration process—without being required to share ownership of property during your lifetime.

Although designating a beneficiary will usually be a simple matter, additional planning will be required for certain types of assets. This is particularly true in the case of retirement accounts and life insurance. With respect to retirement accounts, an attorney or accountant can provide advice on how to transfer the proceeds of these accounts in the most tax-effective manner possible. And with respect to life insurance, an attorney can provide advice on how to structure the purchase and ownership of a life insurance policy so as to minimize insurance law issues as well as any adverse tax consequences. In either case, the advice should be tailored to your individual circumstances.

End-of-Relationship Planning

When different-sex married couples divorce, the law furnishes them with a set of default rules for the division and distribution of their property and the payment of spousal support. The laws of California, Connecticut, the District of Columbia, Massachusetts, New Hampshire, New Jersey, Oregon, and Vermont similarly furnish default rules to same-sex couples when they dissolve their legal relationships.[68] Although Washington law makes no specific mention of the rules that apply with regard to the division and distribution of property and payment of spousal support upon the termination of a domestic partnership, Washington case law indicates that same-sex couples may be entitled to a just and equitable distribution of property acquired during their relationship, provided that it qualifies as a "meretricious relationship" under Washington law.[69]

However, this legal safety net may be pulled out from under same-sex couples who attempt to dissolve their legal relationship outside the state of celebration. At present, there are only a few published decisions in this area, and those decisions provide evidence of only mixed success. On the positive side, an Iowa trial court dissolved a Vermont civil union and ordered the division of the couple's property and debts, notwithstanding the state's mini-DOMA.[70] A Massachusetts trial court, relying in part on the then-recent extension of the right to marry to same-sex couples in that state, similarly dissolved a Vermont civil union and ordered the division of the couple's property.[71] In contrast, a Connecticut appeals court—prior to the enactment of its civil union regime and accompanying mini-DOMA—held that its trial courts were without the power to dissolve a Vermont civil union.[72] Faced with this uncertainty, same-sex couples may wish to return to the jurisdiction of celebration to take advantage of its procedures for dissolving the legal bond between them, especially if one or both members of the couple wish to enter into another legally recognized relationship (because of the potential for this second legally recognized relationship to be considered bigamous). But they should be prepared to stay for more than just a quick court appearance because these jurisdictions generally require a minimum period of residence (in some cases, as much as twelve months) before dissolution may be sought.[73]

A couple that has not entered into a legal relationship—and, therefore, cannot rely on a comprehensive set of default rules—may enter into a written agreement governing property division in the event of a breakup. This "domestic-partnership" agreement (also called a "living together" or "cohabitation" agreement) can cover a wide variety of subjects in addition to the division of property, including the pooling of income and assets during the relationship, the division of responsibility for household chores and expenses, the division of parental rights and responsibilities (if the couple has or plans to have children), and whether one partner will provide support payments to the other (and any children) upon dissolution of the relationship.[74] A domestic-partnership agreement may also specify the method for resolving disputes between the partners; for example, some couples choose to avoid the judicial system and opt instead for mediation or arbitration of their disputes in order to save time, money, and the need to confront a hostile legal system.[75]

Even a couple that has entered into a legal relationship may wish to enter into a domestic-partnership agreement. Such an agreement will be necessary for those who enter into a reciprocal beneficiary relationship in Hawaii or a domestic partnership in Maine or Washington because those states provide no mechanism for dividing and distributing property upon the termination of the relationship.[76] In the other states that legally recognize same-sex relationships, a domestic-partnership agreement will be advisable if the couple wishes a different division of their property than would be dictated by the default rules.[77]

Couples who decide to enter into a domestic-partnership agreement should enlist the aid of an attorney to draft the agreement. Ideally, each member of the couple should be represented by a separate attorney in this process. Separate attorneys can help to protect the parties' respective interests and will enhance the value of the agreement as reinforcement for the couple's estate plan (because the agreement can serve as evidence of the existence of the relationship, and of the absence of undue influence, in a later will contest or other legal proceeding).[78] An attorney can also help to minimize the potential tax consequences of the agreement. The benefit of an attorney is further underscored by (1) the need to ensure that the document recites an "acceptable" form of consideration for the agreement (e.g., all references to the sexual aspects of a relationship must be expurgated from the document lest it be deemed an unenforceable contract for prostitution),[79] (2) the existence of a handful of states that refuse to enforce contracts between unmarried cohabitants,[80] and (3) another handful of states that have enacted mini-DOMAs worded so broadly as to call into question the validity of even powers of attorney and wills that name a same-sex partner.[81]

Tax Planning

Most people are familiar with the federal income tax from their first-hand experience of filing a return every April 15th. For those not familiar with it, the federal income tax is imposed on a taxpayer's income (e.g., wages, rents, interest, dividends, and gain on the sale or disposition of property), less any deductions to which the taxpayer may be entitled for certain expenses (e.g., home mortgage interest, state and local taxes, or medical expenses). Fewer people are probably familiar with the federal gift and estate taxes because they are imposed on only a relative few among us. The federal gift and estate taxes are imposed on wholly or partly gratuitous transfers of property, either during life or at death. These taxes are imposed on the person who transfers the property, and the taxes are imposed on the full value of the property (or portion of the property) transferred gratuitously.

It is important to note, however, that not all gratuitous transfers will trigger the actual payment of gift or estate taxes. For example, the gift tax "annual exclusion" permits you (in legal terminology, the "donor") to give away a certain amount of property each year ($12,000 in 2007) to each of as many donees (the legal term for the recipient of a gift) as you wish— without paying any gift tax at all.[82] You are also allowed a credit (the so-called unified credit) against any gift or estate tax that you might owe after application of the gift tax annual exclusion; in effect, this credit permits you to transfer a certain amount of property over your lifetime without paying gift or estate tax. For the foreseeable future, the amount of property that you can transfer over your lifetime free of gift tax under the unified credit is capped at $1 million.[83] Currently, the credit for estate tax purposes is higher (e.g., those who die in 2007 are allowed to transfer $2 million worth of property free of tax).[84] But note that both of these figures are cumulative. As the Internal Revenue Service (IRS) explains: "Any unified credit you use against your gift tax in one year reduces the amount of credit that you can use against your gift tax in a later year. The total amount used during life against your gift tax reduces the credit available to use against your estate tax."[85] Due to the combination of the gift tax annual exclusion and the unified credit, the gift and estate taxes are meant to be paid by only the wealthiest among us.

Each state has its own tax system as well. Most states impose some form of an income tax, often patterned on the federal income tax. Fewer states impose gift and estate taxes.

Given the multiplicity of different taxes that can apply to a single transaction and the complexity of the tax laws, tax advice must necessarily be tailored to the specific circumstances of the individual taxpayer and should be provided by an accountant or an attorney who is familiar with the tax laws *and* who can evaluate your personal situation. Thus, in the remainder of this section, rather than provide specific advice, my goal is to sensitize you to some of the difficult tax issues that lesbian and gay taxpayers face and to highlight the ways in which the tax laws can be (and, in fact, are) used to express disapproval of homosexuality and to oppress and harass lesbians and gay men.

Federal Taxation
From Default to Discrimination. The federal tax laws reflect—and reward— a traditional view of "marriage." When you look at marriage through the prism of the federal tax laws, what you see is a husband and wife who pool their income and assets and act together as a single economic unit, with one spouse engaging in paid labor out in the job market while the other takes care of the house and children.[86] Supporting this view, the tax laws generally ignore transactions that occur between husbands and wives and often treat all of the property owned by one spouse as owned by the other. Moreover, the very rate structure of the federal income tax is designed to reward one-earner couples with a marriage "bonus" (i.e., they pay less tax than if they each filed as "single" taxpayers) and to penalize two-earner couples (i.e., they pay more

tax than if they each filed as "single" taxpayers).[87] A number of other provisions exacerbate the marriage penalty for two-earner couples, including the home-mortgage interest deduction, the deduction for educational loan interest, the credit for household and dependent care services, and the earned income tax credit.[88] In these ways, the tax laws protect and promote a 1950s, "Ozzie and Harriet" model of marriage and the family.

On a practical level, this view both produces tax benefits for and imposes tax limitations on different-sex married couples. Married couples count among the benefits (1) the ability to transfer property to each other free of income, gift, and estate taxes[89] and (2) an exemption from income tax for fringe benefits that one spouse's employer provides to the other spouse (recall the health insurance example from Chapter 5).[90] Among the limitations imposed on married couples are (1) the inability to take an income tax deduction for losses on the transfer of property between spouses[91] and (2) having the stock owned by one spouse attributed to the other for purposes of a number of antiabuse rules.[92] Tax planning for married couples entails no more than maximizing the available benefits and minimizing the impact of the limitations.

Until 1996, the federal tax laws defined marriage by reference to state law.[93] Because no state recognized same-sex marriage prior to that time, the federal tax laws, by default, did not recognize same-sex marriage either. Congress was content with this arrangement until same-sex couples began to make progress in their fight for marriage. As explained in Chapter 6, the Hawaii Supreme Court's decision in *Baehr v. Lewin* raised the specter of legalized same-sex marriage for the first time in the United States. While that case was pending, Congress enacted the Defense of Marriage Act in 1996 to limit the potential impact of any outcome favorable to same-sex couples.[94] DOMA provides, in part, that only different-sex couples can be considered "married" for purposes of federal law; thus, DOMA ensures that a same-sex couple can never be treated as married for federal tax purposes—even if their relationship is legally recognized by one or more of the several states.[95]

From a tax planning perspective, DOMA makes same-sex couples the mirror image of different-sex couples. On the one hand, same-sex couples do not reap any of the tax benefits bestowed upon different-sex married couples. For example, because same-sex couples are treated as legal strangers for tax purposes, transfers of property between the members of the couple may trigger income, gift, and/or estate tax. And, as described in Chapter 5, they must pay income tax on employer-provided domestic-partner benefits such as health insurance coverage. On the other hand, same-sex couples are not subject to the limits imposed on married different-sex couples that stem from their being treated as one economic unit for tax purposes. For example, same-sex couples can deduct "paper" losses and arrange their business affairs in ways that artificially minimize taxes without worrying about spousal attribution rules. Consequently, tax planning for same-sex couples involves no more than maximizing this inverse set of available benefits and minimizing the impact of these inverse burdens.

Tax Limbo. On closer inspection, however, the task becomes more complicated. Recall that transactions between husbands and wives are ignored for tax purposes—meaning that there is no income tax on any gain, no income tax deduction for any loss, and no gift or estate tax on the transfer—all based on the assumption that married couples act together as a single economic unit. Through DOMA, Congress has confirmed that it will not treat same-sex couples similarly, even when they do operate as a single economic unit. But refusing to treat same-sex couples as "married" raises more questions than it answers.

Inevitably, transfers will occur between members of a same-sex couple; however, because the federal government does not recognize same-sex relationships, the couple cannot simply ignore these transfers in the way that a different-sex married couple can. Instead, a same-sex couple must grapple with fitting the transfers between them into some recognized tax classification (e.g., a transfer between donor and donee, creditor and debtor, employer and employee, or business partners).[96] Choosing the right classification is important because the tax results of a transfer often depend on the circumstances in which it occurs.

This situation can pose particularly significant problems for same-sex couples who pool income and investments (and, as we will see, even for those who don't). If one partner contributes more to the pool than the other, then the couple must determine the character of the difference both for income- and gift tax purposes because the partner who contributes more to the pool has effectively made a transfer to the partner who contributes less. (Because differing contributions commonly result from differing salary levels, I will refer to the partner who contributes more as the "higher-earning partner" and to the partner who contributes less as the "lower-earning partner.") In the following paragraphs, we will consider the potential characterizations of the transfer from the higher-earning partner to the lower-earning partner, first for income tax purposes and then for gift tax purposes. We will finish by considering how these income tax and gift tax characterizations can interact with each other in rather unpleasant ways.

For income tax purposes, there is a variety of different potential characterizations for the transfer between the partners. For example, the higher-earning partner might be treated as making a gift each time the utility bills are paid, a trip is made to the grocery store, or a withdrawal is made from the ATM.[97] If so, the higher-earning partner would continue to pay income tax on her wages,[98] and the lower-earning partner would pay no income tax on those gifts.[99] Alternatively, the pooling might be characterized as a support arrangement.[100] In that case, the higher-earning partner would still be subject to income tax on her wages, whereas the lower-earning partner would again pay no income tax on the support payments.[101] A more frightening alternative would require *both* partners to pay income tax on the transfer—on the ground that it technically constitutes "income" to each of them.[102] Yet another possibility is that the transfer could represent some combination of the above (e.g., part support, part gift; part support, part income; or part gift, part income).

Already nauseated by the dizzying array of potential income tax characterizations for the transfer from the higher-earning partner to the lower-earning partner, we now have to consider that same transfer from a gift tax perspective. For gift tax purposes, there is likewise a variety of different potential characterizations for the transfer between the partners—some similar to the income tax characterizations, some not—each with their own specific tax consequences. For example, the transfer might be treated as a gift from the higher-earning partner to the lower-earning partner.[103] Although the recipient of a gift is not taxed on its value under the income tax, the person who makes a gift is taxed on its transfer under the gift tax.[104] Alternatively, the transfer might be considered to have been made in exchange for domestic services rendered by the lower-earning partner to the higher-earning partner or in exchange for a transfer of property from the lower-earning partner to the higher-earning partner. In either case, the transfer will escape gift tax but may trigger income tax (i.e., the payment for services would be taxable wages, and the transfer of property might result in a taxable gain).[105] Another possibility is that the transfer might be characterized as a support payment, which would escape gift tax (just as it escapes income tax).[106] Yet another possibility is that the transfer could represent some combination of the above (e.g., part nontaxable support payment, part taxable gift, or part nontaxable payment for services, part taxable gift).

You might be inclined to dismiss the gift tax complications on the ground that, as I described earlier, the gift and estate taxes are designed to be imposed on only the wealthiest among us. But if gift tax were imposed on transfers between members of a same-sex couple—that is, on every rent or mortgage payment, on every purchase of clothing, and even on purchases of food—then this transfer tax on the wealthy would effectively become a sales tax imposed on a broad swath of the lesbian and gay community. As soon as the total amount of transfers from the higher-earning partner to the lower-earning partner exceeded the gift tax annual exclusion ($12,000 in 2007), the higher-earning partner would begin spending down her unified credit, which, as mentioned earlier, is the amount that she can pass free of gift tax during her entire lifetime and is currently capped at $1 million.[107] Any same-sex couple with jointly held property and a significant disparity in income (e.g., one-earner couples like my sister and Cindy) could easily exceed the annual exclusion and spend down the unified credit each year. Once the unified credit has been exhausted, which is a distinct possibility over the course of a long-term relationship (or a series of long-term relationships), the higher-earning partner would begin paying gift tax at the eye-popping rate of 41 percent.[108] Thus, for same-sex couples, gift taxation is a possibility whose importance should not be trivialized or ignored.

To finish our trip through tax limbo, we need to consider together the income and gift tax consequences of the transfer from the higher-earning partner to the lower-earning partner. Because the income tax and the gift tax operate independently, the characterization of a single transfer need not be consistent across these taxes.[109] In other words, just because a transfer is characterized as a gift for gift tax purposes does *not* mean that it must be characterized as a gift for income tax purposes. In practice, this results in the further multiplication of the potential tax characterizations for a single transfer within a same-sex couple. It also opens the door to the possibility of truly punitive taxation of same-sex couples. For example, a transfer might be characterized as income to *both* partners for income tax purposes *and* as a taxable gift from the higher-earning partner to the lower-earning partner for gift tax purposes.[110] This would result in a portion of the income of the higher-earning partner being subject to *triple* taxation. While you are pondering this terrifying possibility, I would remind you that different-sex married couples need not worry about any of this because transfers between husband and wife are essentially ignored for federal tax purposes.

Tax Hell. Faced with a veritable constellation of potential tax characterizations and high financial stakes, same-sex couples who pool their income and investments must examine all of the possibilities and settle on the appropriate tax treatment for any transfer between them. Their task is not made any easier by Congress or the IRS, both of whom have been conspicuously silent on the question of how the tax laws apply to same-sex couples. Yet, despite this lack of guidance, the tax laws attach a presumption of correctness to whatever treatment the IRS deems appropriate (after the fact and without any advance public notice) and place the burden on same-sex couples to prove that their chosen treatment is correct.[111] If, on audit, the couple fails to carry this burden, they may find themselves liable not only for additional tax but also for interest and penalties (if they cannot show reasonable cause for the failure).[112]

Even if the couple manages to win the battle with the IRS over an alleged failure appropriately to characterize the transfer between them, they may find that the war is far from over. In addition to settling on an appropriate tax characterization for the transfer, same-sex couples must comply with record-keeping and reporting requirements that are ostensibly designed to help verify the accuracy of their tax returns. For income tax purposes, each taxpayer is required to "keep such permanent books of account or records . . . as are sufficient to establish the amount of gross income, deductions, credits, or other matters required to be shown by such person in any return."[113] Likewise, for gift tax purposes, each taxpayer is required to "keep such permanent books of account or records as are necessary to establish the amount of his total gifts . . . together with the deductions allowable in determining the amount of his taxable gifts, and the other information required to be shown in a gift tax return."[114] Furthermore, if a taxpayer makes gifts to a person in excess of the annual exclusion, she is required to list separately on her gift tax return *each and every gift* made during the calendar year to that person, including gifts that are not taxed because of the annual exclusion.[115]

In practice, these requirements impose an impossible compliance burden on same-sex couples. The tax laws essentially require these couples to keep records documenting every penny that they spend, save, or give away. Every trip to the grocery store, the clothing store, and the bank must be documented to determine who spent what and on whom. Without these records, the couple will find it difficult, if not impossible, to counter IRS assertions about the size or character of the transfer between them. Even couples who avoid pooling or carefully avoid differing contributions to the pool may be tripped up by these recordkeeping requirements because, without the appropriate records, the couple may find it difficult to disprove the existence of an asserted transfer between them.

Simply put, these recordkeeping and reporting requirements are demeaning and oppressive. Think for a moment of the mountain of receipts that you collect every month. Then think of having to catalog each of those receipts according to what was spent and on whom. Then think about having to tally up the total at the end of the year. Then think about having to list every one of these transactions on a tax return, showing the particulars of what was given, by whom, and to whom. Finally, think about having to find a place to store this small mountain of paper for six or more years (depending on the relevant statute of limitations)[116] in order to provide support for the claimed amount and tax characterization of any transfer.

For same-sex couples, these recordkeeping and reporting requirements represent not only an onerous burden but also a severe invasion of privacy. After *Lawrence v. Texas*,[117] the government can no longer break into our bedrooms to determine with whom and how we have sex, but it can still use the tax laws to knock on the front door, come in, and probe our every move with our partners. In contrast, the tax laws effectively afford married different-sex couples a privileged zone of privacy by treating them as one economic unit— because transactions within the couple generally have no tax consequences, the government has no need to inquire about them.

Such a crushing (not to mention insulting) recordkeeping and reporting burden can only breed noncompliance. Whether intentional or unintentional, this noncompliance may give the IRS an opportunity to increase the amount of additional tax owed and to impose penalties. Furthermore, there is the potential for criminal liability for those who either throw up their hands at the impossibility of the task or who refuse to acquiesce in their own oppression. In this way, the uncertainty of tax limbo quickly and easily gives way to the unremitting punishment of what I like to refer to as the lesbian and gay circle of tax hell.[118]

Sodomy Statutes Still Exist. Given the array of civil and criminal penalties that the IRS has at its disposal, same-sex couples are nearly assured that they will not escape an IRS audit unscathed. In this way, the tax laws act much the same as sodomy statutes did prior to *Lawrence v. Texas*. Like a sodomy statute, the tax laws target and punish gay sex, albeit indirectly through the proxy of gay coupling. And despite being underenforced,[119] the tax laws and their civil and criminal penalties nonetheless "hang as an ominous Sword of Damocles over the heads of lesbians and gay men throughout the country."[120]

Moreover, as is the case with a sodomy statute, the impact of the tax laws on lesbians and gay men is not confined to the civil and criminal penalties that may be imposed on the occurrence of the rare audit or prosecution. The tax laws can also harm us in other ways. As one of the more prominent applications of DOMA, the tax laws are overtly hostile to lesbians and gay men. The tax laws clearly attempt to banish our relationships from sight by creating every incentive for same-sex couples to retreat to the closet (i.e., to file returns and statements with the IRS that do not connect one partner with the other in any way) in an effort to avoid detection and punishment. This overt hostility toward same-sex couples stigmatizes us by branding our relationships inferior to those of different-sex couples. In effect, the tax laws contribute to the feedback loop discussed at the end of Chapter 2 by embodying and perpetuating societal prejudice, discrimination, and hostility toward lesbians and gay men and by giving such activity the imprimatur of the federal government.

State Taxation

Because most states with income or gift taxes pattern them after federal law,[121] state taxes usually exacerbate the problems identified in the previous section. In fact, even among the jurisdictions that legally recognize same-sex relationships, only California, Connecticut, the District of Columbia, Massachusetts, New Jersey, Oregon, and Vermont limit further damage by recognizing same-sex relationships for income and (where applicable) gift tax purposes.[122]

Out of Sight, Out of Mind

As this chapter illustrates, society has constructed a safety net of legal default rules that provides little or no protection to lesbians and gay men. By operating for the nearly exclusive benefit of heterosexuals, these default rules reflect and reinforce heterosexual privilege and manifest society's disapproval of homosexuality. And this is no accident; it is the result of a conscious choice. When squarely faced with its failure to address the legal needs of lesbians and gay men, society has generally chosen to ignore us—to keep us out of sight and out of mind. For example, when it appeared that the legal safety net would be extended to cover lesbians and gay men, Congress and most state legislatures and/or voters passed "defense of marriage" measures to ensure that any success would be of limited effect and that they could rest assured that the legal mechanisms for expressing their disapproval of homosexuality would be left undisturbed.[123]

To be sure that this disapprobation is unmistakably felt, society employs the law to render the lives of lesbians and gay men both more difficult and more expensive than those of heterosexuals. To replicate the ready-made medical, financial, and tax plans that heterosexuals can purchase at the bargain price of a marriage license, same-sex couples must hire an attorney to engage in significant and potentially expensive legal planning on their behalf. Even when couples have the means to plan ahead, legal rules may curtail or eliminate their ability to effectuate their wishes. For instance, the tax laws impose burdensome costs on same-sex couples who dare to pool their income and investments, and certain mini-DOMAs are so broadly written as to cast doubt on the validity of powers of attorney or wills that name a same-sex partner. Besides, the failure to take our relationships into account only emboldens hostile family members to attack our planning documents because, if their attacks are successful, the default rules will award them power over our bodies and/or our property.[124]

If same-sex relationships were legally recognized, the need for advance planning would be greatly reduced because lesbians and gay men could rely on the existing network of default rules in the same way that heterosexuals now can. We would also be able to arrange our affairs in ways that more closely track our personal preferences because legal limits such as the tax rules and mini-DOMAs previously mentioned would no longer restrict our planning options. At the same time, recognizing our relationships would reduce hostile family members' incentives to attack our planning documents because our partners (rather than those family members) would be the ones recognized as most naturally entitled to make decisions for us or to receive our property at death.[125]

To this end, and as described more fully in Chapter 6, it is important that we counter society's attempts to banish our relationships to social and legal invisibility. In this chapter, I have elaborated on the costs of allowing society to push our relationships out of sight and out of mind, hopefully demonstrating that these costs are quite simply intolerable. But we cannot expect others to understand the intolerability of this burden unless we explain the nature and extent of these costs to those around us. By making the costs both concrete and personal, we can hopefully open heterosexuals' eyes to the many ways in which our relationships are disadvantaged by the heterosexual privilege that is embedded in our laws.

Notes

1. Ellen D. B. Riggle, Sharon S. Rostosky, and Robert A. Prather, "Advance Planning by Same-Sex Couples," *J. Fam. Issues* 27 (2006): 758, 760–761, 766 tbl. 1; Ellen D. B. Riggle, Sharon S. Rostosky, Robert A. Prather, and Rebecca Hamrin, "The Execution of Legal Documents by Sexual Minority Individuals," *Psychol. Pub. Pol'y and L.* 11 (2005): 138, 139–141, 149 tbl. 2.

2. T. P. Gallanis, "Default Rules, Mandatory Rules, and the Movement for Same-Sex Equality," *Ohio St. L.J.* 60 (1999): 1513, 1522.

3. Ibid., 1523–1524.

4. *Cruzan v. Dir., Mo. Dep't of Health*, 497 U.S. 261, 269 (1990); see also Fay A. Rozovsky, *Consent to Treatment: A Practical Guide*, 4th ed. (New York: Aspen Publishers, 2007), §1.01[D][1]–[4].

5. *Cruzan*, 270.

6. Ibid., 278.

7. If you choose to create a "springing" power, you may nevertheless wish to include a provision (or look for a form with a provision) that immediately designates the person as your agent for purposes of the new federal Health Insurance Portability and Accountability Act (HIPAA) privacy regulations. 45 C.F.R. §164.502(g)(1) (2007). Particularly if your agent is also your partner, this will facilitate your doctor's ability to share medical information with your partner.

8. Alan Meisel and Kathy L. Cerminara, *The Right to Die: The Law of End-of-Life Decisionmaking*, 3d ed. (New York: Aspen Publishers, 2006), §8.04.

9. Ibid., §8.01, at 8-3.

10. See, for example, Unif. Health-Care Decisions Act §5 cmt., *U.L.A.* 9 (2005), 112.

11. Cal. Prob. Code §4716 (2007); Conn. Gen. Stat. §§19a-570(9), -571, 46b-38nn, -38oo (2007); D.C. Code §21-2210 (2007); Haw. Rev. Stat. §327E-2, -5 (2007); Me. Rev. Stat. tit. 18-A, §5-805 (2007); N.M. Stat. §24-7A-5 (2006); Or. Rev. Stat. §127.635 (2005); Act of May 9, 2007, ch. 99, §9, 2007 Ore. HB 2007 (Lexis) (see Chapter 6 for an explanation of the effective date of this act); Act of April 20, 2007, §11, 2007 Wash. Adv. Legis. Serv. 156 (S.B. 5336) (to be codified at Wash. Rev. Code §7.70.065).

12. Rebecca K. Glatzer, "Equality at the End: Amending State Surrogacy Statutes to Honor Same-Sex Couples' End-of-Life Decisions," *Elder L.J.* 13 (2005): 255, 269.

13. *In re Guardianship of Sharon Kowalski*, 478 N.W.2d 790, 791 (Minn. Ct. App. 1991).

14. Gallanis, "Default Rules," 1517.

15. Ibid.

16. Matthew R. Dubois, "Legal Planning for Gay, Lesbian, and Non-Traditional Elders," *Alb. L. Rev.* 63 (1999): 263, 304.

17. Meisel and Cerminara, *The Right to Die*, §7.10(J).

18. Ibid., §7.10(A).

19. See, for example, Glatzer, "Equality at the End," 255–256.

20. Meisel and Cerminara, *The Right to Die*, §7.10(H).

21. William M. McGovern Jr. and Sheldon F. Kurtz, *Wills, Trusts, and Estates*, 3d ed. (St. Paul, MN: West Group, 2004), 350, §9.2; John J. Regan, *Tax, Estate, and Financial Planning for the Elderly* (New York, NY: Matthew Bender, 2006), §13.03(1).

22. Karen E. Boxx, "The Durable Power of Attorney's Place in the Family of Fiduciary Relationships," *Ga. L. Rev.* 36 (2001): 1, 7, 12.

23. Jennifer Tulin McGrath, "The Ethical Responsibilities of Estate Planning Attorneys in the Representation of Non-Traditional Couples," *Seattle U. L. Rev.* 27 (2003): 75, 96.

24. Regan, *Tax, Estate, and Financial Planning,* 1, §13.03(5).

25. Complaint, *Flanigan v. Univ. of Md. Med. Sys. Corp.* (Baltimore City Cir. Ct., February 26, 2002), www.lambdalegal.org/our-work/in-court/briefs/flanigan-v-university-of.html.

26. Cal. Health and Safety Code §1261 (2007); Conn. Gen. Stat. §46b-38nn (2007); D.C. Code §32-704 (2007); Haw. Rev. Stat. §323-2 (2006); N.J. Rev. Stat. §§26:8A-6(f), 37:1–32(j) (2007); Vt. Stat. tit. 15, §1204(e)(10) (2006); Act of April 20, 2007, §8, 2007 Wash. Adv. Legis. Serv. 156 (S.B. 5336); *Goodridge v. Dep't of Pub. Health,* 798 N.E.2d 941 (Mass. 2003).

27. N.Y. Pub. Health Law §2805-q (2007).

28. 410 Ill. Comp. Stat. 50/3.2 (2006); La. Rev. Stat. §40:2005(A) (2006); Me. Rev. Stat. tit. 22, §1711-D (2006); Neb. Rev. Stat. §71-20,120 (2006); Nev. Rev. Stat. §449.715 (2005); R.I. Gen. Laws §23-17-19.3 (2006).

29. Mich. Comp. Laws Serv. §333.20201(2)(k) (2006); Minn. Stat. §144.651(21), (26) (2006); N.H. Rev. Stat. §151:21(XII) (2006); N.C. Gen. Stat. §131E-117(8) (2006); W. Va. Code §16-5B-15 (2007); Act of March 26, 2007, 2007 Va. Laws ch. 516 (H.B. 2730) (to be codified at Va. Code §32.1-127).

30. Joint Commission on Accreditation of Healthcare Organizations (JCAHO), *Hospital Accreditation Standards* 148 (Oak Brook Terrace, IL: JCAHO, 2006).

31. Ibid., 398.

32. T. P. Gallanis, "Inheritance Rights for Domestic Partners," *Tul. L. Rev.* 79 (2004): 55, 56, 60; Amy D. Ronner, "Homophobia: In the Closet and in the Coffin," *Law and Ineq.* 21 (2003): 65.

33. Mary Louise Fellows, Monica Kirkpatrick Johnson, Amy Chiericozzi, Ann Hale, Christopher Lee, Robin Preble, and Michael Voran, "Committed Partners and Inheritance: An Empirical Study," *Law and Ineq.* 16 (1998): 1, 11–13.

34. Gallanis, "Default Rules," 1523.

35. See Fellows et al., "Committed Partners and Inheritance," 31–52, 65–91.

36. Cal. Fam. Code §297.5(c) (2007); Cal. Prob. Code §6401 (2007); Conn. Gen. Stat. §§45a-437, 46b-38nn (2007); D.C. Code §19-302 (2007); Haw. Rev. Stat. §560:2-102 (2006); Mass. Gen. Laws ch. 190, §1 (2007); Me. Rev. Stat. tit. 18-A, §2-102 (2006); N.H. Rev. Stat. §561:1(I) (2007); Act of June 4, 2007, §1, 2007 N.H. Adv. Legis. Serv. ch. 58 (to be codified at N.H. Rev. Stat. §457-A:6, effective January 1, 2008); N.J. Rev. Stat. §§3B:5-3, 37:1–32(a) (2007); Or. Rev. Stat. §§112.025, .035 (2005); Act of May 9, 2007, ch. 99, §9, 2007 Ore. HB 2007 (Lexis) (see Chapter 6 for an explanation of the effective date of this act); Act of April 20, 2007, §27, 2007 Wash. Adv. Legis. Serv. 156 (S.B. 5336) (to be codified at Wash. Rev. Code §11.04.015); Vt. Stat. tit. 14, §§401, 461, 474, 551 (2006); ibid., tit. 15, §1204(e)(1); *Goodridge,* 941.

37. Cal. Fam. Code §297.5(c) (2007); Cal. Prob. Code §§100-105, 21,610-21,612 (2007); Conn. Gen. Stat. §§45a-257a, -436, 46b-38nn (2007); D.C. Code §19-113 (2007); Haw. Rev. Stat. §560:2-202, -301 (2006); Mass. Gen. Laws ch. 191, §§9, 15 (2007); N.H. Rev. Stat. §560:10 (2007); Act of June 4, 2007, §1, 2007 N.H. Adv.

Legis. Serv. ch. 58 (to be codified at N.H. Rev. Stat. §457-A:6, effective January 1, 2008); N.J. Rev. Stat. §§3B:5-15, :8-1, 37:1-31(a), -32(a), (c), -33 (2007); Or. Rev. Stat. §112.305 (2005); Act of May 9, 2007, ch. 99, §9, 2007 Ore. HB 2007 (Lexis) (see Chapter 6 for an explanation of the effective date of this act); Vt. Stat. tit. 14, §§401, 402, 461, 474, 551 (2005); ibid., tit. 15, §1204(e)(1); *Goodridge,* 941. Compare Me. Rev. Stat. tit. 18-A, §2-201, -301 (2006); Act of April 20, 2007, 2007 Wash. Adv. Legis. Serv. 156 (S.B. 5336) (failing to amend Wash. Rev. Code §11.12.095 to include domestic partners).

38. John E. Wallace, "The Afterlife of the Meretricious Relationship Doctrine: Applying the Doctrine Post-Mortem," *Seattle U. L. Rev.* 29 (2005): 243.

39. Wash. Rev. Code §11.04.015 (2007); Act of April 20, 2007, §27, 2007 Wash. Adv. Legis. Serv. 156 (S.B. 5336) (amending Wash. Rev. Code §11.04.015 to include registered domestic partners).

40. *Restatement (Second) of Conflict of Laws* (St. Paul, MN/American Law Institute Publishers, 1969), §§236, 260 and cmt. b.

41. *Howard v. Reynolds,* 283 N.E.2d 629, 630 (Ohio 1972); *In re Estate of Gould,* 140 N.E.2d 793, 796 (Ohio Prob. Ct.), aff'd, 140 N.E.2d 801 (Ohio Ct. App. 1956).

42. Ohio Rev. Code §§2105.06, 3101.01 (2006).

43. *Howard,* 631.

44. Ohio Rev. Code §3101.01(C)(3) (2006).

45. Ohio Const., art. XV, §11.

46. *Restatement (Third) of Property: Wills and Other Donative Transfers* (St. Paul, MN/American Law Institute Publishers, 1999), §3.1 cmts. f–r.

47. Bruce L. Stout, "Handwritten Wills May Be Valid If Certain Requirements Are Met," *Est. Plan.* 30 (2003): 174.

48. McGovern and Kurtz, *Wills, Trusts, and Estates,* 504–506, §12.2.

49. Karin J. Barkhorn, "Wills and Revocable Inter Vivos Trusts: A Comparison," in *Basic Will Drafting,* PLI Tax Law and Estate Planning Course Handbook Series 318 (New York: Practising Law Institute, 2002), 21, 24.

50. Merrianne E. Dean, "Estate Planning for Non-Traditional Families," in *32nd Annual Estate Planning Institute,* PLI Tax Law and Estate Planning Course Handbook Series 309 (New York: Practising Law Institute, 2001), 1087, 1101.

51. McGrath, "The Ethical Responsibilities of Estate Planning Attorneys," 92 and n.80; Christine A. Hammerle, "Free Will to Will? A Case for the Recognition of Intestacy Rights for Survivors to a Same-Sex Marriage or Civil Union," *Mich. L. Rev.* 104 (2006): 1763, 1769–1771.

52. Dubois, "Legal Planning," 313–314; Hammerle, "Free Will to Will?" 1770–1771.

53. McGrath, "The Ethical Responsibilities of Estate Planning Attorneys," 92; Dubois, "Legal Planning," 314–315; Hammerle, "Free Will to Will?" 1769–1770.

54. Barkhorn, "Wills and Revocable Inter Vivos Trusts," 23–24; Dubois, "Legal Planning," 321–322.

55. McGovern and Kurtz, *Wills, Trusts, and Estates,* §9.1, 342–345; Barkhorn, "Wills and Revocable Inter Vivos Trusts," 24–26.

56. McGovern and Kurtz, *Wills, Trusts, and Estates,* 342, §9.1.

57. McGrath, "The Ethical Responsibilities of Estate Planning Attorneys," 93; Dubois, "Legal Planning," 322–323; see McGovern and Kurtz, *Wills, Trusts, and Estates,* 342–343, §9.1.

58. Barkhorn, "Wills and Revocable Inter Vivos Trusts," 24; McGrath, "The Ethical Responsibilities of Estate Planning Attorneys," 93–94.

59. McGovern and Kurtz, *Wills, Trusts, and Estates,* §9.1, 343; Barkhorn, "Wills and Revocable Inter Vivos Trusts," 27.

60. See Barkhorn, "Wills and Revocable Inter Vivos Trusts," 29–30.

61. I.R.C. §§671, 676, 677 (2007).

62. Ibid., §§2036, 2038.

63. A third form of co-ownership—tenancy by the entirety—is similar to joint tenancy with right of survivorship but is available only to married couples. Not all states recognize tenancies by the entirety. See Richard R. Powell, *The Law of Real Property,* rev. ed. (Newark, NJ: Matthew Bender, 2006), 7, §52.01(3) (indicating that California, Connecticut, Maine, New Hampshire, and Washington do not recognize this form of co-ownership). Nonetheless, Hawaii, Massachusetts, New Jersey, Oregon, and Vermont permit legally recognized same-sex couples to form tenancies by the entirety. Haw. Rev. Stat. §509-2 (2006); Mass. Gen. Laws, ch. 184, §§7–8 (2007); N.J. Rev. Stat. §37:1-32(a) (2007); Or. Rev. Stat. §§91.020, .030, 108.090 (2005); Act of May 9, 2007, ch. 99, §9, 2007 Ore. HB 2007 (Lexis) (see Chapter 6 for an explanation of the effective date of this act); Vt. Stat. tit. 15, §1204(e)(1) (2006); *Goodridge,* 941.

64. Powell, *The Law of Real Property,* 7, §51.02(1).

65. Patricia A. Cain, "Tax and Financial Planning for Same-Sex Couples: Recommended Reading," *Tul. J.L. and Sexuality* 8 (1998): 613, 640.

66. I.R.C. §2040 (2007); Treas. Reg. §25.2511-1(h)(5) (as amended in 1997).

67. For example, Cal. Veh. Code §5910.5 (2007); Kan. Stat. §8-135(c)(10) (2006); Mo. Rev. Stat. §301.681 (2006); Ohio Rev. Code §2131.13 (2006).

68. Cal. Fam. Code §297.5(a)–(b) (2007); Conn. Gen. Stat. §§46b-38nn, -3800 (2007); D.C. Code §§16-910, -911, -916 (2007); Act of June 4, 2007, §1, 2007 N.H. Adv. Legis. Serv. ch. 58 (to be codified at N.H. Rev. Stat. §457-A:7, effective January 1, 2008); N.J. Rev. Stat. §37:1-31(b) (2007); Act of May 9, 2007, ch. 99, §9, 2007 Ore. HB 2007 (Lexis) (see Chapter 6 for an explanation of the effective date of this act); Vt. Stat. tit. 15, §1204(d) (2006); *Goodridge,* 941.

69. Act of April 20, 2007, §6, 2007 Wash. Adv. Legis. Serv. 156 (S.B. 5336); *Gormley v. Robertson,* 83 P.3d 1042, 1046 (Wash. Ct. App. 2004).

70. See *Alons v. Iowa Dist. Ct.,* 698 N.W.2d 858 (2005).

71. *Salucco v. Alldredge,* 17 Mass. L. Rep. 498 (Mass. Super. Ct. 2004).

72. *Rosengarten v. Downes,* 802 A.2d 170 (Conn. App. Ct.), review granted, 261 Conn. 936, review dismissed as moot, SC 16836, order (Conn. December 31, 2002), available at www.domawatch.org/stateissues/connecticut/rosengartenvdownes.html (for a description of the procedural history of this case, see Op. Att'y Gen. 2004-006, 2004 Conn. AG Lexis 5, *6 n.2 [May 17, 2004]); see also *Lane v. Albanese,* 39 Conn. L. Rptr. 3 (Conn. Super. Ct. 2005).

73. For example, Conn. Gen. Stat. §46b-44 (2007); D.C. Code §16-902 (2007); Mass. Gen. Laws, ch. 208, §5 (2007); N.H. Rev. Stat. §458:5 (2007); Vt. Stat. tit. 15, §592 (2006).

74. See, for example, Frank S. Berall, "Estate Planning Considerations for Unmarried Same- or Opposite-Sex Cohabitants," *Quinnipiac L. Rev.* 23 (2004): 361, 380, 383–386, 388–389; S. Jeanne Hall, "Estate Planning for Domestic Partnerships," in *Valuation, Taxation, and Planning Techniques for Sophisticated Estates,* PLI Tax

Law and Estate Planning Course Handbook Series 332 (New York: Practising Law Institute, 2005), 389, 412–421.

75. See Mark J. Hanson, "Moving Forward Together: The LGBT Community and the Family Mediation Field," *Pepp. Disp. Resol. L.J.* 6 (2006): 295; Clark Freshman, "Privatizing Same-Sex 'Marriage' Through Alternative Dispute Resolution: Community-Enhancing Versus Community-Enabling Mediation," *UCLA L. Rev.* 44 (1997): 1687.

76. Haw. Rev. Stat. §572C-7 (2006); Me. Rev. Stat. tit. 22, §2710(4) (2006); Act of April 20, 2007, §6, 2007 Wash. Adv. Legis. Serv. 156 (S.B. 5336).

77. Freshman, "Privatizing Same-Sex 'Marriage,'" 1704.

78. See Berall, "Estate Planning Considerations," 379–380; Hall, "Estate Planning for Domestic Partnerships," 421; McGrath, "The Ethical Responsibilities of Estate Planning Attorneys," 85.

79. For example, *Marvin v. Marvin*, 557 P.2d 106, 116 (Cal. 1976); see McGrath, "The Ethical Responsibilities of Estate Planning Attorneys," 84 n.26.

80. For example, *Rehak v. Mathis*, 238 S.E.2d 81 (Ga. 1977); *Hewitt v. Hewitt*, 394 N.E.2d 1204 (Ill. 1979); see also *In re Estate of Hall*, 707 N.E.2d 201, 205–206 (Ill. App. Ct. 1998).

81. For example, Va. Code §20-45.3 (2006); Mont. Code §40-1-401(4) (2005).

82. I.R.C. §2503(b) (2007).

83. Ibid., §2505.

84. Ibid., §§2001, 2010. The unified credit for estate tax purposes will be undergoing nearly annual changes (i.e., increases) over the next several years, leading up to what is currently scheduled to be a one-year repeal of the estate tax in 2010. Ibid., §2010.

85. Internal Revenue Service, Department of Treasury, Pub. 950, Introduction to Estate and Gift Taxes (2006), 3.

86. Boris I. Bittker and Lawrence Lokken, *Federal Taxation of Income, Estates, and Gifts*, 3d ed. (Boston: Warren, Gorham, and Lamont, 1999), 4 §111.3.2; Grace Blumberg, "Sexism in the Code: A Comparative Study of Income Taxation of Working Wives and Mothers," *Buff. L. Rev.* 21 (1971): 49, 52; Nancy C. Staudt, "Taxing Housework," *Geo. L.J.* 84 (1996): 1571, 1571–1572.

87. Dorothy A. Brown, "The Marriage Bonus/Penalty in Black and White," *U. Cin. L. Rev.* 65 (1997): 787.

88. Theodore P. Seto, *The Assumption of Selfishness in the Internal Revenue Code: Reflections on the Unintended Tax Advantages of Gay Marriage*, Loyola Law School Legal Studies Paper 2005-33 (2005), 18–19.

89. I.R.C. §§1041, 2056, 2523 (2007).

90. For example, ibid., §§105(b), 106(a), 119(a), 132(h)(1)–(2); Treas. Reg. §1.106-1 (1960); ibid., §1.132-1(b)(3)(iii) (as amended in 1993).

91. I.R.C. §§267(a)(1), 1041 (2007).

92. For example, ibid., §§267(c)(4), 318(a).

93. *Boyter v. Comm'r*, 668 F.2d 1382, 1385 (4th Cir. 1981).

94. H.R. Rep. 104-664 (1996), 2, 4, reprinted in 1996 U.S.C.C.A.N. 2905, 2906, 2908.

95. 1 U.S.C. §7 (2007).

96. Adam Chase, "Tax Planning for Same-Sex Couples," *Denv. U. L. Rev.* 72 (1995): 359, 373–389.

97. Patricia A. Cain, "Same-Sex Couples and the Federal Tax Laws," *Tul. J.L. and Sexuality* 1 (1991): 97, 114–115.

98. See *Lucas v. Earl*, 281 U.S. 111, 114–115 (1930); I.R.S. Chief Couns. Mem. 2006-08-38 (February 24, 2006); but see Patricia Cain, "Relitigating *Seaborn*: Taxing the Community Income of California Registered Domestic Partners," *Tax Notes* 111 (2006): 561; Dennis J. Ventry Jr., "No Income Splitting for Domestic Partners: How the IRS Erred," *Tax Notes* 110 (2006): 1221.

99. I.R.C. §102 (2007).

100. Cain, "Same-Sex Couples and the Federal Tax Laws," 115–116.

101. Bittker and Lokken, *Federal Taxation of Income, Estates, and Gifts* 1, §10.2.6; Cain, "Same-Sex Couples and the Federal Tax Laws," 116.

102. Bruce Wolk, "Federal Tax Consequences of Wealth Transfers Between Unmarried Cohabitants," *UCLA L. Rev.* 27 (1980): 1240, 1244–1262; see also Cain, "The Income Tax: Taxing Lesbians," *S. Cal. Rev. L. and Women's Stud.* 6 (1997): 471, 476.

103. See Cain, "Same-Sex Couples and the Federal Tax Laws," 125; Nancy J. Knauer, "Heteronormativity and Federal Tax Policy," *W. Va. L. Rev.* 101 (1998): 129, 174; Wolk, "Federal Tax Consequences of Wealth Transfers," 1275–1281.

104. I.R.C. §§102, 2501 (2007).

105. Treas. Reg. §25.2512-8 (as amended in 1992).

106. Rev. Rul. 68-379, 1968-2 C.B. 414.

107. I.R.C. §§2503(b), 2505(a) (2007).

108. Internal Revenue Service, Department of the Treasury, Instructions for Form 709 (2006), 12.

109. See, for example, *United States v. Davis*, 370 U.S. 65, 69 n.6 (1962); *Comm'r v. Beck's Estate*, 129 F.2d 243, 246 (2d Cir. 1942).

110. See Cain, "Same-Sex Couples and the Federal Tax Laws," 124–125; Chase, "Tax Planning for Same-Sex Couples," 375.

111. See Tax Ct. R. 142(a)(1); *United States v. Janis*, 428 U.S. 433, 440 (1976); *Welch v. Helvering*, 290 U.S. 111, 115 (1933).

112. Anthony C. Infanti, "The Internal Revenue Code as Sodomy Statute," *Santa Clara L. Rev.* 44 (2004): 763, 790–797.

113. Treas. Reg. §1.6001-1(a) (as amended in 1990).

114. Ibid., §25.6001-1(a) (as amended in 1977).

115. Ibid., §25.6019-3(a) (as amended in 1994).

116. Internal Revenue Service, Department of the Treasury, Pub. 552, Record-keeping for Individuals (2005), 6.

117. *Lawrence v. Texas*, 539 U.S. 558 (2003).

118. Anthony C. Infanti, "*Homo Sacer*, Homosexual: Some Thoughts on Waging Tax Guerrilla Warfare," *Unbound: Harv. J. of the Legal Left* 2 (2006): 27, 29.

119. See General Accounting Office, Rep. GAO-03-378, *Tax Administration: IRS Should Continue to Expand Reporting on Its Enforcement Efforts* 38 (2003): app. III, tbl. 6. But underenforcement does not mean no enforcement at all. See Patricia A. Cain, "Death Taxes: A Critique from the Margin," *Clev. St. L. Rev.* 48 (2000): 677, 696–697.

120. Evan Wolfson and Robert S. Mower, "When the Police Are in Our Bedrooms, Shouldn't the Courts Go in After Them? An Update on the Fight Against 'Sodomy' Laws," *Fordham Urb. L.J.* 21 (1994): 997.

121. *All States Tax Handbook* (Englewood Cliffs, NJ: Prentice-Hall, 2006) §273; Harley T. Duncan, Federation of Tax Administrators, "Relationships Between Federal and State Income Taxes" (2005), 1–2, available at www.taxreformpanel.gov/meetings/pdf/incometax_04182005.pdf.

122. See Act of September 30, 2006, 2006 Cal. Legis. Serv., ch. 802 (S.B. 1827); Conn. Gen. Stat. §46b-38pp (2007); D.C. Code §47-1803.02(a)(2)(W), -1805.01(f) (2007); N.J. Rev. Stat. §37:1-32(n) (2007); Act of May 9, 2007, ch. 99, §§9(8), 11, 2007 Ore. HB 2007 (Lexis) (see Chapter 6 for an explanation of the effective date of this act); Vt. Stat. tit. 15, §1204(e)(14) (2006); ibid., tit. 32, §5812; Department of Revenue, Commonwealth of Mass., Tech. Info. Rel. 04-17 (July 7, 2004).

123. See also American Law Institute, *Principles of the Law of Family Dissolution: Analysis and Recommendations* (Newark, NJ: LexisNexis, 2002), ch. 6; E. Gary Spitko, "The Expressive Function of Succession Law and the Merits of Non-Marital Inclusion," *Ariz. L. Rev.* 41 (1999): 1063, 1094–1096.

124. For example, Spitko, "The Expressive Function of Succession Law," 1075.

125. Ibid.

8
Parenting

One of the scariest—and happiest—days of my life was the day that my niece Olivia Grace was born. From the start, my sister, Elyse, had had a relatively easy pregnancy. She and Cindy had picked a sperm donor and found a fertility clinic, and Elyse had become pregnant after only one round of intrauterine (commonly referred to as "artificial") insemination. Elyse was very happy and active during her pregnancy; she went so far as to resod—yes, you read that right—the entire back yard while she was eight months pregnant. When I received a call from Elyse in the wee hours of the morning to tell me that she had gone into labor, I expected that she would have an easy delivery as well.

But then hours passed with no call. I began to worry. All I could think of was that something had gone horribly wrong. As I was falling back to sleep after Elyse's call, I dreamed that there were complications in the delivery. I began to think that my crazy dream had been a premonition. Both of our parents passed away years ago, so Elyse is the only family I have left, and I was distressed at the thought of losing her. I tried calling, but no one answered. Finally, almost twelve hours later, the phone rang. Olivia had been born, and Elyse was fine. It turned out that the labor had lasted for quite some time, and neither of us had been able to get through to the other because the cellular telephone reception in much of the hospital was poor to nonexistent.

Over the past few years, I have watched Olivia grow and learn. She now talks to me on the telephone (however sheepishly), always has a hug and a kiss for me, and adores my dog Kasha (whom she amusingly called "Kaka" for quite a while). At the same time, I have watched Elyse quickly grow into her role as a full-time mother, and I never cease to be amazed by her motherly aplomb. I had hoped to start this chapter with a narrative from Cindy or Elyse giving you their perspective on parenting; however, Elyse became pregnant again just as I began work on the chapter, and unfortunately, this pregnancy did not go as easily as the last.

This time, Elyse underwent cycle after cycle of intrauterine insemination, to no avail. Then she moved on to the riskier and more expensive in vitro fertilization. She was given a series of injections to increase egg production and then underwent an egg-retrieval procedure. The doctors retrieved more than ten eggs, which they then fertilized and allowed to grow for five days before inserting two embryos into Elyse's uterus and freezing another four for later use. Both embryos implanted. But Elyse experienced complications from the egg-retrieval procedure and then was ill and in bed for weeks. Cindy had to balance work with taking care of Olivia, fortunately with a great deal of help from family and friends. Things gradually normalized a bit during the middle of the pregnancy, but then Elyse was put on bed rest again at the end of the pregnancy. Yet, despite the emotional roller coaster, the two of them never wavered in their desire to have another child, and a few months before this book went to press, they actually had two new arrivals—my niece Emma and my nephew, Jake.

You might be wondering whether I have ever thought about having children of my own. This is a question I have wondered a lot about myself. While Michael and I were together, we often talked about having children. Michael wanted one of us to have a child using a surrogate mother (so that the child would be biologically related). At that point, I was hesitant to have children because I did not feel sufficiently stable in my career. Also, I was morally troubled by the idea of hiring a woman to bear our child, and I felt that the financial costs and legal risks involved in surrogacy arrangements outweighed any benefit of having a biologically related child. Instead, I preferred to adopt a child because my parents had adopted Elyse and me, and I thought I should do for someone else what my parents had done for us. In addition, I realize that, to some extent, social pressure influenced my thinking. There is clearly no social expectation that two gay men will have children; indeed, every stereotype points in exactly the opposite direction. If we were to have a child, we would all inevitably have to contend with hostility from those who neither expected nor wished us to have children.

In the end, Michael and I split up without ever resolving this impasse. More recently, Hien and I have discussed having children. Hien is more open to the idea of adoption, and I now feel stable enough in my career and life to care for a child and comfortable enough in my own skin to handle any hostility that might come our way. What worries me, though, is the thought that it might now be too late. As I sit writing this, I have just turned thirty-eight years old. My mother was the same age when she adopted me.

Although I am grateful for having been adopted and will always love my parents, I still can't help but think about how my mother passed away when she was sixty-nine years old. She might not have reached a ripe old age, but she did not pass away at an unusually young age either. At thirty years old, I found myself making funeral arrangements for my mother and having to care for my seventy-five-year-old father, who had Alzheimer's disease. When I looked around at my friends' parents, I saw that they were still young and could look forward to watching their children marry and have children of their own. A short eighteen months later, my father died.

I'm not sure I want to take the chance that this same course of events might repeat itself. The experience was both painful and unexpected (even if within the realm of possibility): My mother's cancer was extremely aggressive—she passed away only weeks after her illness became truly apparent. I would not want to be the cause of a similar, emotionally scarring experience for my own children. I also feel despair at the thought that none of my children could ever know either of my parents. I have always felt a loss or emptiness because I never really knew my grandparents, the last of whom died before I reached the age of nine and the others much earlier than that. Sometimes I wonder whether, with so many questions and doubts, I truly have the desire to have children. I don't see in myself the same drive and determination that I see in my sister and Cindy. I wonder whether I might be better suited to my role as uncle; maybe my purpose is not to have my own children but to do whatever I can for my nieces and nephews. Or maybe that is just the safer, more socially acceptable choice.

It is clear that I am no closer now to making this decision than I was ten years ago. But I no longer have the same luxury of time that I had back then. If I don't make a decision soon, the decision will be made for me.

It seems appropriate that the last substantive chapter in this book concerns legal issues relating to lesbian and gay parenting. Despite the cliché, there is more than a kernel of truth in the words that Whitney Houston sang more than twenty years ago: "I believe the children are our future; teach them well and let them lead the way."[1] The children of lesbians and gay men, like my niece Olivia (and her new siblings), provide us with hope because they hold the promise of a more accepting future for us all. In fact, studies suggest that children raised by lesbians and gay men may actually be more open-minded in matters relating to sexuality and more tolerant of diversity than children raised by heterosexuals.[2] Unfortunately, that may be exactly what reactionaries fear.

When reactionaries speak about lesbian and gay parenting, they do not use words such as "hope" and "promise"; instead, they describe it as "dangerous" or liken it to "experimentation" on children. For example, in 2003, the Vatican's Congregation for the Doctrine of the Faith issued a statement containing the following passage on lesbian and gay parenting: "Allowing children to be adopted by [same-sex couples] would actually mean doing violence to these children, in the sense that their condition of dependency would be used to place them in an environment that is not conducive to their full human development. This is gravely immoral."[3]

Because of such ingrained heterosexism, "no aspect of contemporary discussion about parenting and the family has produced as much controversy as the issue of lesbians and gay men raising children."[4] This controversy has manifested itself "in state and federal courts and legislatures, in the electoral arena, and in culture wars over efforts to extend to nonheterosexuals equal rights to marriage, child custody, adoption, foster care, and fertility services."[5] In the battle over lesbian and gay parenting, some of the most contested terrain lies in the emerging body of social science research on the effect of parents' sexual orientation on their children.[6]

Each side in this debate has been accused of manipulating the science to serve its own political ends.[7] The research in favor of lesbian and gay parenting "almost uniformly" supports the conclusion that "gay parents and their children do not differ significantly from the norm."[8] Based on this body of research, mainstream medical organizations such as the American Academy of Pediatrics and the American Psychological Association have issued statements supportive of lesbian and gay parenting.[9] A small but vocal group opposes the views of these mainstream medical organizations. Prominent among these opponents is the psychologist Paul Cameron, who heads the Family Research Institute and has published a number of articles that bolster "traditional" or "commonsense" views of lesbian and gay parenting.[10] For example, Cameron has asserted that lesbians and gay men are less child-oriented than heterosexuals; "homosexual parents are associated disproportionately with homosexual children" (this finding was reported under the heading "contagion"); lesbians and gay men are more than fifty times more likely to molest their children than heterosexuals; the children of lesbians and gay men disproportionately experience divorce and disproportionately report the circumstances of their childhood as emotionally harmful; and, based on a survey of obituaries in the *Washington Blade,* the children of lesbians and gay men are at a higher risk of losing a parent (to AIDS or other causes) during their childhood years.[11]

Naturally, each side has attacked the methodological flaws and biases in the other's research.[12] However, the most trenchant critique of this research is aimed at both sides and calls into question the heterosexist assumptions that undergird *all* of the research. Both sides in this debate start from the premise that parenting by married heterosexual couples is the standard against which all other parenting is measured.[13] Critics have asked why lesbian and gay parenting must be scientifically proven to match the results of parenting by married heterosexual couples before it will be deemed acceptable. In other words, why is difference necessarily bad? To turn this question around: If, as studies seem to suggest, lesbian and gay parents produce children who are more open-minded when it comes to matters of sexuality and who are more tolerant of diversity, why is parenting by married heterosexual couples not deemed deficient by comparison?

Yet we can only expect the battle over lesbian and gay parenting to grow more intense in coming years. Fueled by successful campaigns to ban same-sex marriage, the reactionary right is poised to push for legal bans on lesbian and gay parenting. Having branded lesbian and gay relationships inferior, reactionaries now wish to take what they view as the natural next step: branding lesbian and gay households legally unacceptable environments for raising children. In fact, the Human Rights Campaign reported "an exponential increase in 2005 in the number of measures that would have prohibited or restricted the ability of GLBT people to adopt children or to serve as foster parents. . . . Fortunately, none of these bills passed."[14]

In late 2005, a legislator in Indiana proposed a bill that would have significantly restricted access to assisted reproduction in that state, making it a crime for a doctor to help same-sex couples, single people, and even certain married couples to reproduce through intrauterine insemination or in vitro fertilization. After this proposal was quickly shot down, the same legislator introduced a bill in early 2006 that would authorize the state's health finance commission to study the issue.[15] At the same time, there were reports that in 2006, legislators in as many as sixteen states would introduce laws or constitutional amendments banning lesbians and gay men from adopting or foster parenting. In the end, only a single bill was introduced, and it quickly died without a hearing.

Interestingly, these legislative efforts failed despite the fact that lesbian and gay parenting remains a divisive issue. A March 2006 survey by the Pew Research Center for the People and the Press indicated that respondents were nearly evenly divided on the question of adoption by lesbians and gay men.[16] Nonetheless, lesbian and gay parenting—especially through adoption and foster parenting—has not proven to be as inflammatory an issue as same-sex marriage. The issue seems to have been defused by a shift in the debate away from the rights of the parents and toward the needs of the children.

This is, however, more than just a rhetorical shift, because abstract talk about legal rights can obscure the practical impact of turning lesbian and gay families into a battleground in the reactionary right's culture war. When society places legal impediments in the way of lesbian and gay parenting, it not only prevents lesbians and gay men from fulfilling their desire to parent but it also has a negative impact on children. For example, it may deprive children from prior heterosexual relationships of an adequate connection with a parent whom they know and love, or it may deprive children who are in foster care or up for adoption of any parent at all.

With this glimpse of two potential futures—and the stakes of the looming battle over them—firmly in mind, we can now turn to look around (and behind) us to get a sense of the current lay of the land. The discussion in this chapter is divided into two parts: The first part focuses on child custody and visitation issues that arise following the dissolution of a former heterosexual marriage; the second part focuses on the emerging area of parenting by same-sex couples or single lesbians and gay men.

Children from Former Heterosexual Marriages

The "Best Interest of the Child" Standard

Some lesbians and gay men realize or acknowledge their (homo)sexual orientation only after entering into a different-sex marriage and having children. In any ensuing divorce and child custody dispute, a court will apply the "best interest of the child" standard to determine which parent shall have custody and whether (and under what circumstances) to grant visitation to the noncustodial parent.[17] Under this standard, a judge may consider some or all of the following factors when deciding on the most appropriate living arrangements for a child:

> (1) the child's physical, emotional, mental, religious and social needs; (2) each parent's ability and desire to meet those needs; (3) the child's preference, provided that the child is of sufficient age to articulate and comprehend such a preference; (4) the parents' preferences; (5) the child's interaction with her parents and siblings; (6) whether one parent is the primary caretaker; (7) the bond between the child and each parent; (8) the suitability of the existing custody and visitation arrangement, including whether it has provided a stable environment to which the child is well-adjusted; (9) the parent's ability and willingness to encourage the child's relationship with the other parent and cooperate in decisions regarding the child's welfare; (10) any history of domestic violence, child abuse or child neglect; (11) substance abuse by a parent or member of the household; (12) each parent's criminal record; (13) the mental and physical health of all involved; (14) a parent's bad faith, coercion, or duress in negotiating the custody agreement; (15) the child's age and sex; (16) each parent's moral fitness; and (17) the child's cultural background.[18]

Through this assortment of factors, state law affords judges a great deal of flexibility in fashioning custody arrangements. Thus, depending on the types of custody awards permitted under state law, a judge may decide that it is in the best interest of the child to award sole legal and physical custody to one parent, normally with visitation being granted to the other; joint legal custody to both parents, enabling them to each participate in major decisions concerning the child (e.g., regarding education, medical care, religious training, and discipline); joint physical custody to both parents, requiring the child to spend "a significant amount of time with each parent"; or some combination of these different options (e.g., joint legal and physical custody, joint legal custody to both parents but sole physical custody to one parent, or joint physical custody to both parents but sole legal custody to one parent).[19] Most states permit the court to modify its initial order only if there has been a significant or material change in circumstances—a threshold that, it is worth noting, has often been met merely by a parent's coming out or living openly as a lesbian or gay man.[20] And, because the trial court judge actually sees the parties to the case and hears their testimony directly, appellate courts generally defer to the trial judge's decision, absent some clear showing of an abuse of discretion.[21]

This combination of flexibility and deference empowers the trial judge to tailor custody and visitation arrangements to the circumstances of each case.[22] At the same time, it introduces a much-criticized level of indeterminacy into custody and visitation decisions. Of particular concern to lesbians and gay men, this flexibility and deference opens the way for judges to impose their own moral values and to (overtly or covertly) consider a parent's sexual orientation when making custody and visitation decisions.[23]

Sexual Orientation and the Best Interest of the Child

In the past, a parent's (homo)sexual orientation "meant no possibility of . . . obtaining custody from the courts and lessened the chances of obtaining even visitation."[24] Today, there is a clear trend among the states to "demand evidence of harm before a parent's sexual orientation will be held against him or her in matters of custody or in awarding visitation."[25] Some courts scrupulously apply this "nexus" test, looking for a direct impact on the child and avoiding reliance on the "'mere possibility of negative impact on the child.'"[26] Indeed, the District of Columbia forbids its courts to use a parent's sexual orientation as a "conclusive consideration" when making custody and visitation awards.[27] Courts in some states have even described sexual orientation as a "nonissue" or as "irrelevant" to the best interest of the child analysis.[28]

Notwithstanding these salutary developments, some courts still presume that a parent's homosexuality will be detrimental to the child and place the burden on the lesbian or gay parent to prove that his or her sexual orientation will *not* harm the child.[29] Other courts continue to indulge their prejudices by paying lip service to the nexus test and then proceeding to deny custody to a lesbian or gay parent on the basis of harm that is more imagined than real. For example, in *Tucker v. Tucker,*[30] the Utah Supreme Court upheld a trial judge's decision to award sole physical custody of a couple's child to the heterosexual father. Faced with two admittedly "good" parents, the trial judge decided to grant custody to the father based in part on the lesbian mother's lack of moral fitness. The trial judge specifically found that the mother's sexual orientation "'does not bear directly on her parenting abilities, and the court finds that she should not be deprived of custody of her minor child based upon her sexual preference.'"[31] Yet, in the very next paragraph, the trial judge stated:

[The mother] has chosen to act out her sexual preference by conducting a relationship with a woman companion involving cohabitation without benefit of marriage in the same home with the minor child. The court finds that this can be analyzed and should be analyzed similarly to a situation involving cohabitation with a member of the opposite sex without benefit of marriage in the presence of a minor child. The court finds that this conduct on the part of [the mother] during the pendency of this action and prior to the custody trial in this matter demonstrates a lack of moral example to the child and a lack of moral fitness.[32]

The Utah Supreme Court upheld this finding despite a state ban on same-sex marriage that makes it impossible for the child's mother ever to set an "appropriate" moral example for her child.

A dwindling group of states still employ a "per se" or equivalent rule that treats homosexuality as invariably detrimental to a child's best interest. These states either mandate discrimination or freely allow trial judges to openly discriminate against lesbian or gay parents. For example, the Missouri Supreme Court has eschewed forthrightly adopting the per se rule, holding that "[a] homosexual parent is not *ipso facto* unfit for custody of his or her child, and no reported Missouri case has held otherwise."[33] Nonetheless, in making custody decisions, the Missouri courts have presumed that a parent's homosexuality will cause damage to the child.[34] One Missouri judge has characterized this as "an absolute or conclusive presumption of detriment" because no actual evidence of damage to the child is required; rather, it is sufficient in Missouri for a court merely to speculate about potential harm due to the social stigma attached to homosexuality:

> Any doubt as to the irrebuttable or conclusive presumption based on what "may" or "possibly" result from a child in the custody of a homosexual parent, would . . . be here dispelled by an affirmance based on these facts. The mother provides the child with his own room in a well kept house, enrolls him in a preschool, has a steady nursing job, cares about the child, and, despite sleeping with and occasionally hugging a woman, has stated under oath she would discourage her son from emulating her sexual preference. The father has limited education, an income of $6500 and lives in basically a one room cabin containing a toilet surrounded by a curtain; the child sleeps in a fold-up cot by a woodstove and plays in an area littered with Busch beer cans, collected by the father's "slow" sister, who was ordered by the trial court not to care for the boy while alone. The 75 year old paternal grandmother helps care for the little boy.
>
> To say it is in the best interests of this little boy to put him in the sole custody of the father, who was pictured leering at a girly magazine, solely on the basis of the mother's sexual preference, would be and is a mistake. To tip the scales solely on the basis of what "may" befall the child because of the mother's sexual preference results in this high stakes decision on the child's welfare being made on less than complete information and renders it suspect.[35]

It should come as no surprise then that, in Missouri, "circumstances have been consistently found to require that a child not be placed or remain in the custody of a homosexual parent and that visitation of a homosexual parent be restricted or terminated."[36]

The Alabama Supreme Court has been far less oblique in articulating its hostility toward lesbian and gay parenting. In *Ex parte J.M.F.*,[37] the court upheld a trial judge's decision removing a child from the custody of her lesbian mother, who had ceased living "discreetly" with her partner (i.e., the two had begun to share a room in the home where the child lived). To obtain custody, the court held that the father did not need to show that the child's relationship with her mother was having a detrimental effect on her but only needed to show that granting him custody would "materially promote the child's best interests."[38] The court had no difficulty finding that the father had met this standard because he and his new wife had "established a two-parent home environment where heterosexual marriage is presented as the moral and societal norm," in contrast with the child's mother, who had "chosen to expose the child continuously to a lifestyle that is 'neither legal in this state, nor moral in the eyes of most of its citizens.'"[39] In a later case, then Chief Justice Roy Moore (the notorious "Ten Commandments judge") filed a concurring opinion in which he underscored this point:

> Homosexual conduct is, and has been, considered abhorrent, immoral, detestable, a crime against nature, and a violation of the laws of nature and of nature's God upon which this Nation and our laws are predicated. Such conduct violates both the criminal and civil laws of this State and is destructive to a basic building block of society—the family. The law of Alabama is not only clear in its condemning such conduct, but the courts of this State have consistently held that exposing a child to such behavior has a destructive and seriously detrimental effect on the children. It is an inherent evil against which children must be protected.[40]

In view of such antigay animus, some commentators have argued that the per se approach may be unconstitutional. As former U.S. Supreme Court Justice Sandra Day O'Connor has remarked, "the States [do not] have unfettered power to regulate families. The States are subject to constitutional constraints, and the Supreme Court has, when appropriate, struck down state laws that intrude on the core functions of the family or on the individual liberties of family members."[41] In this vein, commentators maintain that the per se approach may run afoul of the U.S. Supreme Court's decisions in *Romer v. Evans*,[42] which held that laws motivated only by antigay animus are unconstitutional, and *Lawrence v. Texas*,[43] which recently reaffirmed *Romer* in the course of striking down state sodomy laws and holding that private, consensual same-sex sexual conduct is constitutionally protected from government interference.[44]

But reports of the death of the per se approach appear to be premature. In *L.A.M. v. B.M.*,[45] the Alabama Civil Court of Appeals read *Lawrence* narrowly, confining it to its peculiar facts. Based on this narrow reading, the court held that *Lawrence* did not overrule the Alabama Supreme Court's decision in *Ex parte J.M.F.* because it embraced the per se rule in a different context (that is, in a dispute over modification of a child custody order and the best interest of the child at issue). The decision in *Lawrence* did, however, persuade the Idaho Supreme Court to adopt the nexus test when it faced this issue for the first time.[46] But, even while shunning a facially discriminatory rule, the Idaho Supreme Court upheld the decision of a trial judge who, in a move described as both "unusual" and a "cause for legal concern," clearly "reached for reasons to help [the heterosexual mother] succeed in her claim when the primary reason stated in her petition to modify custody, homosexuality, is not a legally permissible consideration."[47]

Custody and Visitation Restrictions

There is a similar trend toward using the nexus test in determining whether to impose restrictions on a lesbian or gay parent's activities while in custody of or visiting with a child.[48] For example, in *Downey v. Muffley*,[49] the Indiana Court of Appeals overturned an order awarding custody to a lesbian mother but prohibiting her partner from spending the night when the children were present. The court clearly stated that "visitation and custody determinations must be determined with respect to the best interests of the children, not the sexual preferences of the parents."[50] The court held that such an overnight restriction cannot be imposed as a standard restriction; rather, the restriction "can be justified only when it is based upon a finding of harm to the children on a *case-by-case basis*."[51]

In reaching its decision, however, the court approvingly discussed an earlier case, *Marlow v. Marlow*.[52] In that case, another division of the Indiana Court of Appeals upheld an overnight restriction on a gay father's visitation rights that was similar to the one disapproved in *Downey*, along with an accompanying prohibition on taking the children to "any social, religious or educational functions sponsored by or which otherwise promote the homosexual lifestyle."[53] The court imposed these restrictions because the father lived with his partner in a one-bedroom apartment and had taken the children to a conference sponsored by Parents and Friends of Lesbians and Gays; a performance by a lesbian chorus; and a baptismal service for a gay man, which, according to the trial court, had led to emotional difficulties for the children and demonstrated "a specific intent by [the father] to orient the children to the gay lifestyle."[54] Based on this record, the trial court felt, and the court of appeals agreed, that the father was "overemphasizing the issue of homosexuality with the children" and that the children were "in need of a balanced environment both physically and emotionally stable, and one in which they can find safe retreat from a complex world."[55] But, as one commentator has noted, "this is ultimately just an argument against exposing children to openly gay people. Such people—presumed too confusing, alien, or deviant for the young to comprehend—must under this logic be kept from children. Homosexuality thus reduces to an unpleasant reality in our 'complex world' from which children require a 'safe retreat' into the arms of heterosexuals."[56]

Courts in other states still commonly impose restrictions on a lesbian or gay parent's activities in the name of protecting "the child from some imagined harm the child may be subjected to in the future."[57] For example, in *Taylor v. Taylor*,[58] the Arkansas Supreme Court upheld a temporary award of custody to a lesbian mother that was conditioned on her same-sex partner moving out of her home but allowed the partner to care for the children on nights when the mother was working. In reaching its decision, the court noted that Arkansas law "has never condoned a parent's unmarried cohabitation, or a parent's promiscuous conduct or lifestyle, when such conduct is in the presence of the child."[59] Accordingly, the Arkansas courts routinely impose noncohabitation restrictions on parents, regardless of their sexual orientation, in order "to promote a stable environment for the children and . . . not . . . merely to monitor a parent's sexual conduct."[60] What the court failed to note, however, is that heterosexual parents can easily and quickly free themselves of noncohabitation restrictions by marrying, whereas lesbian and gay parents cannot.

In addition, in *Ex parte D.W.W.*,[61] the Alabama Supreme Court upheld severe restrictions placed on a lesbian mother's visitation rights. The mother was permitted to visit her children every other weekend and one night during the intervening week; however, that visitation could take place *only* at the maternal grandparents' home and "under their supervision and control"—and in no event was the mother's partner to be present during visitation. A majority of the court found that, "even without . . . evidence that the children have been adversely affected by their mother's relationship, the trial court would have been justified in restricting . . . visitation, in order to limit the children's exposure to their mother's lesbian lifestyle. When a noncustodial parent is involved in a continuing homosexual relationship, restrictions on that parent's visitation rights have been widely held to be proper."[62]

A dissenting justice criticized the majority for being "more interested in providing social commentary than in protecting the best interests of these parties' two children," and he bluntly stated "that the trial court's decision appears to be founded primarily on prejudice."[63] In fact, the dissenting justice pointed out, the trial court went out of its way to protect the children from the mother's lesbianism but had awarded full custody to the children's father—who had a history of alcohol abuse, numerous citations for driving while under the influence (on one occasion, he totaled a car while driving under the influence with his twenty-three-month-old child, who had not even been secured in a safety seat), and several formal charges of domestic abuse against him (along with a number of other incidents that were not reported to the police). Furthermore, the father had shut one of the children inside a clothes dryer and had threatened to kill the mother and children. His care was also having a noticeable impact on the children's health: There were complaints from the school about the daughter's poor hygiene after visits with the father, the children returned from visits with the father with flea bites, and both children contracted scabies after visiting with the father.

Third-Party Intervention

In a custody contest between a child's legal parents, both parents are initially presumed to be equally qualified for custody. They then vie with each other to show the court which of them will more effectively further the best interests of the child.[64] In contrast, when a third party (i.e., anyone other than a legal parent, including a grandparent or other relative) seeks to remove a child from the custody of a biological or adoptive parent, there is generally no equivalent presumption that both contestants are equally qualified to take custody of the child. This difference is due, at least in part, to the fact that the U.S. Supreme Court has recognized that the constitutionally protected right to have and raise children is a fundamental right that "cannot be abridged by the state unless the state can bear 'especially high burdens of justification for the infringement.'"[65] Thus, there is generally a "parental preference" in custody disputes between a parent and a third party. In other words, custody will be awarded to the biological or adoptive parent unless the third party can show, by clear and convincing evidence or a similar heightened standard of proof, that the legal parent is unfit or that extraordinary circumstances justify taking the child away from her parent.[66]

The infamous case of Bottoms v. Bottoms[67] is probably the most widely publicized instance of a court awarding custody to a third party due to the biological parent's (homo)sexual orientation. In Bottoms, the Virginia courts awarded custody of a child to his maternal grandmother and granted restricted visitation rights to his mother. The grandmother sought custody shortly after her daughter informed her that she was involved in a lesbian relationship. The trial court found that the parental preference had been overcome in that case because the mother's lesbianism rendered her per se an unfit parent. The court of appeals reversed the trial court's decision, but the Virginia Supreme Court reinstated that decision. In upholding the trial court's decision, a majority of the Virginia Supreme Court relied on the speculative harm that the mother's lesbian relationship would cause the child and then scoured the record for further evidence to buttress its decision—evidence that, incidentally, the court of appeals had dismissed as insufficient to overcome the parental preference.

Commentators have argued that the U.S. Supreme Court's recent decision in Troxel v. Granville[68] will provide lesbian and gay parents with "ammunition to fend off third-party custody claims."[69] Although Troxel narrowly addressed the constitutionality of applying a Washington statute to grant visitation to grandparents over a mother's objection, the plurality opinion described "the liberty interest at issue in this case—the interest of parents in the care, custody, and control of their children—[as] perhaps the oldest of the fundamental liberty interests recognized by this Court."[70] In the course of its discussion, the plurality further stated that "so long as a parent adequately cares for his or her children (i.e., is fit), there will normally be no reason for the State to inject itself into the private realm of the family to further question the ability of that parent to make the best decisions concerning the rearing of that parent's children."[71] And, given the traditional presumption that a fit parent acts in the best interests of her children, the plurality decried the trial court's failure to accord special weight to the mother's decision concerning visitation by the grandparents.

But even under the strictest of legal standards, a court may still choose to act on its sexual prejudice and award custody of a child to a third party, as happened in the *Bottoms* case.[72] Yet, as law professor Nancy Polikoff has remarked, "in spite of this danger, the articulation of a strict standard before a parent can be deprived of custody is the only protection a lesbian or gay parent has against the homophobic claims of relatives and other third parties."[73]

Asserting Our Rights

As this survey indicates, tightening of the legal standards applicable to custody and visitation decisions has not ineluctably led to an improvement in the results reached by individual judges. Judges still retain wide-ranging discretion, and their "ignorance and prejudice too frequently combine to distort the analysis."[74] Indeed, a particularly virulent form of heterosexism manifests itself in these cases: Judges reward parents for being "discreet" (i.e., closeted) and punish them for "flaunting" their sexual orientation in front of their children;[75] judges reward parents for separating themselves from the lesbian and gay community and punish them for being involved in their community or for merely having lesbian and gay friends and acquaintances;[76] and judges reward parents for saying that they would prefer their children to grow up to be heterosexual and punish them for failing to "discourage the child from adopting a homosexual lifestyle."[77] In the end, courts often appear to be more concerned with ensuring that parents toe the heterosexual line than they do with furthering the best interests of children.[78]

Both academic commentators and legal advocates for lesbian and gay parents maintain that these judges routinely violate parents' constitutional rights—from the fundamental right of parents to the care, custody, and control of their children to the parents' right to liberty, as elucidated in *Lawrence v. Texas;* the parents' Fourteenth Amendment rights to due process of law and equal protection of the law; and the parents' First Amendment rights to freedom of speech and association.[79] Courts have not, however, readily accepted these arguments, which may be due, in part, to the way in which they are framed: "In many cases in which parents articulated their claims in terms of rights—whether relying on specific constitutional principles, an overarching concept of fundamental rights of parents, biological status, or contractual family ties—the discourse of rights was rejected as altogether unacceptable and irrelevant in the child custody context. There was a subtle but distinct suggestion . . . that judges interpreted rights claims on the part of parents to be selfish and not aimed at meeting the needs of their children."[80] Instead of focusing purely on violation of the parents' rights and the resulting harm to them, we may therefore be more successful if we also draw on the children's right to have a relationship with their parents and the harm caused if this right is denied or unduly restricted.[81]

In this way, we might achieve a more balanced approach that centers not on individual rights (ostensibly pitting parent against child) but on the protection of the family bond (turning the parent and child into legal allies against a hostile judiciary).[82] As noted in the introduction to this chapter, shifting the debate from lesbian and gay rights to the needs of children has been a successful strategy in the political arena to prevent the enactment of legal bans on lesbian and gay parenting. This strategy may bear fruit in the judicial arena as well because it will force judges to see their actions as breaking up a family rather than as foiling the lesbian or gay parent's attempt to turn child custody into a political issue. In any event, as Polikoff has noted, we have little choice but to assert our rights and the rights of our children because these legal rights—however imperfectly observed—are the only protection that we have in child custody and visitation proceedings.

Parenting by Single Lesbians and Gay Men and Same-Sex Couples

Starting a Family

Single lesbians and gay men and same-sex couples can pursue several different paths to parenthood: foster parenting, adoption, or assisted reproduction. Foster parenting is a temporary arrangement to provide care for a child whose birth family cannot care for her. A child remains in foster care until she either can be returned to her family or becomes eligible for adoption (because return to the family is not possible).[83] Adoption may also occur through the direct placement of a child, usually an infant—as was the case with Elyse and me—and not an older child, who would more typically go through the foster care system.[84] In most cases, lesbians and gay men will be foster parenting or adopting children who are not biologically related to them; in contrast, when using assisted reproduction (e.g., intrauterine insemination, in vitro fertilization, or surrogacy), at least one lesbian or gay parent will typically be biologically related to the child.

These three paths to parenthood are the same ones that are pursued by single heterosexuals and reproductively challenged different-sex couples; however, which of these paths are actually open to lesbians and gay men varies from state to state. In this section, I briefly describe both the legal barriers that some states erect to close off these paths to lesbian and gay parents and the efforts that other states make to ease the way for us to become parents.

Foster Parenting. Despite the difficulty encountered in recruiting and retaining qualified foster parents,[85] several states persist in barring or restricting lesbian and gay foster parenting. In 1995, the director of the Nebraska Department of Social Services issued an administrative memorandum banning "persons who identify themselves as homosexuals" from serving as foster parents.[86] An addendum issued a few months later clarified that exceptions could be made on a case-by-case basis if the homosexual individual were a relative of the child.[87] Because the department never issued an official regulation or policy adopting this ban, I sent an e-mail and follow-up letter to determine whether the department continues to adhere to this policy. In response, I was informed that neither the administrative memorandum nor the addendum has been revoked or modified, which evidently means that they continue in force.[88]

Other states do not bar all lesbians and gay men from foster parenting, but only those in relationships. For example, Utah law permits single individuals and legally married couples to serve as foster parents; however, a single individual who cohabits with another person in a relationship that is not a legal marriage under Utah law is ineligible to serve as a foster parent.[89] By regulation, Alabama similarly requires foster parents who are "living together in a relationship" to be married, and Mississippi prohibits "unrelated adults" from living in the foster home.[90] A North Dakota regulation bans unmarried different-sex couples from serving as foster parents;[91] I sent an e-mail and follow-up letter to the North Dakota Department of Human Services to determine whether it applies this ban to same-sex couples as well but never received a response.

Although the restrictions in Alabama, Mississippi, and Utah apply equally to same-sex and different-sex couples, these states afford only different-sex couples the option to marry and free themselves of the restriction. Indeed, the Utah legislation is widely viewed as having been aimed at excluding lesbians and gay men from parenting—its broader coverage was intended to be no more than a buttress against constitutional attacks.[92] More conspicuously, North Dakota enacted legislation in 2003 that sanctions discrimination against lesbians and gay men by permitting child placement agencies to refuse to be involved in placements that violate their religious or moral convictions or policies.[93]

In 1999, the Arkansas Child Welfare Agency Review Board promulgated a regulation prohibiting an individual from serving as a foster parent "if any adult member of that person's household is a homosexual."[94] In 2006, the Arkansas Supreme Court struck this regulation down as a violation of the separation of powers under the state constitution. The court noted that the legislature had authorized the board only to promulgate regulations that promote the health, safety, and welfare of children in foster care. Based on the trial judge's findings of fact, the court concluded that this regulation "does not promote the health, safety, or welfare of foster children but rather acts to exclude a set of individuals from becoming foster parents based upon morality and bias."[95] Because the board was acting outside the scope of its authority, the court found that the regulation constituted an attempt by the board to usurp the power of the legislature by legislating "with respect to public morality."[96]

Early in 2007, Arkansas lawmakers considered legislation that would have replaced the board's ban on foster parenting by lesbians and gay men—and would have added to it a ban on adoption by lesbians and gay men. However, after passing the Arkansas Senate, this legislation died in the Arkansas House of Representatives. In the wake of the legislature's failure to pass this ban on lesbian and gay foster parenting and adoption, a conservative Christian organization has taken steps to bring a measure directly before Arkansas voters in 2008 that would ban foster parenting and adoption by unmarried couples.[97] In any event, existing Arkansas rules contain a clear preference for foster homes headed by married, different-sex couples, allowing exceptions to be made for single-parent households only "on the basis of the applicant's special qualifications to fulfill the needs of a particular foster child."[98]

Until 2006, the Missouri Department of Social Services had a policy of refusing to license lesbians and gay men as foster parents, although it did not actively investigate applicants' sexual orientation.[99] The department took the position that lesbians and gay men could not meet the requirement in its regulations that all foster parents must be of "reputable character."[100] Because Missouri had criminalized same-sex sexual contact, the department reasoned that lesbians and gay men, as presumptive criminals, could not be of reputable character. In February 2006, a Missouri trial court judge granted summary judgment to a lesbian who had challenged the policy and reversed the department's denial of a foster care license to her. Following the U.S. Supreme Court's decision in *Lawrence v. Texas*, the judge held that Missouri's criminalization of consensual same-sex sexual contact is unconstitutional and unenforceable and, therefore, cannot serve as a basis for drawing conclusions about anyone's character.

The Missouri attorney general dropped the appeal of the trial judge's decision in this case after the state formally repealed its sodomy law in early June 2006.[101] Following the attorney general's decision, the department withdrew the offending regulation and replaced it with a rule that is intended to allow lesbians and gay men to be licensed as foster parents.[102] Nonetheless, department officials have warned that "just because gays may get licensed doesn't automatically mean they will become foster parents."[103] Under these rules, the department will ask new foster parents their sexual orientation and take it into account when making placement decisions.

Connecticut derogates from its general public policy of prohibiting discrimination on the basis of sexual orientation by similarly allowing sexual orientation to be considered when making foster care placement decisions.[104] But even in the absence of such an explicit policy, lesbians and gay men still experience discrimination at the hands of child welfare agencies: They are forced to fight denials of their initial applications to foster parent, to endure longer waiting periods than heterosexual foster parents before a child is placed in their home, and to prove that they are "exceptional" parents.[105] Overall, "the child welfare system is not a friendly or welcoming place for many prospective or active LGB foster parents."[106]

To address these problems, California, Massachusetts, New Jersey, and Wisconsin prohibit child welfare agencies from discriminating on the basis of sexual orientation when making foster care placements.[107] In a few states, child welfare agencies have taken these efforts a step further; for example, the Massachusetts Department of Social Services and agencies in Los Angeles, San Francisco, New York, Philadelphia, and Houston have actively recruited lesbians and gay men (and supportive straights) to serve as foster parents for lesbian and gay youth.[108] Finding accepting and welcoming homes (as well as appropriate role models and mentors) for these lesbian and gay youth is important because in foster care, they all too commonly experience antigay harassment and violence, are forced to undergo "conversion" or "reparative" therapies, are isolated or find their activities unduly restricted, are moved from placement to placement—or simply give up on a child welfare system that fails them and decide to live on the streets.[109]

Adoption. Although Florida does not formally restrict foster parenting by lesbians and gay men, it is the only state with a legal ban on adoption by lesbians and gay men.[110] The courts have, however, narrowly interpreted this ban to prohibit only "practicing" (i.e., sexually active) homosexuals from adopting.[111] So interpreted, the courts have upheld the ban against state and federal constitutional challenges.[112]

Surprisingly, the most recent of these decisions—issued by the U.S. Court of Appeals for the Eleventh Circuit—came *after* the U.S. Supreme Court's decision in *Lawrence v. Texas*. Recall that *Lawrence* affords constitutional protection to private, consensual same-sex sexual contact, which is precisely the type of contact that triggers Florida's adoption ban. In fact, one commentator has remarked that the Eleventh Circuit "seemed almost willful in its refusal to follow *Lawrence*. Basically, it is as if the Eleventh Circuit was throwing down the gauntlet and challenging the Court to either stand by or repudiate *Lawrence*."[113] Unfortunately, the Supreme Court failed to take up this challenge. It declined to review the Eleventh Circuit's decision,[114] which still stands as good law and provides encouragement to reactionaries who are determined to enact similar bans in other states. For example, the proponents of the Arkansas ban on lesbian and gay foster parenting and adoption (discussed earlier) have dismissed questions about its constitutionality by referring to the Eleventh Circuit's decision.[115]

A few states restrict, but do not ban, adoption by lesbians and gay men. For instance, Mississippi and Utah both prohibit same-sex couples (but not singles) from adopting.[116] Similarly, although Alabama law explicitly permits "any adult person" to adopt,[117] the Alabama legislature has passed an act expressing its "intent to prohibit child adoption by homosexual couples."[118] In most states, a child may be placed for adoption through a licensed child placement agency or directly through private adoption (but, in either case, a court must approve the adoption). In the case of agency adoptions, Connecticut specifically permits the agency to take sexual orientation into account when placing a child for adoption, and North Dakota permits the agency to refuse to be involved in placements that violate its religious or moral convictions or policies.[119] Conversely, a growing number of states— including California, Maine, Maryland, Massachusetts, Nevada, New Jersey, and New York—prohibit agencies from discriminating on the basis of sexual orientation when making adoption placements.[120]

Even in the absence of an explicit policy, lesbians and gay men still experience discrimination in the agency adoption process, as "the degree to which they are considered, recruited, approved, and supported as adoptive . . . parents may depend greatly on a given agency's attitudes and informal practices."[121] In a recent study of public and private adoption agencies, nearly 40 percent of responding agencies indicated that they would *not* be willing to accept applications from lesbians and gay men.[122] Of the responding agencies, 5.4 percent erroneously reported that their states' laws barred adoption by lesbians and gay men, and another 9.9 percent were "unsure" about whether lesbians and gay men are permitted to adopt under their states' laws.[123] Even among the agencies that indicated that they were willing to accept adoption applications from lesbians and gay men, only a "very few reported attempting to recruit prospective adoptive parents from the homosexual community."[124] Beyond any difficulties that prospective lesbian and gay adoptive parents might encounter with agencies, commentators have identified a number of states whose courts are considered to be hostile to lesbian and gay adoptions, including Alabama, Arizona, Arkansas, Louisiana, Missouri, Nebraska, North Carolina, Texas, Wisconsin, and Virginia.[125]

Assisted Reproduction. In contrast to foster parenting and adoption, which are both creatures of statute and highly regulated by the state, access to assisted reproductive technology (ART) has largely been left unregulated by state legislatures.[126] The courts have therefore been left to wrestle with the complex legal issues surrounding the use of ART on a case-by-case basis, which has resulted in a flexible, if inconsistent, body of law.[127] For lesbians and gay men who wish to become parents using ART, this means that the government has thus far refrained from interfering with their ability to have children. Nevertheless, even if the government were to interfere with access to ART, its intervention might very well be struck down as a violation of the constitutional right to procreative freedom.[128]

A lack of government interference with lesbian and gay access to ART should not, however, be equated with unfettered access to that technology. Lesbians and gay men may encounter individual physicians who refuse to perform ART procedures on religious or moral grounds. But, as described in Chapter 2, lesbians and gay men may have legal recourse in these situations if they live in a jurisdiction with a public accommodations law that covers medical offices and that protects against discrimination on the basis of sexual orientation. In this regard, you may recall that a lawsuit is pending before the California Supreme Court in which a lesbian is claiming that her physician violated the state public accommodations law by refusing to provide her fertility treatment on religious grounds.

Even when access to ART is not an issue, lesbians and gay men should nonetheless consult a lawyer experienced in these matters early on in the process. A lawyer can help the intended parent(s) to minimize the risk that the legal results of employing ART will fail to correspond with their expectations for how their incipient family will function.

For those using a sperm or egg donor, a lawyer can provide advice on the type of donor (i.e., known or anonymous) that should be used and on the advisability of having a licensed physician perform any intrauterine insemination. These choices may determine whether a donor is afforded visitation rights or is subject to child support obligations.[129] For example, because a licensed physician inseminated my sister, New Jersey law treats the (anonymous) donor "as if he were not the father of [the] child thereby conceived and [he] shall have no rights or duties stemming from the conception of [the] child."[130]

For those using a surrogate, a lawyer can help to navigate the state law treatment of surrogacy arrangements, which varies widely. In some states, surrogacy is sanctioned, and there are specific procedures for creating an enforceable surrogacy contract or specified limits on the terms of such contracts; in other states, surrogacy arrangements are flatly prohibited; in other states, surrogacy arrangements are not prohibited, but neither are they legally enforceable; and in yet other states, there simply is no law of any kind addressing surrogacy arrangements, and those who choose this method of assisted reproduction operate in uncharted legal territory.[131] To complicate matters further, some states actually employ a combination of these approaches (e.g., addressing certain types of surrogacy arrangements but not others). In the face of often uncertain state law, a lawyer can work both to reduce the risk that a surrogate will breach an agreement and to minimize the adverse effects of a breach should one occur.

Completing the Family

When a same-sex couple creates a family, the law often sees only a part of that family. The law usually recognizes only one member of the couple as a legal parent, either because only that parent was permitted to adopt or because only that parent is biologically related to the child. The other parent is treated as a legal stranger to the child. This can create problems for both the "nonlegal" parent and the child in everyday interactions with medical personnel and hospitals, school officials, and day care organizations—not to mention upon the death of the legal parent or the couple's breakup, when the nonlegal parent will have no obvious right to custody or visitation, and the child may, as a result, find his relationship with one of his parents unexpectedly severed.[132] It also deprives the child of the ability to obtain the tangible benefits of being legally related, including the ability to be named on the nonlegal parent's health insurance policy, to be financially supported by the nonlegal parent should the parents dissolve their relationship, and to inherit from the nonlegal parent and to receive survivor benefits (e.g., Social Security) when she dies.[133] Normally, the only way to complete this family in the eyes of the law and to resolve these problems is for the nonlegal parent to adopt the child through a "second-parent" (or "coparent") adoption.

Second-Parent Adoption. As mentioned earlier, adoption is a creature of statute. Traditionally, adoption statutes required the existing parents to relinquish all parental rights before a child could be adopted by new parents.[134] In response to the increasing prevalence of divorce and remarriage, however, state legislatures created an exception for stepparent adoptions.[135] Accordingly, in a stepparent adoption, a parent's new spouse is allowed to adopt the child without terminating that parent's rights (although the ex-spouse is required to relinquish his or her parental rights before the stepparent may adopt).[136] Using stepparent adoption as a model, the National Center for Lesbian Rights originated the concept of "second-parent" adoption in the early 1980s, when parenting within same-sex relationships became more common and the problems engendered by recognizing only one legal parent became evident.[137] Advocates of second-parent adoption have argued that "the legal device [i.e., stepparent adoption] available to married couples raising a child should also be available to lesbian couples raising a child, as it would advance the policy goal of promoting the interests of children raised in lesbian families."[138]

Efforts to legally sanction second-parent adoption have met with somewhat mixed results. Encouragingly, four states—California, Colorado, Connecticut, and Vermont—have amended their adoption laws to sanction second-parent adoptions.[139] Although California's statutory second-parent adoption provision covers only adoptions by registered domestic partners, the California Supreme Court has independently construed the state's adoption laws to permit second-parent adoptions by any same-sex couple, whether or not registered as domestic partners.[140] Appellate courts in several other jurisdictions have likewise broadly construed existing adoption laws to embrace second-parent adoptions, including courts in the District of Columbia, Illinois, Massachusetts, New Jersey, New York, and Pennsylvania.[141] Trial-level courts in parts of at least fifteen other states have granted second-parent adoptions, even in the absence of guidance from the state legislature or the state's appellate courts.[142]

To the contrary, appellate courts in three states—Nebraska, Ohio, and Wisconsin—have held that second-parent adoptions are not permitted by their adoption laws.[143] Moreover, shortly following several appellate court decisions sanctioning second-parent adoptions in Indiana,[144] the state legislature amended its adoption laws in 2005 in an attempt to reverse those decisions and to prohibit second-parent adoptions in Indiana.[145]

Beyond Second-Parent Adoption. A small group of states has further eased the task of forming or completing a family headed by a same-sex couple. Through their legal recognition of same-sex couples, California, Connecticut, Massachusetts, New Hampshire, New Jersey, Oregon, and Vermont have all made the stepparent adoption process available to legally recognized same-sex couples.[146] Opening stepparent adoptions to same-sex couples is helpful because second-parent adoptions do not benefit from the same streamlined procedures (e.g., routine waiver of home studies and waiting periods in uncontested adoptions) that render stepparent adoptions both simpler and less costly than second-parent adoptions.[147]

Collapsing the steps of family formation and completion, California, Connecticut, Massachusetts, New Hampshire, New Jersey, Oregon, and Vermont all permit legally recognized same-sex couples who form (or add to) a family through adoption to petition for joint adoption.[148] In California, New Jersey, Oregon, and Massachusetts, state court decisions or administrative rules further extend the availability of joint adoption to same-sex couples whose relationships are not legally recognized.[149] Generally reserved for married couples,[150] the joint adoption process allows both members of the couple to petition for adoption simultaneously, rather than one after the other. Joint adoption is preferable to either second-parent or stepparent adoption because it not only reduces the costs of forming and completing the family but also eliminates the period in the two-step adoption process during which one of the parents is treated as a legal stranger to the child.

Several jurisdictions that have approved second-parent adoptions through court decisions have likewise allowed same-sex couples to petition for joint adoption. These jurisdictions include the District of Columbia, Illinois, and New York.[151] The Maine Supreme Judicial Court also recently allowed a same-sex couple to petition for joint adoption; at the same time, it implicitly sanctioned the possibility of second-parent adoptions in that state.[152] And, notwithstanding the Indiana legislature's apparent statutory reversal of several appellate decisions sanctioning second-parent adoption, a state appellate court recently decided that same-sex couples may nonetheless file joint petitions to adopt because the legislature only addressed sequential (and not simultaneous) adoptions when it amended the statute.[153] It further appears that joint adoption may be possible in Pennsylvania, where the state supreme court has approved second-parent adoptions.[154]

For legally recognized lesbian couples starting a family using the medical technique of intrauterine insemination, California and New Jersey (and possibly Connecticut, Massachusetts, New Hampshire, and Oregon) have similarly collapsed the steps of family formation and completion by eliminating the need for a second-parent adoption following the birth of the child.[155] Usually, when a different-sex married couple has a child with the aid of this technology, "both spouses automatically are treated as the child's legal parents, even if one spouse lacks a biological connection to the child. Until recently, however, when same-sex couples have used assisted reproduction to have children, only one of the partners was considered the child's legal parent until an adoption was completed by the nonbirth or nonbiological parent."[156] By applying the parentage rules for married couples to legally recognized same-sex couples, California and New Jersey (and possibly Connecticut, Massachusetts, New Hampshire, and Oregon) treat both members of a legally recognized lesbian couple as the child's legal parents, without the need for adoption or other time-consuming and costly court proceedings.[157]

The California Supreme Court recently applied these parentage rules to a lesbian couple who had not registered as domestic partners but who had consciously chosen to conceive children through intrauterine insemination, to raise the children together as coparents, and to hold themselves both out as the children's parents.[158] The court, relying in part on the rules applicable to registered domestic partners, explicitly found that a child can have two legal "mothers" under California law; accordingly, in that case, both the biological and the nonbiological mother were held to be the legal parents of the children. And, even before the New Jersey Supreme Court's extension of the rights and obligations of marriage to same-sex couples, a lower court had held that a lesbian couple who qualified as domestic partners under New Jersey law could benefit from the presumption of parentage in the state's intrauterine insemination statute, and it ordered both members of the couple to be treated as legal parents as of the date of the child's birth.[159]

Interminably "Incomplete" Families. As one commentator has noted, children born to different-sex married couples benefit from the protection of a thick legal security blanket, whereas the children of same-sex couples are protected by no more than "a bare patchwork quilt."[160] Despite some encouraging progress, second-parent adoption and its more expeditious alternatives (i.e., stepparent adoption, joint adoption, and the presumption of parentage) are widely available in only a handful of states—in most cases, same-sex couples can legally complete their families only if they happen to live in the right part of a state. And nearly half of the states afford same-sex couples no opportunity to legally complete their families at all.

When the law turns a blind eye to lesbian and gay parents, same-sex couples find it necessary to seek the help of a lawyer to replicate the legal protections enjoyed by the families of married different-sex couples.[161] To achieve this end, a lawyer may revise or rewrite documents that you already have—for example, a will or domestic-partnership agreement—to take into account the addition to your family. The lawyer may also draft new documents, such as a shared-parenting or coparenting agreement that reflects your commitment to raise the child together as a couple and addresses custody, visitation, and support issues in the event of a breakup; a nomination of guardian for the child in the event of the legal parent's death or incapacity; and an authorization to consent to medical treatment on behalf of the child should the legal parent be unavailable. At best, however, a lawyer can only partially replicate the legal protections that are automatically conferred on the families of married different-sex couples.

In this regard, it is important to recognize both the legal limits of, and the practical possibilities associated with, these documents. In some states, courts may refuse to enforce the custody and visitation provisions in a shared-parenting agreement, as has occurred in Florida.[162] The specter of such judicial hostility to lesbian and gay parenting influences some couples to employ mediation as a first step in attempting to resolve parenting disputes.[163] Nevertheless, shared-parenting agreements do have their uses, even if they are not specifically enforceable. For instance, in a growing number of states, a shared-parenting agreement may serve to bolster the nonlegal parent's case for applying existing legal doctrines (e.g., *in loco parentis,* de facto parenthood, or psychological parenthood) that "allow a person who is not a legal parent, but who has functioned as a child's parent, to have some legally protected rights to maintain visitation or custody with the child after the parents' relationship dissolves."[164] (It is worth noting, however, that when these doctrines are applied—usually only *after* the couple's breakup—the precise contours of the legal rights and obligations conferred on the relationship between the child and the *in loco,* de facto, or psychological parent are often unclear, especially outside the realm of custody, visitation, and support.)[165] Additionally, shared-parenting agreements can be a useful tool for convincing third parties (e.g., schools) to respect intact lesbian and gay families and to communicate and interact with both parents.

False Choice Revisited. Despite their admitted shortcomings, these documents may prove to be a necessary legal backstop for all same-sex couples with children—even if their home state legally recognizes both parents. Some uncertainty hangs over the question of whether one state's recognition of both members of a same-sex couple as the legal parents of a child will be

respected by other states.[166] The portability of legal recognition from one state to another promises to be an active front in the looming battle over lesbian and gay parenting.

In 2004, the State of Oklahoma enacted a statute that prohibits the state, any of its agencies, or any of its courts from recognizing an out-of-state or foreign adoption "by more than one individual of the same sex."[167] The Oklahoma legislature enacted this statute in response to an opinion from the state's attorney general, who had opined that Oklahoma law and the Full Faith and Credit Clause of the U.S. Constitution required the legal recognition of two parents of the same gender.[168] The law was promptly challenged, and in May 2006, a federal district court struck the law down on the ground that it violates the Full Faith and Credit, Equal Protection, and Due Process Clauses of the U.S. Constitution.[169] Fortunately, in August 2007, the U.S. Court of Appeals for the Tenth Circuit affirmed this decision.[170]

A related question concerns the impact of the federal Defense of Marriage Act (DOMA) on the application of the Full Faith and Credit Clause to adoptions by same-sex couples. DOMA explicitly permits states to refuse "to give effect to any . . . judicial proceeding of any other State . . . respecting a relationship between persons of the same sex that is treated as a marriage under the laws of such other State . . . or a right or claim arising from such relationship."[171] As one commentator has noted, "some have suggested that the federal DOMA's reference to judicial proceedings calls into question the longstanding conclusion that the Full Faith and Credit Clause obliges states to honor other state's judgments," including judgments confirming the adoption of a child.[172] Indeed, relying on DOMA, the Louisiana attorney general has opined that the state's vital-records registrar can refuse a request by a married same-sex couple to complete a new birth certificate listing both of them as parents of a child born in Louisiana whom they have adopted in another state that, unlike Louisiana, legally recognizes their relationship.[173]

Yet thornier questions may arise with regard to the application of presumptions of parentage—this time in the context of pitched, interstate battles over custody and visitation, as in *Miller-Jenkins v. Miller-Jenkins*.[174] In that case, Lisa and Janet Miller-Jenkins, a lesbian couple from Virginia, traveled to Vermont in December 2000 to enter into a civil union. In 2001, based on a joint decision by the couple to become parents, Lisa began to receive intrauterine insemination using the sperm of an anonymous donor, became pregnant, and gave birth to a daughter in April 2002. When their daughter was about four months old, the Miller-Jenkinses moved to Vermont, where they lived until 2003, when Lisa and Janet decided to separate. Lisa moved back to Virginia, taking the baby with her, and Janet remained in Vermont.

A few months after the breakup, Lisa filed a petition to dissolve the couple's civil union with a court in Vermont. In 2004, the court issued a temporary order granting visitation to Janet in Vermont. Although Lisa at first allowed the child to visit Janet, she soon changed her mind, cut off Janet's visits with the child, and filed an action in a Virginia court requesting it to determine the child's parentage. Despite the ongoing legal proceedings in Vermont, the Virginia trial court held that it had jurisdiction to determine the child's parentage and the existence of any parental rights. The Virginia court sided with Lisa, finding that Janet's parental rights were based on the Vermont civil union law, which was "null and void" in Virginia. Consequently, the Virginia court held that Lisa was the sole parent of the child and, in direct conflict with the Vermont court's previous order, further held that Janet had no claim to visitation with the child. The Vermont court later definitively ruled that both Lisa and Janet had parental rights with respect to the child and categorically refused to give full faith and credit to the decision of the Virginia court. Lisa appealed the Vermont ruling, and the Vermont Supreme Court upheld the trial court's decision in August 2006. Lisa then appealed the Vermont Supreme Court's ruling to the U.S. Supreme Court, which declined to hear the appeal.

In November 2006, the Virginia Court of Appeals reversed the Virginia trial court's ruling and ordered it to honor the custody and visitation orders issued by the Vermont courts. The court of appeals found that DOMA did not preempt an earlier federal law governing the application of the Full Faith and Credit Clause to child custody and visitation orders.[175] Lisa appealed this ruling to the Virginia Supreme Court, which, as of this writing, has rejected one appeal on procedural grounds but still has another of Lisa's appeals pending before it.[176]

The resulting cloud of uncertainty surrounding the portability of a same-sex couple's parental rights engenders the same false choice problem that I discussed in Chapters 6 and 7 with respect to the portability of legal recognition of same-sex relationships. Because of this uncertainty, same-sex couples who live in states that recognize both partners as the legal parents of their children are nonetheless forced to act as if they lived in a state that does not do so. The mobility of modern society (after all, who knows where a job or a trip may take you?) essentially demands that these same-sex couples incur the expense of having a lawyer draw up a web of documents that is designed to replicate, to the extent possible, protections that they should already have. This is a duplicative and unnecessary cost that society imposes on same-sex couples but not on married different-sex couples. Once again, you might reconceptualize this cost as a penalty tax—this time on the purchase of legal recognition for same-sex families—that is intended to reduce our—now "after-tax"—civil rights gains.

Shaping Change

"Can family caregiving be a form of political resistance or expression?"[177] This provocative question begins a recent article by law professor Laura Kessler. In answering "yes" to this question, Kessler singles out lesbian and gay parenting as an example of what she calls "transgressive caregiving" because the very existence of lesbian and gay families represents a "radical challenge to heterosexual reproduction and family relations."[178] At the same time that it challenges heterosexist norms, lesbian and gay parenting also calls into question a host of negative stereotypes, particularly about gay men.[179] Thus, in the hands of lesbians and gay men, the simple (and, some critics might say, assimilationist) act of parenting becomes a defiant, political act.

Whether we know it or not, our everyday lives can take on a radical cast. For example, my sister and Cindy may not view their daily activities with my nieces and nephew as political, radical, or extraordinary; yet, through those activities, they are constantly creating the potential for political and social transformation. Every day, they challenge the notion that a family headed by a married different-sex couple is the only milieu in which children can thrive. And it is not only those among us who choose to be parents who contribute to the radicalness of lesbian and gay parenting: Those among us who, like me, do not have children of our own but who form part of the support networks of lesbian and gay friends and family who are raising children also do our part in creating this potential for transformation by rejecting the traditional "nuclear" family model in favor of extended kinship networks.[180] In fact, I know there have been many times when Elyse and Cindy have been grateful for the help and support of my nieces' and nephew's many aunts and uncles.

Nevertheless, in the coming legal battles, if we are to be successful, we must draw attention not to ourselves but to the best interests of our children.[181] When the focus is on the power of lesbian and gay families to destabilize heterosexist norms, legislators and judges, frightened by the idea of change, can quite easily give free rein to their ingrained sexual prejudices. Experience teaches us, however, that it is more difficult for those in power to vent their animosity toward lesbian and gay parents when they are confronted with the reality that their decisions will also cause direct and tangible harm to innocent children by, for example, depriving those children of parents whom they know and love (or, in some cases, of any parents at all), health insurance, adequate means of support, or the right to inherit.

With the passage of time, the changes occurring on the social and political levels will further influence legal decision-making and continue to ameliorate the legal context within which lesbian and gay families operate. One commentator has noted that "in many of these cases, the inequitable outcomes stem not from statutes or common law. The inequity stems from the inability of judges to imagine a world with gay parents and gay families. It is this lack of imagination, not statutory restrictions that lead to uninformed and often mean-spirited opinions."[182] Viewed in this light, the most important step that we can take to shape long-term change may be for lesbian and gay families (including their extended kinship networks) to simply live their daily lives openly and visibly so that lesbian and gay parenting becomes both more commonplace and more firmly ensconced in the imaginations of judges, legislators, and others who influence the creation and application of family law.

Notes

1. Whitney Houston, "Greatest Love of All," on *Whitney Houston* (Arista Records, 1985).

2. See Norman Anderssen, Christine Amlie, and Erling André Ytterøy, "Outcomes for Children with Lesbian or Gay Parents: A Review of Studies from 1978 to 2000," *Scandinavian J. Psychol.* 43 (2002): 335, 344; Andrew McLeod and Isiaah Crawford, "The Postmodern Family: An Examination of the Psychological and Legal Perspectives of Gay and Lesbian Parenting," in Gregory M. Herek, ed., *Stigma and Sexual Orientation: Understanding Prejudice Against Lesbians, Gay Men, and Bisexuals* (Thousand Oaks, CA: Sage Publications, 1998), 211, 214; William Meezan and Jonathan Rauch, "Gay Marriage, Same-Sex Parenting, and America's Children," *Future of Children* 15 (2005): 97, 103; Ellen C. Perrin and Committee on Psychosocial Aspects of Child and Family Health, "Technical Report: Coparent or Second-Parent Adoption by Same-Sex Parents," *Pediatrics* 109 (2002): 341, 343; Judith Stacey and Timothy J. Biblarz, "(How) Does the Sexual Orientation of Parents Matter?" *Am. Soc. Rev.* 66 (2001): 159, 177–178.

3. Congregation for the Doctrine of the Faith, "Considerations Regarding Proposals to Give Legal Recognition to Unions Between Homosexual Persons" (2003), §7, available at www.vatican.va/roman_curia/congregations/cfaith/documents/rc_con_cfaith_doc_20030731_homosexual-unions_en.html.

4. Victoria Clarke, "'Stereotype, Attack, and Stigmatize Those Who Disagree': Employing Scientific Rhetoric in Debates About Lesbian and Gay Parenting," *Feminism and Psychol.* 10 (2000): 152.

5. Stacey and Biblarz, "(How) Does the Sexual Orientation of Parents Matter?" 160.

6. Ibid.; see also Clarke, "'Stereotype, Attack, and Stigmatize Those Who Disagree,'" 153; McLeod and Crawford, "The Postmodern Family," 211–212, 220–221.

7. Clarke, "'Stereotype, Attack, and Stigmatize Those Who Disagree,'" 153; Meezan and Rauch, "Gay Marriage, Same-Sex Parenting, and America's Children," 100.

8. McLeod and Crawford, "The Postmodern Family," 211; see also Anderssen et al., "Outcomes for Children with Lesbian or Gay Parents," 349; Stacey and Biblarz, "(How) Does the Sexual Orientation of Parents Matter?" 160.

9. American Psychological Association, "Resolution on Sexual Orientation, Parents, and Children," in Ruth Ullmann Paige, "Proceedings of the American Psychological Association for the Legislative Year 2004," *Am. Psychol.* 60 (2005): 436, 499–500; Committee on Psychosocial Aspects of Child and Family Health, American Academy of Pediatrics, "Coparent or Second-Parent Adoption by Same-Sex Parents," *Pediatrics* 109 (2002): 339.

10. See Clarke, "'Stereotype, Attack, and Stigmatize Those Who Disagree,'" 154–155. In the early 1980s, the American Psychological Association dropped Cameron from its membership for failing to cooperate with an investigation into

complaints about his use of questionable methodologies in his studies. A few years later, the *Advocate* dubbed Cameron the "most dangerous antigay zealot in the United States." Dave Walter, "Paul Cameron," *Advocate* (October 29, 1985): 28, 29.

11. Paul Cameron and Kirk Cameron, "Homosexual Parents," *Adolescence* 31 (1996): 757; Paul Cameron, Kirk Cameron, and Thomas Landess, "Errors by the American Psychiatric Association, the American Psychological Association, and the National Education Association in Representing Homosexuality in Amicus Briefs About Amendment 2 to the U.S. Supreme Court," *Psychol. Reps.* 79 (1996): 383.

12. For example, Paul Cameron and Kirk Cameron, "Did the APA Misrepresent the Scientific Literature to Courts in Support of Homosexual Custody?" *J. Psychol.* 131 (1997): 313; Gregory M. Herek, "Bad Science in the Service of Stigma: A Critique of the Cameron Group's Survey Studies," in Herek, ed., *Stigma and Sexual Orientation,* 223.

13. Stacey and Biblarz, "(How) Does the Sexual Orientation of Parents Matter?"

14. Human Rights Campaign Foundation, "Equality from State to State: Gay, Lesbian, Bisexual and Transgender Americans and State Legislation in 2005" (2005), available at www.hrc.org/Template.cfm?Section=About_HRC&Template=/Content Management/ContentDisplay.cfm&ContentID=32564, 20.

15. S.B. 273, 114th Gen. Assem., 2d Reg. Sess. §9 (Ind. 2006).

16. Pew Research Center for People and Press, "Less Opposition to Gay Marriage, Adoption and Military Service" (March 22, 2006).

17. Jeff Atkinson, *Modern Child Custody Practice,* 2d ed. (New York: Lexis Publishing, 2005), 1, §4-2; John P. McCahey, Sandra Morgan Little, et al., *Child Custody and Visitation Law and Practice* (New York: Matthew Bender, 2006), 2, §10.06[1]–[2][a].

18. Donald K. Sherman, "Sixth Annual Review of Gender and Sexuality Law: Family Law Chapter—Child Custody and Visitation," *Geo. J. Gender and L.* 6 (2005): 691, 697–701 (footnotes omitted).

19. Sherman, "Sixth Annual Review of Gender and Sexuality Law," 702; see American Law Institute, *Principles of the Law of Family Dissolution: Analysis and Recommendations* (Newark, NJ: LexisNexis, 2002), §2.02 cmt. c; McCahey et al., *Child Custody and Visitation Law and Practice,* 2, §§10.03, 13.04.

20. Atkinson, *Modern Child Custody Practice,* 1, §§10-3, -5; Elizabeth Trainor, Annotation, *Custodial Parent's Homosexual or Lesbian Relationship with Third Person as Justifying Modification of Child Custody Order,* 65 A.L.R. 5th 591, §§2(a), 3(a) (1999).

21. McCahey et al., *Child Custody and Visitation Law and Practice,* 4, §26.06.

22. American Law Institute, *Principles of the Law of Family Dissolution,* §2.02 cmt. c.

23. Ibid.; Sherman, "Sixth Annual Review of Gender and Sexuality Law," 692–693.

24. McCahey et al., *Child Custody and Visitation Law and Practice,* 2, §10.12[2][c].

25. Patricia M. Logue, "The Rights of Lesbian and Gay Parents and Their Children," *J. Am. Acad. Matrimonial Law.* 18 (2002): 95, 101; see also Sherman, "Sixth Annual Review of Gender and Sexuality Law," 706.

26. *Jacoby v. Jacoby,* 763 So. 2d 410, 413 (Fla. Ct. App. 2000) (quoting *Maradie v. Maradie,* 680 So. 2d 538, 543 [Fla. Ct. App. 1996]).

27. D.C. Code §16-914(a)(1) (2007).

28. *In re Marriage of Cupples,* 531 N.W.2d 656, 657 (Iowa Ct. App. 1995); *Bezio v. Patenaude,* 410 N.E.2d 1207, 1215–1216 (Mass. 1980).

29. For example, *Barron v. Barron,* 594 A.2d 682, 687 (Pa. Super. Ct. 1991).

30. *Tucker v. Tucker,* 910 P.2d 1209 (Utah 1996).

31. Ibid., 1213.

32. Ibid.

33. *J.A.D. v. F.J.D.,* 978 S.W.2d 336, 339 (Mo. 1998).

34. For example, *J.P. v. P.W.,* 772 S.W.2d 786, 792 (Mo. Ct. App. 1989); *G.A. v. D.A.,* 745 S.W.2d 726 (Mo. Ct. App. 1987); *S.E.G. v. R.A.G.,* 735 S.W.2d 164, 166 (Mo. Ct. App. 1987).

35. *G.A. v. D.A.,* 728–729 (Lowenstein, J., dissenting). There is some debate over whether this is even a constitutionally permissible concern. See *Palmore v. Sidoti,* 466 U.S. 429 (1984). Compare, for example, *Jacoby v. Jacoby,* 410, 413 (applying *Palmore*), with *S.E.G. v. R.A.G.,* 166 (refusing to apply *Palmore*).

36. *J.P. v. P.W.,* 793.

37. *Ex parte J.M.F.,* 730 So. 2d 1190 (Ala. 1998).

38. Ibid., 1194.

39. Ibid., 1195, 1196 (quoting *Ex parte D.W.W.,* 717 So. 2d 793, 796 [Ala. 1998]).

40. *Ex parte H.H.,* 830 So. 2d 21, 26 (Ala. 2002) (Moore, C.J., dissenting).

41. Sandra Day O'Connor, "The Supreme Court and the Family," *U. Pa. J. Const'l L.* 3 (2001): 573, 575.

42. *Romer v. Evans,* 517 U.S. 620 (1996).

43. *Lawrence v. Texas,* 539 U.S. 558 (2003).

44. Matt Larsen, "*Lawrence v. Texas* and Family Law: Gay Parents' Constitutional Rights in Child Custody Proceedings," *N.Y.U. Ann. Surv. Am. L.* 60 (2004): 53; Jennifer Naeger, "And Then There Were None: The Repeal of Sodomy Laws after *Lawrence v. Texas* and Its Effect on the Custody and Visitation Rights of Gay and Lesbian Parents," *St. John's L. Rev.* 78 (2004): 397.

45. *L.A.M. v. B.M.,* 906 So. 2d 942, 946–947 (Ala. Civ. App. 2004).

46. *McGriff v. McGriff,* 99 P.3d 111, 117 (Idaho 2004); see Susan M. Moss, "*McGriff v. McGriff:* Consideration of a Parent's Sexual Orientation in Child Custody Disputes," *Idaho L. Rev.* 41 (2005): 593, 594.

47. *McGriff v. McGriff,* 124 (Kidwell, J., dissenting); see Moss, "*McGriff v. McGriff,*" 595.

48. Logue, "The Rights of Lesbian and Gay Parents and Their Children," 102–105; McCahey et al., *Child Custody and Visitation Law and Practice,* 3, §16.09(1).

49. *Downey v. Muffley,* 767 N.E.2d 1014 (Ind. Ct. App. 2002).

50. Ibid., 1021.

51. Ibid.

52. *Marlow v. Marlow,* 702 N.E.2d 733 (Ind. Ct. App. 1998).

53. Ibid., 735.

54. Ibid., 736–737.

55. Ibid., 737.

56. Larsen, "*Lawrence v. Texas* and Family Law," 80.

57. McCahey et al., *Child Custody and Visitation Law and Practice,* 2, §10.12[2][c]; see also Logue, "The Rights of Lesbian and Gay Parents and Their

Children," 103; Nancy G. Maxwell and Richard Donner, "The Psychological Consequences of Judicially Imposed Closets in Child Custody and Visitation Disputes Involving Gay or Lesbian Parents," *Wm. and Mary J. of Women and L.* 13 (2006): 305, 306–317.

58. *Taylor v. Taylor,* 47 S.W.3d 222 (Ark. 2001).

59. Ibid., 225.

60. Ibid.

61. *Ex parte D.W.W.,* 793.

62. Ibid., 796.

63. Ibid., 797 (Kennedy, J., dissenting).

64. McCahey et al., *Child Custody and Visitation Law and Practice,* 2, §11.01.

65. Mark Strasser, "Fit to Be Tied: On Custody, Discretion, and Sexual Orientation," *Am. U. L. Rev.* 46 (1997): 841, 843 (quoting Gerald Gunther, *Constitutional Law,* 12th ed. [Westbury, NY: Foundation Press, 1991], 446).

66. McCahey et al., *Child Custody and Visitation Law and Practice,* 2, §§11.01, .03; Atkinson, *Modern Child Custody Practice,* 1, §§9-1, -2.

67. *Bottoms v. Bottoms,* 457 S.E.2d 102 (Va. 1995).

68. *Troxel v. Granville,* 530 U.S. 57 (2000).

69. For example, Nancy D. Polikoff, "The Impact of *Troxel v. Granville* on Lesbian and Gay Parents," *Rutgers L.J.* 32 (2001): 825, 852; Brooke N. Silverthorn, "When Parental Rights and Children's Best Interests Collide: An Examination of *Troxel v. Granville* as It Relates to Gay and Lesbian Families," *Ga. St. U. L. Rev.* 19 (2003): 893, 906–907.

70. *Troxel v. Granville,* 65 (plurality).

71. Ibid., 68.

72. Polikoff, "The Impact of *Troxel v. Granville,*" 854.

73. Ibid., 854–855.

74. Julie Shapiro, "Custody and Conduct: How the Law Fails Lesbian and Gay Parents and Their Children," *Ind. L.J.* 71 (1996): 623, 625.

75. For example, *Ex parte D.W.W.,* 793, 796.

76. Compare, for example, *Van Driel v. Van Driel,* 525 N.W.2d 37–40 (S.D. 1994), with *Marlow v. Marlow,* 733.

77. Compare, for example, *Barron v. Barron,* 682, 684, with *Ex parte J.M.F.,* 1190, 1195.

78. Nadine A. Gartner, "Lesbian (M)otherhood: Creating an Alternative Model for Settling Child Custody Disputes," *Tul. J.L. and Sexuality* 16 (2007): 45, 58–61; Shapiro, "Custody and Conduct," 646–647; see also Maxwell and Donner, "The Psychological Consequences of Judicially Imposed Closets," 318–330 (discussing the psychological harm that this form of heterosexism can cause to the children involved).

79. For example, Kimberly D. Richman, "(When) Are Rights Wrong? Rights Discourses and Indeterminacy in Gay and Lesbian Parents' Custody Cases," *Law and Soc. Inquiry* 30 (2005): 137; Eugene Volokh, "Parent-Child Speech and Child Custody Speech Restrictions," *N.Y.U. L. Rev.* 81 (2006): 631; Larsen, "*Lawrence v. Texas* and Family Law."

80. Richman, "(When) Are Rights Wrong?" 163.

81. Ibid., 157–162; Maxwell and Donner, "The Psychological Consequences of Judicially Imposed Closets," 318–330; Shapiro, "Custody and Conduct," 626.

82. See Richman, "(When) Are Rights Wrong?" 172.

83. Joan H. Hollinger, ed., *Adoption Law and Practice* (New York: Matthew Bender, 2005), 1, §3.02(2).

84. Ibid., 1, §3.02(3).

85. See, for example, A. Chris Downs and Steven E. James, "Gay, Lesbian, and Bisexual Foster Parents: Strengths and Challenges for the Child Welfare System," *Child Welfare* 85 (2006): 281, 282; Sandra Stukes Chipungu and Tricia B. Bent-Goodley, "Meeting the Challenges of Contemporary Foster Care," *Future of Children* 14 (2004): 75, 83–84.

86. Administrative memorandum from Director of Nebraska Department of Social Services Mary Dean Harvey to District and Division Administrators, Human Services no. 1-95, January 23, 1995; see also Nancy Hicks, "Agency Program Excludes Same-Sex Issues," *Lincoln Journal Star,* May 6, 2007, C1 (describing how Nebraska Health and Human Services excluded a lesbian parent from speaking at a diversity event).

87. Administrative memorandum from Human Services Division Administrator Christine M. Hanus to District and Division Administrators, Addendum to Human Services no. 1-95, March 8, 1995.

88. Letter from Acting Director Christine Z. Peterson, Nebraska Department of Health and Human Services, to author, September 11, 2006.

89. Utah Code §§62A-4a-602(5)(b), 78-30-1(3) (2007).

90. Ala. Admin. Code r. 660-5-29-.02(1)(b)(1) (2006); 11-111-001 Miss. Code R. app. A, §III(A)(4) (2005).

91. N.D. Admin. Code 75-03-14-04(5) (2006).

92. Laura T. Kessler, "Transgressive Caregiving," *Fla. St. U. L. Rev.* 33 (2005): 1, 34.

93. N.D. Cent. Code §§50-12-03, -07.1 (2005).

94. *Dep't of Human Servs. v. Howard,* 05-814, 2006 Ark. Lexis 418, *2 (Ark. June 29, 2006).

95. Ibid., *12.

96. Ibid., *19.

97. Laura Kellams, "Proposal: No 'I Do,' No Taking in Youths," *Arkansas Democrat-Gazette,* August 23, 2007.

98. Division of Children and Family Services, Arkansas Department of Human Services, Publication 22, "Standards for Approval of Family Foster Homes" (2002), 7.

99. See *Johnston v. Mo. Dep't Soc. Servs.,* 0516CV09517, slip op. at 5 (Mo. Cir. Ct., February 17, 2006).

100. Mo. Code Regs. tit. 13, §40-60.030(2) (2005).

101. 2006 Mo. Legis. Serv. H.B. 1290.

102. Mo. Code Regs. tit. 13, §§35-60.030, 40-60.030 (2007); Emergency Rescission, 13 CSR 40-60.030, 31 Mo. Reg. 1297 (September 1, 2006); Emergency Rule, 13 CSR 35-60.030, 31 Mo. Reg. 1296 (September 1, 2006).

103. Tim Hoover, "State Eases Policy on Gay Parents," *Kansas City Star,* July 19, 2006, A1.

104. Conn. Gen. Stat. §45a-726a (2007).

105. See Downs and James, "Gay, Lesbian, and Bisexual Foster Parents," 294–295.

106. Ibid., 295.

107. Cal. Welf. and Inst. Code §16,013 (2007); 110 Code Mass. Reg. §1.09(1), (3) (2007); N.J. Admin. Code §10:122B-1.5(b) (2007); Wis. Admin. Code HFS 56.04(6) (2007).

108. For example, James W. Gilliam Jr., "Toward Providing a Welcoming Home for All: Enacting a New Approach to Address the Longstanding Problems Lesbian, Gay, Bisexual, and Transgender Youth Face in the Foster Care System," *Loy. L.A. L. Rev.* 37 (2004): 1037, 1041–1042, 1047.

109. Rob Woronoff, Rudy Estrada, and Susan Sommer, Child Welfare League of America and Lambda Legal Defense and Education Fund, "Out of the Margins: A Report on Regional Listening Forums Highlighting the Experiences of Lesbian, Gay, Bisexual, Transgender, and Questioning Youth in Care" (2006), available at http://data.lambdalegal.org/pdf/693.pdf; Anne Tamar-Mattis, "Implications of AB 458 for California LGBTQ Youth in Foster Care," *Tul. J.L. and Sexuality* 14 (2005): 149, 157.

110. Fla. Stat. §63.042(3) (2007).

111. *Lofton v. Sec'y of the Dep't of Children and Family Servs.*, 358 F.3d 804, 807 (11th Cir. 2004).

112. Ibid.; *Cox v. Fla. Dep't of Health and Rehabilitative Servs.*, 656 So. 2d 902 (Fla. 1995).

113. Mark Strasser, "Rebellion in the Eleventh Circuit: On *Lawrence, Lofton,* and the Best Interests of Children," *Tulsa L. Rev.* 40 (2005): 421.

114. *Lofton v. Sec'y, Fla. Dep't of Children and Families,* 543 U.S. 1081 (2005).

115. Laura Kellams, "2008 Bid Set on Banning Care by Gays," *Arkansas Democrat-Gazette,* June 13, 2007.

116. Miss. Code §93-17-3(5) (2007); Utah Code §78-30-1(3)(b) (2007).

117. Ala. Code §26-10A-5(a) (2007).

118. Act of April 29, 1998, 1998 Ala. Legis. Serv. 439.

119. Conn. Gen. Stat. §45a-726a (2007); N.D. Cent. Code §§50-12-03, -07.1 (2005).

120. Cal. Welf. and Inst. Code §16,013 (2007); Me. Rev. Stat. tit. 5, §§4553(8)(K), 4591–4592 (2006); Md. Code Regs. 07.05.03.09(A)(2), .15(C)(2) (2007); 110 Code Mass. Reg. §1.09(1), (3) (2007); Nev. Admin. Code §127.351 (2006); N.J. Admin. Code §10:121C-2.6, -4.1(c) (2007); N.Y. Comp. Codes R. and Regs tit. 18, §421.16(h)(2) (2007); see also *Butler v. Adoption Media, LLC,* 486 F. Supp. 2d 1022 (N.D. Cal. 2007); Henry K. Lee, "Gay Couple Win Lawsuit Against Adoption Web Site," *San Francisco Chronicle,* May 23, 2007, B12 (announcing a settlement of *Butler v. Adoption Media, LLC* in which the adoption web site operators will phase out postings by California residents rather than offer their services equally to same-sex couples and different-sex married couples).

121. Devon Brooks and Sheryl Goldberg, "Gay and Lesbian Adoptive and Foster Care Placements: Can They Meet the Needs of Waiting Children?" *Soc. Work* 46 (2001): 147, 152; see also Hollinger, ed., *Adoption Law and Practice,* 1, §3.06[6] n.77.

122. David M. Brodzinsky and the Staff of the Evan B. Donaldson Adoption Institute, "Adoption by Lesbians and Gays: A National Survey of Adoption Agency Policies, Practices, and Attitudes" (2003), 20–21, available at www.adoptioninstitute.org/whowe/Lesbian%20and%20Gay%20Adoption%20Report_final.doc.

123. Ibid., 19.

124. Ibid., 36.

125. Molly Cooper, "What Makes a Family? Addressing the Issue of Gay and Lesbian Adoption," *Fam. Ct. Rev.* 42 (2004): 178, 182; Lambda Legal, "Overview of State Adoption Laws" (2007), available at www.lambdalegal.org/our-work/issues/marriage-relationships-family/parenting/overview-of-state-adoption.html.

126. Charles P. Kindregan Jr. and Maureen McBrien, *Assisted Reproductive Technology: A Lawyer's Guide to Emerging Law and Science* (Chicago: American Bar Association, 2006), 24–25, 193–196.

127. Ibid., 24–25, 196.

128. John A. Robertson, "Gay and Lesbian Access to Assisted Reproductive Technology," *Case W. Res. L. Rev.* 55 (2004): 323, 326–348; Richard F. Storrow, "Rescuing Children from the Marriage Movement: The Case Against Marital Status Discrimination in Adoption and Assisted Reproduction," *U.C. Davis L. Rev.* 39 (2006): 305, 327–328.

129. See Kindregan and McBrien, *Assisted Reproductive Technology*, 36–46, 90–91.

130. N.J. Rev. Stat. §9:17-44(b) (2007).

131. Kindregan and McBrien, *Assisted Reproductive Technology,* 145–182, 208–212.

132. Alona R. Croteau, "Voices in the Dark: Second Parent Adoptions When the Law Is Silent," *Loy. L. Rev.* 50 (2004): 675, 679.

133. Ibid., 678–679.

134. Julie Shapiro, "A Lesbian-Centered Critique of Second-Parent Adoptions," *Berkeley Women's L.J.* 14 (1999): 17, 26.

135. Croteau, "Voices in the Dark," 681.

136. Hollinger, ed., *Adoption Law and Practice*, 1, §2.10[3].

137. Jeffrey G. Gibson, "Lesbian and Gay Prospective Adoptive Parents: The Legal Battle," *Hum. Rts.* (Spring 1999): 7, 10; National Center for Lesbian Rights, "Second Parent Adoptions: A Snapshot of Current Law" (2003), available at www.nclrights.org/publications/2ndparentadoptions.htm.

138. Shapiro, "A Lesbian-Centered Critique of Second-Parent Adoptions," 28. Because stepparent adoption was used as the model, any other existing legal parent (e.g., a sperm or egg donor with legally recognized parental rights) must normally relinquish his or her parental rights before a second-parent adoption may take place. Ibid., 27.

139. Cal. Fam. Code §9000(b) (2007); Act of May 14, 2007, ch. 214, 2007 Colo. HB 1330; Conn. Gen. Stat. §45a-724(a)(3) (2007); Vt. Stat. tit. 15A, §1-102(b) (2006).

140. *Sharon S. v. Super. Ct.,* 73 P.3d 554 (Cal. 2003).

141. *In re M.M.D.,* 662 A.2d 837 (D.C. 1995); *In re Petition of K.M.,* 653 N.E.2d 888 (Ill. Ct. App. 1995); *Adoption of Tammy,* 619 N.E.2d 315 (Mass. 1993); *In re Adoption of Two Children by H.N.R.,* 666 A.2d 535 (N.J. Super. Ct. App. Div. 1995); *In re Jacob,* 660 N.E.2d 397 (N.Y. 1995); *In re Adoption of R.B.F.,* 803 A.2d 1195 (Pa. 2002); *Adoption of M.A.,* 2007 ME 123 (implicitly sanctioning second-parent adoptions by allowing a same-sex couple to file a joint petition to adopt).

142. Hollinger, ed., *Adoption Law and Practice*, 1, §3.06[6]; Human Rights Campaign, "Parenting Laws: Second Parent Adoption" (June 2007), available at www.hrc.org/Template.cfm?Section=Your_Community&Template=/ContentManagement/ContentDisplay.cfm&ContentID=13383.

143. *In re Adoption of Luke*, 640 N.W.2d 374 (Neb. 2002); *In re Adoption of Doe*, 719 N.E.2d 1071 (Ohio Ct. App. 1998); *In re Angel Lace M.*, 516 N.W.2d 678 (Wis. 1994).

144. For example, *In re Adoption of Infant K.S.P.*, 804 N.E.2d 1253 (Ind. Ct. App. 2004); *In re Adoption of M.M.G.C.*, 785 N.E.2d 267 (Ind. Ct. App. 2003).

145. Act of May 4, 2005, §9, 2005 Ind. Acts 130 (codified at Ind. Code Ann. §31–19–15–2(b) [2006]); see *In re Infant Girl W.*, 845 N.E.2d 229, 247–251 (Ind. Ct. App. 2006) (Najam, J., dissenting).

146. Cal. Fam. Code §9000(b), (g) (2007); Conn. Gen. Stat. §§45a-724(2), -731(5)–(7), 46b-38nn, -38oo (2007); Mass. Gen. Laws ch. 210, §2A(C) (2007); N.H. Rev. Stat. §§170-B:4(IV)(a), -B:25(II) (2007); Act of June 4, 2007, §1, 2007 N.H. Adv. Legis. Serv. ch. 58 (to be codified at N.H. Rev. Stat. §457-A:6 effective January 1, 2008); N.J. Rev. Stat. §§9:3-48, -50, -55, 37:1-32(d) (2007); Or. Rev. Stat. §109.041(2) (2005); Act of May 9, 2007, ch. 99, §9(3), 2007 Ore. HB 2007 (Lexis) (see the discussion of Oregon's domestic partnership regime in Chapter 6 for an explanation of the effective date of this provision); Vt. Stat. tit. 15, §1204(e)(4) (2006); ibid., tit. 15A, §3-301(c); *Goodridge v. Dep't of Pub. Health*, 798 N.E.2d 941 (Mass. 2003).

147. Hollinger, ed., *Adoption Law and Practice*, 1, §3.06[6]; Storrow, "Rescuing Children from the Marriage Movement," 336–338, 343–344.

148. Cal. Fam. Code §297.5(a) (2007); Conn. Gen. Stat. §§45a-732, 46b-38nn, -38oo (2007); Mass. Gen. Laws ch. 210, §1 (2007); N.H. Rev. Stat. §§170-B:4(I) (2007); Act of June 4, 2007, §1, 2007 N.H. Adv. Legis. Serv. ch. 58 (to be codified at N.H. Rev. Stat. §457-A:6 effective January 1, 2008); N.J. Rev. Stat. §§9:3-43(a), 37:1-32(d) (2007); Or. Rev. Stat. §109.309 (2005); Act of May 9, 2007, ch. 99, §9(3), 2007 Ore. HB 2007 (Lexis) (see the discussion of Oregon's domestic partnership regime in Chapter 6 for an explanation of the effective date of this provision); Vt. Stat. tit. 15, §1204(e)(4) (2006); ibid., tit. 15A, §3-301(b); *Sharon S. v. Super. Ct.*, 73 P.3d 554, 564 (Cal. 2003); *Goodridge v. Dep't of Pub. Health*.

149. *Sharon S.*, 73 P.3d, 554; *Adoption of Tammy*, 315, 318–319; Or. Admin. R. 413-120-0200(3) (2007); see Gibson, "Lesbian and Gay Prospective Adoptive Parents," 11.

150. See, for example, Op. Att'y Gen. 7160, 2004 Mich. AG Lexis 15 (September 14, 2004) (same-sex couples married in other states [e.g., Massachusetts] are ineligible to petition for joint adoption in Michigan because Michigan law permits only married couples to jointly adopt a child and does not recognize out-of-state same-sex marriages).

151. *In re M.M.D.; In re Petition of K.M.*, 888; *In re Adoption of Carolyn B.*, 774 N.Y.S.2d 227 (N.Y. App. Div. 2004).

152. *Adoption of M.A.*, 2007 ME 123.

153. *In re Infant Girl W.*, 229, transfer denied, 851 N.E.2d 961 (Ind. 2006).

154. *In re Adoption of R.B.F.*, 1195, 1203; see also Maureen B. Cohon, "Where the Rainbow Ends: Trying to Find a Pot of Gold for Same-Sex Couples in Pennsylvania," *Duq. L. Rev.* 41 (2003): 495, 501.

155. Surrogacy, which involves the participation of a birth mother who is not intended to be a parent, involves thornier questions that may require a later adoption or a judicial decree to unequivocally establish parentage. Kindregan and McBrien, *Assisted Reproductive Technology*, 131–132, 136–138, 144–145; see also Susan Frelich Appleton, "Presuming Women: Revisiting the Presumption of Legitimacy in the

Same-Sex Couples Era," *B.U. L. Rev.* 86 (2006): 227. But see *K.M. v. E.G.*, 117 P.3d 673 (Cal. 2005).

156. Courtney G. Joslin, "The Legal Parentage of Children Born to Same-Sex Couples: Developments in the Law," *Fam. L.Q.* 39 (2005): 683, 684.

157. Cal. Fam. Code §§297.5(d), 7613 (2007); N.J. Rev. Stat. §§9:17-44, 37:1–31(e) (2007); see also Conn. Gen. Stat. §§45a-774, 46b-38nn, -38oo (2007); Mass. Gen. Laws ch. 46, §4B (2007); *Goodridge v. Dep't of Pub. Health*, 941; N.H. Rev. Stat. §168-B:3 (2007); Act of June 4, 2007, §1, 2007 N.H. Adv. Legis. Serv. ch. 58 (to be codified at N.H. Rev. Stat. §457-A:6 effective January 1, 2008); Or. Rev. Stat. §109.243 (2005); Act of May 9, 2007, ch. 99, §9(3), 11, 2007 Ore. HB 2007 (Lexis) (see the discussion of Oregon's domestic partnership regime in Chapter 6 for an explanation of the effective date of this provision). The Vermont Supreme Court has taken a narrow view of its statutory presumption of parentage, concluding that the presumption was intended to apply only for purposes of child support actions. Nonetheless, the court has indicated that, at least in the context of a visitation proceeding, a lesbian "couple's legal union [i.e., civil union] at the time of the child's birth is extremely persuasive evidence of joint parentage." *Miller-Jenkins v. Miller-Jenkins*, 2006 VT 78, ¶¶41-63 (2006), cert. denied, 127 S. Ct. 2130 (2007).

158. *Elisa B. v. Super. Ct.*, 117 P.3d 660 (Cal. 2005).

159. *In re Parentage of Child of Kimberly Robinson*, 890 A.2d 1036 (N.J. Super. Ct. Ch. Div. 2005).

160. Jennifer L. Rosato, "Children of Same-Sex Parents Deserve the Security Blanket of the Parentage Presumption," *Fam. Ct. Rev.* 44 (2006): 74, 75; see also Deborah L. Forman, "Same-Sex Partners: Strangers, Third Parties, or Parents? The Changing Legal Landscape and the Struggle for Parental Equality," *Fam. L.Q.* 40 (2006): 23, 48–49.

161. Frank S. Berall, "Estate Planning Considerations for Unmarried Same- or Opposite-Sex Cohabitants," *Quinnipiac L. Rev.* 23 (2004): 361, 388–390; Croteau, "Voices in the Dark," 677–678.

162. *Wakeman v. Dixon*, 921 So. 2d 669 (Fla. Ct. App. 2006); see also Cohon, "Where the Rainbow Ends," 503–504 (indicating that shared-parenting agreements are of doubtful enforceability in Pennsylvania); Forman, "Same-Sex Partners," 40–41.

163. See Jeffrey A. Dodge, "Same-Sex Marriage and Divorce: A Proposal for Child Custody Mediation," *Fam. Ct. Rev.* 44 (2006): 87; William Mason Emnett, "Queer Conflicts: Mediating Parenting Disputes Within the Gay Community," *Geo. L.J.* 86 (1997): 433; Gartner, "Lesbian (M)otherhood," 66–74; Betsy J. Walter, "Lesbian Mediation: Resolving Custody and Visitation Disputes When Couples End Their Relationships," *Fam. Ct. Rev.* 41 (2003): 104.

164. Joslin, "The Legal Parentage of Children Born to Same-Sex Couples," 693; compare, for example, *E.N.O. v. L.M.M.*, 711 N.E.2d 886, 892 nn.9–10 (Mass. 1999), with *Jones v. Barlow*, 2007 UT 20, ¶¶29, 42 (refusing to adopt the de facto parent or psychological parent doctrines and further permitting the legal parent to terminate the *in loco parentis* status of the nonlegal parent at will). Courts have generally distinguished the U.S. Supreme Court's decision in *Troxel v. Granville* when considering claims of *in loco*, de facto, or psychological parent status. Sherman, "Sixth Annual Review of Gender and Sexuality Law," 713–714.

165. Joslin, "The Legal Parentage of Children Born to Same-Sex Couples," 696.

166. See, for example, Linda S. Anderson, "Protecting Parent-Child Relationships: Determining Parental Rights of Same-Sex Parents Consistently Despite Varying Recognition of Their Relationship," *Pierce L. Rev.* 5 (2006): 1.

167. Okla. Stat. tit. 10, §7502-1.4(A) (2006).

168. Op. Att'y Gen. 04-8, 2004 Okla. AG Lexis 8 (March 19, 2004); see *Finstuen v. Edmondson*, CIV-04-1152-C, 2006 U.S. Dist. Lexis 32122, *4 (W.D. Okla. May 19, 2006).

169. *Finstuen v. Edmondson.*

170. *Finstuen v. Crutcher*, 06-6213 and 06-6216, 2007 U.S. App. Lexis 18500 (10th Cir. August 3, 2007); see also Barbara Hoberock, "State Won't Fight Same-Sex Adoption Ruling," *Tulsa World,* August 17, 2007, A9.

171. 28 U.S.C. §1738C (2007).

172. Deborah L. Forman, "Interstate Recognition of Same-Sex Parents in the Wake of Gay Marriage, Civil Unions, and Domestic Partnerships," *B.C. L. Rev.* 46 (2004): 1, 79.

173. Op. Att'y Gen. 06-0325, 2007 WL 1438453 (La. April 18, 2007). It is worth noting that this opinion comes to the same conclusion with respect to adoptions by unmarried same-sex couples.

174. *Miller-Jenkins v. Miller-Jenkins,* 2006 VT 78, cert. denied, 127 S. Ct. 2130 (2007).

175. *Miller-Jenkins v. Miller-Jenkins*, 637 S.E.2d 330 (Va. Ct. App. 2006).

176. "Va. High Court Rejects Civil-Union Custody Appeal," *Richmond Times Dispatch,* May 12, 2007, B-7.

177. Kessler, "Transgressive Caregiving," 2.

178. Ibid., 38.

179. E. Gary Spitko, "From Queer to Paternity: How Primary Gay Fathers Are Changing Fatherhood and Gay Identity," *St. Louis U. Pub. L. Rev.* 24 (2005): 195.

180. Kessler, "Transgressive Caregiving," 43.

181. See Lauren Schwartzreich, "Restructuring the Framework for Legal Analyses of Gay Parenting," *Harv. Blackletter L.J.* 21 (2005): 109; Barbara Bennett Woodhouse, "Waiting for Loving: The Child's Fundamental Right to Adoption," *Cap. U. L. Rev.* 34 (2005): 297.

182. Christopher Carnahan, "Inscribing Lesbian and Gay Identities: How Judicial Imaginations Intertwine with the Best Interests of Children," *Cardozo Women's L.J.* 11 (2004): 1, 35.

9

Parting Thoughts

Uniformity breeds conformity, and conformity's other face is intolerance.

—Zygmunt Bauman[1]

In the first chapter of this book, I described the current situation of the lesbian and gay movement as a "predicament." To extricate ourselves from this predicament, we have largely pursued a strategy that attempts to effect social change from within the legal system. We have, for example, sought legal recognition for our relationships and our families; the passage of laws that prohibit discrimination on the basis of sexual orientation in employment, housing, and public accommodations; and the passage of laws that enhance punishment for bias crimes. As I acknowledged in Chapter 1, our attraction to this civil rights approach is quite natural given the "immediate, concrete appeal"[2] of securing legal rights. But this attraction is no more natural than the backlash that we have experienced from a society in which heterosexism has been entrenched for centuries. If nothing else, I hope that the ensuing chapters have shown that the time is ripe for lesbians and gay men to reconsider their relationship to the law and for us to alter our approach to effecting change.

To start, we must come to terms with the fact that the law has been—and continues to be—no great friend of lesbians and gay men. For instance, we have seen that the law of public accommodations establishes the ability to discriminate as the default rule. And the default rules in many other areas of the law—including medical decision-making, hospital visitation, the division of property upon the termination of a relationship, and intestate succession—codify discrimination by ignoring our relationships and providing a safety net for the nearly exclusive benefit of heterosexuals.

Moreover, a critical perspective reveals that the law often does more (to harm) or less (to help) than appearances indicate. Under the rubric of laws that do less (to help), you may recall the discussion of President Clinton's executive order that grants unenforceable employment discrimination protections to lesbian and gay federal employees. Or you may recall that, notwithstanding the adoption of state and local laws that prohibit employment discrimination on the basis of sexual orientation, lesbians and gay men continue to be paid less than their heterosexual counterparts for equal work. Conversely, "Don't Ask, Don't Tell" (DADT) does far more (to harm) than appearances indicate. DADT was sold to the public as an improvement over the prior ban on lesbians and gay men in the military. But DADT is no better than the prior ban; in fact, it is arguably worse because it operates as a trap for the unwary, who are led to believe that lesbians and gay men are now welcome to serve in the military so long as they do so silently. Furthermore, in the child custody and visitation area, the trend toward abandoning the per se rule in favor of a nexus test (i.e., one that requires proof of harm before a parent's (homo)sexual orientation can be held against her in custody and visitation decisions) means little when individual judges are still able to act on their sexual prejudices after paying lip service to the ostensibly stricter nexus test. Naturally, these are just a few examples of a wider problem that is illustrated throughout this book.

We must further recognize that even if the law were friendlier to lesbians and gay men, the law simply *cannot* grant us the unqualified acceptance that we seek from society. As numerous legal commentators have remarked, "the attainment of formal equality under the law does not translate into complete equality for subordinate groups."[3] Merely changing the law will not ineluctably lead to a change in the way that straight people think about or interact with lesbians and gay men. In other words, our fight must be about more than changing laws; it must be about changing minds.

The key to success in that endeavor is to keep the need for legal change in proper perspective. To change the way that straight people think about and interact with lesbians and gay men—to get them to accept us without reservation—will require a long, hard struggle. The law provides no clear and easy path around that struggle. Yet it is difficult to deny that the law plays a (welcome or unwelcome) part in each of our lives; for example, we have observed inextricable links between the law and lesbian and gay parenting. Recognizing the law's role in our lives, we must attempt to strike an appropriate balance between efforts to effect legal change and efforts to effect social change, because these two realms influence each other: Just as changes in the law can create opportunities for social change, social change can alter how the law is applied and interpreted.[4]

Thus, rather than viewing the law as some sort of shortcut to unqualified acceptance, we should view it as a utilitarian tool or weapon in our struggle for acceptance. Changes in the law should no longer be seen as an end in themselves but as no more than a means for achieving our ends. In this regard, it is worth noting that not every legal battle needs to result in a "win" to advance us toward our goal. Even when we "lose," we can still win because we achieve a measure of success every time we bring our oppression out into the open by forcing society to forthrightly articulate and squarely face its antigay prejudices. Legal losses help to demonstrate how everyday law for gays and lesbians is more like an everyday legal obstacle course. The courts are an especially useful means for drawing attention to such problems; indeed, there is "a long tradition of litigators and movements using the courts as platforms for arguing controversial positions and garnering public support for them."[5] In short, we should not hesitate to use and manipulate the law—in mundane, novel, and even radical ways—to our greatest possible advantage.[6]

There certainly will also be times when the law will be of little use in furthering our struggle. At those times, we should not hesitate to abandon legal approaches in favor of other (e.g., social, political, or economic) approaches that can more effectively advance our struggle. For precisely this reason, I eschewed a narrow focus on legal strategies and solutions to problems throughout the course of this book, instead providing advice that attempts to strike a balance between legal and nonlegal approaches to effecting change.

And, in keeping with the notion that our individual narratives are a powerful (but underutilized) tool for effecting change, I have attempted to broaden the focus of our energy to include efforts at both the organizational and the individual levels. Accordingly, much of the advice in this book has centered on how best to deploy our individual narratives in order to foster understanding of—and empathy for—the plight of lesbians and gay men. Sometimes we are best served by working together to tell our stories in a coordinated effort, such as when we work together to lobby for the passage of a law that benefits us. Other times we are best served by telling our stories separately, such as when we explain our individual experiences of discrimination to a court in an attempt to obtain legal redress or to family, friends, and coworkers in an effort to help them understand what it is like to live life as a lesbian or gay man in a generally hostile society.

In keeping with this broadened focus, we must come to understand that we cannot merely rely on others—whether lesbian and gay organizations or our straight allies—to effect change on our behalf. When a relative few demand change, the heterosexual majority can simply ignore them as radicals, outliers, or elites that do not represent the masses, or it can pacify them by tinkering at the margins to make "change" that has no real impact on the majority or on its attitudes toward lesbians and gay men. In contrast, if we all simultaneously express our dissatisfaction with the status quo and demand change, the heterosexual majority will have little choice but to confront the problems engendered by the divide that it has created between gay

and straight. For this reason, it is important that we all become activists by
working for change every day, in ways big and small and both individually
and collectively.

At the same time, by broadening the focus to include efforts at the individual level, we will begin the process of breaking down stereotypes by encouraging the telling of a multiplicity of stories that reveal the diversity of
the lesbian and gay community. Straight people will see that we are of all
different races, ethnicities, genders, and social classes. They will see the
many ways in which we are both similar to and different from them. And,
hopefully, they will come to realize that we are human beings and not just
some undifferentiated "other" that can be easily marginalized, demonized,
stigmatized, or just forgotten. In these ways, we increase the likelihood that
our efforts might actually change the minds of heterosexuals.

For some among us, the intersection of sexual orientation with these
other characteristics (e.g., race, gender, and/or class) will render the task of
becoming an activist more costly than it is for others. To address these differential burdens, we should come together as a community to discuss ways
of evening out the burdens of individual activism and addressing other
forms of discrimination. Furthermore, not everyone in our diverse community will be personally affected by every one of the issues discussed in this
book. Nevertheless, we should each work for change even when we are not
directly affected by an issue because any assault on the lesbian and gay community necessarily affects all of us by contributing to the general culture of
heterosexism.

In the end, we will all benefit if only we refuse to accede to the ever-
present pressure to remain silent—to pass as straight or to cover our
(homo)sexual orientation—so as not to upset the tacit privileging of heterosexuality in our society. To effect lasting, positive change, we need to resist
the temptation to take the easy road of conforming to heterosexual expectations. Instead, we must engage in the more difficult task of actively overturning and destabilizing the privileging of heterosexuality in our society.
We must strive not only to "come out" but to "be out"—to tell our own
stories, in our own words, and in the most effective way possible.

Notes

1. Zygmunt Bauman, *Globalization: The Human Consequences* (New York:
Columbia University Press, 1998), 47.

2. Diane Helene Miller, *Freedom to Differ: The Shaping of the Gay and Lesbian
Struggle for Civil Rights* (New York: New York University Press, 1998), 140.

3. Darren Lenard Hutchinson, "Dissecting Axes of Subordination: The Need for
a Structural Analysis," *Am. U. J. Gender Soc. Pol'y and L.* 11 (2003): 13, 17.

4. See Ellen Ann Andersen, *Out of the Closets and into the Courts* (New York:
New York University Press, 2005), 140–142, 199–202, 210–213.

5. Jules Lobel, "Courts as Forums for Protest," *UCLA L. Rev.* 52 (2004): 477, 560.

6. For some radical thoughts on ways in which lesbians and gay men can use the law to their advantage, see Anthony C. Infanti, "*Homo Sacer,* Homosexual: Some Thoughts on Waging Tax Guerrilla Warfare," *Unbound: Harv. J. of the Legal Left* 2 (2006): 27.

Appendix: Resources

American Civil Liberties Union (ACLU)
125 Broad Street, 18th Floor
New York, NY 10004
General web site: www.aclu.org
Web site for LGBT Project: www.aclu.org/lgbt/index.html

The ACLU advocates for the protection of individual rights, and it has a specific project dedicated to lesbian, gay, bisexual, and transgender rights. The ACLU's LGBT rights project brings lawsuits in state and federal courts in cases concerning discrimination, parenting, relationships and marriage, and youth and schools. The ACLU's web site contains information and reports on action that it has taken as well as a list of local chapters with their contact information. To request assistance from the ACLU, contact must be made at the state or local level.

Caring Connections
National Hospice and Palliative Care Organization
1700 Diagonal Road, Suite 625
Alexandria, VA 22314
Toll-free help line: 800-658-8898
Toll-free help line in Spanish: 877-658-8896
Email: caringinfo@nhpco.org
Web site: www.caringinfo.org

Caring Connections is a program of the National Hospice and Palliative Care Organization. Caring Connections is designed to be "a national consumer engagement initiative to improve care at the end of life." Among other things, Caring Connections provides on its web site free advance directive form documents and helpful explanations for each state in the nation.

Family Pride
1725 K Street, N.W., Suite 212
Washington, DC 20006

or

P.O. Box 65327
Washington, DC 20035-5327
Phone: 202-331-5015
Fax: 202-331-0080
E-mail: info@familypride.org
Web site: www.familypride.org

Family Pride is an organization whose goal is creating equality for all families, but it maintains a special focus on lesbian, gay, bisexual, and transgender families and parents. Family Pride's web site contains tools and publications dealing with topics such as making schools inclusive, talking to children about political attacks on nontraditional families, and starting a parents' group.

Freedom to Marry
116 West 23rd Street, Suite 500
New York, NY 10011
Phone: 212-851-8418
Fax: 646-375-2069
E-mail: info@freedomtomarry.org
Web site: www.freedomtomarry.org

As its name indicates, Freedom to Marry is an organization that works to achieve marriage equality nationwide. Freedom to Marry's web site hosts a very interesting "Story Center" that allows individuals to share their stories of discrimination and how it affects their lives.

Gay and Lesbian Advocates and Defenders (GLAD)
30 Winter Street, Suite 800
Boston, MA 02108
Phone: (617) 426-1350 (Boston area); 1-800-455-GLAD (New England)
E-mail: gladlaw@glad.org
Web site: www.glad.org

GLAD describes itself as "New England's leading legal rights organization dedicated to ending discrimination based on sexual orientation, HIV status and gender identity and expression. Providing litigation, advocacy, and educational work in all areas of gay, lesbian, bisexual and transgender civil rights and the rights of people living with HIV, GLAD has a full-time legal staff and a network of cooperating attorneys across New England." GLAD operates a "legal infoline" (telephone numbers listed above) that is operated by trained volunteers who work with callers to provide information, support, and referrals.

Gay and Lesbian Alliance Against Defamation (GLAAD)
5455 Wilshire Boulevard, Suite 1500
Los Angeles, CA 90036
Phone: 323-933-2240
Fax: 323-933-2241

and

248 West 35th Street, 8th Floor
New York, NY 10001
Phone: 212-629-3322
Fax: 212-629-3225
General web site: www.glaad.org

GLAAD is a media watchdog that "is dedicated to promoting and ensuring fair, accurate and inclusive representation of people and events in the media as a means of eliminating homophobia and discrimination based on gender identity and sexual orientation." GLAAD's web site contains resources for reporting incidents of defamation in print and electronic media. GLAAD also trains volunteers to assist in monitoring local television, newspaper, and radio programming, and it issues alerts and calls to action when instances of defamation occur.

Gay and Lesbian Medical Association (GLMA)

459 Fulton Street, Suite 107
San Francisco, CA 94102
Phone: 415-255-4547
Fax: 415-255-4784
E-mail: info@glma.org
Web site: www.glma.org

GLMA works to achieve equality in health care for lesbian, gay, bisexual, and transgender individuals. GLMA works with health care providers by training them to render "sensitive and competent care to LGBT people." It also maintains a list of health care providers who "have indicated a commitment to non-judgmental care of LGBT patients."

Gay, Lesbian, and Straight Education Network (GLSEN)

90 Broad Street, 2nd Floor
New York, NY 10004
Phone: 212-727-0135
Fax: 212-727-0254
E-mail: glsen@glsen.org
Web site: www.glsen.org

GLSEN is an organization that works to ensure that schools are safe for all students, regardless of sexual orientation or gender identity. GLSEN has a fairly extensive online library with information for educators (in the areas of law and policy, curriculum, and training) and for students (on starting a gay-straight alliance and student organizing).

Human Rights Campaign (HRC)

1640 Rhode Island Avenue, N.W.
Washington, DC 20036-3278
Phone: 202-628-4160
Phone (TTY): 202-216-1572

Phone (toll-free): 800-777-4723
Fax: 202-347-5323
E-mail: hrc@hrc.org
Web site: www.hrc.org

HRC describes itself as "America's largest civil rights organization working to achieve gay, lesbian, bisexual and transgender equality." In addition to the many educational documents and links on its web site, HRC tracks the laws and legislation in each state that affect lesbian, gay, bisexual, and transgender individuals.

Human Rights Watch (HRW)
325 West Huron, Suite 304
Chicago, IL 60610
Phone: 312-573-2450
Fax: 312-573-2454
E-mail: chicago@hrw.org

and

11500 West Olympic Boulevard, Suite 441
Los Angeles, CA 90064
Phone: 310-477-5540
Fax: 310-477-4622
E-mail: hrwlasb@hrw.org

and

350 Fifth Avenue, 34th Floor
New York, NY 10118-3299
Phone: 212-290-4700
Fax: 212-736-1300
E-mail: hrwnyc@hrw.org

and

100 Bush Street, Suite 1812
San Francisco, CA 94104
Phone: 415-362-3250
Fax: 415-362-3255
E-mail: hrwsf@hrw.org

and

1630 Connecticut Avenue, N.W., Suite 500
Washington, DC 20009
Phone: 202-612-4321
Fax: 202-612-4333
E-mail: hrwdc@hrw.org
General web site: www.hrw.org

HRW "is dedicated to protecting the human rights of people around the world." Among the areas that HRW focuses on are lesbian, gay, bisexual, and transgender rights. HRW's web site contains publications on LGBT issues in the United States (including a report on binational same-sex couples and a report on violence against LGBT students) as well as information on LGBT issues in other countries.

Immigration Equality
40 Exchange Place, 17th Floor
New York, NY 10005
Phone: 212-714-2904
Fax: 212-714-2973
Web site: www.immigrationequality.org

Immigration Equality "works to end discrimination in U.S. immigration law, to reduce the negative impact of that law on the lives of lesbian, gay, bisexual, transgender and HIV-positive people, and to help obtain asylum for those persecuted in their home country based on their sexual orientation, transgender identity or HIV-status." Immigration Equality provides free legal services to low-income individuals seeking asylum in the United States and maintains a list of LGBT-friendly attorneys for those who do not qualify for their free legal services. In addition to providing such legal services, Immigration Equality also answers general informational questions about U.S. immigration law and maintains a wide variety of resources on its web site for individuals and for attorneys.

International Gay and Lesbian Human Rights Commission (IGLHRC)
80 Maiden Lane, Suite 1505
New York, NY 10038
Telephone: 212-268-8040
Fax: 212-430-6060
E-mail: iglhrc@iglhrc.org
Web site: www.iglhrc.org

IGLHRC's "mission is to secure the full enjoyment of the human rights of all people and communities subject to discrimination or abuse on the basis of sexual orientation or expression, gender identity or expression, and/or HIV/AIDS status." IGLHRC responds to human rights violations on the basis of sexual orientation, documents those violations, and mobilizes "communities to bring to bear pressure and scrutiny in order to end discriminatory and abusive laws, policies, and practices." IGLHRC also has an education component to its mission. It compiles reports on human rights conditions for sexual minorities in specific countries, compiles reports that cover issues across countries (e.g., its report on the rights of LGBT parents and children), and maintains a web site with links and information on research resources and referrals.

Lambda Legal
120 Wall Street, Suite 1500
New York, NY 10005-3904
Phone: 212-809-8585
Fax: 212-809-0055
Web site: www.lambdalegal.org

Lambda Legal describes itself as "a national organization committed to achieving full recognition of the civil rights of lesbians, gay men, bisexuals, transgender people and those with HIV through impact litigation, education and public policy work." In addition to helpful information on a variety of issues (from adoption and parenting to employment to relationship recognition), Lambda Legal operates a "help desk" with staff that assist individuals who are seeking legal information or assistance. The appropriate contact information and times of operation for the help desk, which vary by geographical area of the country, are listed on Lambda Legal's web site under "Help Desk."

Legal Services Corporation (LSC)
3333 K Street, N.W., 3rd Floor
Washington, DC 20007-3522
Phone: 202-295-1500
Fax: 202-337-6797
E-mail: info@lsc.gov
Web site: www.lsc.gov

LSC describes itself as "a private, non-profit corporation established by Congress to seek to ensure equal access to justice under the law for all Americans by providing civil legal assistance to those who otherwise would be unable to afford it." On its web site, LSC maintains a directory of legal assistance programs throughout the country with contact information.

Michael D. Palm Center
Aaron Belkin, Director
Michael D. Palm Center
University of California–Santa Barbara
Santa Barbara, CA 93106-9420
Phone: 805-893-5664
Web site: www.palmcenter.org

The Michael D. Palm Center was formerly known as the Center for the Study of Sexual Minorities in the Military. The center describes itself as "committed to sponsoring state-of-the-art research to enhance the quality of public dialogue about critical and controversial issues of the day." The center continues the work of the Center for the Study of Sexual Minorities in the Military by placing a priority on its "Don't Ask, Don't Tell" project, which is designed to "improve the quality of information available to public deliberations about the military policy." On its web site, the center provides access to publications written by its staff and senior research fellows.

National Center for Lesbian Rights (NCLR)
870 Market Street, Suite 370
San Francisco, CA 94102
Phone: 415-392-6257
Fax: 415-392-8442
E-mail: info@nclrights.org
Web site: www.nclrights.org

NCLR is a nonprofit, public-interest law firm that works to "advance the legal and human rights of lesbian, gay, bisexual, and transgender (LGBT) people and their families across the United States" through a combination of "impact litigation, public policy advocacy, public education, collaboration with other social justice organizations and activists, and direct legal services." In addition to a number of helpful publications on its web site, NCLR operates a help line for the general public that can be accessed either through its web site (under "Need Help?") or by calling the telephone number listed above. NCLR also offers technical assistance to attorneys who are representing LGBT clients.

National Coalition of Anti-Violence Programs (NCAVP)
240 West 35th Street, Suite 200
New York, NY 10001
Phone: 212-714-1184
Fax: 212-714-2627
E-mail: info@ncavp.org
Web site: www.ncavp.org

NCAVP describes itself as "a coalition of programs that document and advocate for victims of anti-LGBT and anti-HIV/AIDS violence/harassment, domestic violence, sexual assault, police misconduct and other forms of victimization." On its web site, NCAVP maintains a list of local antiviolence programs with contact information as well as copies of its annual reports on anti-LGBT hate violence and LGBT domestic violence.

National Gay and Lesbian Task Force (NGLTF)
1325 Massachusetts Avenue, N.W., Suite 600
Washington, DC 20005
Phone: 202-393-5177
Phone (TTY): 202-393-2284
Fax: 202-393-2241
E-mail: thetaskforce@thetaskforce.org
Web site: www.thetaskforce.org

NGLTF describes its mission as building "the political power of the lesbian, gay, bisexual and transgender (LGBT) community from the ground up." NGLTF trains activists, organizes lobbying efforts, and operates a think tank that provides research and policy analysis in support of its work. In addition to information on a variety of issues (including aging, the "anti-gay industry," faith, hate crimes, relationship recognition, nondiscrimination, parenting and families, and racial and economic justice), NGLTF has an "activist center" on its web site that provides information on how individuals can become politically involved and that, under the "Act Locally" tab, lists political issues and organizations (with web site addresses) by state.

National Lesbian and Gay Law Association (NLGLA)
601 Thirteenth Street, N.W., Suite 1170 South
Washington, DC 20005-3823
Phone: 202-637-6384

E-mail: info@nlgla.org
Web site: www.nlgla.org

NLGLA is a national association of lawyers, judges and other legal professionals, law students, activists, and affiliated LGBT legal organizations. "NLGLA promotes justice in and through the legal profession for the LGBT community in all its diversity." Each year, NLGLA holds its "Lavender Law" conference, with substantive programs on the law as it affects LGBT individuals as well as a career fair for LGBT law students.

Servicemembers Legal Defense Network (SLDN)
P.O. Box 65301
Washington, DC 20035-5301
Phone: 202-328-3244 or 202-328-FAIR
Fax: 202-797-1635
E-mail: sldn@sldn.org
Web site: www.sldn.org

SLDN describes itself as "a national, non-profit legal services, watchdog and policy organization dedicated to ending discrimination against and harassment of military personnel affected by 'Don't Ask, Don't Tell' and related forms of intolerance." SLDN offers free legal services to service members who have legal issues relating to the "Don't Ask, Don't Tell" policy.

Tolerance.org
Web site: www.tolerance.org

Tolerance.org is a web project of the Southern Poverty Law Center (SPLC). SPLC describes Tolerance.org as "a principal online destination for people interested in dismantling bigotry and creating, in hate's stead, communities that value diversity." Sexual orientation is included among the areas covered by the materials on this useful web site.

Williams Institute on Sexual Orientation Law and Public Policy
University of California–Los Angeles School of Law
Box 951476
Los Angeles, CA 90095-1476
Phone: 310-267-4382
E-mail: williamsinstitute@law.ucla.edu
Web site: www.law.ucla.edu/williamsinstitute

The Williams Institute describes itself as a "think tank dedicated to the field of sexual orientation law and public policy. The Institute supports legal scholarship, legal research, policy analysis, and education regarding sexual orientation discrimination and other legal issues that affect lesbian and gay people." On its web site, the Williams Institute provides access to policy studies, court documents, and op-ed pieces. It also sponsors an annual speaker series, symposia, continuing legal education for lawyers, and training for judges.

Index

6, 56, 57, 73, 96, 109, 112, 114, 235;
state and local employment and, 112;
story about, 25–26; suffering, 13, 31, 35.
See also Employment discrimination;
Housing discrimination
Disinheritance, 177
District of Columbia, domestic-partner
registry and, 147
District of Columbia Court of Appeals,
Gay Rights Coalition and, 73
Diversity, 4, 127, 142, 238; tolerance for,
201, 202
Divorce, 181–183, 204
DOMA. *See* Defense of Marriage Act
Domestic-partnership agreements, 182,
183, 221
Domestic partnership law, 147, 149–150
Domestic-partnership registry, 146–147,
151–152
Domestic partnerships, 3, 113, 116, 137,
141, 147, 150, 155, 175, 183, 219;
adoption and, 218; benefits and, 127,
151–152, 185; decision-making status
and, 149; defining, 107; entering, 161;
false choice and, 158; intrauterine
insemination and, 220; legal recognition
of, 6, 153, 159; registering, 177;
termination of, 182; visitation and, 149,
175
*Don't: A Reader's Guide to the Military's
Anti-Gay Policy* (Halley), 86
"Don't Ask, Don't Tell" (DADT), 82, 84;
harm from, 236; history, 83;
homosexual acts and, 90; meaning of,
in theory, 85–86; same-sex marriage
and, 89; status-conduct distinction
and, 91
Downey v. Muffley, 208
Due Process Clause, 58, 124, 170, 211,
222

EAA. *See* Equal Access Act
Earned income tax credit, 185
ECHR. *See* European Court of Human
Rights
Education: access to, 55–57;
discrimination in, 56; workplace,
126–127
Educational loan interest, deduction for,
185
Electric shock aversion therapy, 12
Emergency room, story about, 167
Empathy, 22n32, 98, 160
Employee Retirement Income Security
Act (ERISA), 118

Employment discrimination, 8, 12, 116,
119; banning, 112; D.C./state laws/
executive orders/policies against, 113
(table); discussion of, 108; gender-
based, 4; protection against, 115, 236;
sexual orientation and, 4–5, 108–119,
235, 236
Employment Division v. Smith, private
schools and, 56
End-of-relationship planning, 181–183
Equal Access Act (EAA), GSAs and, 72,
79n112
Equal benefits laws, 118
Equal Credit Opportunity Act, 120
Equal pay, receiving, 117
Equal protection, 7, 149, 211, 222;
challenging, 102n91; violation of, 32
Equal Protection Clause, 124
Equality, strides toward, 138
ERISA. *See* Employee Retirement
Income Security Act
Eskridge, William: on regulation of
homosexual activity, 11
Estate planning, 176–181, 183
Estate taxes. *See* Gift and estate taxes
Euphemisms, desexualized (list), 22n32
European Convention for the Protection
of Human Rights and Fundamental
Freedoms, 6, 21n22
European Court of Human Rights
(ECHR), 6
Evolution, theory of, 61
Ex parte D.W.W., visitation and, 209
Ex parte J.M.F., 207, 208
Executive orders, employment
discrimination, 113 (table)

Fags, 52, 53, 54, 105
False choice, 158, 172, 221–222
Family, 55, 62, 124; completing, 218–223; defining, 123,
174, 175, 176; incomplete, 220–221;
law, 225; non-nuclear, 123; regulation
of, 207; starting, 212–217; traditional
notion of, 139
Family Medical Leave Act, 84
Family Research Institute, 202
Federal Bureau of Investigation (FBI),
20nn13, 14
Federal employment: discrimination and,
109; protections for, 109–112
Federal taxation, 183, 184–190
FedEx, ERISA and, 118
Fertility services, 28, 199, 202, 217
Films, homosexual-themed, 12

Kaye, Chief Judge, 153
Kerry, John: same-sex marriage and, 9
Kessler, Laura, 223
Kinship networks, 224
Kowalski, Sharon, 172, 173

Lacy, story of, 80–82, 87, 93
L.A.M. v. B.M., 207–208
Lambda Legal, 15, 24n59; online guide
  by, 127; publication by, 135n125
Last will and testament, execution of,
  178–179
Law: acceptance and, 236; changing, 14–19,
  236; radical thoughts on, 239n6; sexual
  orientation and, vii, viii; society and, 15
Lawrence v. Texas, 4, 6, 7, 94–95, 96, 124,
  189, 190, 211, 214, 215; CAAF and, 95;
  reading of, 207–208; sodomy laws and,
  3, 207
Leadership Conference on Civil Rights,
  125
Leadership Conference on Civil Rights
  Education Fund, 125
Legal concerns, vii, 5–6, 15, 169, 191, 224
Legal protections, 108, 110, 177
Legal recognition, 3, 33–34, 138, 145–156,
  158–159, 160–161, 169, 177, 183, 190,
  219, 220, 235; geographic limitations
  on, 159; portability of, 222
Legal redress: obtaining, 32–35, 116–117,
  125, 126; other forms of, 31–32
Legal relationships, 158, 178
Legal rights, 13, 19, 235
Legitimacy, 140
Lesbian and gay community:
  multidimensional view of, 18; same-
  sex marriage and, 138–139; tax on, 187;
  terrorizing, 45; yellow pages for, 34
Lesbian and gay movement, 8;
  predicament of, 2, 10, 235
Lesbian and gay parenting, 204, 221,
  224–225, 236; ART and, 217; battle over,
  202, 203, 212, 222; "commonsense"
  views of, 202; custody and, 207;
  hostility toward, 207; legal barriers for,
  213; single, 212–223; social science
  research on, 202; visitation and, 207
Lesbian and gay rights organizations, 14,
  237; donations to, 160; hospital
  visitation and, 175
Lesbian and gay students, protecting,
  67–70
Lesbian-baiting, 92
Lesbian, gay, bisexual, and transgendered
  (LGBT) community, vii, 67

"LGBT Anti-Violence Programs" (HRC
  web site), 39
LGBT community. *See* Lesbian, gay,
  bisexual, and transgendered
  community
Library materials, 60, 62, 65
Limited open forum, 72
"Living together" agreement, 182
Living trust, 180
Lobbying, 34–35, 57, 65, 68, 125–126,
  127, 175–176
Lobotomies, 12
Log Cabin Republicans, 95, 103n110
Los Angeles Times, on Owens, 43
Love Makes a Family, 160
Lower-earning partners, higher-earning
  partners and, 186, 187
Lucas, Basil, 42, 43

Maine Supreme Judicial Court, adoption
  and, 219
Manual for Courts-Martial, defining
  sodomy and, 99n10; evidentiary
  privileges and, 102n96
Marginalized groups, 54
Marital status, protections, 27, 113, 120,
  122
Marlow v. Marlow, 208
Marriage: benefits of, 178, 184, 185;
  bigamous/polygamous, 141; civil, 140;
  defining, 61, 118, 155; disadvantages
  of, 140–141; equal rights to, 202;
  "Ozzie and Harriet" model of, 185;
  validation of, 136. *See also* Same-sex
  marriage
Marriage laws, 139, 141, 145
Marriage licenses, 138, 155, 156, 158;
  same-sex couples and, 147, 150
Martin, Viviano Cruz, 43
Martinez, David Leal, 43
Maryland Court of Appeals, same-sex
  marriage and, 154
Maryland State Board of Education,
  homosexuality and, 55
Masculinity, reaffirming, 45
Massachusetts Constitution: civil
  marriage and, 147; group
  classifications and, 148
Massachusetts Department of Social
  Services, 215
Massachusetts Senate, civil unions and,
  148
Massachusetts Supreme Judicial Court,
  147–149, 154; benefits of marriage and,
  139; same-sex marriage and, 6, 144

About the Author

Anthony C. Infanti is associate professor of law at the University of Pittsburgh School of Law. His work focuses on sexual orientation and the law, paying particular attention to the application of the tax laws to lesbians and gay men.